FIFTH EDITION

Elementary Classroom Management

C. M. Charles
San Diego State University, Emeritus

Gail W. Senter
California State University San Marcos

Boston ■ New York ■ San Francisco
Mexico City ■ Montreal ■ Toronto ■ London ■ Madrid ■ Munich ■ Paris
Hong Kong ■ Singapore ■ Tokyo ■ Cape Town ■ Sydney

Senior Editor: Arnis E. Burvikovs
Editorial Assistant: Erin Reilly
Marketing Manager: Erica DeLuca
Editorial Production Service: Omegatype Typography, Inc.
Composition Buyer: Linda Cox
Manufacturing Buyer: Linda Morris
Electronic Composition: Omegatype Typography, Inc.
Cover Administrator: Kristina Mose-Libon

For related titles and support materials, visit our online catalog at www.ablongman.com.

Between the time website information is gathered and then published, it is not unusual for some sites to have closed. Also, the transcription of URLs can result in typographical errors. The publisher would appreciate notification where these errors occur so that they may be corrected in subsequent editions.

ISBN-13: 978-0-205-51071-9   ISBN-10: 0-205-51071-X

Library of Congress Cataloging-in-Publication Data

Charles, C. M.
    Elementary classroom management / C. M. Charles, Gail W. Senter.—5th ed.
        p.   cm.
    Includes bibliographical references and index.
    ISBN 0-205-51071-X
    1. Classroom management.   2. Education, Elementary.   I. Senter, Gail W.   II. Title.

    LB3013.S45   2008
    317.102'4—dc22

                                                                    2006048764

Printed in the United States of America

10   9   8   7   6   5   4   3   2   1   11   10   09   08   07

ABOUT THE AUTHORS

 C. M. Charles was a public school teacher from 1953 to 1959, then moved into higher education and held professorships at the University of New Mexico, Teachers College Columbia University, Pepperdine University, Universidade Federal do Marahao (Brazil), and San Diego State University, where he is now professor emeritus. At San Diego State, Charles directed innovative programs in teacher education and five times received outstanding professor and distinguished teaching awards. He also served on several occasions as advisor in teacher education and curriculum to the governments of Peru and Brazil. Charles has authored or coauthored more than 25 books, many of which have attracted wide audiences in the United States and abroad, with translations into several foreign languages. Those dealing most directly with school discipline are *Teacher's Petit Piaget* (1972); *The Synergetic Classroom: Joyful Teaching and Gentle Discipline* (2000); *Essential Elements of Effective Discipline* (2002); *Classroom Management for Middle-Grades Teachers* (2004); *Elementary Classroom Management* (fifth edition, 2008); *Building Classroom Discipline* (ninth edition, 2008), and *Today's Best Classroom Management Strategies: Paths to Positive Discipline* (2008).

 Gail W. Senter earned her doctorate in Curriculum and Instruction from the University of Southern California. After teaching in public schools, she moved her professional focus to university-level teacher-training programs in Southern California. In that capacity, she has held faculty positions at the San Diego campus of Chapman University, California State University San Bernardino, and California State University San Marcos, working with pre-service and veteran teachers at both the elementary and secondary levels. She assisted C. M. Charles on his book, *Introduction to Educational Research* book, collaborated with Charles on multiple editions of *Building Classroom Discipline* (ninth edition, 2008) and is principal author of *Elementary Classroom Management* (fifth edition, 2008).

CONTENTS

Chapter 3
Managing the Physical Environment of the Classroom   40

PART II: THE FIRST DAYS AND THE FIRST WEEKS   57

Chapter 4
Managing the Psychosocial Environment of the Classroom   57

Chapter 12
Managing the Work of Paraprofessionals, Substitute Teachers, and Student Teachers   245

Chapter 13
Managing Emotional Trauma and Job-Related Stress Productively   267

PREFACE

THE PURPOSE OF THIS BOOK

This fifth edition of *Elementary Classroom Management* continues to focus on the improvement of instruction and learning through good classroom management. When it is done well, classroom management helps establish learning environments and instructional programs that are well organized and efficient, in which communication is good, and in which teachers, students, and others are considerate of each other and dedicated to learning. As teachers improve their skills in classroom management, they find that students also become more cooperative, make responsible choices, and happily engage in learning activities.

RELATING THIS BOOK TO STANDARDS FOR TEACHERS

In recent years, national standards for teacher preparation and performance have been identified by a number of agencies. The purpose of these standards is to help guide the development of new teachers, help in-service teachers improve their performance, and assess both teacher preparation and teacher performance. This book discusses the many subjects that apply to these standards. It also offers examples, case studies, and recommendations for additional sources to further support and connect the standards to the areas of classroom management. Notable efforts include the Interstate New Teacher Assessment and Support Consortium standards (INTASC), the Praxis Series of tests, the National Board for Professional Teacher Standards (NBPTS), and the National Council for Accreditation of Teacher Education (NCATE). In fact, it should be noted that INTASC, NBPTS, and NCATE have worked together to create a compatible set of performance-based standards that span the teaching career. The standards are described briefly in the paragraphs that follow, and their chapter coverage appears on pages xix–xxii.

INTASC Standards

The Interstate New Teacher Assessment and Support Consortium (INTASC) has worked diligently to set forth standards teachers should meet in order to be licensed to teach in public schools. The consortium is composed of more than thirty states that have developed standards and assessment processes for initial teacher certification. The INTASC core standards are based on ten principles of effective teaching, for all subjects and grade levels. The principles focus on effective integration of content knowledge and pedagogical understanding—knowledge of how to teach (INTASC, 2003). Detailed presentations of INTASC can be found on these websites: www.ccsso.org/projects/Interstate_New_Teacher_Assessment_and_Support_Consortium and www.dpi.state.nc.us/pbl/pblintasc.htm.

Praxis Series

The Praxis Series is a series of assessments for beginning teachers. Developed and disseminated by the Educational Testing Service (ETS), the Praxis Series assesses academic skills, subject knowledge, and classroom performance during the early stages of a beginning teacher's career, from entry into teacher education to the first year of teaching. Praxis I measures basic skills in reading, writing, and mathematics and may be used as an admission tool for teacher education programs. Praxis II measures prospective teachers' knowledge of the subjects they will teach, as well as pedagogical skills and knowledge. It includes tests on principles of learning and teaching, specific subject assessments, and multiple subject assessments. Praxis III measures the classroom performance of beginning teachers. It includes instructional planning and teaching, classroom management, and student assessment and may be used as a licensure tool.

Several states have worked to align the INTASC principles and the Praxis criteria. In addition, Charlotte Danielson, one of the Praxis III test developers, was concerned that teachers have or make little opportunity to discuss teaching with others. She created a framework that teachers can use as they discuss their teaching and professional lives. Danielson's books, including *Enhancing Professional Practice: A Framework for Teaching* (2nd ed.) with the newly revised framework, are available at www.ascd.org.

NBPTS Standards

The National Board of Professional Teaching Standards (NBPTS) is an organization that has established standards for highly accomplished teaching, as seen in the National Board's central policy statement, *What Teachers Should Know and Be Able to Do*. NBPTS has developed five core propositions on which voluntary national teacher certification is based (NBPTS, 2003).

NBPTS awards professional certificates to teachers who possess and demonstrate extensive professional knowledge and the ability to perform at a high level. Certification candidates submit a portfolio that includes video or digital tapes of classroom interactions, samples of student work, and the teacher's reflective comments. Trained NBPTS evaluators who teach in the same field as the candidate judge all elements of the assessments.

NCATE Standards

The National Council for Accreditation of Teacher Education (NCATE) is an accrediting agency that serves many institutions with programs in teacher education. The Council has set six criteria of prospective teacher performance in a context of professional and liberal arts studies. Although NCATE standards apply to teacher preparation programs, not to teacher education students per se, NCATE believes that the new professional teachers who graduate from accredited schools, colleges, or departments of education should be able to meet the criteria (NCATE, 2002).

CHAPTER TOPICS AND CONTENTS

This fifth edition of *Elementary Classroom Management* retains the chapters from previous editions, but **infuses and emphasizes further discussions of standards, handling emotions of trauma-related stress, and bullying.** It also adds discussion about managing students with neurological based behavior. Embedded in each chapter are case studies and vignettes for a variety of management concerns, all with focus or reflection questions to illustrate how the techniques can be implemented. Also included in the book are numerous websites and discussions of management concerns related to curriculum standards and testing, curriculum mapping, backward design planning, differentiated instruction for teaching all learners, classbuilding and teambuilding, multi-age and looped classes, cooperative learning, authentic assessment, student-led conferences, and the use of technology, including adaptive technology for children with special needs.

The chapters and topics are organized into management concerns to be handled before the school year begins, during the first days and weeks of school, and matters that require ongoing attention. They are sequenced in an order that the authors believe best corresponds to the development of good management skills.

Part I: Before the School Year Begins

Chapter 1 deals with the nature of classroom management.

Chapter 2 shows how to plan out instructional days and the entire school year.

Chapter 3 describes how to organize and manage the physical environment of the classroom.

Part II: The First Days and the First Weeks

Chapter 4 explains how to establish and maintain a positive psychosocial environment in the classroom.

Chapter 5 explores human motivation and motivation management.

Part III: Matters That Require Ongoing Attention

Chapter 6 describes effective ways to organize, differentiate, and present instruction.

Chapter 7 provides suggestions for managing students during work.

Chapter 8 describes the natures and special needs of diverse groups of students.

Chapter 9 explains how to prevent and deal with disruptive student behavior.

Chapter 10 provides suggestions concerning assessment, record keeping, and reporting.

Chapter 11 explains how to establish and maintain good communication with students, caregivers, and others.

Chapter 12 recommends procedures for managing the work of paraprofessionals, substitutes, and student teachers.

Chapter 13 suggests how to deal with emotions of stress that result from unexpected or disastrous events and stress that is related to work.

The **Epilogue** presents activities, including a Capstone activity to pull everything together.

The **Appendixes** are intended as resources for expanding horizons and opportunities for teachers.

■ MANAGEMENT KNOWLEDGE FROM RESEARCH AND EXPERIENCE

A strong body of academic material related to classroom management provides the basis for many of the observations and suggestions presented in this book. In addition, case studies are included to provide an experiential perspective to the topics. Works of special importance in classroom management are cited within chapters and listed at the ends of chapters.

■ HELP TO READERS

The text is written in an informal, inviting tone to make information accessible for readers. Each chapter begins with a Prediction–Review Guide. By responding in the column labeled *Prediction* before reading the chapter, readers are able to record what they know, don't know, think they know, or assume about the chapter topics. After reading the chapter, readers can reflect on their earlier responses by responding to the same statements in the *Review* column. Many of the statements are intentionally worded to not be true or false; consequently, reflective discussions can be organized for use in class based on these statements and reader responses. Websites, along with case studies and vignettes, are infused in the chapters to provide additional resources and experiential perspectives and discussions. To help readers strengthen their learning and acquire a sense of progressive accomplishments, checklists, practice applications, and discussion questions are included at the ends of chapters.

MyLabSchool

(mylabschool is a collection of online tools for your success in this course, on your licensure exams, and in your teaching career. Visit www. mylabschool.com to access the following:

- Video footage of real-life classrooms, with opportunities for you to reflect on the videos and offer your own thoughts and suggestions for applying theory to practice
- An extensive archive of text and multimedia cases that provide valuable perspectives on real classrooms and real teaching challenges
- Allyn & Bacon's Lesson and Portfolio Builder application, which includes an integrated state standards correlation tool
- Research paper assistance using Research Navigator™, which provides access to three exclusive databases of credible and reliable source material: EBSCO's ContentSelect Academic Journal Database, The *New York Times* Search by Subject Archive, and "Best of the Web" Link Library
- Career Center with resources for Praxis exams and licensure preparation, professional portfolio development, and job search and interview techniques

HELP TO INSTRUCTORS

The following features are included in the Instructor's Manual that accompanies the text to help instructors manage the course or topics effectively and efficiently:

- Suggestions for introducing the textbook to students
- Course organization options, including both goals and calendar considerations
- Additional activities
- Evaluation procedures and expectations

In light of current reform efforts concerning teacher preparation and performance and the No Child Left Behind Act of 2001, both the text and the **Instructor's Manual** (available online by contacting your Allyn & Bacon representative) include a quick guide to the chapters in the text where you will find reference to these guidelines

"SOME DAYS I THINK THEY CAN UNDERSTAND EVERY WORD I SAY."

- The Interstate New Teacher Assessment and Support Consortium (INTASC) standards
- Danielson's Framework for Teaching
- The National Board for Professional Teaching Standards (NBPTS)
- The National Council for Accreditation of Teacher Education (NCATE)

Additionally, in *MyLabSchool* instructors and students can apply the content of the textbook to visual footage of classroom situations. Short video clips show real teacher–student interactions across grade levels and in varied school settings. The clips are followed by interactive questions for reflection and response.

ACKNOWLEDGMENTS

The authors wish to thank the following teachers who shared their experiences in previous texts: Gloria Anderson, Kim Anderson, Eileen Andreoli, Jearine Bacon, Kay Ballantyne, Frank Barnes, Janet Beyea, Scott Boyens, Mary Brewer, Dyanna Burak, Bernardo Campos, Della Casteñeda, Ruth Charles, Tim Charles, Sherry Coburn, Debbie Comer, Keith Correll, Marilyn Cox, Rebecca Cumming, Elizabeth Davies, Ginger DeNigro, Hollie Foster, Stacy Ganzer, Devora Garrison, Jennifer George, Jan Gretlein, Lynne Harvey, Carolyn Hasslett, Ellen Hodgers, Beth Johnson, Lisa Johnston, Rose Mary Johnston, Pam Klevesahl, Kathryn Krainock, Ginny Lorenz, Cathy McCloud, Cynthia McDermott, Carol Mercer, Janet

Mulder, Karen O'Connor, Patti Peterson, Roberta Revetta, Charlotte Rodzach, Ronda Royal, Jamie Ruben, Karen Runyon, Nancy Rutherford, Rebecca Santibanez, Ted Saulino, David Sisk, and Candace Young.

Professional Analysts

The quality of any textbook is heavily dependent on critical analyses and suggestions made by knowledgeable experts. Among the professionals whose suggestions have helped improve this book are the following, to whom the authors express their sincere gratitude: Dr. C. Bobbi Hansen, University of San Diego; Dr. Kimberly Woo, California State University San Marcos; and Jo Sylvester.

We would also like to thank the reviewers of this edition: Alison Critchfield, Midway College; Janice Gail Janz, University of New Orleans; Donald Maas, California Polytechnic State University; Melinda Schoenfeldt, Ball State University; and Penelope Wong, California State University Chico.

The authors also gratefully acknowledge the assistance provided by Arnis Burvikovs, Editor at Allyn and Bacon, and Erin Reilly, Editorial Assistant at Allyn and Bacon.

On this journey
You will encounter all different paths:
paths of hardships,
paths of beauty,
paths of trial,
and paths of error.
You may get lost,
but if you give up,
you will not reach your destination.
If you did not want to reach your destination,
why did you begin the journey?
Be strong.
Keep faith.
The journey,
you know in your heart,
is worth it.

Written by Dyanna Burak during teacher training.
Dyanna is now a second-grade teacher.

INTASC STANDARDS

INTASC stands for Interstate New Teacher Assessment and Support Consortium (see www.ccsso.org/projects/Interstate_New_Teacher_Assessment_and_Support_Consortium). This consortium, which consists of more than thirty states that have developed standards and assessment procedures for initial teacher certification, has issued licensing standards that should be met in order to teach in public schools. The INTASC core standards are based on ten principles of effective teaching, which focus on integration of content knowledge and pedagogical understanding.

INTASC Standards	Chapter Coverage
1. **Knowledge of Subject Matter** The teacher understands the central concepts, tools of inquiry, and structures of the subject being taught and can create learning experiences that make these aspects of subject matter meaningful for students.	2, 6, 8
2. **Knowledge of Human Development and Learning** The teacher understands how children learn and develop and can provide learning opportunities that support their intellectual, social, and personal development.	4, 5, 8, 9
3. **Adapting Instruction for Individual Needs** The teacher understands how students differ in their approaches to learning and creates instructional opportunities that are adapted to diverse learners.	3, 6, 8
4. **Multiple Instructional Strategies** The teacher uses various instructional strategies to encourage students' development of critical thinking, problem solving, and performance skills.	6, 8
5. **Classroom Motivation and Management** The teacher uses an understanding of individual and group motivation and behavior to create a learning environment that encourages positive social interaction, active engagement in learning, and self-motivation.	5, 9
6. **Communication Skills** The teacher uses knowledge of effective verbal, nonverbal, and media communication techniques to foster active inquiry, collaboration, and supportive interaction in the classroom.	4, 11, 12, 13
7. **Instructional Planning Skills** The teacher plans instruction based on knowledge of subject matter, students, the community, and curriculum guides.	2, 6, 7

8. **Assessment of Student Learning** 10
The teacher understands and uses formal and
informal assessment strategies to evaluate and
ensure the continuous intellectual, social, and
physical development of the learner.

9. **Professional Commitment** 1, 11, 12, 13,
The teacher is a reflective practitioner who continually Appendixes
evaluates the effects of his or her choices and actions on
others (students, parents, and other professionals in the
learning community) and who actively seeks out
opportunities to grow professionally.

10. **Partnerships** 11, 12
The teacher fosters relationships with school colleagues,
parents, and agencies in the larger community to support
students' learning and well-being.

Source: The Interstate New Teacher Assessment and Support Consortium (INTASC) standards were developed by
the Council of Chief State School Officers and member states. Copies may be downloaded from the Council's
website at www.ccsso.org.

Council of Chief State School Officers. (1992). Model standards for beginning teacher licensing, assessment, and
development: A resource for state dialogue. Washington, DC: Author. www.ccsso.org/ content/pdfs/corestrd.pdf.

PRAXIS SERIES AND DANIELSON'S FRAMEWORK FOR TEACHING

The Praxis Series is a series of tests developed and disseminated by the Educational Testing Service (ETS) for assessing skills and knowledge of each stage of a beginning teacher's career, from entry into teacher education to actual classroom performance. It measures basic skills in reading, writing, and mathematics, as well as professional education and subject matter knowledge. Teaching skills measured include instructional planning, teaching, classroom management, and assessment of student learning.

Praxis I assesses reading, writing, and mathematics skills and may be used for admission to a teacher education program.

Praxis II measures prospective teachers' knowledge of the teaching and learning process and the subjects they will teach. It includes tests on Principles of Learning and Teaching, specific subject assessments, and multiple subject assessments.

Praxis III focuses on classroom performance assessment and usually is taken by teachers in their first year of teaching.

Several states have worked to align the INTASC principles and the Praxis criteria. Consult the following website to see one such example from the Utah State Department of Education: www.ed.utah.edu/TandL/NCATE/correlationINTASC-PRAXIS.pdf.

Charlotte Danielson, one of the Praxis III test developers, was concerned that teachers have or make little opportunity to discuss teaching with each other. Consequently, she devised a framework, shown here, of four domains that teachers can use for discussions to enrich their professional lives and teaching. In the second edition of Danielson's book, *Enhancing Professional Practice: A Framework for Teaching,* you will find a revised framework of domains, components, and elements. For more about Danielson's efforts and books, consult www.ascd.org.

Danielson's Framework for Teaching	Chapter Coverage
1. Planning and Preparation • Demonstrating knowledge of students • Selecting instructional goals • Demonstrating knowledge of resources • Designing coherent instruction	2, 6, 7
2. The Classroom Environment • Creating an environment of respect and rapport • Establishing a culture for learning • Managing classroom procedures • Managing student behavior • Organizing physical space	3, 4, 9, 13
3. Instruction • Communicating clearly and accurately • Using questioning and discussion techniques • Engaging students in learning • Providing feedback to students • Demonstrating flexibility and responsiveness	5, 6, 7, 8, 10, 13
4. Professional Responsibilities • Reflecting on teaching • Maintaining accurate records • Communicating with families • Contributing to the school and district • Growing and developing professionally	1, 10, 11, 12, 13, Appendixes

Source: Charlotte Danielson. The original edition of the Framework for Teaching was published in 1996 by ASCD and has been used by hundreds of educators worldwide to structure professional conversations. The second edition (Feb. 2007) includes a number of updates on both the domains and components, and the levels of performance.

NBPTS STANDARDS

The National Board for Professional Teaching Standards (NBPTS) has established standards for highly accomplished teaching, which are outlined in the board's central policy statement, *What Teachers Should Know and Be Able to Do.* Based on NBPTS principles, teachers can earn voluntary national certification (see http://nbrc.stanford.edu/align/standards.html).

This board issues professional certificates to master teachers—those with vast professional knowledge and highly developed teaching skills. A certification candidate submits a portfolio that includes videotapes or CDs of classroom instruction, samples of student work, and the teacher's comments.

NBPTS Standards	Chapter Coverage
1. Teachers are committed to students and their learning.	4, 8, 13
2. Teachers know the subjects they teach and how to teach those subjects to students.	5, 6, 7
3. Teachers are responsible for managing and monitoring student learning.	3, 6, 8, 9, 10
4. Teachers think systematically about their practice and learn from experience.	1, 2, 10
5. Teachers are members of learning communities.	11, 12, Appendixes

Source: Reprinted with permission from the National Board for Professional Teaching Standards. www.nbpts.org. All rights reserved.

NCATE STANDARDS

The National Council for Accreditation of Teacher Education (NCATE) is an accrediting agency that provides guidance to many teacher preparation programs. The Council has set six criteria of prospective teacher performance in professional and liberal arts studies. Although NCATE standards apply to programs, not to individual teacher education students, NCATE believes that the new professional teacher who graduates from an accredited teacher preparation program should be able to meet the criteria (see www.ncate.org/public/standards.asp).

NCATE Standards	Chapter Coverage
Help all pre-kindergarten through twelfth grade (P–12) students learn.	2, 5, 6, 8, 9
Teach to P–12 student standards set by specialized professional associations and the states.	Appendixes
Explain instructional choices based on research-derived knowledge and best practice.	6
Apply effective methods of teaching students who are at different developmental stages, have different learning styles, and come from diverse backgrounds.	3, 4, 5, 7, 8, 9
Reflect on practice, act on feedback, and integrate technology into instruction effectively.	1, 10, 11, 12, 13

Source: Reprinted with permission from the National Council for Accreditation of Teacher Education. All rights reserved.

CHAPTER 1

Classroom Management
Problems and Promises

You make the path when you walk.
> —Loosely translated from Spanish poet Antonio Machado

Prediction–Review Guide

Before you read the chapter, take a minute to put a check mark in the Prediction column next to any statement with which you agree.

		Prediction	Review
1.	A primary purpose of classroom management is efficiency and effectiveness in teaching.	❑	❑
2.	The *psychosocial environment* refers to class parties and other social events that occur in the classroom.	❑	❑
3.	*Feedback* is a term used to indicate student responses to a teacher's questions.	❑	❑
4.	When new teachers fail in their jobs, most often it is because their management skills are fine but their content knowledge is weak.	❑	❑
5.	The Cardinal Principles mainly have to do with how teachers should organize and present lessons.	❑	❑
6.	Three fundamental questions in education are: What should students learn? How do they learn? and How should they be taught?	❑	❑
7.	It is suggested that students begin each day with a quiet activity.	❑	❑
8.	The term *monitor* is used to indicate a student who helps with chores in the classroom.	❑	❑
9.	Lesson management, like other management chores, requires ongoing attention.	❑	❑
10.	In addition to their classroom responsibilities, teachers are expected to handle extracurricular duties.	❑	❑

1

Support for specific standards found in this chapter:

INTASC Standards

9. Professional Commitment

   The teacher is a reflective practitioner who continually evaluates the effects of his or her choices and actions on others (students, parents, and other professionals in the learning community) and who actively seeks out opportunities to grow professionally.

Danielson's Framework for Teaching

4. Professional Responsibilities
   - Reflecting on teaching
   - Maintaining accurate records
   - Communicating with families
   - Contributing to the school and district
   - Growing and developing professionally

NBPTS Standards

4. Teachers think systematically about their practice and learn from experience.

NCATE Standards

Reflect on practice, act on feedback, and integrate technology into instruction effectively.

This book is about managing the elementary classroom. It explores selected skills of management that lead toward artistry in teaching and pleasure in learning. These skills, among the most important you will encounter in all of teaching, rarely occur naturally and cannot be taken for granted. They can, however, be taught and learned. Some can be acquired quickly, whereas others are built up over time. Beginning teachers, in particular, often struggle because their management skills have not yet developed adequately. Such was the case for Janna Smart, a promising new teacher who found that teaching involved considerably more than she anticipated.

■ A MODERN PARABLE: THE BEGINNER

Janna Smart decided to follow in the footsteps of her mother, Mercedes Bright, who had taught school when Janna was growing up. Many of Janna's teachers were friends of her mother. While Janna did homework, her mother worked on her own schoolwork—grading papers, planning lessons, and preparing materials. Sometimes Janna followed the directions for a project so Mercedes could check that they were clear enough for her students. Later Janna enjoyed seeing the children's finished work. She often listened when Mercedes spoke with her friends about school, their work, and the children they taught. Thus it was little surprise that when Janna earned her Bachelor of Arts degree, she continued for an additional fifth year to earn her elementary teaching credential.

Late summer following her certification, Janna was called to three interviews. However, it wasn't until late September, after school had been in session for several weeks, that Janna was offered a position to teach a multi-age class of first and second graders. Because her district supported smaller classes for primary grades, her class had only twenty-two students. She accepted the position without hesitation.

Janna knew she was qualified. In addition to all the hours she had volunteered in her mother's classroom, Janna had worked hard and seriously while she was in school. She completed her teacher-training program with honors, and in doing so attracted attention. One professor even called her a natural, and both her cooperating teachers in student teaching ranked her a very strong teacher candidate. Her fellow classmates often came to her for ideas and support because of her resourcefulness and ability to gather materials for good units. Because she liked children and felt they responded well to her, she felt very comfortable about teaching. For Janna, as for her mother before her, all the pieces seemed to fall into place.

Janna was hired on a Thursday morning and would first meet her students the following Monday—she had only three and one half days to prepare! That day she looked at the room that would be her classroom, walked around the school with the principal, and met two of her team members. Over the weekend she reviewed the curriculum and standards for both the first and second grades and planned activities that would help everyone get acquainted. Luckily, some of her friends helped with her room. They made attractive bulletin boards and an inviting art exhibit with a related project based on fall colors and autumn leaves. They arranged a reading center with large, colorful pillows. They put the several computers in different spots about the room. They created a nature center with some plants, an aquarium of guppies and snails, and a cage with two hamsters, food and water dishes, tunnels, and places for the hamsters to nest.

When her students, along with some parents, arrived on Monday morning, Janna was nervous, but she greeted them all warmly. The students were quite well behaved, although they were a little uneasy and reserved. She taught them how to enter the room in a polite and orderly manner. She told them about herself, and she learned everyone's name by playing a memory game. At the end of the day, Janna felt that she had made a good beginning.

She was confident that the second day would be even better, but to her dismay things did not go perfectly. Some of the students remembered how to enter the room as she had taught them, but most did not. It took her much longer than expected to get them settled. As the day went on, those who had at first been cooperative became slow to follow directions. When she tried to work with the first graders on their curriculum, the second graders fooled around. That made her uneasy, and it hurt her feelings when some began showing disrespect.

By the third morning, Janna was struggling. She had several confrontations with students who talked, called out, wandered out of their seats, would not listen to directions or pay attention, sharpened pencils needlessly, and repeatedly asked to go to the restroom. When dismissed for recess, three boys raced out of the room and down the corridor. As the day progressed, almost every child had splashed in the aquarium, and it seemed they simply could not leave the hamsters alone.

The fourth day moved toward chaos. Every boy seemed bent on snatching another's paper and every girl on tattling. No one seemed at all willing to listen to Janna or do as she requested. When Janna worked with the second graders, the first graders played or wandered around the room. When assigned seatwork had been completed (or not completed, or completed incorrectly, or messed up impossibly), students shouted, waved their arms, and annoyed the few who still were trying to work. Many seemed never to have heard of standards of human decency, much less of classroom behavior. Janna's efforts to plan for two grades and the curricular expectations for each child only added to her struggles.

By the fifth day, Janna began to despair. Students now blatantly broke rules and seemed unaffected by her kindest, most sincere counseling. It was not so much that they were cruel or hostile toward her—they simply disregarded her and clowned, giggled, fussed, fought, and shouted. She was frustrated with the double curricula and the broad ranges of age and maturity within the two grades.

Other surprises caught Janna off-guard as well. On Wednesday, two mothers stayed to help in the room, but because Janna didn't know what to have them do, they spent the day watching her sweat and struggle. On Thursday, a child with learning disabilities was brought in to be included in her room. The student called out incessantly and made noises, which the other students found bizarre and delightedly mimicked. Two new girls arrived on Friday; one spoke little English and the other spoke none at all. One of them vomited during the math lesson, which made everyone laugh. Unable to get the class back into the lesson, Janna shouted at the students about being cruel and inconsiderate and made them put their heads down on their desks.

These events almost obscured the fact that, by Friday, a third of the scissors had disappeared; the computers were making distracting noises; all of the guppies were dead, evidently killed by something put in the water, and no one knew where to find one of the hamsters that was missing from its cage. That afternoon a parent confronted her, swearing and complaining that her son was being bullied on the playground and demanding that Janna put a stop to it. Two boys got into a fight and ruined a new shirt, and Janna was called to the phone after school and was reprimanded by the parent about the cost of shirts and her lack of control. She also received a note in her mailbox informing her that her support provider, an experienced teacher assigned by the district's Beginning Teacher Support Assistance program to work with Janna during her first year, intended to visit her classroom the following week.

Janna dragged herself home, her spirits crushed and her mind in turmoil. She now doubted that she would ever get those six-, seven-, and eight-year-olds to behave like civilized boys and girls, much less learn. She cried for two hours, seriously contemplating moving to Australia, before she called a friend. They went to a coffeehouse, and Janna talked and cried some more. That took her mind off escaping to Australia, however, and by the next morning she found a trace of determination returning.

During the night she faced the fact that most of the problems had to do with three things: her own instruction, her curriculum planning and organization, and her ability to manage the class.

Previously she had been confident about her ability to instruct. Now she knew her lessons were not running smoothly. Some were too long, some too short, and most too difficult. Though interesting to Janna, some were obviously boring the students. She could see why they might lose interest and look for something more stimulating. In addition, the two grade levels of curricula and standards only added to her challenge.

She realized, too, that she was having trouble monitoring seatwork while she worked with one grade or the other and with small groups. Students, often several at a time, were forever coming up to her with questions, usually about what she had carefully explained only minutes before. Also, she noticed that most anything took the students off-task, and she could hardly get them back.

While at her university, she remembered hearing about using technology in the classroom, about curriculum standards, and about teacher and student rights. She realized now how little she knew about technology. While she was aware of the standards in general, she was not overly familiar with the specific standards for first and second grades. She also realized that she knew little about the rights and responsibilities that applied to her situation and her students. She knew that English language learners and students with special needs had rights that would affect her decisions and ability to include them in her class and her ability to instruct them so they could be successful.

On Saturday morning she made three phone calls—one to her mother, one to a teacher who had been at the school a few years, and the third to her support provider. With all three she swallowed her pride and confessed her difficulties. She learned that her experiences were hardly unusual and she accepted a number of suggestions for redoing the operations of her classroom. She went to school that afternoon and there, in the calm solitude, began her new arrangements.

When students returned on Monday, Janna seated them farther apart and separated those who had been encouraging each other's disruptive behavior. She had moved all the computers to a separate area in the room, moved her desk to the back of the room, and repositioned the small-group area so she would be closer to the rest of the class. She found she was better able to quickly reach all her students with this new arrangement. She set up a signal system using colored cups and kinesthetic signs that students could use to ask for help. This allowed her to go to them, not vice-versa, and gave the students fewer opportunities to get into trouble. She also planned several classbuilding and teambuilding activities to bring everyone together, and was prepared with quick brain and movement energizers for when students showed signs of needing a break.

She installed a new system of distributing and collecting materials, with students assigned

"WE WORKED WITH GLUE TODAY. THIS IS MY SEAT MATE, BILLY."

to help. In fact, she assigned special responsibilities to every student in the class. She added more structure to her lessons and organized them so students were quickly and actively involved. She printed simple directions on the board, using separate areas and different colors for each grade, and referred students to them. She resolutely began to follow through on insisting that students complete their work and fulfill their obligations, and she set up record keeping and parent communication systems to ensure that they did so. She also put into place a system of incentives and activities for students when they worked and behaved appropriately. Although she initially hated such systems because it seemed to her that she was bribing students, Janna soon discovered their value. By using activities for learning and for incentive, she encouraged the students to save time by working hard and behaving well, and she allowed them to do fun learning activities that she wanted to include anyway, if time permitted. Most of her changes worked, and by the end of the second week Janna was almost back to where she had started, which she considered a grand achievement.

THE LESSON: THE WEIGHT OF MINOR DETAILS

Janna's trials point to one of the most significant realities in teaching, one that is especially important to beginning teachers. The reality is, no matter how much you know of philosophy, child psychology, and the subject matter you teach, teaching will inevitably dump in your lap an enormity of minor details that can, if not dealt with quickly, overwhelm everything else you are trying to do.

Fortunately, Janna had the determination to withstand defeat. She also was helped in that effort by a story that had inspired her mother and by some readings in her university courses. Her mother often had repeated a story that she had read in *Teacher and Child* (1972), a book by Haim Ginott. The story was about a river boatman who was ferrying a passenger across the river. The passenger, a scholar, asked the boatman, "Do you know philosophy?" "I can't say I do," answered the boatman. "Then you have lost a third of your life," declared the scholar. After a time the scholar asked, "Do you know literature?" "I can't say I do," answered the boatman. "Then you have lost another third of your life," said the scholar. A bit farther along the boat was seized by the current and dashed against a boulder, whereupon it split and began to sink. The boatman asked the scholar, "Do you know how to swim?" "No," cried the scholar. "Then," concluded the boatman, "you have lost all your life." Janna knew the philosophy and the subject matter and was determined that she would also learn how to swim.

In her own education classes, Janna had read about Jesse Stuart and Marva Collins. Stuart told his story in *The Thread That Runs So True*, first published in 1949. The book detailed his twenty years of teaching in the mountain region of Kentucky, but seemed to be almost a mini-history of education in the United States. Just a few years older than some of his students, he had only a teaching certificate and three years in high school when he entered his first one-room school. These qualifications did little to prepare him for the ruffian group of older students—boys who delighted in the fact that they had "run off" their previous teachers. Though the boys set out to make the new teacher's life miserable, Stuart was determined to give them the best he had and to never be chased out of the school, no matter what they tried to do to him. Janna decided that she, too, would not be chased away.

In *Marva Collins' Way* (1990), Collins told about how she had turned hopeless, hostile youngsters into eager and ambitious achievers. It was her attitude that made children learn, her constant "You can do it" that convinced students there was nothing they could not achieve. Collins greeted her children daily with endless encouragement. "The first thing we are going to do here, children, is an awful lot of believing in ourselves." Inspired and determined, "I can do it" became Janna's mantra.

Janna knew she could and would succeed, just as Mercedes had done years before. She knew that doing so meant preventing as many problems as possible and immediately handling those that did arise and threaten to drag her under. She knew (or thought she knew) how to create a class team and how to prepare and present good lessons for one grade level, but not for two grades at the same time. She also realized that she knew very little about the other things that required her attention during the day: taking attendance, collecting lunch money, keeping paper and other supplies available and in good order, distributing and collecting worksheets and other materials, moving students from one place to another, timing the day's activities, correcting student work in helpful ways, ensuring that students kept materials and displays in good order, and generally nipping disruptive behavior in the bud. She realized that somehow or another the plants had to be watered, the fish fed and the water changed, the hamster habitat cleaned, the audiovisual equipment dealt with, the notices sent out, the duplicating done, classroom visitors dealt with in positive ways, and provisions made for students with special needs or with limited English proficiency. She found she was spending enormous amounts of time cajoling students and then waiting exasperatedly for them to follow directions. She added insult to her own injuries by spending evenings, though exhausted, reading papers, preparing material for the next day, and contacting parents or guardians about a myriad of matters. Her schooling hadn't prepared her for all of that. She discovered quickly how heavy the mass of minor details could be.

WHAT TEACHERS TRY TO ACCOMPLISH, AND HOW

Certainly, lists of specific things teachers try to accomplish during a year would fill the remaining pages of this book. Instead of lists, what you will find here is highly summarized information and examples that are important to your understanding of the linkage between teacher intentions and the managerial tasks that make their accomplishment possible. We'll begin with some very general goals and move toward a few specific examples.

In very broad terms, teachers want to help their students become productive citizens, able to live life fully and well. Teachers everywhere sincerely want their students to make responsible choices and to discriminate between right and wrong. They would like for their students to be healthy and to appreciate life's beauty and joy, but also to be able to deal with adversity. Teachers want all of this for the students they teach. (Of course, teachers also wouldn't mind a bit of appreciation, fond regard, and remembrance, though they don't expect too much of it.)

In more specific terms, teachers aim their efforts toward the goals that have guided modern education for decades. These goals were well articulated in the 1918 *Cardinal Principles of Secondary Education,* though they certainly were evident before that publication. The 1918 goals were (1) health, (2) command of the fundamental processes (communication and math), (3) worthy home membership, (4) vocation, (5) civil education (good citizenship), (6) worthy use of leisure, and (7) ethical character. These goals are not equally emphasized now, if indeed they ever were. While little attention presently is given to worthy home membership or worthy use of leisure, the remaining five goals still figure strongly in the curriculum.

The very specific outcomes of teaching—as well as the procedures designed to bring them about—are published in curriculum guides and statewide standards and frameworks that describe what is to be accomplished at each grade level and in every area of the curriculum. And now in response to the No Child Left Behind Act of 2001 (NCLB), twenty-one states (most notably California, Texas, and Florida) have statewide textbook adoptions that dictate the textbooks schools and districts can use. The states select the textbooks they deem to most closely correspond with curriculum standards and frameworks. As a result, major publishing houses now tailor books and other materials accordingly.

■ THE INSTRUCTIONAL PACKAGE: CONTENT, INSTRUCTION THROUGH EXPERIENCE, AND MANAGEMENT

Management is of crucial importance to teaching—in fact, classroom teaching hardly can occur in its absence. As will become evident in later chapters, the management component of teaching varies according to subject, grade level, and method of teaching. A sixth-grade classroom is run quite differently from a kindergarten; multi-age classes are run differently from single-grade rooms. Reading is done differently from art, music differently from math, spelling differently from social studies. Record keeping, activities, groupings, materials, and even expectations and work products for students are likely to differ.

It is difficult, if not impossible, to describe in precise detail exactly what is included and what transpires in the totality of classroom teaching. Identifiable key elements of teaching can be thought of as decision points that call on teachers to decide how they should proceed in the classroom. Let us examine some of teaching's key considerations and decision points by analyzing the following statement:

> Education begins with three fundamental questions that, when considered in light of learner traits and conditions, link to structures called elements of teaching, which have certain identifiable characteristics and certain typical focuses.

Think of it this way—education begins with three fundamental questions that are entwined with learner traits and conditions.

1. *What should learners know?* The answer to this question is determined by deciding what is best for individuals and society. What learners should know—the contents and curricula of education currently identified by the content standards—is a central question in philosophy.

2. *How do learners learn?* The answer to this question is determined by investigating the processes by which individuals acquire, remember, and put knowledge to use. It is a central question in educational psychology. For further enlightenment, this question of how students learn must be considered in light of certain learner traits and conditions known to affect learning. Chief among these are

- Intelligence and aptitude, which include inborn abilities and proclivities that vary from student to student
- Individual learning styles and rates
- Motivation as indicated by students' willingness to work at the experiences and activities provided them
- Group behavior, which differs significantly from individual behavior
- Social and economic realities, which are known to affect individual ability and motivation to learn

3. *How should learners be taught?* The answer to this question is determined by which experiences, instructional strategies, activities, and materials best promote student learning. It is a central question in pedagogy, or methods of teaching.

Consideration of these questions links to structures called elements of teaching, which are the content to be taught (what learners should learn according to content standards) and the instruction through experiences and activities (how learners learn and how they should be taught). Underlying these elements is another element—management—the primary focus of this book. When everything is taken into account, it becomes clear that for a classroom to run smoothly, management techniques must fit the activities and expectations of specific subjects, students' ages, and ability levels. In other words, curriculum, instruction, and management must go hand in hand.

These three elements of teaching are judged against the following criteria:

- Content must be worth learning in itself and further contribute to the overall goals of education.
- Instruction through experiences must be given clearly, must guide and assist learning, must be relevant to both subject matter and students' lives, and must be attractive and enjoyable.
- Management must help teaching run more smoothly and efficiently.

2ND GRADE
MS. SMART

" BLESS HER HEART."

Further, these criteria can be linked as follows: Worthwhile *content or curricula* are delivered through instructional strategies, which include *experiences and activities* that are relevant and attractive, clear and helpful, with the entire process enhanced through *management* that promotes smoothness and efficiency.

JANNA SMART REVISITED

Mindful of the difficulties Janna Smart experienced, and with the introduction to classroom management now completed, let us see how Janna might have minimized the troubles she encountered. We will give attention to what she could have done before the school year began, or in this case before she first met her students; during the first days and weeks; and as a continual process through the year. This presentation is general for now but will be elaborated in chapters to come.

Before the School Year Begins

Before students are scheduled to arrive, teachers need to take care of several matters, of which the following five are especially important. First, teachers should familiarize themselves with the school facilities and meet as many of the school personnel as possible—administrators, clerical and custodial staffs, and other teachers. Janna Smart did this well: As the principal introduced her and showed her around the school on the morning she was hired, she quickly began to establish friendly relationships with him, the staff, and the teachers she met. She learned the locations of the library, playgrounds, restrooms, the cafeteria, the nurse's office, the custodians' station, and the teacher workroom and lounge. She introduced herself to people at school whenever possible.

Second, teachers should familiarize themselves with the curriculum and content standards for their particular grade level, and with textbooks and other materials provided them. Janna did this fairly well. She reviewed curriculum guides and standards for both first and second grades, studied the various textbooks and familiarized herself with materials present or typically used in her room, and reviewed and began ordering available media.

Third teachers should lay out a tentative calendar for the year, with specific detailed plans for the first two or three weeks. Janna, who prided herself on attention to detail, had the first month of topics and lessons broadly outlined before her first day with the students. She later found it necessary to modify her plans substantially, but most teachers frequently do.

Fourth, teachers should organize and set up the physical environment of the classroom to include flexible seating; convenient work areas adjacent to needed materials; any special areas in the room such as science corners, computer areas, or reading centers; and storage centers for materials and equipment. Janna thought her well-meaning friends had done a good job of this, though she soon found they had included things that were too distracting (hamsters and an aquarium). She soon realized she had put too much emphasis on classroom appearance and not enough on efficiency of procedures, activities, and student movement.

Fifth, teachers should give thought to the kind of psychosocial climate that they hope to establish and maintain, together with the procedures designed for bringing it about. It was here that Janna made a major mistake. She knew that students needed to feel a sense of belonging, especially because they were moved so abruptly to a new class with a new teacher after the school year had begun. They also needed to experience pleasure in their work. Janna thought she could establish those feelings simply by being nice to students and accepting what they did, believing they would reciprocate in kind. When she found they didn't, she had no effective means for putting an immediate end to disrespect, poor manners, inconsiderate behavior, and irresponsible choices. She had to learn that order and consideration to others must be firmly established and taught before a class can move ahead.

The First Days and the First Weeks

What teachers do in the beginning is crucial in setting tone, expectations, and likelihood of compliance. Good managers make sure the first few days of school are orderly, which calls for tight structure. They explain rules and procedures, introduce materials and various parts of the classroom, monitor students closely, and let them know when they are behaving responsibly and appropriately. They explain and practice routines, a first step in making them habitual. They use a few appropriate classbuilding activities to help create a caring community for the students. The teacher also talks with students about how they must accept responsibility for their own conduct. Janna did not do this well. Of course everything in the program can't be introduced on the first day of school, but by the end of the first week, several issues should be settled.

Attendance and Opening Procedures.   Students should begin the day, from the first day onward, with a quiet activity either at their seats or at a designated area in the room. During this time the teacher should take attendance while walking around and observing the students.

Older students should learn at once that they are to go to their assigned seats and begin work immediately. They can be given specific assignments such as five-a-day math problems, journal writing, or reading their library books. Younger students, not yet able to work on their own, are taught to go directly to the circle (kindergarten) or to their seats. In the past, on the first morning students were told: "Now we are in school, and the first thing we do here is sit down, fold our hands, and close our lips. If we need to say anything, we must raise our hand." The teacher then went directly into calling the roll and other opening activities, such as flag salute, calendar counting, song, or sharing. When students showed themselves capable of doing other activities with self-control, the teacher may have changed the opening. In any case, the beginning tone was businesslike and was quickly made routine. Considerable reminding and practice were necessary at first, but quiet self-control was—and still is—essential to everything else in the program.

Jones (2007), Kagan (1994), and others encourage teachers to greet students in a manner similar to this (and yes, it is all right to smile): "Welcome everyone. I'm very glad you are with me this year. I know we will have fun and learn a lot, and learning will be fun. There will be time for you to talk and move, and also time to sit. I will use a quiet signal like this when I want your attention on me." Every day teachers should give their students structured activities that allow them to move and talk—two basic human needs.

Seating Arrangements and Orientation to the Classroom.   Teachers should explain seating arrangements. Introductions to the uses of the various parts of the classroom, including interest centers and work areas, the materials they contain, and what is to be done there, can be accomplished with teacher demonstration or guided student exploration and discovery. Older students may enjoy a scavenger hunt of the classroom and its resources.

Class Rules and System of Discipline.   On the first day teachers should go over the expected rules of responsible student behavior. There should be no more than four rules for younger children and six for older children; greater numbers cannot be remembered. Have in mind what is acceptable to you, but encourage students to give input, ask questions, or discuss the various rules, incentives, and consequences. Make sure students understand the rules, the reasons behind them, and enforcement procedures you will use, and make sure they see the system as fair. If students are old enough, have them sign their names on a sheet of paper containing the rules to indicate they understand the rules, find them fair, and fully intend to abide by them.

Orientation to the School and School Rules.   Most older students, unless new to the neighborhood, will already be acquainted with the buildings and grounds. Still, it is advisable to spend time orienting students to restrooms, drinking fountains, playgrounds, the cafeteria, the library, the principal's office, the reception desk, and the nurse's station. Many teachers take their students on a walking tour of these places sometime during the first or second day of school.

Students are expected to follow certain rules that pertain to the school, as distinct from those of the classroom. These rules tell how to behave in common areas such as corridors, on the playground, in the library, in the cafeteria, at bus and parking areas, and at street crossings. It is the teacher's responsibility to thoroughly familiarize students (and aides and visiting parents and guardians as well) with these school regulations and procedures.

The Daily Schedule.   The daily schedule should be explained in a way that makes clear what activities are to occur during each part of the day and how students are to work and behave for each. The schedule should be posted where students easily can see it for reference. Along with a discussion of the schedule and activities, the teacher previews books and materials to be used on a regular basis—where they are located, how they are obtained, how they are cared for, and how they are returned after use.

Monitors (Classroom Helpers).   Many teachers use class members to help with the numerous classroom chores. Often called *monitors,* these helpers are selected during the first week of classes and changed several times during the year. Some teachers assign monitors to their duties, while others take applications, ask for volunteers, or make prized assignments (such as feeding a classroom animal) contingent on special accomplishment. A list of duties for which monitors can be particularly helpful can be found in Chapter 7. It is desirable to assign some special job to every student in the class, in order to increase interest and promote a sense of ownership and responsibility.

Miscellaneous Needs.   Students continually need help while working independently. They also need to sharpen pencils, get drinks, go to the restroom, and call their parents or guardians. Procedures and routines must be established and practiced for all such matters, so students understand how they are to proceed.

Traffic Patterns.   Students must be instructed and given opportunity to practice how to enter the classroom, how to leave when dismissed, what to do during emergency drills, and how to move from one area to another. Congestion, prevalent around the teacher's desk and classroom animals, should be eliminated by instructing students on how they are to move about and how many may be out of their seats at a given time.

Paraprofessionals and Volunteers.   Many teachers have aides and volunteers working in their rooms, and perhaps even cross-grade partners and cross-age tutors. Some experienced teachers have student teachers assigned to them. The duties of each should be very clear, as should the extent to which they are to correct and discipline students. When assigned to do clerical work, paraprofessionals should be provided a comfortable workstation with appropriate materials.

Preparing for Substitute Teachers.   Every teacher must rely on a substitute from time to time. The class should be able to continue with its normal routines under the direction of a substitute. To make this possible, the teacher must prepare the class to work with, not against, the new teacher. Discussions with the class can clarify students' responsibilities in helping the process. Whenever possible, complete lesson plans should be left for the substitute, and one or two class monitors should be assigned to inform substitutes of routines, locations of materials, and normal work procedures.

Managerial Matters That Require Ongoing Attention

To the extent possible, matters just described should be discussed with the class and put into place during the first week of school. In addition, several managerial matters require ongoing attention throughout the year. Having regained control of her classroom, Janna placed herself in a position from which she could attend to these matters. Such ongoing matters are mentioned here briefly and are discussed more fully in later chapters.

Curriculum Management.   The curriculum is the program for learners, which is aligned to standards that are described by the state and the school. Its management entails the selection, organization, and presentation of subject matter, plus arrangements for student work and accountability. These matters fluctuate through the year and require continual adjustment.

Lesson Management.   Lesson management involves selecting and organizing learning activities, grouping students, giving explanations and directions, providing for student accountability, monitoring and giving feedback, assessing performance, and reteaching as necessary. In such management, teachers find that the pacing of lessons is very important. Pacing means that lessons cover what is intended, with immediate student participation, within the allotted time, with steady momentum but without rush or delay. Also very important are the transitions between lessons, which should be made smoothly and quickly, allowing for no dead time.

Record Keeping, Assessment, and Reporting.   Records should be kept that tell student, teacher, caregivers, or administrator, at a glance, a student's achievement levels, work in progress, strengths and weaknesses, and future needs. This requirement is most easily met by keeping records sheets for the entire class plus separate records folders for each individual student. The folders should include individual progress charts together with samples (good and poor) of student work. As for reporting, each school district has its own system. Most use report cards to show achievement made in different subjects and may also include effort expended by the student and general behavior or comportment.

Special Groups.   Teachers now teach students with diverse abilities and in varied settings. All teachers are expected to welcome, value, and educate all students, including those with special needs. Teachers who teach in inclusive classrooms, multi-age classrooms, or have students with language and cultural diversities, have additional management challenges related to curriculum and lessons, record keeping, and paraprofessionals. Teachers, students, and caregivers all have rights and responsibilities that affect these matters.

Communication.   Teachers are constant communicators. They direct, instruct, and motivate students through lessons. They work with paraprofessionals, support providers, volunteers, and substitute teachers, all of whom have potential to enrich lessons. They communicate with caregivers in a variety of ways. They also interact with administrators and colleagues.

Extracurricular Activities.   Teachers' duties range far beyond those of simply organizing and presenting lessons. The following are a few of the important tasks they frequently perform that contribute to children's education but rarely are considered part of teaching.

Plays and Performances.   Teachers are called on to organize, coach, direct, and stage various types of performances, which usually involve organizing help from parents and volunteers.

Field Trips.   When the class is able to leave the school to visit places of special interest, the teacher must oversee transportation, permission slips from parents and guardians, volunteers to help supervise students, and advance preparation to make the trip smooth and beneficial.

Fairs and Carnivals.   Many schools put on fairs, carnivals, and other money-raising activities. Even when such events are under the direction of the parent–teacher organization, teachers are called on for planning, preparation, and work at the events.

Back-to-School and Open House.   Almost all schools have one or more evenings during the year in which caregivers and the public are invited to visit the school and classrooms. At these events, teachers describe their programs, activities, and expectations for the year, and display samples of student work.

Assemblies.   Teachers sometimes are put in charge of assemblies for their school, which requires much planning and organization. At other times they are responsible only for the movement of their class to and from the assembly, as well as the behavior of their students while there.

Clubs.   Teachers often assume leadership roles for special clubs or other activities such as student council, safety patrol, cheerleading, athletics, photography, scouts, science groups, after-school recreation, and so forth. Occasionally these extra tasks bring a little extra pay, but typically they are an expected part of the teacher's overall duties.

Here we end our introductory chapter on classroom management, having laid the groundwork for what is to come. The next chapter will deal with how to manage the curriculum and the calendar. Before proceeding to that topic, take a moment to consider these parting thoughts then review and reflect on what has been presented so far.

Parting Thoughts

What is important is not what happens to us, but how we respond to what happens to us.

—J. Sarte

If you have built castles in the air, your work need not be lost; that is where they should be. Now put foundations under them.

—Thoreau

SUMMARY SELF-CHECK

Check off the following as you either understand or become able to apply them.

❏   Three fundamental questions about education
- What should students know?
- How do learners learn?
- How should learners be taught?

❏   Aspects of classroom management that require attention
- Before the year begins: familiarity with personnel and facilities, curriculum and content standards, calendar; preparation of the classroom; planning for the emotional tone of the class
- First days and weeks of school: attendance and opening procedures; seating arrangements and classroom orientation; class rules and system of discipline; orientation to the school, classroom and school rules; the daily class schedule; books and materials; selection of student helpers (monitors); routines for sharpening pencils, getting drinks, and using the restroom; traffic patterns and regulations; use of volunteers and paraprofessionals; preparation for substitute teachers

- Continual attention throughout the year: curriculum selection and organization; lesson management; special groups; record keeping, assessment, and reporting; extracurricular activities

ACTIVITIES FOR REFLECTION AND DISCUSSION

1. Take a moment to review the statements in the Prediction–Review Guide at the beginning of this chapter. Put a check mark in the Review column next to any statement with which you now agree. How have your thoughts changed since reading this chapter?

2. Interview at least two teachers about the problems they experienced their first year(s) of teaching. What is the best advice from the teachers you interviewed regarding the first days of school or first year of teaching?

3. From what you have seen or heard, how realistic is the Janna Smart story?

4. What distinction, if any, can be made between teaching and management? Describe what you believe each entails. What overlap do you see?

5. Have you known teachers who failed, gave up early, or lived through immense frustration? If so, what seemed to be the major difficulties with which they had to contend?

6. The point was made that the instructional program cannot proceed until a semblance of good order is established, practiced, and maintained in the classroom. Do you agree with that? What if it takes a week or two (or longer) to get the class under control?

7. This first chapter presents a fairly thorough overview of classroom management. Was it worth your time reading it, or did you feel that you more or less knew all these things before you decided to become a teacher?

REFERENCES AND RECOMMENDED READINGS

Bureau of Education. (1918). *Cardinal principles of secondary education* (Bulletin #35). Washington, DC: Department of the Interior, Bureau of Education.

Evertson, C., Emmer, E., Clements, B., Sanford, J., & Worsham, M. (2006). *Classroom management for elementary teachers* (7th ed.). Boston: Allyn & Bacon.

Finn, C. E., Jr., & Ravitch, D. (2004, September 29). *The mad, mad world of textbook adoption.* Washington, DC: Thomas B. Fordham Institute. www.edexcellence.net/institute/publication/ publication.cfm?id=335

Fuery, C. (2005). *The new winning year one: Jump-start student success from day one K–12* (9th ed.). Captiva, FL: Sanibel Sanddollar Publications.

Gilbert, L. (2005, May). What helps beginning teachers? *Educational Leadership, 62*(8), 36–39.

Ginott, H. (1972). *Teacher and child.* New York: Macmillan.

Good, T., & Brophy, J. (2002). *Looking into classrooms* (9th ed.). New York: Allyn & Bacon.

Jones, F. (2007). *Tools for teaching: Discipline Instruction Motivation* (2nd ed.). Santa Cruz, CA: Fredric H. Jones and Associates.

Kagan, S. (1994). *Cooperative learning.* San Clemente, CA: Kagan Cooperative Learning.

Lieberman, A., & Miller, L. (1999). *Teachers—Transforming their world and their work.* New York: Teachers College.

Mandel, S. (2006, March). What new teachers really need. *Educational Leadership, 63*(6), 66–69.

McCann, T., Johannessen, L., & Ricca, B. (2005, May). Responding to new teachers' concerns. *Educational Leadership, 62*(8), 30–34.

Ryan, K., & Cooper, J. (2007). *Those who can, teach* (11th ed.). Boston: Houghton Mifflin.

Useem, E., & Neild, R. (2005, May). Supporting new teachers in the city. *Educational Leadership, 62*(8), 44–47.

Wong, H., & Wong, R. (2001). *How to be an effective teacher: The first days of school* (17th ed.). Mountain View, CA: Harry K. Wong Publications.

Trade Books

Collins, M., & Tamarkin, C. (1990). *Marva Collins' way.* New York: G. P. Putnam's Sons.

Sollman, C., Emmons, B., & Paolini, J. (1994). *Through the cracks.* Worcester, MA: Davis Publications.

Stuart, J. (1949). *The thread that runs so true.* New York: Simon & Schuster.

CHAPTER 2

Laying Out the School Year

A good plan executed right now is far better than a perfect plan executed next week.

—George S. Patton

Prediction–Review Guide

Before you read the chapter, take a minute to put a check mark in the Prediction column next to any statement with which you agree.

	Prediction	Review
1. Curriculum is defined as the contents of textbooks and other materials children use.	❏	❏
2. Teachers are expected to redesign curriculum guides to meet their own specifications.	❏	❏
3. Ideally, teachers should lay out the yearly calendar before they finalize units of instruction.	❏	❏
4. Curriculum maps reveal repetitions and gaps in content and skills.	❏	❏
5. Backward design planning begins with target goals and assessment.	❏	❏
6. Essential or guiding questions are intended to check ongoing student understanding of the fine points of their study.	❏	❏
7. Authorities recommend that, when planning units, teachers begin by listing the broad objectives they hope to have their students attain.	❏	❏
8. Thematic plans integrate several subjects into each unit of instruction.	❏	❏
9. Awareness of what students already know or are able to do provides helpful information to teachers as they plan.	❏	❏
10. How the curriculum is managed is much more important to education than is the subject matter contained in the curriculum.	❏	❏

Support for specific standards found in this chapter:

INTASC Standards

1. Knowledge of Subject Matter

    The teacher understands the central concepts, tools of inquiry, and structures of the subject being taught and can create learning experiences that make these aspects of subject matter meaningful for students.

7. Instructional Planning Skills

    The teacher plans instruction based on knowledge of subject matter, students, the community, and curriculum guides.

Danielson's Framework for Teaching

1. Planning and Preparation

    - Demonstrating knowledge of students
    - Selecting instructional goals
    - Demonstrating knowledge of resources
    - Designing coherent instruction

NBPTS Standards

4. Teachers think systematically about their practice and learn from experience.

NCATE Standards

Help all pre-kindergarten through twelfth grade (P–12) students learn.

One of the first management tasks that awaits teachers—one to be completed at least tentatively before the school year begins—is that of laying out the intended instructional program for the year. This process involves interweaving curriculum with the calendar. Because the reality of schooling is that the curriculum is more flexible than the calendar and time schedules, the curriculum must be adjusted to the dates and times available for instruction.

This task is more challenging for elementary teachers than for secondary teachers, because elementary classes deal with so many different subject areas on a daily basis—reading, grammar, spelling, composition, listening, speaking, mathematics, history, geography, current events, science, health, safety, physical education, music, art, penmanship, and sometimes others. Elementary teachers are challenged to find ways to deal with, and do justice to, all these subjects for all the children they teach. They accomplish this task in two steps. First, they note what the year's calendar allows in terms of instructional days and time. Then they organize their instructional programs to fit within time constraints while providing proper emphasis, duration, and continuity over weeks, semesters, and the entire year.

HOW TO LAY OUT THE YEAR

When you begin considering the curriculum for your grade (or grades, if yours is a multi-age class), you should look at what you are supposed to teach (content and standards), available materials, and your students. Having done that, you will find yourself penciling a calendar for the year. Many lesson plan books furnished by schools, or available for purchase, contain spaces to enter your daily plans week by week. These plan books provide a year's calendar formatted as blank boxes for each day of each month.

National holidays will be shown in your plan book, as well as some nonholidays, such as Halloween, Election Day, and Valentine's Day. As you prepare the calendar, you can mark all the holidays, vacation times, teacher in-service days, and days when students will not be present. Your school district calendar, separate from the plan book, will indicate teaching days, in-service days, parent–teacher conference days, and dates when report cards are due. Your school site calendar will include back-to-school and open house nights, and perhaps dates for school assemblies, school carnival, family math night, and other school or community events. While these events may seem to interfere with teaching continuity, they also can excite and motivate students and provide themes that you can use to good advantage.

Anticipating Upcoming Events

Once you have marked the yearly calendar in this way, you will have a more accurate view of the blocks of time available for teaching. Now you can make additional notations that offer an even more complete picture of what the months will bring. Depending on your actual school year, you will find it helpful to anticipate the following realities.

Summer.   Many districts schedule teacher orientations and workshops in July or August, before the school year begins. New teachers who are hired before the school year begins are expected to attend these events.

Mid-July, Late August, Early September.   In most areas of the United States, school begins the week before or after Labor Day, although in some places school begins as early as mid-July. Everyone is excited, and these first days tend to be a time of fairly good student behavior. Students are unsure of the new setting and usually hope they have a teacher who will treat them well. This is a good time for high-interest units of study; they help you get off to a good start with your students. Because you can expect that the students will test you very early in the year, as they did with Janna Smart in Chapter 1, these first days are the time to establish routines and expectations. This also is a good time for classbuilding activities that will help create a sense of community among the students, and for teambuilding activities that will encourage cooperation. For teachers and students alike, the first days of school usually are a time of watchfulness and promise.

The Jewish New Year and High Holy Days, from Rosh Hashanah to Yom Kippur, occur in September and October. Check with your building principal regarding the school's policy of drawing attention to religious holidays and discussing their history and meaning.

October.   Depending on when the school year began, a back-to-school night usually is scheduled for September or October. You will be expected to describe your program to those who attend, answer questions, talk with caregivers, and show samples of each student's work. Although your program should already have been communicated to parents and guardians through a newsletter, this is a good time for reminders.

Also depending on when school began, parent–teacher conferences are scheduled close to the back-to-school night. In many areas, students are dismissed early or do not have school on those days. These conferences call for considerable preparation on your part (as will be explained in Chapter 11). You will need to plan out what you would like to discuss with each student's parent or guardian. You also will need representative samples of each student's work, showing areas of strength and areas for growth.

Columbus Day is observed the second Monday of October, providing a three-day weekend. Most teachers give some attention to Columbus's efforts through stories and art activities. Halloween is on the last day of the month. Although many schools downplay Halloween, students nevertheless will be excited and distracted by it. Many teachers provide stories and writing and art activities on the Halloween theme. Again, check with your principal about district and school policy and practice. Also around Halloween, most parts of the United States "fall back" the clocks to standard time. This time change affects energy levels of both teachers and students.

November.   Three events of particular interest occur this month. Election Day, the first Tuesday of the month, is not a school holiday, but usually is of interest to older students. Veterans Day, November 11, is a school holiday. It is accompanied by little fanfare in most places, and some school districts move the observance date in order to provide a three-day weekend. In contrast, Thanksgiving, the fourth Thursday of the month, generates much excitement. At least two days (in some districts, three days or even the entire week) are non-school days. Students will be interested in the origins of Thanksgiving, making this a good time for writing, drama, and art activities on that theme.

December.   The last one-third of the month will be given to vacation, and the early two-thirds will be a time of excited anticipation over Hanukkah, Kwanzaa, and Christmas. Check school policy regarding mention of these celebrations, but recognize that, regardless of policy, the children will be thinking about special family celebrations, gifts, travel, special foods and treats, family events, and decorations, and will likely be more excitable and distracted than usual. These weeks are especially good times for activities in art, music, drama, and stories of the season.

January.   Teachers and students return from holiday excitements to the normal school routine with varying degrees of interest, but overall this is a time for everyone to settle back into a productive routine. Martin Luther King Day, celebrating Dr. King's birthday on January 15, normally is scheduled to provide a long weekend in the middle of the month. The days that precede it offer an appropriate time for emphasizing African American and Black heroes in history, music, art, and literature. Many students will be interested in the professional football playoffs, with high interest for the Super Bowl at the end of the month, and the winter Olympic Games if they are held that year. Depending on the locale, wintry weather also will be a topic of interest.

February.   This month marks the approximate midpoint of the school year, and seems to pass especially quickly because it is short and contains long weekends and dates of interest to children. Children usually enjoy Groundhog Day (February 2) and Valentine's Day (February 14). Lincoln's birthday (February 12) and Washington's birthday (February 20) also may spark student interest and often are observed with one, and sometimes two, long weekends. Many schools and teachers enjoy celebrating the one-hundredth day of school with a variety of math, literature, and art activities. Teachers also may have to prepare midyear report cards.

March.   After the fast pace of February, March may seem rather slow, and student enthusiasm may wane. However, with fewer outside distractions, children can concentrate better on schoolwork, making this a good time to complete longer units of study. Dr. Seuss's birthday is March 2, encouraging many elementary teachers and librarians to plan celebration activities on that day. Also, Saint Patrick's Day may receive attention on March 17.

April.   Most schools take a weeklong spring break in late March or early April. Students and families often travel or receive visitors during this time. Also, the month frequently brings commemorations of Passover and Easter. Check with your principal about school policy regarding these holidays. Clocks that were changed in the fall will be moved ahead from standard time to Daylight Savings Time early in the month. Energy levels again are affected because of the time change.

"THERE WAS DANCING IN THE HALLS TODAY WHEN CLASSES LET OUT FOR VACATION. THE KIDS WERE EXCITED, TOO!"

May, June.   Early in May, schools typically extend another invitation for caregivers to visit the school. This is when teachers and students display some of their accomplishments of the year, and classrooms usually are decorated accordingly. Mother's Day occurs in May, and students often do art activities in which they make something to give the special women in their lives. Memorial Day falls on May 30 but usually is observed on the last Monday of the month to make a long weekend. In June, Flag Day and Father's Day may attract some attention.

The end of the traditional school year comes in mid-May or June, depending on when the academic year began. Whenever school ends, the final weeks are a time of activity and distraction. Teachers are concerned about report cards. Students' minds are on summer, and a few are concerned about promotion or moving to another school.

Summer.   In districts with year-round school calendars, Independence Day, July 4, will affect planning for the first week of July. In some years the summer Olympic Games and the national primaries can provide interesting topics of study, particularly for older students.

The yearly calendar is annotated in this manner, not to imply that it is the driving force behind curriculum organization, but to remind teachers of outside forces that can influence instruction. Keep the notations at hand as you use your curriculum guide, grade-level standards, and textbooks to plot out the selected topics of instruction for your students. Use Post-Its or pencil your plans on a separate chart or blank calendar pages. You probably will make a number of changes before you finalize them. A point to remember: To the extent possible, begin instructional units on Mondays (or the Tuesday following a long weekend) and have them end just before holidays, long weekends, or vacation times, because it is difficult to recapture student enthusiasm after such breaks. You may need to shorten or even bypass some of the units or lessons included in your grade and books to fit everything in your schedule.

LAYING OUT THE DAY

Once you have the year's calendar blocked out, but before you begin to plan specific lessons and units, it is a good idea to set up the day's schedule within the structure of the school's schedule, as you would like it to be. The school establishes times for recess, lunch, and dismissal, and your grade-level team may adjust schedules to create team teaching opportunities. Otherwise, you have considerable discretion in deciding on the schedule of teaching you prefer. However, you should view the daily schedule as more than a matter of convenience. Certain subjects, such as math or language arts, are best studied when students are fresh, alert, and able to concentrate for a long while. Other subjects, such as singing or physical education, are best scheduled to relieve tension from long concentration. Still others that might involve cooperation and talking are good for later in the day when students are getting tired.

"First grade's like kindergarten. Only BIG TIME."

Daily Schedules

Stacy Ganzer teaches thirty half-day kindergarten students, many of whom are English language learners. In addition to considering the short attention spans and the language diversity of her students, she must plan all her lessons and activities for a shorter time frame than elementary teachers in other grades.

Stacy's Schedule

7:45–7:50	Students place all their folders in the collection bin; attendance
7:50–8:00	Math problem solving of the day
8:00–8:20	Calendar activities/story
8:20–8:30	Shared writing
8:30–9:30	Reading/math groups (two groups of five children)
9:30–9:55	Snack/PE
9:55–10:10	Story/sharing
10:10–10:20	Daily phonemic awareness activities
10:20–10:50	Language and math centers/English language development groups
10:50–11:00	Free exploration (if time allows)
11:00–11:10	Clean up
11:10–11:12	Line up and dismissal

Reading and math groups alternate days. On Wednesdays, reading and math groups are replaced with a journal writing activity, science lesson, or social studies lesson that the class does as a whole group.

Jan Gretlein is a first-grade teacher. She is with her students all day but follows a schedule that takes into consideration many of the same issues as Stacy's schedule.

Jan's Schedule

8:55	School begins; teacher meets students on the playground and walks with them to the classroom
8:55–9:15	Students read silently; teacher talks to caregivers, takes attendance, and assists individuals or small groups of students, as needed
9:15–9:45	Reading workshop/literacy centers
9:45–10:45	Mini-lessons and guided reading groups that focus on individual and small group reading comprehension activities
10:45–11:00	Recess
11:00–11:45	Writing workshop with varied independent writing activities, such as journal and letter writing, poetry, and fiction and nonfiction stories published in class
11:45–12:45	Math
12:45–1:25	Lunch
1:25–1:45	Reading aloud by teacher
1:45–3:00	Science/social studies/PE
3:00–3:20	Clean up, daily news
3:20	School ends; dismissal

Jan schedules library once a week and computer lab every two weeks. Jan does not begin reading groups in the beginning of the year. First, she establishes routines, sets expectations, and familiarizes children with each of the activities they will use at center time. At the beginning of the year, she plans thirty minutes for literacy centers. Later in the year, this is extended to forty-five minutes. For her reading program, Jan uses many of the activities in *Strategies That Work* (Harvey & Goudvis, 2000) and *Mosaic of Thought* (Keene & Zimmermann, 1997).

Marilyn Cox and Bernardo Campos are partners in a fifth-grade team. In their district, fifth graders may participate in several special programs that must be considered as the team plans the daily schedule.

Marilyn and Bernardo's Schedule

8:55	Students gather on the playground with their classmates and enter their classrooms together to begin the day
9:00–11:05	Reader's workshop and writing
11:05–11:20	Recess
11:20–12:45	Math (students are separated by ability groups, and the teaching team rotates to different groups when units change)
12:45–1:00	Homework assignments and explanations
1:00–1:40	Lunch
1:40–2:00	Reading aloud
2:00–2:20	Word study
2:20–3:00	Social studies/science
3:00–3:20	PE/art
3:20	Dismissal

Library is scheduled for one day a week. The school's computer lab is only available by sign up and often is used for project-related work. Marilyn and Bernardo hope to use a portable computer lab, a cart with thirty laptop computers that can be moved from room to room, more often this year and will need to sign up for it accordingly. Many students serve on Student Council, which meets one day a week before school, or on Safety Patrol (in groups of five each day). Because of their responsibilities, these students arrive shortly after the bell rings in the morning and leave the classroom five to ten minutes prior to general dismissal. Additionally, most of Marilyn and Bernardo's students participate in band as an elective. Band students are grouped according to the instrument they play and meet with the band teacher one day a week. Also, in anticipation of a school Winter Olympics event, the fifth-grade team plans for eight rotations over a three-week period before winter break. Students practice eight of the track and field–type events (relay, dash, and so on) in order to participate in the school Olympics in February or March. The daily schedule will change to allot 2:50–3:30 for these rotations.

Stacy, Jan, and Marilyn and Bernardo teach in elementary schools where they are responsible for the entire curriculum. Some schools, particularly middle schools, also have specialist teachers for physical education, music, art, and occasionally other subjects. These schools may schedule common preparation time for subjects such as social studies and language arts to permit teachers to plan together and then team teach. Other schools may have a regularly scheduled preparation time that teachers use for planning. In middle schools that include sixth grade, teams of teachers may share two or more groups of students every day. In teams of two, one teacher may teach students language arts and social studies while another teaches math and science. Where there are teams of four, teachers may each have separate subjects and simply rotate in order to teach the same content to all the students in the grade.

Sherry Coburn is the social studies teacher for a sixth-grade team at her middle school. Every day she teaches four groups of students for a fifty-six minute period. The other three teachers on her team teach language arts, math, and science. Sherry has a typical weekly plan for when her students study a chapter in their textbook. On Monday, Sherry assigns eight district geography questions. After some whole-class review, students use their textbooks and other resources to search for the answers. At the start of the year, students need a great deal of help with this activity, but they become more proficient as time goes by. On Tuesday and Wednesday students complete activities using vocabulary from the chapter in the textbook. This work is turned in as homework on Thursday. To help students with their reading, Sherry creates study guides that include questions and missing words. Students use class time on Thursday to search the chapter and complete the study guides. On Friday, after a quiz from their reading, students play review games such as vocabulary concentration and Jeopardy.

CURRICULUM FROM THE MANAGEMENT PERSPECTIVE

Our concern here is not with preparing and organizing curriculum, but with managing it. In Chapter 1, classroom management was presented as handling, governing, directing, or controlling so as to bring something about, with prime emphasis on efficiency and effectiveness. In curriculum management, what we intend to bring about is purposeful interaction between students and the information and skills they are intended to learn. We want to accomplish this interaction as effectively and efficiently as possible.

Teachers usually think of curriculum as the basic material that they are expected to teach or the textbooks they use. States now have published standards that describe the specific topics and content for each subject area. Just as you find specific standards connected to each chapter in this book, such material is laid out in the teacher editions of the textbooks designed for the students they are teaching. In preparing those textbooks, authors and publishers do their best to interpret and address the published standards, and they work hard to make the books both effective and easy to use. Frequently, textbooks are supplemented with a variety of excellent ancillary materials, such as transparencies or black lines, CDs, DVDs or videos, and banks of test questions.

However, for the sake of accuracy, it must be noted that textbook contents and curriculum are not synonymous terms. For as long as there have been schools, there has been dispute about what the curriculum ought to be. Even today there is no consensus as to what the term *curriculum* means. It has been defined as experiences under the auspices of the school (Rosales-Dordelly & Short, 1985); a series of planned events intended to have educational consequence (Eisner, 1985); and activities, processes, and structural arrangements intended for and used in the school and classroom as a means of accomplishing the educative function (Goodlad, 2004, 1984). Doll suggests that "curriculum is what happens when the door is closed," although he more formally describes curriculum as formal and informal content and process used to help learners grow in knowledge, understanding, skills, attitudes, appreciation, and values (1995). Ralph Tyler (1949), one of the twentieth century's most influential writers on curriculum, didn't really define it at all. Instead, he devoted his efforts to describing how curriculum is studied, developed, and evaluated.

MANAGING THE CURRICULUM FLOW

Focus Questions

Keith Correll seems to base his decisions regarding curriculum and management on his beliefs and expectations about his students and schooling. How does Mr. Correll's approach help him to manage successfully the curriculum for his sixth graders? What changes might he make to manage curriculum for third graders successfully? For first graders?

Mr. Correll teaches a self-contained sixth grade. It is important to him for things to run smoothly. Mr. Correll provides an organized daily schedule and routine, and he expects students to change quickly from one subject to the next. He believes students should know what is coming and know what to do. He sets aside time during the first part of a particular period for a whole-class activity. For example, the first thing in math always is a one-minute timed exercise. Students know he will quickly say "go," and if they don't have their pencils, scratch paper, and test sheet ready, they are out of luck—they can try again the next day.

Subject matter is very important to Mr. Correll, and he plans and teaches with junior high in the back of his mind. Mr. Correll goes over all the assignments ahead of time so students know exactly what is expected. They know the schedule of tests and what they have to do to earn their grades on the report cards. Assignments are to be completed. If they are not, a note goes home, filled out by the student, stating what was not completed and why, and the work must be made up on the student's own time. Mr. Correll believes all this makes students responsible for their own grades.

Some authorities view curriculum as "explicit" or formal, "implicit" or hidden, or "extra." The *explicit* curriculum is what is published. This aligns with standards and grade-level expectations. The *hidden* curriculum includes socialization and learning environments, rules and guidelines, and behavior. The *extra* curriculum includes athletics, band, clubs, and other such activities.

Now current educational policies and reforms further influence the definition of curriculum. Inspired by NCLB, a contemporary twist to the definition is the idea of "curriculum narrowing." Academic subjects of reading, math, and science are given time and resource priorities over other subjects (social studies, physical education, foreign languages, and the arts). Read more about policy and reform and standards in a minute.

Although there is little agreement about definitions of curriculum, there is perhaps even less agreement about the content of curriculum. Philosophers, educators, politicians, critics, individuals with axes to grind, and an infinity of special-interest groups struggle to shape curriculum contents, as each believes proper. Hirsch and others have published volumes by grade level of what every child should know.

NOW A WORD ABOUT STANDARDS

In the 1980s and 1990s, state and federal governments responded to *A Nation at Risk* by implementing a series of laws for standards-based reform. With the Improving America's

Schools Act of 1994 (IASA) and Goals 2000: Educate America Act, the federal government moved standards-based reform to policy and encouraged states to adopt content standards in the core subject areas of mathematics, English language arts, reading, and science. The No Child Left Behind Act of 2001 made standards-based reform a national education policy. Thus, in light of current reform across the nation, standards have become a driving force for content and curriculum, performance, opportunities-to-learn, and technology. This is particularly true of literacy and math, although now all individual subject areas are identifying content standards as well. States and districts are creating or revising learning goals and identifying benchmarks and competencies to define skills, knowledge, and content mastery for students of varying ages and grades.

MAPPING THE BIG PICTURE

"To make sense of our students' experiences over time, we need two lenses: a zoom lens into this year's curriculum for a particular grade and a wide-angle lens to see the K–12 perspective" (Jacobs, 1997, p. 3). Heidi Jacobs describes a procedure she calls curriculum mapping, which involves individual, team, and whole-school input, and promotes alignment by revealing gaps and redundancies in content and skills. A website that can lead you to more about curriculum mapping is www.curriculumdesigners.com. The curriculum mapping process has seven steps.

1. Each teacher independently identifies the major elements that make up the curriculum—the emphasized standards, processes, and skills; the essential content and topics; and the products and performances.
2. In a first read-through, each teacher scans the maps for the entire building (or team), to gather information and identify areas for future examination. Each teacher notes repetitions (of standards, content, and skills), gaps (between standards and goals and what actually is taught), meaningful assessments, matches with content standards and objectives, potential areas of integration, and timeliness (availability of current materials and resources and knowledge of current best practices).
3. If the curriculum-mapping project is large enough (for a school or the district), teachers who do not teach together then meet in teams of six or eight. They share their individual findings and create a composite list of their observations for review by the larger group.
4. In an all-faculty (or all-team) review, observation findings from the smaller sessions are charted, and focus still is on the nonjudgmental review of what was observed. When teachers begin to edit, revise, and develop, they may remain together as one large group or move into smaller instructional units.
5. Faculty members begin to sift through the data from the observation findings and determine areas that can be revised immediately and easily by faculty members, teams, and administrators.
6. Faculty members also determine areas that require more long-range research and development. These areas may require structural decisions, more in-depth investigation, or more consideration of the potential long-range consequences before changes can be made.

7. The steps in the whole curriculum mapping process then are repeated, because curriculum review is active and ongoing.

BACKWARD DESIGN PLANNING

In an effort to help teachers better plan curriculum and assessments that will result in student *understanding* (as opposed to simple student *knowing*), Wiggins and McTighe (1998) offer another approach to planning. What they call backward design is an alternative to coverage and activity-oriented plans. Teachers plan through three stages. Here's an intentionally simplified explanation. Teachers who use backward design planning first identify the desired results. Then they determine acceptable evidence, the products students will provide to demonstrate their understanding. Finally, teachers plan the instruction and learning experiences.

According to Wiggins and McTighe, teachers must reflect on several things when considering the desired results of the teaching and learning. Teachers must identify the understandings students will gain. They must form essential or guiding questions—broad questions that will guide and focus the teaching and learning. They must identify key knowledge and skills students will acquire as a result of the study. Teachers also must consider the evidence, such as performance, quizzes, tests, work samples, and student self-assessment, and determine what evidence they will expect and use for students to demonstrate their understanding.

Task analyses of performance tasks and assessment greatly help teachers determine acceptable evidence, the second step of backward design. It makes sense in this step to articulate content standards and the desired understandings to be assessed through tasks. It also makes sense to clarify the purpose of the assessment tasks—whether they are diagnostic, formative, or summative. GRASPS is a simple acronym that can help with this: Goals, Role, Audience, Situation, Product or Performance, and Standards (Wiggins & McTighe, 1998). Identifying the criteria as well as the scoring tool for evaluating student products and performances (rubric, checklist, or other) is as important to this step as identifying the assessment tool itself.

Only after teachers identify what they want students to understand and be able to do and consider the evidence they will expect and accept from the students to determine those understandings, are they in a position to plan the learning experiences and instruction. Hence, the process name of *backward design planning*.

THE GOALS OF THE SCHOOL CURRICULUM

The school curriculum is intended to expose students to important subjects and topics, thereby causing them to acquire certain knowledge, skills, attitudes, and values. These goals were partially expressed in the Cardinal Principles mentioned in Chapter 1, especially command of the fundamental processes of communication and mathematics, good citizenship, and health. In addition, the curriculum is intended to produce (1) attitudes of openness to ideas, willingness to try, and acceptance of others; (2) knowledge of facts and their application; and (3) growth in thinking skills such as analysis, synthesis, and evaluation. As

Eisner asserts, "curriculum is and needs to be a course of action that advances understanding" (2002).

All of this is to be worked on in school although, in truth, much of it—especially concerning attitudes and values—occurs more potently in the home and community. Published character-building curricula such as *Character Counts* are available for adoption by districts, schools, or individual teachers. These programs offer guided activities so teachers and schools can focus on a character trait or quality each week. However, for teachers to best help students acquire attitudes of good character, they must imbed these qualities into the way they teach. They also must provide students with constant opportunities to practice the attributes and attitudes of good character within the normal events of their class.

IMPLEMENTING THE CURRICULUM

Activities in teachers' daily schedules are delivered through individual lessons that, in most cases, are episodes within larger units of instruction rather than isolated events. Units consist of closely related lessons that build toward larger understandings, and most are designed to be completed in one to four weeks.

Frequently preorganized units are found in teacher editions of student textbooks, but almost all teachers plan a number of units of their own to better match their students' needs. Unit topics are numerous, and they spread across the spectrum of the curriculum—dinosaurs, weather, the family, pets, poetry, fractions, graphing, physical endurance, landscape drawing, the thirteen colonies, media, and so on. These diverse units are built mostly around concrete concepts. Generally, students do not do well in units on intangibles such as prejudice, self-esteem, or feelings until they are able to think abstractly. Some attention is given in elementary classes to patriotism, freedom, and quality, though mostly in terms of the beliefs and deeds of heroes and heroines such as George Washington, Abraham Lincoln, Martin Luther King, Jr., Harriet Tubman, Clara Barton, and Jade Snow Wong.

Something to Think About
It has long been said that when humans learn they remember approximately

- 10 percent of what they read
- 20 percent of what they hear
- 30 percent of what they see
- 70 percent of what they say
- 90 percent of what they do

And yet education still most strongly emphasizes reading and hearing.

The Organization of Units

Authorities in curriculum and instruction believe that, once the topic is selected, units should be planned as follows:

1. Review the local and state standards to determine which may be addressed in this unit of study.

2. Formulate an overall goal that you want your students to achieve or an essential or guiding question for them to answer. An appropriate goal for a unit entitled "Community" might be: "Students will be able to construct a model of a community that includes physical structures as well as evidence of meaningful services." An appropriate essential or guiding question might be: "How does my community affect my life?" For a unit entitled "Maps as Tools," an overall goal might be: "Students will be able to construct a series of maps offering information about a country or region from which some of their ancestors came." An essential or guiding question might be: "In what ways have maps been useful tools for humans?"

3. Formulate several interim subordinate objectives, whose attainment moves learners progressively toward the overall goal. Interim objectives for the unit on community might ask students to be able to replicate their neighborhood community on a map, list community members and their services, or compare their neighborhood community to one from another time and place in history (such as ancient Greece or Rome, mid 1800s, early 1900s). The unit on maps might call on students to read latitude and longitude, interpret and use maps in reference books, and make population and climatic maps for a selected country such as Peru.

4. Organize instructional activities that lead to the attainment of each of the interim objectives. For the unit on community, this will result in a number of individual lessons on the nature and meaning of community and neighborhood and on local jobs. The community unit could be integrated with the unit on maps with lessons on map reading; interpreting map legends; pinpointing specific buildings, businesses, and services; creating a map of the area where one lives; and learning how different types of maps convey specific information. A variety of materials will be needed for the lessons, as well as appropriate space and arrangements for engaging in the activities. All of this will have to be planned and managed carefully if you are to keep students productively on task.

5. Provide assessment activities that will give the students opportunities to demonstrate what they now understand and how they reached the objective or were able to provide the answer to the essential or guiding question.

Note that while this approach does not follow exactly the three stages of backward design unit planning, it does emphasize the curriculum standards, essential or guiding questions, or the objectives—what you hope students will know or be able to do as a result of their working through the unit.

The Way Many Teachers Organize Units

Although curriculum standards remain a key consideration, many teachers do not organize units from the basis of objectives or essential questions, but rather from a consideration of desirable experiences. In planning, those teachers follow a process of self-questioning somewhat like the following:

VIGNETTE 2.1   Planning for Multi-Age Classes

Lisa Johnston teaches a multi-age fourth- and fifth-grade class. It is important to her that all her students receive adequate instruction in the appropriate grade-level content areas. At the beginning of the year, Lisa decides on the themes that will organize her teaching and provide structure for her students to make meaningful connections throughout the year. She plans her curriculum after she reviews the state and local standards for the two grade levels. In order to engage and help everyone be successful, Lisa then carefully considers her students. She mentally divides her students into three categories based on their readiness, interest, and learning profile for the topic or concept: advanced, average, and struggling learners. Then she plans different ways to approach the topic for each of the three groups. For example, she might provide different reading materials to differentiate the content. She might vary the process by which students make sense out of their study. Or she might suggest different ways for students to demonstrate their understanding and extend their learning.

Upon Reflection

Lisa Johnston groups her students into three categories. What are your thoughts about heterogeneous rather than homogeneous grouping within the class for planning and delivering the curricula? What are the challenges of both? The advantages of both?

1. What topics do the textbook, curriculum guide, achievement tests, and my personal beliefs and experiences suggest that I ought to cover this year?
2. What beneficial experiences or activities can I provide for my students within each of these topics? What will students find enjoyable and worthwhile? What books, pictures, media, and other materials and objects (and maybe even guests) can I use?
3. Which district, state, and federal standards will be addressed through these activities?
4. How can I organize these activities to fit into the time allotments I have available?
5. How will I evaluate my students' work, and how can I let them show their parents and others how much they have learned?

You can see that this procedure for organizing instructional units proceeds from a list of experiences or activities that teachers believe good for their students, not from a list of objectives. The teachers still have objectives or outcomes in mind, but they think first about quality experiences.

It is important to note here that the backward design process can be applied to multiple levels of planning. Teachers can use the process to organize the overview of the entire year, as well as to develop unit plans. It even can be used to plan single lessons. The process is the same: First, identify the desired results of the study. Then determine acceptable evidence to demonstrate student understanding. Finally, plan the instruction and learning experiences.

Organizing Thematic Units of Instruction

Thematic units of instruction that integrate teaching from several different subject areas are strongly popular and can be highly efficient. To show how thematic units are planned, let's consider a unit entitled "Lands and Peoples of South America." For this unit we want to integrate social studies, reading, language arts, science, art, and music, all having to do with the regions being studied—and all contributing to a greater breadth of understanding of South American peoples and geography.

We begin by selecting the broad central theme, "Lands and Peoples of South America." That theme can be visualized as the hub of a wheel, whose spokes are composed of the various subjects to be integrated, such as social studies, reading, language arts, science, art, and music. Figure 2.1 is a template for such a thematic curriculum wheel. Figure 2.2 is a template for curriculum design with the multiple intelligences in mind.

First, list separate regions of South America on the hub of the wheel. These might include the high Andes, the Amazon basin, the northern region, the Patagonian grasslands, and the Chilean coastline. Next, make balanced associations between these hub regions and the spoke subjects in order to identify lesson topics on languages, lifestyles, customs, art, and music. Included in the lessons might be words that are important in the study of South America; stories and nonfiction accounts of life in South America; family life in areas of dense and sparse populations; popular music, folk songs, and instruments; illustrations of typical clothing, dwellings, and artifacts; map study with depiction of populations, ethnic distribution, and distances between cities and landmarks; and the study of animals indigenous to the various areas.

A review of state and local standards will help identify appropriate reading, writing, and math, as well as social studies and science standards that should be addressed in this grade level and the unit of study. Once the standards and lesson topics are identified, specific

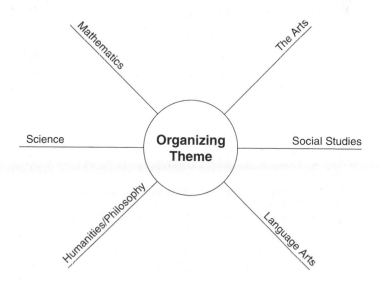

FIGURE 2.1   Interdisciplinary Concept Model

Source: From *Interdisciplinary Curriculum: Design and Implementation* edited by Heidi Hayes Jacobs. Alexandria, VA: Association for Supervision and Curriculum Development. Copyright © 1989 Thomas Armstrong. Reprinted by permission. The Association for Supervision and Curriculum Development is a worldwide community of educators advocating sound policies and sharing best practices to achieve the success of each learner. To learn more, visit ASCD at www.ascd.org.

FIGURE 2.2 Curriculum Wheel

Source: So Each May Learn: Integrating Learning Styles and Multiple Intelligences by H. Silver et al., Alexandria, VA: Association for Supervision and Curriculum Development. © 2000. Reprinted by permission. The Association for Supervision and Curriculum Development is a worldwide community of educators advocating sound policies and sharing best practices to achieve the success of each learner. To learn more, visit ASCD at www.ascd.org.

activities and materials can be selected and time segments allotted. Because activities are the crux of all units, the planning process involves questions about activities and materials such as

- What can the children read?
- What can they look at?
- What can they listen to?
- What can they construct?
- What can they write?

VIGNETTE 2.2   Smoothing and Sparkling

Units should be organized to alternate between times of quiet routine work and tasks that have higher excitement and interest value. Consider how Carol Mercer, a fourth-grade teacher, uses *smoothers* and *sparklers* as she plans her units.

Carol refers to alternations between quiet routine work and high interest, high excitement tasks as smoothers and sparklers. She explains: By smoothers I mean the things I do to provide calm, purposeful work, routine, but necessary. For example, for *smoothers* in my math units I

1. Establish skill groups and assign them names
2. Establish routine schedules and procedures
3. Use monitors to distribute and collect materials
4. Begin all skill lessons in the same way
5. Give explicit directions
6. Post all assignments on the board
7. Allow time for follow-up work

For sparklers in my math units I

1. Use games, flash cards, fun sheets, and puzzles
2. Relate math skills to other areas of the curriculum
3. Post a math riddle and special problem each day
4. Use department store advertisements for various applications of math skills
5. Have students act out math processes
6. Let students solve puzzles cooperatively

Upon Reflection

What other sparklers and smoothers can you think of to help you manage students as they work on routine and high excitement tasks throughout the day? Which of these are more appropriate for lower grades? Intermediate or upper grades?

- What can they discuss?
- What can they work on individually? Cooperatively?
- What can they perform, produce, or display?
- What evidence will indicate their degree of learning and enjoyment?

A Word about Individual Lessons

Units of instruction are accomplished through the individual lessons that comprise each unit. These individual lessons should be planned carefully so that activities, materials, work, space, procedures, homework, and means of assessment all can be communicated clearly to students.

Suggestions for planning, sequencing, and communicating lessons to all concerned are presented in Chapter 6. Before considering such detailed aspects of instructional management, we need to explore several other management concerns. For example, the physical environment of the classroom should be organized and managed, and that is the topic of Chapter 3. However, before proceeding to Chapter 3, take time to explore these end-of-chapter activities.

Parting Thought

Here is the truth about making a plan: It never works. (Not in the way you plan it, that is.) If, however, you do make a plan, the chances of getting what you want significantly increase.
—John-Roger and Peter McWilliams

SUMMARY SELF-CHECK

Check off the following as you either understand or become able to apply them.

- ❑ Before planning a year's program of studies, mark published and important dates on a calendar (vacations, celebrations, special events, school assemblies, conferences, and report card dates) and make note of themes and available blocks of time.

- ❑ In curriculum management we hope to bring about a purposeful and efficient interaction between students and what they are supposed to learn in school.

- ❑ *Curriculum maps* help identify redundancies and gaps in standards, content, and skills.

- ❑ In the *backward design* process of planning, teachers identify desired results and determine acceptable evidence for demonstrating understandings before they plan the learning experiences and instruction.

- ❑ *Curriculum standards* help define skills, knowledge, and expected content mastery for students.

- ❑ A large portion of elementary teaching is done through *instructional units,* which are related lessons that work together to build larger learnings.

- ❑ Before planning specific units of instruction, first decide on the daily and weekly schedules, and then overlay the desired instructional units for the year.

- ❑ Appropriate national, state, and district standards must be considered when planning instructional units.

- ❑ Often preorganized units are found in teacher editions of student textbooks, but most teachers plan many units of their own.

- ❑ Objectives are statements of what students should know or be able to do because of their study.

- ❑ Essential or guiding questions are broad questions—rather than fact-based questions—related to the topic of study that guide and focus the teaching and learning.

❑ Authorities recommend planning units by
- Identifying standards most appropriate for the unit of study
- Formulating overall goals or essential or guiding questions
- Formulating interim objectives
- Selecting and sequencing activities and materials for the achievement of each interim objective
- Evaluating student learning in terms of stated objectives

❑ Many teachers plan their units by
- Identifying important topics
- Identifying appropriate state and district standards
- Thinking of beneficial activities and materials related to the topics
- Fitting those activities into lessons and time slots
- Deciding how students are to be evaluated
- Deciding how students will demonstrate their accomplishments and learning

❑ *Thematic units* that integrate several subject areas are popular.

❑ Backward design planning can be used for planning the year's curriculum, as well as for unit planning and daily lessons.

❑ Activities are of prime importance for all units. When planning units, teachers should think continually in terms of the following questions:
- What can the children read?
- What can they look at?
- What can they listen to?
- What can they construct?
- What can they write?
- What can they discuss?
- What can they work on individually? Cooperatively?
- What can they perform, produce, or display?
- What evidence will indicate their degree of learning and enjoyment?

ACTIVITIES FOR REFLECTION AND DISCUSSION

1. Take a moment to review the statements in the Prediction–Review Guide at the beginning of this chapter. Put a check mark in the Review column next to any statement with which you now agree. How have your thoughts changed since reading this chapter?

2. Interview at least two teachers about their planning. What do they consider for their personal situations regarding the organization of their days? What advice do these teachers offer regarding how best to plan the school year? Units? Daily lessons? How does their planning align with what authorities recommend?

3. In Chapter 1, Janna Smart had to learn the standards and curricula and plan for a multi-age class. Check the first and second grade standards and curricula for your state. What suggestions can you make to her regarding this challenge?

4. Suppose that January 2 falls on Monday. Lay out the January calendar to determine teaching days and any celebration days that might influence your curriculum.

5. How do lessons, instructional units, and thematic units differ? How are they similar? Why is so much of the elementary curriculum organized into units? Illustrate your conclusions by summarizing what might be done in a short primary-grade unit on dinosaurs, first as a traditional unit and then as a thematic unit.

6. Suppose you want to plan a very short unit (perhaps consisting of only a lesson or two) on the life cycle of the trumpeter swan. Do your planning in two ways:

   First, make a plan beginning with two or three specific objectives, written in terms of what you later can actually see or hear students do as a result of what they learn (e.g., "Students will demonstrate understanding of the trumpeter swan's habitat by describing the unique environment in which it lives and indicating its nesting area on a map of North America."). Your lesson activities should be aimed directly at helping students reach your stated objectives.

   Second, make a plan beginning with two or three experiences you'd like your students to have concerning the trumpeter swans. Your lesson activities and materials should be expressions of the experiences you named.

   What do you see as the comparative advantages and disadvantages of these two planning approaches?

7. For a grade level of your choosing, work in teams to outline the major elements of the language arts/literacy curriculum found in an area district or school. This is step one of the curriculum mapping. List the standards, processes, skills, essential content and topics, and the products and performances that are expected to demonstrate student learning.

REFERENCES AND RECOMMENDED READINGS

Doll, R. (1995). *Curriculum improvement: Decision making and process* (9th ed.). Boston: Allyn & Bacon.

Eisner, E. (1985). *The educational imagination: On the design and evaluation of school programs* (2nd ed.). New York: Macmillan.

Eisner, E. (2002). *The arts and creation of mind.* New Haven, CT: Yale University Press.

Evertson, C., Emmer, E., Clements, B., Sanford, J., & Worsham, M. (2006). *Classroom management for elementary teachers* (7th ed.). Boston: Allyn & Bacon.

Goodlad, J. (2004, 1984). *A place called school: Prospectives for the future.* New York: McGraw-Hill.

Harvey, S., & Goudvis, A. (2000). *Strategies that work: Teaching comprehension to enhance understanding.* New York: Stenhouse Publishers.

Jacobs, H. (1989). *Interdisciplinary curriculum: Design and implementation.* Alexandria, VA: ASCD.

Jacobs, H. (1997). *Mapping the big picture: Integrating curriculum and assessment K–12.* Alexandria, VA: ASCD.

Jacobs, H. (2004). *Getting results with curriculum mapping.* Alexandria, VA: Association for Supervision and Curriculum Development (ASCD).

Keene, E., & Zimmermann, S. (1997). *Mosaic of thought: Teaching comprehension in a reader's workshop.* Portsmouth, NH: Heinemann.

McWilliams, P. (1995). *The portable life 101.* Los Angeles: Prelude Press.

Newmann, D. (1997). *The compleat teacher's almanack: A daily guide to all 12 months of the year.* New York: Fine Communications.

Rosales-Dordelly, C., & Short, E. (1985). *Curriculum professors' specialized knowledge.* Lanham, MD: University Press of America.

Silver, H., Strong, R., & Perini, M. (2000). *So each may learn: Integrating learning styles and multiple intelligences.* Alexandria, VA: ASCD.

Thousand, J., Villa, R., & Nevin, A. (2002). *Creativity and collaborative learning: The practical guide to empowering students, teachers, and families* (2nd ed.). Baltimore: Paul H. Brookes.

Tomlinson, C. (1999). *The differentiated classroom: Responding to the needs of all learners.* Alexandria, VA: ASCD.

Tomlinson, C., & McTighe, J. (2006). *Integrating differentiated instruction and understanding by design: Connecting content and kids.* Alexandria, VA: ASCD.

Traver, R. (1998). What is a good guiding question? *Educational Leadership, 55*(6), 70–73.

Tyler, R. (1949). *Basic principles of curriculum and instruction.* Chicago: University of Chicago Press.

Wiggins, G., & McTighe, J. (1998). *Understanding by design* (expanded 2nd ed.). Alexandria, VA: ASCD.

Websites

Character Counts!
http://charactercounts.org

Curriculum Designers
www.curriculumdesigners.com

Managing the Physical Environment of the Classroom

A bare room is like a boring teacher. Both lack the pizzazz which is the soul of teaching.

—Kathy Paterson

Prediction–Review Guide

Before you read the chapter, take a minute to put a check mark in the Prediction column next to any statement with which you agree.

	Prediction	Review
1. The main purpose of bulletin boards should be to beautify the room.	❑	❑
2. Experience has taught that the overall best class environment emphasizes the chalk- or whiteboard and rows of student seats.	❑	❑
3. Ceiling space is an important but often forgotten facet of the physical environment.	❑	❑
4. Modular clusters seem to provide the greatest seating advantages, including benefits for students with special needs.	❑	❑
5. A main disadvantage of modular clusters is that they encourage students to talk and interact with others, even when talking is not appropriate.	❑	❑
6. Ambience, in reality, is a synonym for teacher personality.	❑	❑
7. Any music can be used effectively in the classroom, as long as the children like it.	❑	❑
8. The main principle underlying management of physical space is that the physical classroom should enhance the activities included in the curriculum.	❑	❑
9. An important guideline for managing the physical environment is to keep it clean and in good order.	❑	❑
10. All students should have responsibilities for helping to maintain the physical environment.	❑	❑

Support for specific standards found in this chapter:

INTASC Standards

3. Adapting Instruction for Individual Needs

   The teacher understands how students differ in their approaches to learning and creates instructional opportunities that are adapted to diverse learners.

Danielson's Framework for Teaching

2. The Classroom Environment
   - Creating an environment of respect and rapport
   - Establishing a culture for learning
   - Managing classroom procedures
   - Managing student behavior
   - Organizing physical space

NBPTS Standards

3. Teachers are responsible for managing and monitoring student learning.

NCATE Standards

Apply effective methods of teaching students who are at different developmental stages, have different learning styles, and come from diverse backgrounds.

Once the calendar and curriculum have been interwoven and tentatively set, the next step in overall classroom management is to organize the interior of the classroom so it not only reflects but also substantially contributes to the learning and behavior goals of the program. This can be done in elementary school classrooms better than anywhere else (with the possible exception of secondary school laboratories and athletic facilities). Some classrooms are works of art, richly equipped and beautifully laid out, in which you would consider children fortunate to spend their days. Other rooms are austere, dull, and uninspiring; you would pity students trapped in them.

Classrooms often reflect the personality of the teacher. However, beautiful classrooms can be run by teachers who are punitive, harsh, and cold, and uninspired classrooms can be the domains of warm and nurturing teachers. This fact reminds us that quality of teaching cannot be judged solely on the basis of room appearance. That, however, does not detract from this basic point:

> The physical environment can and should be organized so as to further the program of instruction and activity.

This bears repeating, and should be understood before you read on. What you put into your classroom should have instructional purpose. There is little point in loading it with decorations that have no instructional value and do not contribute to the program, except perhaps to charm parents and administrators. But the classroom just as easily can be made attractive—and more usefully so—by setting it up with interesting activities and stimulating materials. Teachers have a free hand in setting up their workplaces—almost anything is permitted, within reason of course, and it begins with their own mental image of the classroom.

Take a minute to reread the description in Chapter 1 of Janna's room arrangement, and keep this in mind as you continue reading this chapter.

Upon Reflection
Janna Smart's friends set up her room while she reviewed curriculum and planned for her first days with her students. While the room looked interesting and attractive, what were some of the inherent problems in their room arrangement?

THE PICTURES WE HOLD IN OUR HEADS

All of us hold some mental picture of what school classrooms should look like. Many of us imagine rows of desks with chalkboard and teacher in front, one or two doors on the side wall, perhaps a coatroom in the back, and windows with shelves of dusty reference books. While such classrooms have been used to advantage by thousands of teachers over the decades to teach millions of students, there are better ways of setting up the classroom—ways that affect attitudes, efficiency, and overall learning. Suppose for example, you plan to have your students do the following:

- Make stick puppets to use in retelling a story
- Write and share original haiku poems
- Create a *Who's Who* book of class members
- Write letters to a class in a foreign country
- Build a model of a community
- Make graphs of daily weather phenomena
- Monitor and record the growth cycles of plants from seeds
- Learn a folkdance from another country
- Compare the latitudes of foreign capital cities
- Make a video of life in the school or classroom

As you consider these activities, you begin finding hints for organizing the room. The essential or guiding question might be: How can my room best help me do justice to what I want my students to experience and learn?

As the question suggests, the classroom should be made to accommodate and to further a variety of educational activities. Math and language arts, for example, may require students to work quietly at their seats with furnished materials. Social studies may call for active collaborative work in construction, drawing, or discussion. Science and art often require special workspaces and materials. Dance, music, and drama require open space for movement. Each type of activity calls for its own space, seating, movement, materials, and interactions.

Just how classrooms can be made both rich and flexible will be explained presently, but let us first take a moment to remind ourselves of a seldom-remembered but fundamentally important fact: The room should be set up for the teacher's pleasure, too. Some teachers are more comfortable—and possibly more effective—when working in highly structured programs that hold students under tight supervision and that direct them through assignments. Other teachers are more comfortable—and possibly more effective—when giving students leeway in selecting activities, obtaining and using appropriate materials, and working cooperatively with fellow students. We go too far when we expect all teachers to teach in a single, specified way, especially when that certain way changes from year to year, as is often the case. Teachers are different and have different styles, and most of them would benefit from being allowed to use their talents to their fullest.

Remember, too, that just as teachers show different styles of teaching, so will they set up their classrooms differently. Some prefer their rooms to be richly furnished with materials, charts, pictures, animals, decorations, and slogans, believing that this keeps the classroom fully stimulating. Others prefer their rooms to be clean and efficient, with materials at hand only when relevant to what is being studied at a particular time. These teachers find heavily decorated classrooms distracting and believe students find them distracting, too. Effective teaching can occur in both these physical settings, which again suggests the desirability of allowing serious-minded teachers to rely on their own best judgments. Regardless of their differing styles, teachers should consider all areas of the classroom when they organize the physical environment.

SIX FACETS OF THE PHYSICAL ENVIRONMENT

This analysis breaks the physical classroom into six components: (1) floor space, (2) wall space, (3) countertop space, (4) shelf space, (5) cupboard and closet space, and (6) ambience. Many teachers use a seventh facet as well—the ceiling. While the ceiling does offer many possibilities, it is not considered here because attaching materials to it may increase fire hazard and often is a violation of local fire codes. Let's explore some of the possibilities offered by the other six facets.

Floor Space

One of the first things a teacher has to decide is how to position students for the various activities that involve individual work and group interactions. This not only affects seating arrangements but also traffic patterns and work/activity areas (including interest centers and the teacher's station). Because today's classrooms are inclusive and teachers can expect physical and language diversity among their students, it also is important to consider floor

"YOU'LL NOTICE YOUR DESKS HAVE A NEW FEATURE TODAY. SIT DOWN AND BUCKLE UP."

space as it relates to any special needs for students, including proximate space for related service providers.

Seating.   In the not-so-distant past, student desks were anchored to wooden or metal runners, where they remained unmoved until rusted out or ripped up. You probably won't see that now except in museums. Seating in today's schools is intended to be flexible so various groupings can be made and space opened for multiple purposes, according to the needs of the subjects taught. Teachers arrange seating at their discretion, keeping in mind two cautions: First, students shouldn't be placed so they have to look directly into strong light—the resulting strain causes tension and makes concentration difficult. Investigators, including Hathaway, Hargreaves, Thompson, and Novitsky (1992), Chan and Petrie (1998), Freiberg (1999), and Berry (2002) have documented possible health effects of lighting. Second, when students are asked to rearrange their desks and tables, they show a penchant for shoving, bumping, making noise, and pestering each other. Accept this as a fact of teaching, and when you ask students to rearrange their seating areas, remind them in a positive tone to do so in accordance with class rules and procedures.

When students are taught as a total group, they should be seated as near to the teacher as feasible, facing a chalkboard or dry erase board. Primary students may come together on a small carpet area for whole-group instruction. The teacher may sit with them on the carpet or in a chair, often near a small board or an easel. Well-behaved students can be placed close together, but some students may have to be separated a bit. Designating marks or colored carpet squares on the room carpet is a common method of separation and arrangement. During guided study, students sometimes will be asked to work alone and sometimes in cooperative groups. Normally the teacher will circulate among students to monitor and help. For ease of movement, aisles and gaps in seating should be maintained, but the distance between the teacher and the farthest student should be as minimal as possible.

When students are taught in small groups, they may be called to a special area where extra chairs are kept or to which they bring their own chairs. Ideally, the floor arrangement will keep the teacher, while interacting with the small group, in fairly close proximity to students working at their desks. The teacher must be able to oversee everyone in the class, and this watchfulness should be evident to students.

Popular seating arrangements include rows, circles, semicircles, and long tables. Jones (2007) advocates creating an interior loop or walkway, with the least distance and fewest barriers between the teacher and every student in the classroom, so the teacher can easily and efficiently "work the crowd" (see Figure 3.1). Others find that modular clusters seem to best meet the demands of modern classrooms, where large- and small-group instruction, cooperative group- and teamwork, and individual seatwork routinely are interchanged. Kagan (1994) recommends group arrangements that enable students to engage in classbuilding and teambuilding activities for successful cooperative learning. For example, four students sitting in pairs on opposite sides of a table (or with their desks touching and placed so students face each other) can work as shoulder partners, as face partners, or as teams of four. Kagan further suggests that placing students with comparable language and achievement abilities on the same side of the table so they can work as shoulder partners ensures the best mix for partnering and processing information and tasks (see Figure 3.2).

Modular clusters of five or six students afford fairly good eye contact among students and between the teacher and individual students, enable easy transition into cooperative work, allow good traffic flow, and provide the flexibility for obtaining extra floor space when needed. Such small group clusters also are most effective in facilitating the inclusion of students with disabilities. Figure 3.3 shows an example of modular seating for thirty-six students.

Work and Activity Areas. These areas are affected by the room's seating arrangement. Compact seating makes space available to begin with and rearranging the seats provides still more space. Of course, you don't need extra space for all activities. Frequently reading, math, spelling, handwriting, and guided seatwork are conducted with students in their assigned seats. Activities in social studies, science, art, music, drama, and dance often involve movement and require extra space.

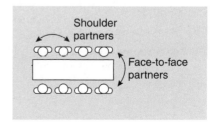

FIGURE 3.2 Kagan encourages group arrangements so students can interact with shoulder partners, face partners, and teams of four

FIGURE 3.1 Jones's interior loop: Walkways that allow teachers to "work the crowd" with the fewest steps are created by bringing students forward and packing them sideways

Source: Fred Jones *Tools for Teaching,* 2007, www.fredjones.com. Reprinted by permission.

Modular Clusters

Advantages

Better face-to-face positioning than with traditional seating

Very easy to regroup into 2's, 4's, 6's, 12's

Compact, requiring little floor space

Disadvantages

Some students must turn to see the teacher

Somewhat awkward to re-form into total group with good face-to-face positioning

Invites collaboration when talking may not be appropriate

FIGURE 3.3   Modular Cluster Seating

Space is needed for other purposes as well. Most teachers like to include one or more special centers, corners, or interest areas. An art center with easels may be present. Freestanding learning centers may be on the floor, though they are placed more commonly on tables or countertops. Frequently special corners for quiet reading, science projects, map and globe study, or individual investigations are seen. Most classrooms also have at least one computer for students to use in writing, math, and other areas. Because of their operating noise, lighting needs, and potential distractibility, computers require additional considerations. Teacher Jearine Bacon, who makes extensive use of computers in her primary classroom, describes some of the cautions to keep in mind concerning the classroom computer:

> Classroom computers are extremely motivating and useful in the classroom, but care should be taken in their use. The computer should be away from liquids, dust, and extreme heat, and some distance from the chalkboard. The screen should be shielded from other students so that it will not be a distraction, and students should be reminded frequently of the rules for use and care of the computer. Computers are expensive to repair and frustrating to use when not working properly.

VIGNETTE 3.1   Modular Cluster Seating

Beth Davies prefers modular cluster seating in her fifth-grade classroom. Initially she chooses the places where the children sit. Once they become acquainted she lets them contract to sit by a person of their choice, but still within their original cluster. By this time they understand about Beth's right to teach and their right to learn without disruption. The students know that Beth will immediately move any person who abuses the contract. In each cluster of desks Beth tries to balance the lower-achieving students with the higher-achieving, in order to mix minds and provide help during group work.

Upon Reflection
Based on your personal experience and your observations, what are your thoughts about cluster seating versus rows or other configurations?

"I CAN HEAR SCRAPING SOUNDS...
I THINK SHE'S MOVING HER DESK
IN FRONT OF THE DOOR."

Some teachers also like to set aside a special space in the classroom as a reward for responsible student behavior or good work. Here teachers sometimes put cushions, a thick rug, a computer, interesting books and magazines, individual slide viewers, and headsets for listening to music or stories.

While today's teachers are up and moving among students throughout the entire day, most still have a desk somewhere in the classroom. Their station—normally a desk—should be placed in a position that oversees the entire class, ideally to the side or the back of the room. It is a good idea to make the teacher's station attractive and special, as it enhances one's position as authority and can help students feel honored when called there. It should begin with a clean desk (a good example for students), an attractive file cabinet, and shelves for a small collection of personal books. Photographs of family, friends, former students, or pets add touches that students like. Artifacts, weavings, and art prints contribute tastefully. One or two articles of high prestige for students can be kept there, such as a puppet, a sports team pennant, or a large toy animal. A special chair for students can provide a pleasant place for individual conferencing.

Traffic Patterns.   Student movement around the room must be given careful attention, because congestion, waiting, and unnecessary contact usually lead to disruptive behavior. For students with disabilities, traffic patterns must be free from barriers and allow easy access to materials. Students routinely enter and exit the room, obtain and return materials, sharpen pencils (some teachers keep a supply sharpened to exchange when needed), get drinks, go to learning centers, feed the fish, approach the teacher, and so on. Traffic routes for such movements must be kept open, a concern not to be taken lightly when deciding on the layout of the room. Figure 3.4 shows floor space arrangement for a hypothetical elementary classroom.

Wall Space

Classroom walls are rarely used to full advantage, but they offer excellent instructional possibilities. Chalkboards and whiteboards remain among the most valuable of all teaching tools. They are used routinely to post daily information, assignments, math problems, and vocabulary words. Most teachers use them for explanations and demonstrations. Often overlooked, however, is the delight many students have in going to the board to work.

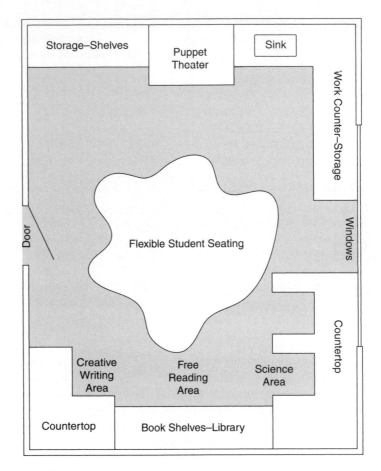

FIGURE 3.4   Floor Space Arrangement

Bulletin Boards.   Bulletin boards, though present in practically every classroom, tend to be used mostly for decoration and rarely for instruction. Decorations can make a room pleasant to look at, but with a bit of thought they also can serve the more important purpose of instruction. More valuable than mere decoration are displays such as puzzles that draw students' attention and make them think, clippings from newspapers and magazines that serve as focal points for class discussion, and interactive and creative ideas and problem situations that stimulate writing and debate. Perhaps best of all, bulletin boards are excellent places for displaying art prints and other visual materials, including student work.

Displays of Student Work.   It's advisable to give all students the opportunity to display samples of their work in the classroom. However, not just any work should be shown, especially when the work is not commensurate with student ability. When excellence is obvious or marked improvement is evident, putting that work on display—with the student's permission—is a good way to provide recognition. This recognition gives students a sense of ownership in their classroom, as well as a sense of accomplishment and the understanding that others care about their performance. It also builds self-esteem and is highly motivating.

Art Prints and Other Visual Materials.   Art prints that relate to the curriculum tend to be overlooked by students unless attention is drawn to them in art lessons. The same can be said for most maps, globes, and charts, though students often enjoy simply exploring maps once they learn how to use them.

VIGNETTE 3.2   Wall Displays

Adelheida Montante Castañeda, a sixth-grade teacher, has a large bulletin board across the room from the entry door, visible to anyone who comes into the room. There she displays four of her favorite posters, which she has treasured over the years because they emphasize positive learning, good citizenship, challenge, and determination.

1. My greatest challenge in life is doing what others think I cannot do.
2. Tell me, I forget.
   Show me, I remember.
   Involve me, I understand.
3. My Classroom Rights
   a. I have the right to be happy and to be treated with compassion in this room. This means that no one will laugh at me or hurt my feelings.
   b. I have a right to be safe in this room. This means that no one will kick me, punch me, push me, or hurt me.
   c. I have a right to hear and be heard in this room. This means that no one will yell, scream, shout, or make noises.
   d. I have a right to learn more about myself in this room. This means that I will be free to express my feelings and my opinions without being interrupted or punished, as long as the rights of others are not infringed.
4. How to Get Better Grades
   a. Be on time and ready to work.
   b. Follow directions.
   c. Work neatly and accurately.
   d. Ask for help when you need it.
   e. Check your work.
   f. Find a time and place to study.
   g. Take responsibility for yourself.

Upon Reflection
Take time to visit some elementary classrooms in the area. What visual displays do you see on the walls? What purpose do they have in the classroom?

Idea: Take pictures of what you see with a camera phone, digital, or disposable camera, and create a personal file for future reference.

Wall space should be used for posting graphic models, visual instruction plans, and reminders. Such materials are chronically underutilized given the help they provide students and teachers. These visual materials illustrate and help explain products or procedures such as parts of a business letter, elements of sentences and paragraphs, steps in long division, proper use of the computer, proper editing notations and publishing procedures, and any number of explanations and reminders that teachers must otherwise repeat, sometimes to the point of exasperation.

You also may consider posting inspirational slogans and class mottoes, class rules, reminders on how to help substitute teachers, and a synopsis of the class goals for the year.

Countertop Space

A good deal of useful space is available in most classrooms on the countertops that often run beneath windows. Because they are near natural light, these countertops are well suited to many kinds of science activities, especially those involving living plants. They also are good places for aquariums and terrariums if the outside light is not too strong or hot. Other kinds of science projects find useful placement here as well—experiments; projects in progress; and models of human torsos, sense organs, skeletons, dinosaurs, atoms, molecules, and the like. Kits of various kinds that are in most classrooms, often on countertops, typically contain science projects or materials to supplement instruction in reading, spelling, social studies, and mathematics. Globes fit nicely on countertops and can be wonderful instructional devices since they show not only the shape of the earth but also the relative locations of and distances between landmasses, oceans, countries, and cities. They are important to the study of history, geography, astronomy, and current events.

Shelf Space

Shelves, if not built into classrooms, can be added inexpensively by stacking pine boards on concrete blocks. Typically, textbooks, reference books, class libraries, and other special materials are stored or displayed on shelves.

Textbooks usually accompany the core curricular areas: reading, language arts, mathematics, social studies, and science. Many teachers keep the textbooks on shelves and distribute them to students when needed.

Reference books are heavily used for studies above primary grades. Normally they are kept on shelves and typically include dictionaries, encyclopedias, almanacs, atlases, thesauruses, and special reference books such as the *Guinness Book of Records, The Farmer's Almanac,* and the *Golden Library.*

If not kept on a book carousel, a small class library often is found on classroom shelves. A class library usually consists of easy-to-read books of high interest to students, plus magazines such as *National Geographic Kids* and *Ranger Rick.* Teachers look into many sources to find such materials at low prices, and students' caregivers often donate to class libraries. The library also may include student-written materials that are laminated or bound into small books and often contain illustrations by the authors.

Special materials to motivate and extend students' experiences are kept on shelves in most classrooms. Examples include video and audio CDs and tapes, games, puzzles,

VIGNETTE 3.3   Student Publishing

Rebecca Cummins has taught third grade for many years. She has her students publish and share their stories.

Rebecca's third graders write, illustrate, and bind their own stories into books. They read the books aloud to the class and then take them home to read to their parents. When the books are returned, they are placed on a special shelf in the classroom library. When children finish their work, they may select a classmate's book to read. These books are treated like genuine treasures. At the end of the year, the children take their books home, though Rebecca always begs to keep a few to show next year's class.

Upon Reflection

What goals—academic and social—can be met when students write, publish, and share their stories?

puppets, toys, photo collections, collections of shells and fossils, and the like. Some teachers create a lending library that includes videotapes or CDs of the children as they work on projects and activities during the year. Of course, before children are taped, parents or guardians must grant permission, and when taping, equal time must be given for every child. The tapes are kept on a library shelf and checked out to be viewed at home by parents, grandparents, and others who are not able to be in the classroom during the day. You will read more about this in Chapter 11.

Cupboard and Closet Space

Classroom cupboards and closets are useful places for keeping student supplies, work sheets, audiovisual equipment, physical education or subject-specific equipment, and cleaning materials. They also are good places to store materials used for special occasions such as sports days and certain times of the year such as the winter holidays.

Student supplies include such things as writing paper, construction paper, pencils, scissors, glue, paints, crayons, rulers, and pens. In most schools, smaller quantities of supplies are kept in classroom cupboards while larger quantities are stored in a central teachers' supply or workroom.

Manipulatives for math are kept in appropriately sized storage containers. Plastic boxes that are the same size, stackable, and clear for easy viewing of the contents work well for this purpose and can be purchased on sale at many stores.

Worksheets are used—overused, many believe—in great quantities in most classrooms. Usually the teacher, aide, or volunteer duplicates them. Worksheets are useful for drilling skills and preparing students for timed tests, but they are of little value when used only to keep children busy.

Usually audiovisual equipment is kept in a central area of the school and checked out when needed. If not provided by the school, many teachers bring their own CD player or boom box to their classroom. Many classrooms now have their own television and VCR, either mounted on a wall or on a moveable cart. Classrooms also may have overhead projectors, tape recorders, smaller three-dimensional models, and sometimes slide viewers. Some of these are kept on tables and others in cabinets, to be brought out when needed. More expensive items, such as micro-projectors, larger models (such as human torsos), large art collections, motion picture projectors (although these mostly have been replaced by VCRs), and so forth, are checked out from a central repository for short-term use.

Often equipment used for specific content areas is kept in containers and stored in closets. Physical education equipment, usually consisting of little besides balls and jump ropes, with the room number clearly written on each, is kept in closets, frequently in large plastic garbage bins.

Each room's personal set of cleaning materials also is found in the classroom closet and usually includes a broom, dust cloths, cleanser, paper towels, and rags. A small vacuum cleaner is very useful but probably will not be provided by the school. These materials permit students and teachers to take care of routine spills, dusting, and other necessary cleaning that is beyond what the custodians are available to do. Student monitors can be helpful in this regard.

Finally, collections of special materials for Presidents' Day, Valentine's Day, Saint Patrick's Day, Thanksgiving, winter and spring holidays, and other themes are usually kept in large, clearly labeled plastic or cardboard file boxes, and stored in or on top of closets.

Ambience

Ambience refers to the totality of intangible impressions that pervade the physical classroom—an atmosphere that at its best conveys excitement, aesthetics, comfort, security, and pleasure. It is created in large part by the contents of the room, which many teachers further enhance with art and music. Most schools or district media centers make available prints, carvings, weavings, and photographs, which provide focal points for learning about artists and media. CDs and cassette tapes can provide music that is excellent for relaxation and mood setting, not to mention the opportunity they provide for learning about composers and performers.

Music.   Research, including the "Mozart Effect" study (Rauscher, Shaw, Levine, Ky, & Wright, 1993; see also Campbell, 2000, 2002), is being conducted to investigate the effectiveness and use of music in the classroom. We now know that music effects changes in the mind and body. With this knowledge, teachers can play the right type of music for the desired objective: thinking, relaxing, learning, destressing, concentration, inspiration, and productivity.

Appropriate music can help reduce stress and can heighten alertness, excitement, relaxation, and emotional well-being, as well as creativity. Sometimes we want students to reflect and relax. Music with 50 to 60 beats per minute, as well as environmental sounds of birds, waterfalls, and the like, work best for this. Sometimes we want students to work independently or quietly, for example, during journal or creative writing or problem solving. For these times we should use music that is 60 to 70 beats per minute. Best for this is baroque-style music and some of the "gentle modern classics" of the nineteenth and twentieth centuries by Beethoven, Chopin, Debussy, and others. Sometimes we want to energize students. We know that upbeat music with 120 beats per minute, such as many of the songs of the 1960s and 1970s, works well for energizing and managing transitions.

We know that music contributes to the classroom ambience. As an aside, it is important to be knowledgeable about the ethics and legalities of using music. If you use music only with your students and in your classroom, you do not need a license. If, however, you use music in other venues (workshops or other presentations), a license may be required. When in doubt you should contact the performing rights organization. You can email questions to Broadcast Music, Inc. (BMI) at genlic@bmi.com or call them directly at 877-264-2137.

Special Themes.   Many teachers enhance ambience through special themes built around children's literature, professional athletes, popular music, cartoon characters, favorite motion pictures—whatever seems to attract students' interest. Both the room and lessons can reflect elements of the selected theme—characters, emblems, photographs, drawings, colors, sayings, music, and so forth. Students respond well to such themes and often like to help in their selection and organization.

Other Special Touches.   Finally, a number of special touches and events add to the room ambience—videos, popcorn parties, classroom pets, favorite plants, class murals or quilts, and time lines that depict the history of the year's dates, events, and accomplishments. Ambience deserves this attention because it helps teachers provide students comfort, enjoyment, stimulation, and satisfaction.

CONFUSING OR ENGAGING?

Attention to physical environment should not result in a confused mess, and it is the teacher's responsibility to ensure that it does not. Each of the six facets that comprise the classroom's physical environment should be considered carefully and used to best advantage. As mentioned, best advantage for some teachers means keeping the environment relatively lean, efficient, and nondistracting, whereas others may see it differently. It depends on the teacher and students. In any case, the physical environment should always be kept clean and in good order.

Toward that end and to the extent their maturity allows, students should be given major responsibility in taking care of the classroom and the materials it contains. As they keep things orderly and clean, students have the opportunity to build sound values of aesthetics, ecology, and responsibility.

This brings us to the end of our brief exploration of purposes, arrangements, and contents of the physical environment of the classroom. It also concludes our attention to considerations teachers should tend to *before* the school year begins. Now we are ready to shift attention to what teachers attend to once the school year begins and they meet their students. Before proceeding to Chapter 4, which deals with the psychosocial environment of the classroom, take time to explore these end-of-chapter activities.

Parting Thought

Vision is the ability to make a dream a reality.

SUMMARY SELF-CHECK

Check off the following as you either understand or become able to apply them.

☐ The physical environment of the classroom should be arranged and managed so as to enhance the activities called for in the curriculum. Keeping in mind preferences of teachers and students, give attention to six facets of the physical environment:

- Floor space: seating, work, and activity areas; teacher's station; special centers; traffic patterns; students with disabilities and special needs
- Wall space: chalk- and whiteboards; bulletin boards and display areas; student work, prints, maps, and charts
- Countertop space: science projects, kits, models, and globes
- Shelf space: textbooks, reference books, popular library books, special materials
- Cupboard and closet space: student supplies, worksheets, audiovisual equipment, physical education or subject-specific equipment, cleaning materials, special decorations or collections
- Ambience: art objects, background music, themes, other special touches

ACTIVITIES FOR REFLECTION AND DISCUSSION

1. Take a moment to review the statements in the Prediction–Review Guide at the beginning of this chapter. Put a check mark in the Review column next to any statement with which you now agree. How have your thoughts changed since reading this chapter?

2. Interview at least two teachers about their room arrangements, or visit and photograph several elementary classrooms. How do the teachers design the physical organization of their classroom to support their program?

3. Again review the description in Chapter 1 of Janna Smart's room as her friends had set it up for her the weekend before she met her students. Also reread the section that describes the changes she made the following week. How will these changes better serve the needs of Janna and her students? How do they align with the suggestions that are described in this chapter?

4. Discuss your feelings concerning the degree to which you'd like your classroom to include various items (materials, photos, models, collections, and so on). Comment on (1) your personal preferences concerning richness/leanness of classrooms you have attended, (2) student interest, involvement, and motivation, and (3) how you would manage the types of items you would use.

5. From which aspects of physical classroom management would you assign student responsibilities, not only to help but also to increase the sense of student ownership of the classroom. Consider how the responsibilities need to vary depending on grade level, age, and maturity of your students.

6. The statement was made in the text that "the room should be set up for the teacher's pleasure, too." To what specifically do you think that statement refers? Why do or don't you consider it a valid point?

7. Suppose you teach a third-grade class. In the afternoons you like to rearrange the seating to provide additional floor space for movement activities. Describe specifically how you would train your students to move furniture so that everything is done quickly, correctly, and with no horseplay.

8. Schools provide custodians whose duties include cleaning the classrooms. To what extent, if any, would you want your class (and yourself) to be responsible for cleaning and tidying the room? Justify your opinion in terms of its value to students and their program.

REFERENCES AND RECOMMENDED READINGS

Berry, M., principal investigator. (2002). Healthy school environment and enhanced educational performance, prepared for Carpet and Rug Institute. Report is available at www.jjcommercial.com/pdf/10-CharlesYoungElementary.pdf.

Campbell, D. G. (2000). *The Mozart Effect for children: Awakening your child's mind, health, and creativity with music.* New York: HarperCollins

Campbell, D. G. (2002). *The Mozart Effect: Tapping the power of music to heal the body, strengthen the mind, and unlock the creative spirit.* New York: HarperCollins.

Chan, T., & Petrie, G. (1998). The Brain Learns Better in Well-Designed School Environments. www.nea.org/teacherexperience/braik030312.html.

Evertson, C., Emmer, E., Clements, B., Sanford, J., & Worsham, M. (2006). *Classroom management for elementary teachers* (7th ed.). Boston: Allyn & Bacon.

Freiberg, J. H. (Ed.). (1999). *School climate: Measuring, improving and sustaining healthy learning environments.* New York: RoutledgeFalmer.

Hathaway, W., Hargreaves, J., Thompson, G., & Novitsky, D. (1992). *A study into the effects of light on children of elementary school age—A case of light robbery.* Unpublished manuscript, Planning and Information Services, Alberta Department of Education, Edmonton, Alberta, Canada.

Hebert, E. (1998, September). Designing matters: How school environment affects children. *Educational Leadership, 56*(1), 69–70.

Jensen, E. (1998) *Teaching with the brain in mind.* Alexandria, VA: ASCD.

Jensen, E. (2000). *Music with the brain in mind.* San Diego: The Brain Store.

Jones, F. (2007). *Tools for teaching: Discipline Instruction Motivation* (2nd ed.). Santa Cruz, CA: Fredric H. Jones and Associates.

Kagan, L. (2003). *The successful dynamic trainer: Engaging all learners course workbook.* San Clemente, CA: Kagan Publishing.

Kagan, S. (1994). *Cooperative learning.* San Clemente, CA: Kagan Cooperative Learning.

Rauscher, R., Shaw, G., Levine, L., Ky, K., & Wright, E. (1993). Music and spatial task performance. *Nature, 365,* 611.

Udavari-Solner, A. (1995). A process for adapting curriculum in inclusive classrooms. In R. Villa & J. Thousand (Eds.), *Creating an inclusive school* (pp. 110–124). Alexandria, VA: ASCD.

Villa, R., & Thousand, J. (2005). *Creating an inclusive school* (2nd ed.). Alexandria, VA: ASCD.

CHAPTER 4

Managing the Psychosocial Environment of the Classroom

Don't be out in front of them to rescue or over them to punish, but as they are falling down, stand beside them and guide them. One of the ways we guide them is with the six critical life messages: I believe in you . . . I trust you . . . I know you can handle this . . . you are listened to . . . you are cared for . . . and you are very important to me.

—Barbara Coloroso

Prediction–Review Guide

Before you read the chapter, take a minute to put a check mark in the Prediction column next to any statement with which you agree.

	Prediction	Review
1. The qualities of good character should be embedded into the way we teach rather than taught as separate lessons.	❑	❑
2. *Looping* is a modern concept in which teachers and students stay together for two or more years.	❑	❑
3. Students cannot learn in an environment that is harsh, cold, punitive, and rejecting.	❑	❑
4. In addition to words, teachers communicate with tone of voice and body language.	❑	❑
5. Giving regular personal attention to students is best done by speaking with them individually every day about their schoolwork and academic progress.	❑	❑
6. Verbal reinforcement should be directed at students' character traits rather than at their efforts.	❑	❑
7. Teachers should help students acknowledge that learning is their main responsibility in school.	❑	❑
8. Modeling refers to teaching through example so students can learn through imitation.	❑	❑
9. When teachers team-teach, students have the opportunity to have two teachers present the lesson together to everyone.	❑	❑
10. It is the students' responsibility (with teacher guidance) to maintain a warm, pleasant, and supportive environment.	❑	❑

Support for specific standards found in this chapter:

INTASC Standards

2. Knowledge of Human Development and Learning

   The teacher understands how children learn and develop and can provide learning opportunities that support their intellectual, social, and personal development.

6. Communication Skills

   The teacher uses knowledge of effective verbal, nonverbal, and media communication techniques to foster active inquiry, collaboration, and supportive interaction in the classroom.

Danielson's Framework for Teaching

2. The Classroom Environment

   - Creating an environment of respect and rapport
   - Establishing a culture for learning
   - Managing classroom procedures
   - Managing student behavior
   - Organizing physical space

NBPTS Standards

1. Teachers are committed to students and their learning.

NCATE Standards

Apply effective methods of teaching students who are at different developmental stages, have different learning styles, and come from diverse backgrounds.

Psychosocial environment encompasses the overall emotional climate or "feeling tone" that exists in every classroom, a mixture of pleasure, distress, intrigue, boredom, happiness, sadness, excitement, love, fear—all human emotions seem to be included. This environment is intangible, yet all teachers and students are aware of it. Its effects on learning, productivity, and self-concept are even more powerful than those exerted by the classroom's physical environment.

Think about this as it applies to you. Like most other people asked to recall their educational experiences, don't you find yourself remembering your most intense interactions with teachers or groups of students—those who enlivened, invigorated, and supported your efforts, or those who embarrassed or threatened you? As you read on, the essential or guiding question might be: What decisions and actions can I make to best create a positive psychosocial environment for my students?

▇ THE POSITIVE AND NEGATIVE SIDES OF THE PSYCHOSOCIAL ENVIRONMENT

Most of us during our years as students have experienced or witnessed the extremes—both positive and negative environments. The positive side of the psychosocial environment is the warmth, caring, and support that make the classroom a friendly, pleasant, encouraging place. Most students flourish best in such an environment. But the psychosocial environment can have a negative tone as well—cold, uncaring, harsh, punitive, aloof, and sarcastic—further burdening children whose psychological well-being already is threatened by social ills outside the school, and even fear from bullies in school.

Individuals who intentionally instill fear in others are bullies; they intend to hurt, and they enjoy it. Bullies frequently engage in activities that are verbal or physical, often while bystanders do nothing to stop them—or even encourage them. However, not all bullying takes place through obvious activities. Relational bullying, which is more difficult to recognize, undermines the bullied child's sense of self by shunning, isolating, excluding, or ignoring.

When the climate feels threatening because of the actions or attitudes of other children or the teacher, students fear making errors, hope they will not fail or be embarrassed, and pray that if they make mistakes the teacher will not take reprisals against them. Few students do well in such environments, though there are exceptions. For most, achievement in such climates is suppressed and pleasure is nonexistent.

Perhaps you recall from experience that learning can occur rapidly within a climate of fear, provided the fear is not paralyzing. Fear has long been used to motivate learners, but it is doubtful that fear of physical or psychological hurt should ever be used in today's classrooms. At best it has a short-term effect, and it is known to produce detrimental side effects of stress, anger, and resentment, all of which are counterproductive to what we hope to accomplish with young learners. Teachers who succeed in making their classroom enjoyable, engaging places in which to work and learn leave positive impressions on their students.

MEMORIES

CASE STUDY 4.1

Focus Questions
Take time to recall a teacher who had an effect on you. What do you remember about the teacher and the class? Based on your memories of how the teacher looked, sounded, and acted, are your memories positive or negative?

Carlos Bachicha doesn't remember much about his fourth-grade teacher or school, except that he rode on the same bicycle with his brother and carved a soap elephant that looked much like a pig. His sixth-grade year is even more blank. But his fifth—that's a different story. His teacher was Miss Osborne, and she had red hair and freckles and was forever having her students do something interesting in class. They performed plays while wearing paper costumes they cut and stapled together—and the students thought they looked real enough. They parched corn and smashed it into cornmeal, and a mom baked it and they ate it with butter. One day Miss Osborne took Carlos and his classmates to her house to run a spinning wheel, a real one. Carlos was stung on his toe by a bee—she must have let them go barefoot. That was a long time ago, but Carlos remembers her and that year like they were yesterday.

◼TOWARD AN OPTIMAL PSYCHOSOCIAL ENVIRONMENT

Fraser and O'Brien (1985) found that psychosocial classroom environments tend to focus on five factors: satisfaction, friction, competitiveness, difficulty, and cohesiveness. While it is the teacher's responsibility to establish and maintain a positive psychosocial environment, students can and should help in this effort. Teachers may proceed safely on the premise that classrooms function best when they provide a positive and structured climate, one that reflects warmth, support, and pleasant circumstances with very low levels of fear. Fear should be limited to anxiety of not living up to one's own potential, of letting other people down, or of not acting in one's own best interest. It should never be a fear of personal danger.

However, before you conclude that such climates are devoid of structure, expectations, or enforcement, be assured that this is not the case. In fact, it is doubtful that a positive climate can be maintained in the absence of well-enforced regulations governing interpersonal conduct.

Because establishing a positive climate is the teacher's responsibility and because such a climate usually is best for enhancing learning and building good self-concept, this chapter explores what you can do to ensure that your classroom environment provides the warmth and support prized by students and teachers alike.

VIGNETTE 4.1   Setting the Tone

Second-grade teacher Cynthia Scott begins each school year by setting the tone in her classroom. First she describes her expectations for the year. She tells the children that she considers them her "school family," and she explains that just as in any family they might not always agree on everything. She also tells them that she always will care about them, that each and every one of them is special and important to her, and that she wants them to have the best possible school year. Cynthia then tells her students that she will not tolerate any cruelty or unkindness to each other, and that she expects them to be the best-behaved and most well-mannered class in the entire school, both in the classroom and on the playground. She explains that good behavior really is just good manners, because it shows respect for others, whether children or adults.

Cynthia then goes over the Golden Rule and makes a bulletin board on that theme. She refers to the Golden Rule as the class motto, and she discusses with them how it covers everything: If you don't want to be called names, then don't call other people names. If you want people to listen to you, then be sure to listen to others. And most important, if you want to have friends, then be a friend. The Golden Rule is the only rule in Cynthia's second-grade class.

Upon Reflection
Cynthia Scott begins each school year by setting the tone in her class. List reasons why her class probably will run smoothly.

Gloria Anderson has taught every elementary grade. However, when she teaches fifth or sixth grade, she explores the psychosocial environment in an unusual way.

> I begin the year with an unusual writing prompt. I show students a *No Hunting* sign, the kind you can buy in a sporting goods store. The students are to write about what they think about the sign and why I have it in the classroom. The next day, after I have read all the quick writes, the students and I discuss what the sign means in their room. This discussion leads to their development of class rules and expectations.

■ A QUICK LOOK AT LOOPING

Looping, a concept that dates back to the one-room schoolhouse, is reappearing in some areas of the country. In looping, a teacher keeps the same class of students for two or more consecutive years. The first year of looping is very typical—teacher and students get to

CASE STUDY 4.2

BENEFITS OF LOOPING

Focus Question

When Marilyn Cox and neighborhood students moved into a new school, she was able to loop with her fourth graders from the year before. She found the experience to be rewarding for everyone. Here she describes several advantages when she looped with her students; list them. What other advantages can you think of?

What a wonderful experience this year has been. I've taught for thirty years, but this is my first fifth-grade class. Being new to fifth grade has been infinitely easier because I brought my students along with me. (Last year I taught them in fourth grade in another nearby school.) As school started I didn't lose the usual chunk of time from my schedule needed to build the classroom environment. It was established last year. We just caught up on each other's summer experiences and moved right into fifth grade.

This is my first experience with looping. Having the privilege of starting a brand new school at a brand new grade level gave me the opportunity to take a risk on an entirely new concept to me! It has been wonderful to see how great the students have responded to this new environment. Our relationship, established last year, gave us a history to build on. We didn't have to start from dirt and build up from there. Our structure was already in place.

Not only did I know the students and their strengths and weaknesses, I also knew their parents, and I wasn't the least bit hesitant about contacting them. Back-to-School Night was very well attended. In the past it has been the rule that parent participation goes down drastically by the time students get to fifth grade. That hasn't been true with this class. At parent conference time all meetings went smoothly, due in no small part of their having done this with me last year. Parent helpers are coming out in droves to help in the classroom. Forms are returned faster. It seems incredible that we continue to work as such a tight team. Having the same parent group for two years has afforded me a tight relationship with the families. And having the same students again definitely has kept unacceptable behavior in the classroom down to a minimum.

know one another. The second year, however, has some unique benefits, several of which are related to the psychosocial environment: familiarity, stability, continuity, and strong communication. During the second year they are together, teachers know the strengths, contributions, and abilities of their students, and students know the teacher's expectations and routines. Looping provides stability, particularly for children who might be experiencing difficulties outside the school. Teachers, students, and caregivers have more opportunity and a longer time to bond and work together as a team for the children's success.

FACTORS THAT CONTRIBUTE TO THE PSYCHOSOCIAL ENVIRONMENT

Many factors contribute to and significantly influence the psychosocial environment of the classroom. Factors under control of the teacher can be grouped into three categories: human relations skills, teacher and student responsibilities in human relations, and maintenance of the psychosocial environment.

Human Relations Skills

Good human relations enable people to interact pleasantly and productively, both of which are essential to a participative environment that promotes learning. Four aspects of human relations skills merit attention here: (1) general human relations skills, (2) human relations skills with students, (3) human relations skills with colleagues, and (4) human relations skills with parents and guardians.

General Human Relations Skills.   Certain skills in human relations are pertinent to all people in almost all situations. Those skills involve being friendly, maintaining a positive attitude, demonstrating the ability to listen, and offering genuine compliments.

Friendliness is a trait that is admired everywhere, yet many of us have difficulty being friendly toward others, especially when we find ourselves in threatening situations or with people we dislike. We can, however, learn to be friendly even toward people who do not please us, by smiling, speaking in a considerate way, using their names, asking how they are, and inquiring about family and work. When we do these simple things, we find that others tend to respond to us in the same manner.

Maintaining a positive attitude is a skill that should be kept foremost in mind. Generally we show it by looking on the bright side of things and by avoiding complaining, backbiting, faultfinding, or hurtful gossiping—behaviors known to undermine positive climates. We maintain a positive attitude by remembering that although all of us have difficulties in our lives, we also have some measure of control over how those difficulties affect us. People with positive attitudes believe that no problem exists that cannot be solved, and they focus on dealing with problems rather than complaining or making excuses for them.

Ability to listen is a skill we appreciate in others but often have trouble practicing. Most of us would rather talk than listen, but demonstrating the ability to listen is very helpful in promoting good relationships. It shows genuine interest in the other person, indicates that the other's experiences and observations are valued, and enhances the quality of communication by bringing about a genuine exchange of ideas.

Ability to compliment genuinely is not often discussed but is a skill of considerable power. Both the giving and receiving of compliments make most of us uncomfortable for a time, partly because people sometimes use compliments to manipulate others. Too often, compliments are worded to sound like criticisms rather than acknowledgments or appreciations for what someone does. But it is evident that most people like to receive compliments, even when unable to accept them gracefully, and that they react positively toward individuals who compliment them.

Effective compliments are both genuine and explicit. For example, when complimenting someone on a presentation, we might say, "I found your talk entertaining and helpful, especially your suggestions on conducting evaluation conferences between principals and teachers." Ask yourself how you react to people who give you genuine compliments. In all likelihood, you not only feel good but you also feel more interested in working with and associating with those persons.

Human Relations Skills with Students.   General human relations skills can be applied in all situations, but when dealing with students there are additional skills that serve teachers well. Before all else, teachers should (1) infuse qualities of good character into the way they teach. They also should (2) model courtesy and good manners, (3) give regular attention, (4) display genuine caring, (5) show continual willingness to help, and (6) use verbal and behavioral reinforcers.

When teachers infuse qualities of good character into the way they teach, they go beyond lessons that teach about specific ideals. Lessons are single events. Teachers too often miss opportunities for students to acquire and practice qualities of good character when they simply teach about ideals. For example, when they teach about honesty, they merely provide students with a definition that may or may not be learned. On the other hand, when teachers uphold honesty as an ideal of good character and provide opportunities for students to practice being honest, honesty is more likely to become a characteristic of each student.

Modeling courtesy and good manners closely complements this way of

The topic for today's faculty meeting is 'Credibility Between Student and Teacher'

VIGNETTE 4.2   Communicating with Students

Mary Brewer, an itinerant resource specialist, offers several suggestions for communicating with each individual student. Her students use a daily journal entry in which they can express their feelings in a nonthreatening atmosphere via personal written conversations. She also schedules regular "office hours" throughout the week. Students who want to discuss something with her sign up for the time(s) that are best for them.

Students who otherwise are reluctant to express themselves often are eager to draw pictures that illustrate their feelings, and if it's appropriate to do so, Mary uses the services of bilingual personnel to draw out hidden concerns. Students new to the school are reticent about expressing themselves, often because they feel themselves to be "outsiders," unwelcomed in the "in" group. Mary pairs these students with those more at ease and believes that cooperative learning provides many opportunities for this type of pairing.

Upon Reflection

Effective teachers make a point of talking to or interacting with every student every day. Mary Brewer suggests several ways to communicate with individual students; list them. What other ways can you think of?

teaching and is extremely important in establishing a positive classroom climate. Teachers should hold high standards of decency and courtesy and should model these qualities when dealing with students. They should never act cruelly, speak sarcastically, or show favoritism. Nor should they allow students to bully or be cruel or sarcastic. Courtesy and other qualities of good character, when held as ideals, are embedded into the way we teach and practiced at all times. Laughing and joking are not forbidden; they are prized—but never used hurtfully.

Giving regular attention is best done by speaking personally with each student every day, on matters not necessarily related to schoolwork or behavior. In most classrooms, the majority of teacher's attention goes to two small groups of students—those who do exceptionally well academically and those who chronically misbehave. Now that classrooms are inclusive, a third group also requires extra attention—students with disabilities or special needs. This leaves a large group of students who receive relatively little attention. Because this group causes teachers neither special joy nor special annoyance, it is natural that teachers tend to overlook them. If these students are to do their best, however, they too need attention from the teacher.

Some teachers make a point of speaking to students as they first enter the room each day. Others speak with students while taking attendance. Still others speak with them individually during small-group instruction. To help them distribute personal attention equitably, some teachers keep class rosters at hand and put tally marks beside names as attention is given.

Displaying genuine caring should be both verbal and visual. All of us want to believe that we are cared for and that others value what we say and do. Because we want to feel that we belong and are able to contribute to the group, we look and listen for signs from others that this is so. Approximately 20 percent of what a teacher communicates to students is done with words. The other 80 percent is communicated through body language. Teachers need to make sure that what they say and what their body says are really the same. Teachers should be able to say to students, "I care for you and I want to support you in all that you do here," and then be able to show it.

Continual willingness to help is another trait that is universally admired but seldom seen. We almost confer sainthood on people such as Albert Schweitzer and Mother Teresa who devote their lives to helping the abject poor. You should not expect your students to look upon you as saintly (though some will) when you show that you will do whatever you can to help them learn. Let it be enough that your students gravitate to you, admire you, and remember you positively in later years. How often we adults are heard to say of our teachers, "That Mrs. Smith was strict, but she always went out of her way to help us."

Verbal and behavioral reinforcers are the teacher's words and actions that show support, encouragement, and approval. Reinforcers increase student attention and work output. Some teachers use tangible reinforcers such as stars, tokens, and even food and candy. However, in most classes gestures and verbal reinforcers are sufficient—a wink, nod, smile, thumbs up, "Nice going," "I can see how much work you have put into this," "You must have thought about this a great deal," and "You are improving every day."

Again, reinforcement should be given to all students, not only for achievement but also for effort and improvement. Notice the fine distinction between reinforcing a student's *efforts* and reinforcing *character traits*. Be careful of saying things like "You are very intelligent" or "You are a good boy" when commenting on work. Praise of this type often brings undesirable side effects of uneasiness, inhibited communication, and an increased need for personal validation. It is preferable to say, "I see you worked hard. Thank you."

Human Relations Skills with Colleagues.

Every teacher spends a good deal of time working or dealing with colleagues—fellow teachers, administrators, support staff for students with special needs, beginning teacher support providers, student teachers, secretaries, librarians, custodians, nurses, and others. It is very important to be able to interact well with colleagues. In addition to the general skills of friendliness, polite attitude, listening, and complimenting, four additional considerations should be kept in mind: (1) supporting others, (2) sharing the load, (3) compromising, and (4) leading or following as appropriate.

Teachers who work together as partners have an even greater responsibility to practice these skills. Ideally, teaching teams are the result of mutual agreements that highlight the strengths of the partners. Teaming allows teachers to arrange students and instruction in a variety of ways to best support both teaching and learning. In addition to the considerations below, team teaching requires excellent communication, cooperation, mutual respect and trust, and careful planning.

Supporting others means standing behind them and what they are trying to accomplish, unless you absolutely cannot do so. This support can be active, as when actual assistance is given, or passive, as when acceptance and encouragement are shown.

This attitude of support is not found in overabundance, and it seems that the larger the school, the shorter the supply. Unfortunately, all too often school personnel denigrate the work of colleagues, make snide remarks, and belittle efforts and accomplishments—behind the colleague's back, of course. It has been documented that in faculty lounges, about

90 percent of teachers' comments are negative in nature. Negativism such as this is very detrimental to good working environments.

The paucity of support that teachers show for each other probably is due in part to teacher isolation, frustration, and absence of tangible success. When we don't feel the world is treating us fairly, we tend to lash out at others who have little if anything to do with the real problem.

Another unattractive trait of human nature is that we all want to look good, in our own eyes as well as in the eyes of others, and we seem to believe that we can build ourselves up by tearing others down. As they look worse, we think that we look better in comparison. The result, of course, is never what we had hoped. For example, those who gossip and malign in an attempt to show their superiority hardly ever lack an attentive audience. But does that audience hold the complainer in high regard? Rarely. Complainers and backbiters seldom earn the sincere trust of others. As they tear others down, they taint their own reputations. If you want to build yourself up, the way to do so is by building others up. If you learn only one thing from this book, let it be what you have just read.

Sharing the load is one thing you must do if you hope to earn the respect of your colleagues. In any school, there are many jobs to do and tasks to complete: committee work that no one likes very much; team, Individual Education Plan (IEP), and student concern meetings; open houses and parent–teacher meetings; family math nights; school musicals and carnivals; student council and safety patrols; curriculum groups; materials evaluations; and in-service education sessions. Typically a few people carry most of the load while the rest do far less than their share. If we are to get along well with colleagues, and it is essential to our professional lives that we do so, we must undertake our part even when it is unpleasant. Sharing the load builds trust; shirking produces resentment.

Compromising is a way of life for those who get along well with others. Compromise doesn't mean giving in to others any more than it means demanding to have your own way all of the time. It is a matter of give and take, with resolution coming after everyone has had a say. In any professional group there will be strong differences of opinion regarding purpose, procedure, and workload. You will want to express and stick by what you believe, but also try to understand others' feelings and points of view. If a faculty's work is to go forward in a positive way, an acceptable middle ground must be found.

Both *leading and following* are important in any endeavor, especially when undertaken democratically. We should assume leadership roles in which we can effectively plan courses of action, obtain resources, guide decisions, and rally support. When others lead, we should do our best to help make decisions that share the load. This does not mean following the leader's dictates uncritically, but it does imply that criticisms and counter-suggestions should be expressed in open forums, and support should be given once a group decision has been made.

Teaching in teams requires additional considerations to be most effective and efficient. In addition to giving teachers more time for students, team teaching encourages reflection and evaluation of what the partners themselves are doing. In teams, partners have someone to provide feedback on their ideas, someone whose strengths they can build on, and someone who will support their successes and challenges. However, for team teaching to work, partners must share a mutual philosophy, trust, and compatibility. Successful teaching teams require a lot of give and take, and the shared mindset that this is *our* classroom, and we work *together* for the success of our program and our students.

VIGNETTE 4.3   Team Teaching

First-grade teachers Jamie Rubin and Patti Petersen have more than thirty years of combined teaching experience and have shared a teaching contract for many years. They say that the past years have been the most rewarding and the best, and they would not teach any other way. Being friends for six years prior to team teaching helped in making the situation a strong one. Once, when a child was asked the name of the teacher for whom he was running an errand, he replied without pause, "Mrs. Rubinsen."

Jamie: Our teaching styles are very similar and compatible. We both exhibit organization, fairness, structure, and a sense of fun in a fairly strict classroom. We each have our own strengths. One of us has a master's degree in reading and is very strong in language arts. The other loves science and music. When parents ask how their child will be able to balance two teachers in a first-grade classroom, our response is "If the child is lucky enough to have a two-parent family, then so it is in this classroom."

Patti: What makes our partnership work and thrive? First, our friendship. We respect, trust, and love each other. We often try to outdo each other in the kindnesses we perform so that the next day's workload for our partner is lessened. Second is our communication. We email each other daily with information about the day. Rarely is there a time when either of us is left in the dark concerning anything, be it related to parent, student, or peer.

Upon Reflection

What are the advantages of team teaching? What are the disadvantages? What makes a successful teaching team work?

Beginning Teacher Support Programs.   In many school districts, beginning teachers now find themselves communicating directly with district support persons whose attention and efforts help them grow in their professional skills. It's critical that novice teachers are comfortable and able to communicate classroom realities and concerns so support providers can mentor and assist efficiently.

Human Relations Skills with Parents and Guardians.   Teachers have the responsibility to communicate and work with the parents or guardians of the students they teach. Sadly, some teachers avoid this contact as much as possible, though such avoidance, under most circumstances, is counterproductive. Fortunately, many teachers accept the responsibility willingly and capitalize on it. Why? Alliances with caregivers—teachers working with parents or guardians in a collaborative effort—further the goal of supporting the student. Teachers who communicate well with caregivers often find that they enjoy increased home support in matters of discipline and curriculum. As an extra bonus, parents and guardians give higher ratings to teachers who take the trouble to communicate about what caregivers consider the most important element of schooling—their child.

How teachers reach out to caregivers makes a difference in the response they get from them. When communicating with parents or guardians (details of which are presented in Chapter 11), keep in mind the four traits of friendliness, positive attitude, listening, and genuine compliments. Also make sure to (1) communicate regularly and clearly, (2) describe your program and expectations, (3) emphasize the child's progress while downplaying his or her shortcomings, (4) mention future plans for the child's instruction, and (5) arrange for productive parent conferences.

Communicating regularly and clearly establishes a basis of mutual concern about the child. As a general rule, some kind of communication should go to caregivers every week—a note, instructions for homework, a written commentary about a piece of student work, a class newsletter, or a phone call. Parents or guardians of a student with a disability or other special need should be involved actively in their child's educational program. Also, when language diversity is a consideration, arrangements should be made to translate communications into the primary language of the caregivers. The importance of frequent regular communication cannot be overemphasized; a system should be implemented at the beginning of the year and followed thereafter. Fourth-grade teacher Karen O'Connor explains why she routinely calls parents and guardians of her students.

> I still remember a reaction the first year I taught from the mother of a student who was chronically disruptive in class. The mother said resignedly, "Oh, hello, Mrs. O'Connor. What has Bobby done wrong today?" When I reassured her that I had called to tell her what an interesting oral report Bobby had given in front of the class that day, I heard her relief, even disbelief, as she listened to the details.
>
> I think we need to break the "no news is good news" mindset by taking time to make positive phone calls about our students. That one phone call to Bobby's mother turned a potentially adversarial relationship into a partnership that helped both of us support Bobby's efforts.

This regular communication must be done very clearly, with no possibility of parental misunderstanding. Education is filled with jargon and acronyms, such as grade level expectancies, curriculum standards, inclusion, IEP, GATE, SAT, multi-age classrooms, cooperative learning, authentic assessment, portfolios, clinical teaching, inquiry training—you probably can add several others. Don't take it for granted that caregivers understand any of these terms. Avoid such terms if you can, but if you must communicate about them, explain what they mean.

Describe your program and expectations early in your communication, and repeat them occasionally. Some caregivers will forget, but many may prove to be so interested in what you have to say that they will actively help their child achieve your stated goals. Inform them of the daily schedule. Tell them something about the activities you will use to reach your goals. Let them know about homework, the grading system, and anything else central to your program. They will appreciate it and will become more predisposed to cooperate.

Emphasize progress when communicating about the child. Also identify the child's difficulties, indicate your plan for remedying these shortcomings, and ask for parental help. Caregivers' thoughts about their child are fragile. Parents see their child as an extension of themselves, the child's difficulties as their own, and criticism of the child as leveled at themselves. Dwelling on a child's shortcomings probes at parents' most sensitive feelings.

When discussing the child, consider this sequence: (1) mention something positive about the child personally, (2) show progress the child has made and is making, (3) describe plans for producing still greater achievement in the child, and finally, (4) mention difficulties that are interfering with the child's progress. Assure caregivers that you are working to

HOME VISITS

Focus Questions

Compare this style of interaction with students and caregivers to Karen O'Connor's telephone calls to students the night before school begins (described in Chapter 11). What are the challenges and the potential advantages of each approach? What is the policy of your (local) district or school regarding home visits by teachers?

An important part of classroom management is having parents as allies, and it is important to develop a strong working relationship from the beginning. Third-grade teacher Pam Klevesahl goes so far as to communicate with some parents and students prior to the first day of school.

When Ms. Klevesahl receives her class list before the school year begins, she often finds notes regarding behavioral and/or academic concerns by the names of certain children. These are the students who frequently require more teacher time. Addressing these issues prior to the beginning of school pays dividends later.

Ms. Klevesahl tries to meet with each of these students and their families in their home. The week before the first day of school she calls the family, introduces herself, and explains that she would like to come by the house to meet with them and discuss their child. Often they are surprised and inquire about why she wants to come by. She tells them that she tries to meet as many students and families as she can before school begins. In this way Ms. Klevesahl puts parents as well as the student at ease and arranges to stop by their home for approximately twenty minutes.

When she arrives, Ms. Klevesahl introduces herself and then asks the child if he or she is looking forward to the start of school. She tells them a little about the year and the plans she has for learning units. She then asks the child if he or she has any questions about their year together. Following her discussion with the child, Ms. Klevesahl asks the parents if they have any questions or concerns that she can answer. Frequently parents tell her that their child has difficulty paying attention, working quietly, or the like. When she hears this, she turns directly to the child and says, "Oh my gosh! I sure hope that doesn't happen this year." Ms. Klevesahl then explains that the students in her class are growing up and will be expected to work independently, and that if they do not, they will have to complete their work during recess time. In this way she lets the child and the parents know her expectations as well as the consequences. Ms. Klevesahl then returns to the parents and discusses her behavior plan so they understand what will happen if inappropriate behavior occurs. The child, of course, is listening intently and benefits from the discussion as well.

Finally Ms. Klevesahl concludes by saying how much she enjoyed meeting everyone, and that she looks forward to seeing them on the first day of school.

overcome these difficulties, that you have a plan for doing so, that you need their support in your efforts, and that you will appreciate any insights or suggestions they might offer. Caregivers usually respond well when treated in this manner. They want their child to learn and behave in school, and when the teacher shows interest, they usually support and help.

Future plans for individuals and for the entire class should be communicated. If a student has unusual difficulty in math, formulate a definite plan you can share with the student and caregivers. If a child excels in science, plan how that child might stretch that talent or move into other topics. If the class shows unusual ability in music or art, plan to further those abilities, perhaps through a special performance for caregivers.

Conferencing productively with caregivers, although closely related to the points already made, refers specifically to the parent–teacher conferences scheduled early in the school year at most schools. Some schools and districts schedule conferences at each grading period. Have at hand the individual student's folder, which shows progress, strengths, weaknesses, and work samples. Greet the parents or guardians and have them sit at a table beside you, not across from you. Engage them in a few words of small talk and make them feel at ease. Review the child's good qualities, strengths, progress, difficulties, and your plans for increasing strengths and countering the difficulties. Request their help in supporting the child and, if necessary, in working with the child at home. In fact, if possible, help the caregivers create a home action plan that parallels and supports your plan. Assure the parents or guardians that you will do your best for the child and request their cooperation toward that end. Again, if English is not a strong language for the caregivers, consider inviting a translator to join you for the conference. Further details of what should be included and said in parent–teacher conferences are presented in Chapter 11.

Responsibilities in the Psychosocial Environment

The psychosocial environment of the classroom rests on warmth, stimulation, and helpfulness. These qualities are unlikely to occur unless planned for, and an important part of that planning lies in recognizing who is responsible for what.

Teacher Responsibilities.   The teacher is responsible for communicating and modeling the sort of psychosocial environment desired, initiating the conditions that lead to it, and maintaining a good environment once it is achieved.

The *desired environment,* as described previously, is one in which students work hard, help each other, and enjoy success, all in a pleasant setting of encouragement and absence of threat. You will want to talk with your students frequently about these desired conditions, in terms suited to their level of understanding and maturity. They will want the same conditions you do, and if allowed, they will make suggestions for achieving them. They will understand and support your reasoning. However, they will not always abide by what is necessary to keep the environment healthy.

Conditions that indicate and sustain the environment must be set forth by the teacher, through explanations, modeling, classbuilding, and teambuilding. Students closely watch and often imitate the teacher's attitude and behavior. Teachers must set the tone by using appropriate classbuilding and teambuilding activities throughout the year. During classbuilding activities, students meet and interact with all members of the class. Teambuilding activities give students opportunities to interact and support their teammates in positive ways. Kagan and colleagues (1995, 1997) offer numerous classbuilding and teambuilding structures (step-by-step sequences of action) that support a positive and safe class environment. For more information about classbuilding and teambuilding and activity ideas, visit Kagan's website, www.kaganonline.com.

In addition to their own attitudes and behavior, as well as their classbuilding and teambuilding efforts, teachers must demonstrate the following as they establish and maintain a sound emotional environment in their class:

Enthusiasm.   Enthusiasm is a key element to which students react positively. They find it motivating, energizing, and contagious. Students like seeing teachers who enjoy what they do. Teacher enthusiasm should be shown for the curriculum as well as for working with children, in a stable, ongoing manner throughout the day.

Importance of the Individual.   The importance of every individual in the classroom should be established quickly. Teachers should communicate continually that students are worthy and have a place in school and society, that they have contributions to make, and that the class would be diminished without them. The feeling of importance will grow as students assume responsibilities in the classroom, experience success, and receive deserved acknowledgment from others.

Belonging.   Belonging is a primary goal in life—all of us want to know we are important to family, friends, class, and school. When that goal is not reached, students tend either to withdraw or to misbehave, neither of which is good for the teacher, student, or class. Therefore, it behooves the teacher to foster a sense of belonging in every member of the class by stating, and repeating, that every student is important, will be valued, and will be treated fairly. It also helps to follow through with acknowledgment, friendliness, help, support, and assigned responsibility for some aspect of the room or program. Again, classbuilding and teambuilding efforts help affirm belonging and the sense of community.

Important underlying psychosocial values for inclusive classrooms are the ABCs (acceptance, belonging, and community) and the three Rs (reading, writing, and relationships). Inclusive classrooms also focus on how to support the special gifts of every child in the school community and how to meet students' needs to feel welcomed and secure and to become successful (Pearpoint & Forest, 1992).

Fairness.   Fairness is required if the psychosocial environment is to remain positive. Students don't like the teacher to play favorites or enforce rules unevenly. They expect standards but don't want them to be impossibly high. They expect rules and enforcement but don't want them to be harsh. In other words, students will comply with standards and rules if they consider them to be fair.

Responsibility.   Responsibility goes hand in hand with belonging. It is important that all students accept their roles in furthering their own learning, as well as other classroom roles. Classroom monitors can be assigned responsibilities for many of the ongoing requirements of the class. (You will find additional discussion and suggestions for class monitors in Chapter 7.) Mirroring some of today's business practices, some teachers use students as "one-minute managers" to help run the class. Group discussions should emphasize that every student has a stake in making things good for all students collectively, and for the teacher as well, and that this responsibility should carry over to friends and family. Such responsibilities do not weigh students down but instead give them a sense of purpose, with attendant motivation for supporting group endeavors.

Consistency.   Students want to know what to expect from their teachers day to day. They like surprises, but only pleasant ones. When their teacher vacillates between warm and cold or tolerant and harsh, students become uneasy and their behavior becomes unpredictable.

Friendliness.   Friendliness projects the warmth and consideration that contribute to productive work. This is not "best-pal" friendliness, but that which is shown through having a pleasant demeanor, acknowledging individual students, speaking with them regularly and personally, and remembering their birthdays and something about family members or pets. This friendliness dispels any sense of threat and helps reduce fearfulness while increasing willingness to attempt difficult tasks. Irresponsible choices and poor behavior will not be tolerated, and standards will be maintained and enforced in an evenhanded way. Students are not hurtfully punished; logical consequences give them second chances and the opportunity to right their wrongs or make up for them.

Success.   Success should be established and maintained from the beginning. Success is highly rewarding, motivating, and effective in building positive self-concept, although students should not believe that they always will succeed in what they do or that success always comes easily. It is important, however, that every student experience success, especially from diligent effort and improvement.

Understanding.   When students are struggling with personal difficulties, they want to be understood. Understanding includes recognition of illness, discomfort, personal problems, or traumatic occurrences, so that a greater than normal degree of tolerance justifiably can be shown. This is not to be confused, however, with unquestioning acceptance of whatever a student might say or do. We can be understanding of difficulties, excitements, and problems without approving or ignoring a student's disruptive or inappropriate behavior in the classroom.

Humor.   Finally, humor should be a mainstay of the psychosocial environment. Humor is the trait most often identified by older students when asked what they most like in teachers. (Younger children most often identify niceness.) Students like to laugh, share jokes, and find the humor in situations, and they appreciate teachers who make humor a part of the environment. Unfortunately, students also like to laugh hurtfully at each other, and that is a problem. You never should allow your students to laugh at the expense of others. If everyone is enjoying a laugh, fine. But when it is done in demeaning or cruel ways, it is not to be tolerated. Simply point out that students will have a good time in their work and there will be plenty of humor and laughter, but there will be no horseplay, no abject silliness, and no laughing at another's expense.

Organizing the Conditions That Build a Good Environment.   Conditions that include and sustain a positive psychosocial environment must be brought into play in an organized manner. You must be sure to show every student that he or she is cared for and wanted, will be treated fairly, will be encouraged, and will enjoy learning in a nonthreatening environment. Every student should have important responsibilities in the class. You should not leave such matters to chance or assume they will occur because of your good intentions. (Again, think of the description of Janna Smart's first days with her students.) Even the smartest teacher cannot keep in mind all the conditions and responsibilities of a classroom. A checklist, kept in a record book, serves as a useful reminder of the attitudes and conditions just discussed and ensures that they will be given attention thoroughly and consistently.

Student Responsibilities.   Students have responsibilities to the psychosocial environment just as teachers do, and the act of discharging those responsibilities is very powerful in building the classroom environment. Responsibilities should be clarified in class discussions and reemphasized regularly. Students' main responsibilities include the following.

Learning.   Learning is the main reason students are in school. They are there to acquire the skills, attitudes, values, and understandings that will permit them to function to the fullest while contributing to the societal good. This also includes learning to make responsible choices for themselves. They should be helped to recognize that fact and comply with it as their fundamental responsibility in the classroom.

Contribution.   Contribution to the class is a second major responsibility students have in helping maintain a good psychosocial environment. They are to participate in discussions, help with class duties, assist other students and the teacher, and conduct themselves in accord with class expectations and regulations. Students become more productive and secure and gain more from educational experiences when they participate than when they merely serve as passive or reluctant space-fillers.

Making Responsible Choices.   Making responsible choices related to their learning situations as well as their behavior is an important skill for all students. Students benefit from watching teachers model how they make choices to solve situations and problems. Moreover, we all learn from our mistakes. When students are first guided through the process and then trusted to make choices and decisions, they grow through the results of their decisions.

Being Dependable.   Dependability on the part of all students does wonders for the class environment. When they do what they are supposed to do, well and on time, students help create a climate of enjoyment and productivity. Students can help themselves fulfill this responsibility by using self-reminders concerning tasks and deadlines. Older students can employ checklists of duties; younger students can rely on verbal reminders. All students can be asked periodically to evaluate themselves on dependability.

Being Considerate.   Consideration for others should be shown at all times. Everyone—fellow students, teachers, the principal, custodians, and staff—have difficulties, egos, and sensitive feelings. Students profit from practical discussions, and even role-plays, of the Golden Rule that help them decide how they can show friendliness and helpfulness toward others throughout the day.

Supporting Others.   Support for others' efforts, shown through acceptance and encouragement, is another important student responsibility. Students must learn quickly that they are not to be passive captives in the classroom but active members who help each other succeed. They should be helped to understand that the best way to be liked and helped is to like and help others.

Relating Positively.   Finally, relating positively means showing good manners, being polite and courteous, and avoiding words and actions that hurt others. Teachers can help students see that everyone profits when they get along with each other and that they should work to maintain that attitude.

Maintaining the Psychosocial Environment

The preceding discussion emphasized the many responsibilities of teachers and students in fostering a positive psychosocial environment—a place where students can learn in an atmosphere of helpfulness, encouragement, and the absence of threat. Responsibilities that fall mainly to the teacher, especially regarding what can be done to sustain a positive psychosocial environment once it is begun, include modeling, verbal reinforcement, help, class meetings, classbuilding and teambuilding activities, and private discussions.

Modeling.   Modeling refers to teaching through example to help students learn through imitation. In reality, the majority of our life learnings occur through this process. We see how others act, dress, and talk, and we imitate them. Modeling is especially powerful in social learning and making responsible choices, which are central to the psychosocial environment. Teachers should consistently model what they hope to see in their students and provide students with opportunities to practice and model for fellow students as well.

Verbal Reinforcement.   Verbal reinforcement was described earlier as a process in which verbal rewards are given when you see behavior you approve in others. With words such as "Thanks," "Good work," "You tried hard on this," "This work shows a lot of thought," "I appreciate how helpful you've been," and "You showed that you cared about John's feelings," teachers encourage, guide, and support behavior that contributes to the good of the total class. Verbal reinforcers should be short and describe the behavior being approved. Teachers also should teach their students how to give reinforcement to others so when classmates behave in pleasing ways, their behavior can be encouraged.

"My students told me I should lighten up!"

Help.   Help should always be available to students, though it is generally given after they make a serious effort on their own. Knowing that help is available provides a sense of security and support, and engenders positive attitudes. There also can be a downside to providing help. A "helplessness syndrome" occurs when students will not make or sustain effort without constantly seeking attention from the teacher. Often this occurs simply because students like the teacher's attention, and showing helplessness is a way of getting that attention. In this case, teachers should give the student attention when help is *not* needed, for example, when the student makes a good effort.

Class Meetings.   Class meetings, a technique for dealing with class problems devised by William Glasser (1969), call for the identification of concerns, followed by searching for solutions. Teachers and/or students can raise concerns in the meeting, no faultfinding or blaming is allowed, and all focus is on finding positive solutions. Students sit in a tight circle for these discussions so they can see each other face to face. The meetings can deal with social problems in the classroom or school (e.g., noise or playground fighting), academic problems (e.g., lack of class interest, effort, or progress), or problems outside of school (e.g., conditions that interfere with home study). Class meetings also provide an additional setting for discussions and for practicing effective ways to deal with conflicts. Regular class meetings help students carry out their responsibilities in perpetuating a healthy classroom environment. Nelsen, Lott, and Glenn (2000) clarify the process further by detailing eight discrete building-block skill areas to ensure successful and effective class meetings. For additional information about class meetings and the building blocks for success, look at the following website: www.positivediscipline.com.

Classbuilding and Teambuilding.   Classbuilding and teambuilding, according to Kagan, are essential for creating caring, cooperative classrooms and communities. Classbuilding activities, during which students stand up, move around, and interact with someone new, should be done at least once weekly, beginning the first day of school. Random groups can be effective and efficient during the first three weeks as teacher and students get to know each other. Then teambuilding, with fun and easy activities in which everyone can participate, should occur at least twice weekly. Teambuilding activities are nonacademic and can be very quick. Their purpose is to strengthen team functioning.

Private Discussions.   Private discussions should be held with individual students when necessary to solve problems that are not appropriate for group discussions, such as refusal to work, defiance, theft, vandalism, or personal home or health problems. Individual conferences can focus on conflict resolution or on problem solving when appropriate. Kagan, Kyle, and Scott (2004) share numerous step-by-step suggestions, including *Same-Side Chat,* to use with individuals at the moment of disruption, for follow-up, and for long-term solutions. Consider looking at some of their suggestions, found on Kagan's website, www.kaganonline.com.

This concludes our review of purposes and responsibilities in managing a quality psychosocial environment in the classroom. Chapter 5 focuses on encouraging students toward greater effort and productivity in the classroom. Before proceeding to the next chapter, take time to explore these end-of-chapter activities.

Parting Thought

Teachers have the right to teach.
Students have the right to learn.
And no one has the right to interfere with either of these events.

—Author Unknown

SUMMARY SELF-CHECK

Check off the following as you either understand or become able to apply them.

❑ Teachers strive for an emotional tone in their classrooms that is warm, supportive, and pleasant, as opposed to cold, rejecting, and unpleasant.

❑ Because looping keeps teachers and students together for at least two consecutive years, the climate for the second year actually is created during the first.

❑ Achieving the desired emotional tone calls attention to:
- General human relations skills: being friendly, maintaining a positive outlook, demonstrating the ability to listen, offering genuine compliments
- Relations with students: infusing character into the way we teach, setting a good example, giving regular attention, displaying genuine caring, showing helpfulness, providing reinforcement
- Relations with colleagues: being supportive, sharing the load, compromising, leading or following as appropriate, teaching teams, support programs for beginning teachers
- Relations with caregivers: communicating regularly, describing program and expectations, emphasizing the child's progress, giving future plans for the child's instruction, conducting productive parent–teacher conferences
- Teacher responsibilities in the psychosocial environment: communicating the desired environment, classbuilding and teambuilding, setting conditions that initiate and sustain, showing enthusiasm, stressing responsibility, showing consistency, exhibiting friendliness, ensuring success for all, showing understanding, being helpful, showing a sense of humor, doing all in an organized way
- Student responsibility in the psychosocial environment: learning, contributing, making responsible choices, being dependable, showing consideration, being supportive, being positive with others
- Maintaining a good psychosocial environment: modeling desired behavior, providing verbal reinforcement, providing opportunities to practice, holding class meetings, using classbuilding and teambuilding activities to build community, holding private discussions as needed.

ACTIVITIES FOR REFLECTION AND DISCUSSION

1. Take a moment to review the statements in the Prediction–Review Guide at the beginning of this chapter. Put a check mark in the Review column next to any statement with which you now agree. How have your thoughts changed since reading this chapter?

2. Interview at least two teachers about how they establish the feeling tone in their classrooms. How do they look, sound, and act when the school year begins? How do they sustain the tone through the year?

3. Review the description in Chapter 1 of Janna Smart's efforts regarding the psychosocial environment—the feeling tone—of her classroom. What added challenges might she have been facing because the school year began before she first met her students? How do the changes she made her second week with students align with the suggestions that are described in this chapter?

4. Suppose that you are meeting your class (select a grade level) for the first time and you want students to understand (a) the psychosocial environment you want for the class and why it is important, (b) the responsibilities you will assume in establishing and maintaining that environment, (c) and the responsibilities that students need to assume in furthering that environment. What will you say to convey your ideas? To what extent will you hope for student response and input? Also reflect on how your approach might be different if your class is older or younger.

5. Describe how you would begin the year with a class that had looped with you from the previous year.

6. What will classbuilding and teambuilding look like and sound like in your class? Describe some activities that you might use for each.

7. Class meetings and private discussions were suggested for maintaining a good psychosocial environment. List five topics you consider appropriate for each. How do you differentiate between topics to be discussed privately and those to be discussed in a group? What topics, if any, do you consider inappropriate for either class meetings or private discussion?

REFERENCES AND RECOMMENDED READINGS

Albert, L. (1996). *Cooperative discipline.* Circle Pines, MN: American Guidance Service.

Building classroom relationships [Special issue]. (2003, September). *Educational Leadership, 61*(1). Alexandria, VA: ASCD.

Charles, C. (2000). *The synergetic classroom: Joyful teaching and gentle discipline.* New York: Addison Wesley Longman.

Coloroso, B. (1994). *Kids are worth it! Giving your child the gift of inner discipline.* New York: Avon Books.

Coloroso, B. (2002). *The bully, the bullied, and the bystander.* Toronto, Ontario, Canada: HarperCollins.

Fraser, B., & O'Brien, P. (1985). Student and teacher perceptions of the environment of elementary school classrooms. *Elementary School Journal, 85*(5), 567–580.

Freiburg, J. (1996, September). From tourists to citizens in the classroom. *Educational Leadership, 54*(1), 32–36.

Glasser, W. (1969). *Schools without failure.* New York: Harper & Row.

Glasser, W. (1998). *The quality school: Managing students without coercion.* New York: Perennial Press.

Kagan, L., Kagan, M., & Kagan, S. (1997). *Cooperative learning structures for teambuilding.* San Clemente, CA: Kagan Cooperative Learning.

Kagan, M., Robertson, L., & Kagan, S. (1995). *Cooperative learning structures for classbuilding.* San Clemente, CA: Kagan Cooperative Learning.

Kagan, S., Kyle, P., & Scott, S. (2004). *Win-win discipline.* San Clemente, CA: Kagan Cooperative Learning.

Nelsen, J., Lott, L., & Glenn, H. (2000). *Positive discipline in the classroom.* Rocklin, CA: Prima Publishing.

Pearpoint, J., & Forest, M. (1992). Foreword. In S. Stainback & W. Stainback (Eds.), *Curriculum considerations in inclusive classrooms: Facilitating learning for all students* (pp. xv–xviii). Baltimore: Paul H. Brookes.

Schools as safe havens [Special issue]. (1997, October). *Educational Leadership.* Alexandria, VA: ASCD.

Siris, K., & Osterman, K. (2004, December). Interrupting the cycle of bullying and victimization in the elementary classroom. *Phi Delta Kappan, 86*(4), 288–291. Bloomington, IN: Phi Delta Kappa International.

Websites

Discipline
www.positivediscipline.com

Inclusion
www.inclusion.com
www.circleofinclusion.org

Professional Development
www.kaganonline.com

Trade Book

Sollman, C., Emmons, B., & Paolini, J. (1994). *Through the cracks.* Worcester, MA: Davis Publications.

CHAPTER 5

Managing Student Motivation to Learn

Imagination is the true magic carpet.

—Norman Vincent Peale

Mistakes are simply invitations to try again.

—Dian Ritter

Prediction–Review Guide

Before you read the chapter, take a minute to put a check mark in the Prediction column next to any statement with which you agree.

	Prediction	Review
1. Traditional teaching diminishes children's inborn interest in learning.	❑	❑
2. Students don't try very hard in school because lessons usually are not very interesting to them.	❑	❑
3. Unmotivated students rarely misbehave; they just sit and do nothing.	❑	❑
4. When teachers speak of *motivation* as part of their lesson, they refer to students' innate desire to learn.	❑	❑
5. Glasser claims that motivation and discipline cease to be problems when schooling is organized to meet students' needs.	❑	❑
6. Kagan would have teachers motivate students by using cooperative learning activities built around multiple intelligences and classbuilding and teambuilding experiences.	❑	❑
7. Students are better able to engage in instruction and demonstrate their learnings when teaching is enriched with multiple intelligences strategies.	❑	❑
8. Incentives should be given early in the day or week to ensure that students will continue to work hard the rest of the time.	❑	❑
9. With Preferred Activity Time (PAT), students are allowed to do anything they want as an incentive for work and good behavior.	❑	❑
10. True cooperative learning is more complicated than students working in groups.	❑	❑

Support for specific standards found in this chapter:

INTASC Standards

2. Knowledge of Human Development and Learning

   The teacher understands how children learn and develop and can provide learning opportunities that support their intellectual, social, and personal development.

5. Classroom Motivation and Management

   The teacher uses an understanding of individual and group motivation and behavior to create a learning environment that encourages positive social interaction, active engagement in learning, and self-motivation.

Danielson's Framework for Teaching

3. Instruction
   - Communicating clearly and accurately
   - Using questioning and discussion techniques
   - Engaging students in learning
   - Providing feedback to students
   - Demonstrating flexibility and responsiveness

NBPTS Standards

2. Teachers know the subjects they teach and how to teach those subjects to students.

NCATE Standards

Help all pre-kindergarten through twelfth grade (P–12) students learn.

Apply effective methods of teaching students who are at different developmental stages, have different learning styles, and come from diverse backgrounds.

Ask any group of elementary teachers what brings them the greatest professional pleasure and they almost certainly will mention working with students who have good intentions and who try hard to work. Conversely, if you ask those teachers what troubles them most about teaching, they will likely mention disruptive student behavior and an inability to get some of their students interested in learning.

By *learning,* they of course mean school learning, for all students are interested in learning certain things and make intensive efforts to do so. The problem simply is that students' interests in learning often do not correspond with what teachers are required to teach. Most students enter kindergarten eager and open to the entire curriculum, but within a year or two they have clearly distinguished between school activities that intrigue them and those that do not. From that point on, teachers continually search for ways to attract student attention and engage students in learning activities. In other words, they forever look for ways to motivate their students.

◼ WHAT IS MEANT BY MOTIVATION?

The word *motive* comes from a Latin root meaning "to move" and is defined as an emotion, desire, or psychological need that incites a person to do something. Motive is the *why* of behavior. The associated term *motivation* has two meanings that are used rather differently. One of those meanings refers to a condition within individuals that disposes them toward an activity or goal, such as motivation to learn, motivation to succeed, or motivation to gain acceptance. For example, Mr. Garcia's sixth graders routinely forgot most of what they read about the Greeks and the Romans until Mr. Garcia arranged a contest on ancient civilization facts against Ms. Espinosa's class. His students suddenly began to remember the material much better. Their internal motivation to learn and to succeed was increased.

Teachers frequently use a second, and different, meaning for the term *motivation*. This meaning refers to a process by which motives are instilled into students—that is, what one (such as a teacher) does to get students interested in lessons and to facilitate willingness to work at them. When teachers speak of motivation as a component of a lesson, they refer to what *they do* to attract students' interest and engage them more or less willingly in the work provided. Thinking in a short-term sense, they might ask themselves, "What can I do for motivation in this lesson?"

"I'VE TRIED VARIOUS FORMS OF MOTIVATION. I FIND THAT REMOTE CONTROL WORKS BEST."

◼ WHY PEOPLE DON'T DO WHAT WE WANT THEM TO DO

When we ask people to do something, sometimes they will do it, but sometimes they won't. Understanding the reasons why people will or will not do what we ask is a valuable insight for teachers as they think about how best to motivate students. Among reasons why people don't do what we want them to do are the following:

1. **They don't know what to do.** Students without requisite knowledge or who don't understand the expectations are not likely to do what teachers ask.

2. They don't know how to do it. The same is true regarding students' abilities and skills.

3. They don't know why they should do it. Students want to know the reason for and the importance of their work.

4. They aren't suited or matched to the task. For example, a student who is especially energetic will have a difficult time sitting still for a forty-minute lecture.

5. They don't want to. Sometimes it's simply a lack of will.

Recent studies by Paula Cook (2004) and others have identified a type of behavior referred to as *neurological based behavior* (NBB). Simply, this is behavior that is outside the control of the individual. In other words, individuals with NBB behave as they do because of the way their brains work, and consequently, they may not do as we want because their actions are outside their control. Read more about NBB in Chapter 8.

MOTIVATION AND LESSONS

Motivation that resides over time within individuals is *internal* or *self-motivation,* while motivation that is supplied from outside the individual is *external motivation.* Teachers would love to work with students who always are internally motivated to learn, but they know that most of the time they will have to supply at least some of the motivation for their students.

Teachers know that learning is both exciting and fun when it matches the interests and abilities of their students. They also know that most students enjoy hands-on activities. And they know that when they teach the right way, motivation happens by itself.

Consequently, teachers who are good motivators pay close attention to students' known interests, such as animals, sports, cars, entertainers, music, and cartoons. They look for ways to include those interests in lessons, and often are amazed that young students can quickly learn such vast amounts of information about dinosaurs and sports legends.

Sometimes something as simple as a coupon booklet works. Students begin the year or semester with coupons from the teacher (see Figure 5.1). For example, booklets may include forgiveness coupons for single specific assignments, an assignment the student chooses (with teacher approval). Clever clip art designs and colored paper make these a fun gift. Students are allowed to redeem their coupons according to simple directions. For example, a general assignment coupon might read, "This coupon is good for one assignment from any subject. Check with your teacher to see if the assignment is a coupon event. Coupons may be used only once."

Teachers also rely heavily on student wants. *Want* is an imprecise, nonscientific term that simply means something students desire, something they wish to have or do. Some wants stem from *needs,* a scientific term referring to what students require in order to live enjoyably in reasonably good health. As Maslow pointed out in 1943, everyone needs food, water, and air, and most of us need acceptance, love, and association with others. To say we need these things is to say that we feel best when we have them—healthy, content, fulfilled.

Most student wants have little to do with psychological needs. For example, students may strongly want to eat ice cream, watch a film, get a new comic book or video game, or play with a particular person—none of which, if denied, interferes with personal well-being.

FIGURE 5.1   Sample Pages of a Coupon Booklet

Source: Virginia Lorenz. Reprinted by permission.

TABLE 5.1   Age, Wants, and Interests

Age	Wants (things students seek and/or respond well to)	Interests (specific activities)
5 to 8 years	assurance, physical activity, direct sensory experience, encouragement, praise, warmth, patience, concrete learning tasks	relating experiences, stories, dramatic play, pictures, songs, poems, rhythms, and animals to organized games, models, dolls, jokes, gangs and clubs, collecting, comics, adventure books, animals, and foreign lands and people
9 to 10 years	praise, physical activity, group membership, being admired	riddles, jokes, puzzles, sharing, competitive games, trips, reading, maps, letters, animals, arts and crafts
preadolescent	affection, warmth, greater independence, peer group acceptance and belonging	riddles, jokes, puzzles, gangs and clubs, sports, competitive and outdoor games, hobbies, construction, pets, movies, TV, comics, reading, drama
adolescent	acceptance by and conformation to peer group; kind, unobtrusive guidance by adults; security with independence	music, dancing, cars, opposite sex, sports, trips, TV, movies, magazines, gossip, intrigue, adult roles

Nevertheless, such wants play important roles in students' lives, and they provide practical insights into how teachers can motivate students.

The major interests and wants of elementary students of different age levels have been documented and, in general, have remained fairly constant over time. Table 5.1 shows examples of wants and interests that predominate in elementary students.

WHAT DOES MOTIVATE STUDENTS TO LEARN?

The following is a review of information available to teachers about motivation, accumulated from experience and scholarly research. Also included is an examination of contributions by William Glasser, Howard Gardner, Fred Jones, and Spencer Kagan and his colleagues.

Motivation for Elementary Classrooms

Brophy (1987, 1998) offers a helpful synthesis of research on classroom motivation. He presents a number of suggestions for teachers, of which the following are most pertinent to elementary-grade teachers:

- Make yourself and your classroom attractive to students.
- Adapt lessons to students' interests.

- Focus attention on individual and collaborative learning goals.
- Teach things that are worth learning, in ways that help students appreciate their value.
- Include novelty and variety.
- Provide for active, hands-on response.
- Include fantasy and simulations.
- Project your enthusiasm.

Jones (2007) presents an overview of motivation in the classroom setting that he feels is supported adequately by research. He concludes that students become actively involved in lessons to the extent they expect success, value successful completion of the tasks, and find the climate of interpersonal relationships acceptable. Jones presents conclusions for students at all age levels. For elementary students, academic needs would include the following:

- Being quickly and actively involved in lessons
- Experiencing success
- Seeing learning modeled by adults as exciting and rewarding
- Relating the learning to their own lives
- Having positive contact with peers

Tomlinson (1999, 2002) describes what she calls *invitational learning* that embraces five student needs: affirmation (acceptance and significance), contribution, purpose, power, and challenge. Children want affirmation, to feel they are significant in the classroom. They want to contribute and make a difference in the community. Students look for purpose when they come to school. They want to know that what they learn is useful and that their choices contribute to their success. Finally, students want to feel challenged and/or stretched. They want to feel that their work contributes to their success and the growth of others. The learning environment contributes to meeting these five needs.

Consolidating the ideas of Brophy, Jones, Tomlinson, and others, the following generalizations are warranted and offer concrete, practical advice concerning student motivation:

- Students like to work with others at ideas, activities, and objects that they find novel, intriguing, and related to their perceived life concerns.
- Students seek out people and conditions that help meet needs important in their lives.
- Students try their best to avoid associating with people and conditions they find unpleasant.
- Students engage in tasks that are unpleasant to them in order to please people they see as important, including the teacher.

As a teacher, therefore, you are well advised to capitalize on students' needs, interests, abilities, and curiosity. Use these to full advantage. Students will appreciate the effort you make, and because of their excitement, so will you.

But remember that students detest looking bad in front of their peers; they don't want to appear stupid or to have their failures displayed. Therefore, you should encourage your students and help them feel secure. And as you show your helpfulness and support, students will try to please you with effort, good behavior, responsible choices, and quality work.

IF THERE ARE 21 ATTACKING MUTANT SPACE INVADERS AND YOU ZAP -13 OF THEM WITH A NUCLEAR RAY GUN, YOU WILL HAVE 8 REMAINING, FLEEING MUTANTS.

DoveCarpenter.

"HEY, IT'S HELPED ME GET THIS VIDEO GAME GENERATION INTERESTED IN MATH..."

These points generally hold true, and teachers who capitalize on them often accomplish much with their students. Nonetheless, experienced teachers find that these suggestions do not solve all problems of motivation. Consequently, some teachers set up systems of reinforcement for good student work, effort, and behavior. Many, however, are uncomfortable with such a system, feeling that they might be paying students for doing only what they are supposed to do anyway. They wonder if children will learn to depend on others for approval and recognition and ask questions such as the following: What's in it for me? What's the payoff? Does it count for anything? Do you like it? Did you see me do it? Did I do it right? (Coloroso, 1994). But it is evident that elementary students become excited about receiving smiley faces, stickers, popcorn, extra time at recess or the computer, the honor of helping the teacher, the privilege of feeding the class pet, and many other similar rewards for their good effort. In fact, students will study their spelling and arithmetic in order to get these rewards.

Teachers also have learned, many of them through distressing experiences when they themselves were students, that children can be frightened into working. Many students would rather do their homework than get yelled at, study for their tests than get failing grades, or feign paying attention than receive reprimands. But these days not all students will comply out of fear. Regardless of the work or behavior it induces, motivation through fear is an area for teachers to avoid. If you genuinely want your students to make an effort to learn and have a reasonably enjoyable time doing so, don't try to motivate through fear or intimidation. Ultimately the results are not worth the costs. Students won't like you, you won't like them, and worse, you won't feel very good about yourself either.

It is much better to motivate students through what they enjoy and respond to positively, and through things you feel comfortable with as well. Your program doesn't have to be insipidly easy; it can be rigorous and still be enjoyable.

William Glasser's Contributions

William Glasser is a psychiatrist–psychologist who writes and consults on behalf of school students. His landmark books on education are *Schools without Failure* (1969), *Control Theory in the Classroom* (1998b), *The Quality School* (1998c), *The Quality School Teacher* (1998d), and *Every Student Can Succeed* (2000). For Glasser, motivation is virtually

CASE STUDY 5.1

EXPECTATION AND MOTIVATION

Focus Questions

Rose Mary Johnson describes two specific ways she teaches science and geography for her first graders. How can she approach other first-grade curricula such as math, social studies, and language arts? What else regarding the mental and physical development ranges of her primary students must she consider as she plans?

Mrs. Johnson teaches first grade. She believes teachers can be most interesting when they teach about something they love or know well. Consequently, she uses her own interests and love of geography and science to motivate her students. Even though she has observed that most people believe you can't teach much science and geography to first graders, Mrs. Johnson teaches sophisticated theories and processes in ways that are appropriate for her students.

For example, Mrs. Johnson teaches the steps of the scientific process through very simple experiences (such as things that float or sink). For each step of the process, she uses the formal name (observation, experiment, or hypothesis). She also shows the children pictures that go along with the term or that mean the same thing. After she models, she notices that the children slowly begin using the scientific process in dealing with simple problems.

Mrs. Johnson found that the same idea works for geography. Her students learn to recognize the shapes and names of the seven continents and some interesting facts about each of them. She incorporates these experiences into the literature and reading programs, and the children do a number of activities such as making pop-up books of the continents. Thus, Mrs. Johnson is able to accomplish goals of writing, reading, and learning sentence structure in a way that interests her students.

synonymous with needs satisfaction, specifically the needs he emphasizes in his writings. He maintains that when teaching and learning produce needs satisfaction, motivation to work and behave properly follows naturally.

Glasser (1998a) explains that "all of our behavior, everything we do, can be considered our best attempt to control ourselves so as to satisfy our needs" (p. 17). What are these needs we so desperately try to satisfy? According to Glasser they are: (1) to survive and reproduce, (2) to belong, (3) to acquire power, (4) to be free, and (5) to have fun. Glasser contends that these needs are alive and working in every one of us, from the toddler to the elderly, and he says that we can no more deny the urge to fill these needs than we can deny the color of our eyes. He also contends that schools, as traditionally designed, fall quite short of satisfying these needs.

Glasser goes on to say that education—schools, the classroom, and the teaching–learning process—should be reorganized and conducted so that students, while working at lessons, can satisfy their needs. Then students will behave well, take an interest in education, and learn. To this end, Glasser would have students work together in small learning teams and have teachers function as "lead-managers" instead of bosses, emphasize quality in all student work, and transform the classroom environment into what he calls a "friendly workplace."

Glasser distinguishes between "boss style" and the "lead manager" in the Preface to *The Quality School* (1998c):

A boss drives. A leader leads.

A boss relies on authority. A leader relies on cooperation.

A boss says "I." A leader says "We."

A boss knows how. A leader shows how.

A boss creates resentment. A leader breeds enthusiasm.

A boss fixes blame. A leader fixes mistakes.

A boss makes work drudgery. A leader makes work interesting.

Glasser feels that teams are inherently motivating and give students a sense of belonging. Stronger students find it need-fulfilling to help weaker students, and weaker students find it need-fulfilling to contribute to a team that is getting somewhere. Students with disabilities find themselves able to contribute and participate along with the other team members. Teams provide freedom and fun as they work with less dependence on the teacher and are allowed to assume more authority and responsibility for their learning. Many students working in teams find a good deal of belonging, power, freedom, and fun—the very things Glasser says we all seek in life.

Glasser continually refined his thinking and did so again in *Choice Theory in the Classroom* (1998a) and *Every Student Can Succeed* (2000). Consultants and trainers Kathy Curtiss and Steven English (2003) describe practical classroom applications of choice theory. Expanding on Glasser's ideas, they advocate classroom meetings, portfolios, assessment rubrics based on standards, character development as part of the curriculum, and student self-assessment and reflection. They also believe in partnerships between teachers and students and use instructional strategies that support student ownership and responsibility for learning. Visit these websites for additional details of their work and Glasser's choice theory: www.choicetheory.com/links.htm and www.kathycurtissco.com.

Howard Gardner's Contributions

Howard Gardner is a Harvard Professor of Education and the author of several books, including *The Unschooled Mind: How Children Think and How Schools Should Teach* (1991), *Frames of Mind* (1993a), and *Multiple Intelligences: The Theory in Practice* (1993b). In 1983, Gardner first proposed his theory that human beings possess more than a single, fixed intelligence and learn in a variety of ways. He since has identified eight intelligences and asserts that we all possess all eight, although each in varying degrees of strength. He also observes that schools tend to develop only two of these intelligences to any useful extent—verbal/linguistic and logical/mathematical. Overly simplified, the eight intelligences embrace the following understandings:

- *Verbal/linguistic*—capacity to use words and oral and written language effectively
- *Logical/mathematical*—capacity to use numbers effectively and to think in logical patterns and relationships
- *Visual/spatial*—ability to perceive the visual–spatial world accurately, with awareness of color, line, shape, form, space, and the relationships among these elements

- *Bodily/kinesthetic*—expertise in using one's whole body to express ideas and feelings, with specific physical skills of coordination, balance, dexterity, strength, flexibility, and speed
- *Musical*—ability to perceive, discriminate, transform, and express musical forms
- *Naturalist*—ability to perceive and function in nature, with sensitivity to the interdependence of the plant and animal ecologies and to environmental issues
- *Interpersonal*—ability to perceive and make distinctions in the moods, intentions, motivations, and feelings of other people
- *Intrapersonal*—self-knowledge and the ability to act adaptively on the basis of that knowledge

Gardner says teachers should not ask "How smart are my students?" but rather, "In what ways are my students smart?" Many now believe that understanding Gardner's ideas is essential to effective teacher thinking and planning—and key to student motivation.

For several years, Gardner, Spencer Kagan, and Robert Sylwester exchanged and explored ideas about multiple intelligences. If you are interested in reading more, you can find their triologue posted to Kagan's online magazine at www.kaganonline.com.

In the early 1990s, Gardner proposed a radical school restructuring; students would spend most of their time engaged in project-based learning, both in and out of classroom settings. He believes that life is a series of projects and that school matters, "but only insofar as it yields something that can be used once students leave school" (Gardner, television interview, n.d.). By applying Gardner's ideas of multiple intelligences and project-based learning to motivation, students transform into active participants engaged in meaningful experiences that have real-world applications for them. They are motivated.

Fred Jones's Contributions

Fred Jones is a clinical psychologist and consultant who has made extensive field observations of effective teachers, particularly those he describes as "naturals." His observations are translated into ways to improve teacher effectiveness in motivating, managing, and instructing students. Jones gives a prominent place in his program to genuine incentives as a means of motivating students. He found that most effective teachers use incentives systematically. Specifically relating to motivation (and behavior management) is his work that focuses on responsibility training through incentive systems.

Jones and others say that incentives are something outside of individuals that prompt them to act. Incentives are promised as the consequence for desired work or behavior, but they are delayed or provided later. One way teachers can use incentives as motivators is to apply Grandma's Rule to the classroom—students first do what they are supposed to do, and then, for a while, they can do what they want to do. A sort of bonus portion of the incentive encourages students to save time they normally would waste in order to get it back in the form of preferred activities. It gives students a shared interest in cooperating to save time rather than wasting it in small bits throughout the day.

Jones has found that incentives work best when they are integrated within the context of the instructional program and the classroom structure. He describes this Preferred Activity Time, or PAT, as time allotted for activities such as learning games and enrichment activities. PAT activities are ones that students enjoy, such as reading a class book for pleasure, using vocabulary words to play hangman, working on an art project, or working with manipulatives. When selecting activities for PAT, teachers must consider three things. First, the activity should be attractive to the students. Second, students should earn time toward PAT through their work effort and responsible behavior. And third, teachers should choose activities that are acceptable to them.

PAT can be earned in several ways. Mrs. Foster gives her fifth graders three minutes to put away their math work and prepare for language arts. Any unused time from the three minutes is added to their PAT. Mr. Bjorka gives the class two extra PAT minutes if everyone is seated and ready when the bell rings. However, the class loses the amount of wasted time if a few students continue to be noisy. PAT can be used the day it is earned, or it may be saved for the end of the week or for a future activity such as a field trip.

PAT differs from other reward systems as a motivator of incentives. PAT has these important qualities.

- PAT is genuine. In other words, Preferred Activity Time is desired and available to all students, in exchange for making the extra effort to obtain it.
- PAT has educational value because it is found in enrichment activities and team learning games. To say that students get to do anything they want is misleading. PAT activities that students want to do really are linked to a full program of academic work.
- PAT motivates all students by encouraging group concern for everyone to complete assigned work and behave well. Only then can students earn PAT for the entire class.
- PAT can be earned as an individual bonus. Teachers can work individually with the few students who would lose PAT for the class because of their irresponsible choices. With a contract, the teacher can give consequences to the individual student, but also can reward the whole class when behavior improves or the student makes responsible choices.
- PAT is easy for the teacher to implement and manage.
- PAT is as creative as teacher and student imaginations. Visit Jones's website, www.fredjones.com, where teachers continually share their PAT ideas.

Spencer Kagan's Contributions

Spencer Kagan is another clinical psychologist and consultant who specializes in teacher effectiveness in classrooms. He, too, has spent hours observing and researching effective teachers and their methods. Kagan sees close connections among curriculum, instruction, and management, with motivation affecting the success of all three. Kagan's work in classroom management gives considerable attention to using cooperative learning, classbuilding and teambuilding, and the multiple intelligences as ways to motivate students. He also applies theories he has researched about how the brain affects learning to his ideas of classroom management.

So, how is cooperative learning a motivator? We realize that most of life and work involves cooperative interaction with others. Success, however, comes in learning how to work cooperatively. According to Kagan, the basic principles of cooperative learning rest on critical questions, which he refers to as PIES:

- Positive Interdependence: Is a gain for one a gain for another? Is help necessary?
- Individual Accountability: Is individual public performance required?
- Equal Participation: How equal is the participation?
- Simultaneous Interaction: What percent are overtly active at once?

Cooperative learning groups (just like Glasser's learning teams) give students the opportunity to learn and apply these skills. Students collaborate with others on a project or task, with a degree of group autonomy to make decisions about the task, and have fun while they work.

And how are classbuilding and teambuilding motivators? Kagan (Kagan, Robertson, & Kagan, 1995) defined *classbuilding* as "The process by which a room full of individuals with different backgrounds and experiences become a caring community of active learners" (p. vi). Kagan's use of classbuilding as a verb reinforces that it is a process—classbuilding doesn't happen; it is done. Classbuilding activities have students, at least once a week, stand up, move around, and interact about noncontent topics with students they normally don't work with. For example, they may share what they did over the weekend, talk about a favorite book or movie, or describe a favorite celebration or tradition.

According to Kagan, *teambuilding* sets a climate for learning. Teambuilding has five aims: (1) getting acquainted, (2) team identity, (3) mutual support, (4) valuing differences, and (5) developing synergy. Teambuilding activities are essential when students first form teams, but they also can be used effectively when energy lulls. Quick teambuilding takes only a minute or two away from instructional time, but reenergizes the learning potential. Occurring at least twice a week, teambuilding activities are fun, nonacademic, and well within the ability of all children. For example, students may try to find commonalities with their team members, such as favorite foods or places to visit, or they may come up with a team name and a team cheer.

And finally, how are the multiple intelligences motivators? Students are smart in different ways—remember Gardner's eight kinds of smart. Kagan has observed that classrooms seem to come alive when teachers (and students) use multiple intelligences strategies to teach and show their learnings. In *Multiple Intelligences: The Complete MI Book* (Kagan & Kagan, 1998), Kagan describes enriched classrooms that have three MI visions: matching, stretching, and celebrating. The goal of *matching* is to maximize academic success by teaching to the intelligences of the students. The goal of *stretching* is to maximize the development of all intelligences by making each student more intelligent in more ways. The goal of *celebrating* is to applaud the uniqueness of every student and thereby sharpen students' abilities to understand and work with diversity.

Kagan's work ties to student motivation. To motivate students to make responsible choices regarding their work and behavior, Kagan has written literally hundreds of step-by-step structures for teachers to use. Because the structures are content- and activity-free, they can be used in an infinite range of content areas. Visit www.kaganonline.com for ideas.

PERSONALITY TRAITS OF GOOD MOTIVATORS

Teachers who are especially effective in classroom motivation are likely to possess several personality traits. As you reflect on these traits, remember that although nobody shows all of them all of the time, everybody shows some of them some of the time. Students greatly appreciate these traits, and you probably can increase them in your behavior.

Charisma

Charisma is hard to define and harder to acquire, but we have all seen it—that ephemeral quality of personality that attracts and inspires. It is very difficult to say what makes one person more charismatic than another. Reasonably attractive appearance makes one appealing, at first. So does a sparkling personality, though some of the most appreciated teachers could never have been the life of any party. Ability to envision potential helps, as does steadfastness of purpose and faith in students' capabilities. Add to that some wisdom, enlightenment, experience, normal human frailties, a measure of vulnerability, and determination to persist, and you are getting somewhere in the neighborhood of charisma. If you happen to be an individual fortunate enough to possess it, motivation won't be much of a problem for you.

Caring

Practically all teachers would prefer that their students learn and lead happy and productive lives. But caring in teaching implies considerably more than simple concern. It refers to teacher willingness to work on behalf of students, to keep trying when little progress is evident, and to persist even when students show no appreciation for efforts expended on them, as often will be the case. It means showing friendship—not to confuse with being a buddy—to every student, no matter how undeserving the student might seem. Depending on circumstances, it means encouraging, cajoling, supporting, or demanding. It may call for a warm heart or fire in the eye, but it always communicates that you are not willing to let any student drop by the wayside, to let students be less than they should be, or to say, "Oh well, what difference does it make anyway?"

Caring is a matter of effort and persistence, and is within everyone's grasp. It brings occasional reward and frequent disappointment. How well you care depends on your personality, your level of conviction, and your ability to roll with the punches.

Enthusiasm

Up to a point, teacher enthusiasm motivates students. Enthusiasm is contagious, as is lack of it. But enthusiasm must be genuine. Students quickly spot a fraud. If you truly believe in the value of what you are teaching and in the virtue of those with whom you are working, your students will respond to your efforts, though not always exactly as you would like. But remember, it is difficult to achieve significant results overnight.

Trust

Trust has two sides. Students must trust that their teacher will support and guide them and be someone they can count on. Students also must think that their teacher believes in them and will let them make choices, decisions, and mistakes, and learn and grow from the results, without embarrassment, loss of dignity, harm, or reprisal.

Respect

Respect relates closely to trust. In fact, respect often comes from trust. Furthermore, respect should be mutual. Students must respect their teacher as a knowledge facilitator and as an adult who models the good character qualities and the Golden Rule. Teachers must respect a student's right to learn, sometimes by making mistakes, and share responsibility for that learning.

GOOD MOTIVATORS—WHAT DO THEY DO?

Here we move away from the nebulous area of personality traits to the more definitive realm of teaching skills, acknowledging the considerable overlap between the two. With traits of personality set aside, it is obvious that teachers good at motivation also perform certain skill tasks particularly well. These skills can be learned, practiced, and perhaps even perfected. Teachers good at motivation frequently do such things as the following:

1. *Use novelty, mystery, puzzlement, and excitement* to energize their lessons. Mr. Samuel tells his students as they begin their reading lesson, "There may or may not be a double entendre somewhere on this page. If you think you find one and can explain its meaning, raise your thumb so I can see it."

2. *Use color, sound, movement, and student activity* to attract and hold attention. Mrs. Gomez uses songs, rhymes, and skits to help her students practice Spanish vocabulary, pronunciation, and conversation.

3. *Assign individual and group projects* as a means of adding a sense of purpose to what is being learned and encouraging students toward responsibility and self-control. Ms. Eggleston's students select and keep separate writing and art portfolios of some of their work to show their parents or guardians.

4. *State clear, reasonable expectations and requirements* to avoid confusion and enlist student cooperation. Mr. Timken uses visual instructional plans (VIPs), writes assignments on charts, explains them to students, checks understanding by having students describe the assignments back to him, and leaves the VIP or chart on display while students complete their work.

5. *Provide continual support, help, feedback, and encouragement* to assist students over rough spots and keep them on track. As often as she can, Miss Moore teaches her lessons in a cycle. She explains one step at a time, models the step, and then promptly involves her students by having them do the step in the process. Usually students cumulatively practice the steps—they return to the beginning and work through the process to finally include the newest step. As the students work, she circulates quietly among them, making helpful suggestions and giving encouraging comments. Jones (2007) calls this Say, See, Do Teaching.

6. *Listen to student concerns and remain flexible enough to change* when it is warranted. Mr. Proybal holds brief class discussions at the end of each day asking students to comment on the lessons they liked best, those they liked least, and those they found most difficult. He listens to student suggestions and discusses his own ideas for improvement. In addition to asking students to share one idea they learned today,

VIGNETTE 5.1   Focusing Attention

Kim Anderson learned several classroom management techniques during her student teaching experiences. When she taught a multi-age first- and second-grade class, her cooperating teacher taught her a simple technique for managing expectations during instruction. The teacher first would ask the students what she needed from them before she could begin the lesson. Eager to demonstrate their knowledge, the students raised their hands and would list the five needs. The teacher would draw a simple descriptive icon on the board as students described each need.

First she needed students in *listening positions*, and she drew a chair to show that they needed to be sitting up straight. Second she needed students to *raise their hands* if they wanted to speak, and she drew a hand below the chair. Third she needed *mouths closed*, and she drew a set of lips below the hand. Next she needed *eyes on her*, and she drew an eye. Finally she needed students to *listen* to the teacher and to each other. Her last icon was an ear. The icons stayed on the board throughout the entire lesson as easy reminders.

Kim saw that this technique helped focus student attention on the lesson and simplified her management actions. If the students needed to work on one skill, she simply would point to an individual icon.

Kim's second student teaching placement was with a fifth-grade class, and she soon discovered that the technique worked for this level, too. After she taught them the five needs, all Kim had to say was "listening position," and the students immediately straightened up, knowing exactly what she expected of them.

Upon Reflection

Kim found that this technique for managing expectations during lessons worked in both the primary and upper grade classes she taught. Why do you think this is so? How would you teach this to both grade levels for success?

Mrs. Scott asks: "What can you do so you will learn more tomorrow?" and "What do you want me to do to help you?"

7. *Provide numerous opportunities* for students to display their accomplishments to both the class and to larger audiences. Mrs. Cooper regularly displays student science and social studies projects, and toward the end of the year invites caregivers to view the displays.

8. *Emphasize student accountability* concerning behavior, work habits, and production of quality work. Mr. Adams requires his students to keep records of their work and effort and to periodically reflect on their improvement. Similarly, Mr. Wong has students keep private, ongoing charts and rate themselves each day on their behavior and work. He also schedules brief individual conferences with students to discuss the self-ratings. Mrs. Wilder's students are able to describe their own progress and achievement when they participate in student-led parent conferences.

9. *Use student-centered classroom assessment.* Mrs. Jacobs involves her students in student-centered assessment to better prepare them for writing term papers. By analyzing sample term papers, one outstanding and one very poor, students are able to discern the qualities of the outstanding paper and apply their observations and understanding to their own work.

10. *Give students responsibility.* Students are allowed to make decisions about their learning and behavior that may be different from others around them. They know why they make the decisions and are comfortable with the decisions. They are encouraged to be all they can be and are shown that they have options in what they do. And if they make mistakes—and sometimes they will—they experience the consequences the first time and then are given a second opportunity to try again.

11. *Differentiate instruction.* Mrs. Hodgers thinks of alternative ways to provide content instruction, vary the process by which students can make sense of the content, or demonstrate the understanding and learning they take away from the content.

12. *Work to build esprit de corps* which, when successfully accomplished, mobilizes the class for better behavior and achievement. Ms. Iwai uses many classbuilding and teambuilding activities. She challenges her students to surpass expectations, to be their best, and to strive to make their lives works of art, and she pitches in, sharing and discussing their efforts as well as her own.

These are some of the things good classroom motivators frequently do. In fact, many of these suggestions bring the students into the process and make them feel as though they have some control. There are, as well, many things that good motivators diligently try *not* to do.

WHAT GOOD CLASSROOM MOTIVATORS DON'T DO

Most teachers are not born with the ability to be good classroom motivators. In fact, probably observation and experience has taught them to not do a number of things. Consider these six things teachers who are good motivators do not do:

1. *They don't bore students to death.* They plan against boredom, and at its onset they change the topic or activity, give a short brain break, insert a timely energizer, or simply say, "I know this is not very interesting, but it is important, and I need you to hang in with me for five more minutes. Can you do that for me?"

2. *They don't confuse their students.* At least they try not to, though they recognize that all learners become confused at times. They make their directions short and explicit, they give clear explanations, they show examples if they are able to do so, and when possible they use visual instructional plans to show and remind students of the steps. They check understanding: "Bobby, please help us remember the three things we are supposed to do. Tell us what they are."

3. *They don't vacillate.* Hour after hour, day after day, they hold to their expectations and to the way they interact with students. They aren't hot one day, cold the next, a pal now, an enemy later. They work to get procedures correct and hold them steady. This is not to say they shouldn't be flexible enough to change when change is needed or that even the best teachers don't have good and bad days. Illness and personal problems affect all of us, and in turn affect our work and interactions. But there must be a steadying force in the classroom: the teacher.

"I'D LIKE TO OVERWHELM THEM
WITH INSTRUCTIONAL EXCELLENCE,
BUT I'M NOT ABOVE WINNING
THROUGH INTIMIDATION."

4. *They don't frustrate their students.* Frustrated students sooner or later rebel. Frustration can come from two sources—unreasonable demands or work that is boringly difficult. Mr. Thaddeus is unreasonable when he says, "If the entire class doesn't make 100 on this test, nobody goes to recess for the rest of the day." He is unreasonable when he says, "You are to have all this [exorbitant amount of] homework finished by tomorrow or you get an F in the gradebook."

5. *They do not intimidate their students.* Most teachers tend to be intimidating at first and others remain so despite efforts to the contrary. But they do not use a stance of autocratic superiority to make students work and behave, nor do they use sour personality, fierce physical stature, hostility, or thinly veiled threats. Rather, good teachers try to downplay intimidation, knowing that for whatever achievement it might inspire, it certainly will produce a counterdesire to resist, vanish, or become transported elsewhere.

6. *They don't punish their students* for failure or other shortcomings. That is, they don't punish in the sense of inflicting pain, acute embarrassment, or loss of dignity. They do, of course, follow the provisions of the discipline system used in their class, which often invokes unpleasant consequences for irresponsible choices, disruptive behavior, or wanton failure to complete assignments. But that unpleasantness seldom entails more than missing recess or staying after school and, when possible, correcting whatever was done incorrectly. For students the impact comes from the certainty of receiving a consequence, not the fact that the consequence is a reward or a discipline. Good motivators rarely punish students for doing poor quality work. They know they can achieve more through helpful correction than by hurting students' feelings or making them resentfully angry.

WHAT ARE SOME CAUTIONS IN MOTIVATION?

Although most teachers lament the lack of learner motivation, students can, at times, become overmotivated or overstimulated to such a degree that work and behavior suffer. If you bring a pet into the classroom during a lesson on animals, especially one as unusual as a skunk or raccoon, your lesson probably will be lost in the chaos that ensues. If you overemphasize the dire importance of an upcoming achievement test, students may try so hard that they can't relax and think, and they will consequently do worse than if you hadn't mentioned it at all.

Aside from the harmful effects of overmotivation, what teachers do to instill motivation often raises unanswered ethical questions. For example, if novelty, puzzles, intrigue, and excitement are overlaid onto all lessons, do students come to believe that learning is no good unless a wizard performs magic or a toy bounces and sings? If incentives and rewards are used to spur student work, do you perpetuate the belief that work is done only for a tangible reward and not for the personal satisfaction of learning or the sense of responsibility to oneself? Most teachers find such questions troublesome but would rather see students working, even if the reasons do not seem praiseworthy, than find them not working at all. Taking to heart some of the ideas of Glasser, Gardner, Jones, and Kagan can ease such concerns considerably.

Their suggestions are important to keep in mind as we prepare to move into Chapter 6, the topic of which is managing instruction. Before proceeding to the next chapter, take time to explore these end-of-chapter activities.

Parting Thought

Learning is not attained by chance;
it must be sought for with ardor and
attended to with diligence.

—Abigail Adams

SUMMARY SELF-CHECK

Check off the following as you either understand or become able to apply them.

❑ Teachers are more concerned about student motivation than about anything else in teaching, with the possible exception of discipline.

❑ To most teachers, the word *motivation* refers to what teachers do to get students interested in lessons.

❑ People do not do what we want them to for several reasons: they don't know what to do, don't know how to do it, don't know why they should do it, aren't well suited or matched to the task, don't want to, or behave as they do because of the way their brain works.

❑ To motivate students, experienced teachers capitalize on students' known interests by including those interest topics or themes in their lessons. They also try to encourage students, help them feel secure and supported, and use systems of reinforcement for good work and responsible behavior.

❑ Some teachers still motivate through fear and intimidation, but the overall results rarely are satisfying.

❑ William Glasser has made some important contributions to education, including the following contentions concerning motivation:

- All behavior is people's best attempts to control themselves so as to satisfy their needs.
- Of the five predominant human needs, four relate closely to classroom motivation: to belong, to gain power, to be free, to have fun.
- Education should be organized so learning activities enable students to meet some of these four needs and feel they belong.
- This is accomplished when students work in small learning teams, and teachers function as "lead-managers," stress quality in all student work, and transform the classroom into what students perceive as a "friendly workplace."

❑ Howard Gardner's theory of multiple intelligences identifies eight areas of intelligence: verbal/linguistic, logical/mathematical, visual/spatial, bodily/kinesthetic, musical, naturalist, interpersonal, and intrapersonal.
- Teachers should ask: "In what ways are my students smart?"

❑ Fred Jones believes incentives work best when they are mixed with the content of the instructional program and the classroom structure.
- Preferred Activity Time (PAT) is the opportunity for learning and enrichment activities the teacher would have students do anyway, if time allowed.
- PAT is genuine, has educational value, encourages group concern, can work for individuals, and is easy to implement and manage.
- Visual instructional plans (VIPs) use a series of picture prompts to clearly show and guide students through the process or thinking.

❑ Spencer Kagan links motivation to cooperative learning, classbuilding, teambuilding, and multiple intelligences. He also considers how the brain affects learning.
- Three visions of multiple intelligences (MI) are matching, stretching, celebrating.

❑ Traits of teachers good at motivation seem to include charisma, caring, enthusiasm, trust, and respect.
- Teachers good at motivation use many skills as they plan and instruct.
- Teachers good at motivation try *not* to bore, confuse, frustrate, intimidate, or punish students for failure or shortcomings.
- Dangers of motivation include overstimulation of students and questions about the ethics of using rewards as incentives and payoffs.

ACTIVITIES FOR REFLECTION AND DISCUSSION

1. Take a moment to review the statements in the Prediction–Review Guide at the beginning of this chapter. Put a check mark in the Review column next to any statement with which you now agree. How have your thoughts changed since reading this chapter?

2. Interview at least two teachers about how they motivate their students, or describe one of your teachers from the past who seemed especially able to motivate you to work and learn. Which techniques seem better suited for primary grades (K–2), and which seem better suited for intermediate or upper grades (3–6)? What qualities and skills can you identify in that teacher that seem to contribute to student motivation?

3. The contention was made that good motivators do not intimidate their students. Yet good high school and college football coaches everywhere yell, scream, swear, berate, and sometimes even strike their player–students, despite which the players usually try very hard and show great respect for their coaches. How do you account for that? Why or why not would such an approach be effective in the elementary classroom?

4. Glasser contends that students will work at any subject if the process of doing so enables them to meet some of their needs. How would you organize the following social studies lessons to help students meet their needs: (a) a first-grade study of the family, (b) a fourth-grade study of state geography, and (c) a fifth-grade study of U.S. history?

5. Gardner said, "School matters, but only insofar as it yields something that can be used once students leave school." To what extent do you agree or disagree with this statement? Give examples to demonstrate your viewpoint.

6. Describe how you will use classbuilding, teambuilding, and multiple intelligences strategies in a grade of your choice to motivate your students.

REFERENCES AND RECOMMENDED READINGS

Brophy, J. (1987). Synthesis on strategies for motivating students to learn. *Educational Leadership, 45,* 40–48.

Brophy, J. (1998). *Motivating students to learn.* Boston. McGraw-Hill.

Coloroso, B. (1994) *Kids are worth it! Giving your child the gift of inner discipline.* New York: Avon Books.

Cook, P. (2004). Behaviour, learning and teaching: Applied studies in FAS/FAE (Distance Education Curricula). Winnipeg, MB, Canada: Red River College.

Curtiss, K., & English, S. (2003). *Choice theory certification.* Retrieved August 2003 from www.kathycurtisco.com/what_we_do.htm.

Gardner, H. (1991). *The unschooled mind: How children think and how schools should teach.* New York: Basic Books.

Gardner, H. (1993a). *Frames of mind* (10th ed.). New York: Basic Books.

Gardner, H. (1993b). *Multiple intelligences: The theory in practice.* New York: Basic Books.

Gardner, H. (1997). Reflections on multiple intelligences: Myths and messages. *Phi Delta Kappan, 77*(3), 200–209.

Glasser, W. (1969). *Schools without failure.* New York: Harper & Row.

Glasser, W. (1998a). *Choice theory in the classroom.* New York: HarperCollins.

Glasser, W. (1998b). *Control theory in the classroom* (rev. ed.). New York: Harper & Row.

Glasser, W. (1998c). *The quality school* (rev. ed.). New York: HarperCollins.

Glasser, W. (1998d). *The quality school teacher* (rev. ed.). New York: HarperCollins.

Glasser, W. (2000). *Every student can succeed.* Chatsworth, CA: Author.

Johnson, D., & Johnson, R. (1998). *Learning together and alone* (5th ed.). Boston: Allyn & Bacon.

Jones, F. (2007). *Tools for teaching: Discipline • Instruction • Motivation* (2nd ed.). Santa Cruz, CA: Fredric H. Jones and Associates.

Kagan, L., Kagan, M., & Kagan, S. (1997). *Cooperative learning structures for teambuilding.* San Clemente, CA: Kagan Cooperative Learning.

Kagan, M., Robertson, L., & Kagan, S. (1995). *Cooperative learning structures for classbuilding.* San Clemente, CA: Kagan Cooperative Learning.

Kagan, S. (1994). *Cooperative learning.* San Clemente, CA: Kagan Cooperative Learning.

Kagan, S., & Kagan, M. (1998). *Multiple intelligences: The complete MI book.* San Clemente, CA: Kagan Cooperative Learning.

Marshall, M. (2002). *Discipline without stress, punishments, or rewards: How teachers and parents promote responsibility and learning.* Los Alamitos, CA: Piper Press.

Maslow, A. (1943). A theory of human motivation. *Psychological Review, 50,* 370–396.

Tomlinson, C. (1999). *The differentiated classroom: Responding to the needs of all learners.* Alexandria, VA: ASCD.

Tomlinson, C. (2002, September). Invitations to learn. *Educational Leadership, 60*(1), 6–10.

Websites

Fred Jones
www.fredjones.com

Howard Gardner and Project Zero
www.pz.harvard.edu/index.htm

Kathy Curtiss and Choice Theory
www.kathycurtissco.com

Ruby Payne and Students of Poverty
www.educationworld.com/a_issues/chat/cjat119.shtml
www.csba.org/qa/payne.htm

Spencer Kagan
www.kaganonline.com

William Glasser and Choice Theory
www.choicetheory.com/links.htm

CHAPTER 6

Managing Instruction

A teacher must be a prophet who can look into the future, see the world of tomorrow into which the children of today must fit, and then teach and test the necessary skills.

—Anonymous

Prediction–Review Guide

Before you read the chapter, take a minute to put a check mark in the Prediction column next to any statement with which you agree.

	Prediction	Review
1. In essence, teachers and students share responsibility for the curriculum in *direct teaching*, while *facilitative teaching* puts teachers in charge.	☐	☐
2. *Direct teaching* typically has students use lower levels of thought.	☐	☐
3. Teachers who use *Say, See, Do teaching* explain, model, and give students frequent structured practice.	☐	☐
4. The strategy of *concept attainment* works better for older students than for younger students and language learners.	☐	☐
5. Many teachers seem to prefer using cooperative learning over other strategies of instruction.	☐	☐
6. Generally speaking, students find it motivating to work in cooperative learning groups.	☐	☐
7. Productive and successful *cooperative learning* supports positive interdependence, individual accountability, equal participation, and simultaneous interaction.	☐	☐
8. *Projects* are better for primary-grade children (K–2) than for intermediate-grade children (3–6) because projects encourage concrete rather than abstract thinking.	☐	☐
9. Teachers who *differentiate* instruction make modifications to content, process, or product.	☐	☐
10. *Computerized teaching* is an efficient way to instruct large groups of students.	☐	☐

Support for specific standards found in this chapter:

INTASC Standards

1. Knowledge of Subject Matter

   The teacher understands the central concepts, tools of inquiry, and structures of the subject being taught and can create learning experiences that make these aspects of subject matter meaningful for students.

3. Adapting Instruction for Individual Needs

   The teacher understands how students differ in their approaches to learning and creates instructional opportunities that are adapted to diverse learners.

4. Multiple Instructional Strategies

   The teacher uses various instructional strategies to encourage students' development of critical thinking, problem solving, and performance skills.

7. Instructional Planning Skills

   The teacher plans instruction based on knowledge of subject matter, students, the community, and curriculum guides.

Danielson's Framework for Teaching

1. Planning and Preparation

   - Demonstrating knowledge of students
   - Selecting instructional goals
   - Demonstrating knowledge of resources
   - Designing coherent instruction

3. Instruction

   - Communicating clearly and accurately
   - Using questioning and discussion techniques
   - Engaging students in learning
   - Providing feedback to students
   - Demonstrating flexibility and responsiveness

NBPTS Standards

2. Teachers know the subjects they teach and how to teach those subjects to students.

3. Teachers are responsible for managing and monitoring student learning.

NCATE Standards

Help all pre-kindergarten through twelfth grade (P–12) students learn.

Explain instructional choices based on research-derived knowledge and best practice.

The histories of curriculum and instruction are as old as time. Respected authorities have debated and identified areas of study, and teachers have devised and used a plethora of instructional methods believed to be best practice at the time. Some of the methods have endured, while others have faded with the changing needs of society and the world. Ask teachers about best practice and their responses probably reflect what they experienced in their own schooling and what they learned in their own teacher preparation program.

CURRICULUM AND INSTRUCTION

Fostering basic competencies in reading, writing, and arithmetic was established as law by the Massachusetts Bay Colony's Old Deluder Act of 1647 and has been a major ongoing purpose of elementary education in the United States. The law pointed out that Satan intended to lead people away from the paths of righteousness, so it was incumbent upon all citizens to learn to read the Scriptures as a means of thwarting Satan's unholy intentions. Thus the primary schools became an instrument of God in His work against the devil.

For nearly three hundred years thereafter, the content of the elementary curriculum remained much the same, and to a degree still does, although in the 1930s elementary education slowly began to change. Led by Francis Parker and John Dewey, educators radically suggested that schools be made consistent with students' lives here and now and attuned to the daily needs, aptitudes, and interests of young students. Furthermore, schools should help prepare the young for constructive participation in a democratic society that requires cooperation, compromise, group decision making, and personal responsibility. The suggestion that the schools should take the lead in preparing such citizens was revolutionary.

This progressive view gained popularity up through the 1950s. However, in 1957 when the Soviet Union launched *Sputnik*, the first orbital satellite, criticisms were aimed at schools in the United States—it was claimed that schools had gone soft, that they were asking students to do nothing but play, and that they had quit training young minds.

Over the years education has endured fierce criticism, and educators have tried to make things right. What teachers have known all along—to strive for balance between teaching students facts and teaching them to think for themselves—has not changed. They still strive to help children acquire knowledge, skills, and concepts on the one hand, and cooperation, creativity, and good attitudes on the other, while emphasizing all learnings and slighting none.

Can such a balance be accomplished? And if so, how? The answer is deceptively simple. When students are asked to apply what they've learned to real-life situations, they become better at application. When students are asked to analyze problems and come up with solutions, they learn to problem solve. If students are given activities that require cooperation, they become better at cooperating. If students are given opportunities to demonstrate good moral behavior, they are likely to internalize the characteristics. In other words, students usually learn to do what we give them practice in doing. To this end, the intended outcome indicates the instructional approach that teachers should use. Remember backward design planning (Chapter 2). The logic of balance supports the steps of backward design: identify the desired results, determine acceptable evidence, and then plan learning experiences and instruction.

◼ FOUR INSTRUCTIONAL APPROACHES

The term *instructional approach* is used to mean a broad orientation to instruction, a general way of teaching that can lead to a variety of outcomes. Currently four broad instructional approaches—direct teaching, facilitative teaching, technology-assisted teaching, and differentiated instruction—are widely used in education. Numerous instructional strategies, including many of the popular ones that are categorized and described by Joyce and Weil (2003), are used within these four broad approaches. Cruickshank, Jenkins, and Metcalf (2006) describe thirty-one instructional alternatives, which they define as "any teaching maneuver used to facilitate student learning and satisfaction" (p. 492). Let's briefly review the four major instructional approaches and some of the tactics used in each.

Instructional Approach: Direct Teaching

Historically, direct teaching has been at the forefront of teaching practice and still enjoys great popularity. In the late 1970s and early 1980s, several studies focused on basic academic areas of reading, mathematics, and English and found that students instructed with a structured curriculum and direct teacher involvement learned more than students taught with more individualized or discovery methods. Direct teaching continues to be used to advantage when goals are stated very precisely, content coverage is extensive, student performance is monitored closely, and feedback can be given immediately. Generally it's agreed that direct teaching is excellent for skill development and for delivering large amounts of factual and conceptual information, but it is not good for attitude development or for teaching creativity or problem solving.

Direct teaching gives teachers control of all aspects of instruction at all times. Teachers align the curriculum to the standards, set the objectives, plan the program, organize activities, arrange groups, give explanations, direct and correct student work, keep records, and evaluate results. While teachers may discuss all these matters with students, they primarily do so to help students understand what they are being asked to do. Teachers normally do not ask for student suggestions.

Instructional Strategy: Direct Instruction. Direct instruction is referred to by some as the Hunter model or the five- (six-, seven-, or nine-) step lesson plan. Direct instruction is a highly structured strategy that is intended to maximize student learning. The five-step lesson plan normally follows this sequence (Hunter, 1982):

1. Anticipatory set is used at the beginning of the lesson to orient, focus, or intrigue students, as a means of motivating and guiding their work. As its name suggests, this first step helps students anticipate what is to come. Usually the anticipatory set involves a verbal prompt or clue such as

   "Friends, today there is a great surprise in store for us."

   "Class, have you ever wondered what it would be like if you could have your own pet dinosaur?"

   "Boys and girls, today we are going to learn how to write haiku poetry."

Teachers may state objectives, propose the guiding or essential question, or explain the purpose of the lesson here or in step 2.

2. Teacher input of new information or skills follows the anticipatory set. Input possibilities vary. For example, the teacher can present it directly, or it can be contained in written material or visual media the teacher assigns or shows:

> "Boys and girls, watch carefully how I string these beads so you'll know how to string yours." (Teacher explains while demonstrating.)

> "Group Six, you are to use the encyclopedia to find out why dinosaurs are believed to have become extinct."

> "Class, watch the steps I follow when I multiply these fractions." (Teacher explains how the fractions are multiplied while referring to chart or visual instruction plan [VIP] with clearly numbered steps, and then tells students that the chart or visual instructional plan will remain on display as a reminder.)

3. Guided student practice follows teacher input. Students practice related work at their desks, individually or in groups. The teacher circulates and provides guidance and immediate feedback, stopping class work if necessary to re-explain what students seem not to understand.

4. Closure, following guided practice, further checks student understanding. In their own words, students explain concepts, list procedures, suggest how a new skill can be applied, or reflect on the value or purpose of the learning.

5. Independent practice occurs during homework and subsequent lessons where students review learnings and apply them in a variety of ways.

Teacher and Student Roles in Direct Teaching.   The teacher controls and directs instruction by presenting information in sequential steps and providing prompt feedback about students' efforts. Students do as directed and are not expected to give input about content or procedure.

Strengths of Direct Teaching.   This strategy is very effective for teaching information and basic skills to whole classes. It is highly structured and sequential, keeps students closely on task, and gives them immediate feedback. Also, it enables teachers to cover a quantity of information in a relatively short period of time.

Limitations of Direct Teaching.   This strategy tends to emphasize lower levels of thought. Students are not called on to show much initiative, imagination, creativity, or abstract thinking. The strategy's predictability can become boring for teacher and student alike.

Usability of Direct Teaching.   Direct teaching can be used at all grade levels to teach students of all levels of ability. English language learners and others will appreciate the presentation pattern: smaller information segments followed immediately with practice and feedback. Its appropriateness for a given lesson depends on the curriculum standards, the lesson objectives, to some extent student ability, and the time available for teaching.

Instructional Strategy: Concept Attainment.   A concept is a general rule or notion we have about a certain thing—for example, about an object, idea, or procedures. We form this general idea by mentally combining that thing's perceived characteristics. Concepts are the essential elements of thought. To say that we think is to say that we review concepts and combine and manipulate them. Thus, concept attainment—that is, the process by which we acquire and refine concepts—is of prime importance in education.

Concepts begin to develop as we encounter elements of life, whether these elements are tangible or intellectual, and whether we encounter them directly or vicariously. For example, our clear and accurate concept of a dog is the result of numerous experiences with dogs and what they do. Our concept of a tapir may be less clear and accurate because most of us have not had many experiences with that animal. And even less clear and accurate may be our concept of energy release that occurs in nuclear fusion, though most adults do have some idea about it.

We refine our concepts as we compare and contrast examples. For instance, a child refines the concept of an apple by experiencing apples (seeing, tasting, smelling, and touching them), and then contrasting apples' characteristics with those of oranges and bananas.

To help students attain concepts in school, we ask them to categorize objects and ideas on the basis of critical attributes. Apples, based on their attributes, go in one fruit box, and oranges, based on their attributes, go in another. Similarly, nouns go in one category of words, and verbs go in another. To help students further refine their concepts, we give them examples, called *exemplars,* that contain essential traits. In map study, for example, we teach students that representations of the earth's surface are called *maps.* We may show them, as one exemplar, a Mercator projection in which the earth's longitude and latitude are represented as straight horizontal and vertical lines. We may show them, as another exemplar, a polar projection in which the pole is in the center and lines of longitude and latitude look something like a circular spider web. From these exemplars and others, students acquire a concept of map that includes both Mercator and polar projections, but their concept of each differs from the other.

In using concept attainment, teachers first give exemplars and then ask students to develop and test hypotheses about them. Teacher and students then analyze the thinking process used.

Teacher and Student Roles in Concept Attainment.   The teacher selects, defines, and analyzes the concept to be developed, creates the lists of exemplars, and directs the activities. In concept attainment, the teacher controls the lesson but encourages student interaction and discussion.

Strengths of Concept Attainment.   The strategy is valuable when teachers want to introduce or refine a concept or check student understanding of ideas and processes. Concept attainment causes students to use analytical thinking and inductive reasoning. Further, students enjoy lessons in concept attainment because the lessons seem like games to them. The strategy holds their attention and keeps them involved.

Limitations of Concept Attainment.   The strategy is time consuming, and teacher preparation is crucial for success. The teacher must prepare well to avoid the danger of students developing incorrect concepts.

Usability of Concept Attainment.   With grade-appropriate concepts, the strategy can be used for all grade levels and most subjects. It can be used to introduce, identify, or refine and strengthen concepts, and to review and check student understanding. Concept attainment will not work well with students who do not have the vocabulary or basic knowledge to understand and then translate the concept exemplars and definition.

Instructional Strategy: Say, See, Do Teaching.   Say, See, Do Teaching is an interactive technique developed by Fred Jones (2007). For successful teaching and learning, Jones says you have to consider three things—the way we remember, how much we remember, and how long we can remember it. Say, See, Do Teaching does this. Simply put, the Say, See, Do cycle has three steps: explanation (say), modeling (see), and structured practice (do), with frequent repetitions of steps two and three. For example, Mr. Wallace prepares to teach the steps for long division to his fourth graders. To ensure that they understand it, he uses Jones's Say, See, Do Teaching model, along with a visual instructional plan (VIP) that consists of review, partner teaching, and frequent repetitions of the cumulative steps. As he and the class work through the steps of example problems, Mr. Wallace continually has the students repeat the full process to the newest step and then teach their partner as they again repeat the full process.

A visual instructional plan is a series of picture prompts that represents the process or thinking and clearly guides students through the process of the task and performance. As Mr. Wallace prepared his VIP with careful consideration of the complete task of long division, he followed three simple guidelines: one step at a time, a picture for every step, and minimal reliance on words. His VIP for long division looked like Figure 6.1.

We can contrast VIPs with summary graphics and simple visual aids. Summary graphics do not include the individual steps of the lesson. For the lesson in long division, a summary graphic probably would look like Figure 6.2.

Simple visual aids are memory aids. Although they can be useful for test review, they omit information and details needed for students to acquire the skill or knowledge. Thus a visual aid for the same long division lesson would look like Figure 6.3.

VIPs must answer in a concrete and visual manner the question students most ask when they need help: "What do I do next?" Performance illustrations, one type of VIP, are particularly useful for nonreaders because they show the performance steps. The

FIGURE 6.1   A Visual Instruction Plan (VIP) shows every step of the lesson.

Source: Fred Jones *Tools for Teaching*, 2007, www.fredjones.com. Reprinted by permission.

FIGURE 6.2   A summary graphic hides the individual steps of a lesson.

Source: Fred Jones *Tools for Teaching*, 2007, www.fredjones.com. Reprinted by permission.

FIGURE 6.3   A memory aid is useful for test review, but it omits the information needed for acquisition.

Source: Fred Jones *Tools for Teaching*, 2007, www.fredjones.com. Reprinted by permission.

performance illustration in Figure 6.4 shows students the classroom procedure for properly carrying a chair.

Mind maps are another type of VIP. Mind maps are any graphic that shows someone how to organize information or an idea, solve a problem, or perform a series of operations. Thus, mind maps may assume varied forms, such as those shown in Figure 6.5.

Jones has found that visual instructional plans accelerate learning and support independent learning for three reasons. First, VIPs reduce the time needed for teacher prompting because students can be directed quickly to the next step—the explanation is "prepackaged." In other words, teachers can give efficient help, in only a few seconds, by simply saying something like "Look at step five on the board. That's what you do next."

FIGURE 6.4   For students who cannot read, omit words.

Source: Fred Jones *Tools for Teaching*, 2007, www.fredjones.com. Reprinted by permission.

Second, VIPs minimize the need for students to remember what is said because they can see and refer back to them. And third, because VIPs provide the steps for the entire lesson, students can help themselves rather than ask for help from the teacher.

Teacher and Student Roles in Say, See, Do Teaching.   The teacher uses the three-step cycle to reinforce the teaching and learning, frequently repeating steps two and three. As students practice and solve the problems, they review each step completely by teaching it to a partner (partner teaching). All students are engaged actively in the learning process.

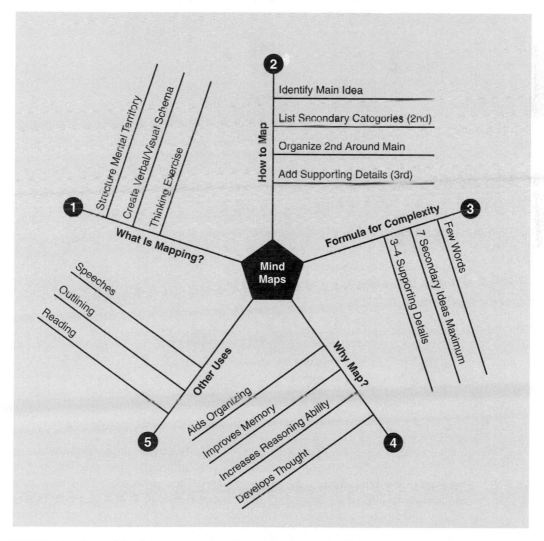

FIGURE 6.5   A mind map shows someone how to organize an idea, solve a problem, or perform a series of operations. In mind mapping, necessity is the mother of invention.

Source: Fred Jones *Tools for Teaching,* 2007, www.fredjones.com. Reprinted by permission.

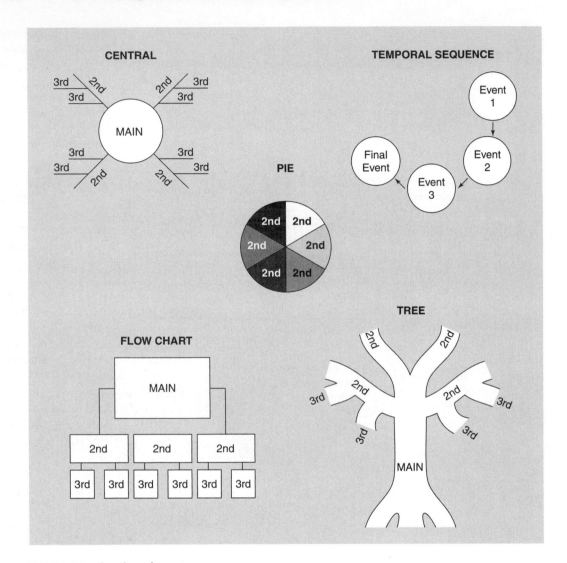

FIGURE 6.5   Continued

Strengths of Say, See, Do Teaching.   Say, See, Do Teaching reinforces the students' abilities to remember by reducing the amount of new information presented at one time and by quickly involving them in the lesson content. The very nature of the practice allows the teacher to observe students and give prompt feedback as it is needed. This is reinforced further when the teacher has students partner teach the material as they review.

Limitations of Say, See, Do Teaching.   The teacher must plan instruction in discrete steps. Also, receiving limited pieces of information at a time can be distracting and disruptive for students who need to see the whole picture in order to master smaller steps.

Usability of Say, See, Do Teaching.   The strategy can be used at all grade levels and in most subjects. Because of its presentation pattern of explanation, modeling, and structured practice, Say, See, Do Teaching can be used to teach new content and skills, as well as to review prior learning. English language learners will appreciate its inherent repetition and structured practice.

Instructional Approach: Facilitative Teaching

In direct teaching, the teacher rather tightly controls instruction. The teacher aligns the curriculum standards, sets objectives, plans and directs the lessons, and evaluates learning. In facilitative teaching, first popularized by Carl Rogers (1969), students have a much more active role in giving input, delving into learning, reflecting on the meaning of what they are learning, and assessing the quality of their efforts. As the label implies, the primary role of the teacher is to facilitate or guide students' efforts and progress. Notice how these two approaches differ in the following lesson on capitalization.

1. *Direct Teaching (Direct Instruction Strategy).* The teacher introduces the lesson by stating rules concerning capitalization of first words in sentences, people's names, and cities and states, and has examples of each rule on a chart to which students can refer. Students do two practice sentences together with teacher direction, then independently complete worksheets while the teacher observes and provides corrected feedback.
2. *Facilitative Teaching (Inquiry Strategy—described later in this section).* The teacher presents a written paragraph containing a number of capitalized words and informs the students that all capitalization is correct. Students read through the paragraph, circle the capitalized words, and then working individually, in pairs, or in teams, attempt to formulate rules that apply to the use of capital letters.

Note that in facilitative teaching the teacher remains in control of the class but does less lecturing and directing and refrains from leading students to conclusions. Instead, students are encouraged to explore problems, come up with their own solutions, and examine the meaning of what they have learned.

Instructional Strategy: Cooperative Learning.   Cooperative learning involves two or more students working together to complete specific tasks. This strategy is used in facilitative teaching because it encourages good cooperation, requires positive give and take, shows the value of collective wisdom, and highlights the contributions that every student can make.

Cooperative learning is a valuable strategy for managing diversity. Students with physical challenges are better able to participate in the learning community because the physical layout of the classroom is planned to best accommodate teams or cooperative learning groups. English language learners are better able and more likely to communicate with their peers in the smaller groupings. As students participate in cooperative activities, they gain confidence in their language skills as well as insights into other cultures.

Spencer Kagan (1994) asserts that teachers' abilities to implement cooperative learning successfully relates to their skills in six key areas:

- *Teams*. Long-term, teacher-formed, and small enough for active participation by all members, teams can be heterogeneous (mixed gender, ethnicity, and ability), homogeneous, or random. Four-member teams can be split for partner work.
- *Will*. Students must have the desire, the will to cooperate. Teambuilding and class-building activities strengthen the will.
- *Management*. Signals, clear responsibility and role expectations, and other management tools help ensure smooth and true cooperative learning experiences.
- *Skills*. Social skills help students work together effectively, and teachers can teach these skills in a variety of ways, including gambits (specific words to say), role-plays, modeling and practice, reflection, and planning.
- *Basic Principles*. Four basic principles support cooperative learning, and all must be present for true cooperative learning to exist. PIES is an easy mnemonic used to remember the four principles: positive interdependence, individual accountability, equal participation, and simultaneous interaction.
- *Cooperative Strategies and Structures*. An abundance of cooperative learning instructional strategies and structures exist, each designed to achieve different objectives and interactions for the instructional content. Kagan (1994) defines structures as content-free steps, the *how* of teaching, and applies them to cooperative learning in two simple formulas: structure + content = activity and a series of activities = a lesson (pp. xii and xiii). He offers hundreds of structures through his materials, trainings, and website, www.kaganonline.

Example of a Cooperative Learning Activity.   Ms. Winston's sixth graders are studying whales. The class is organized into six heterogeneous cooperative learning teams, each of which has five members. From the beginning of the year the students have participated in classbuilding and teambuilding activities. Also, students have learned and practiced a variety of management tools and social skills for successful cooperative learning.

Ms. Winston begins by having students meet as "expert" teams to learn as much as they can about one specific large whale—gray whale, beluga whale, killer whale, blue whale, right whale, or humpback whale. She provides resources for this purpose. When the work is completed, students regroup into five "home" teams with six members each. Each team now contains one expert on each of the six types of whales. Each expert teaches the other five students in the home team about his or her whale: its appearance, where it lives, what it eats, and whether it is endangered. This process continues until all students have served as teacher for the home group. To ensure individual accountability, the other students are asked to listen for specific information. For their final products, every member of the class prepares a booklet of drawings and facts about each whale.

Teacher and Student Roles in Cooperative Learning.   Students principally work in small learning teams on activities that require them to assume various roles in the group. Example student roles might include leader, encourager, questioner, researcher, reporter, artist, summarizer, materials collector, or time manager. The teacher sets up activities, monitors the process, keeps order, and helps—but only when necessary.

Strengths of Cooperative Learning.   Students usually like cooperative activities and engage in them eagerly. In well-planned cooperative activities, all students are able to participate and contribute to their maximum extent. Teams are relatively autonomous, with team members depending on each other. Students learn to think for themselves and show resourcefulness and creativity.

Limitations of Cooperative Learning.   Because students interact in groups, activities can become noisy. Some students move off task easily, and some rely on others to do the work, which causes irritation. Also, the teacher may have difficulty assessing the quality of an individual student's work.

Usability of Cooperative Learning.   Cooperative learning is appropriate for all age levels and most subjects. However, for successful cooperative learning to occur, teachers must take into account the six key areas and the basic principles of PIES. Moreover, cooperative learning is more likely to be successful when activities and projects are designed so every student in the group has a specific role or task to perform. Students must possess adequate skills and self-control for appropriate behavior. With some guidance, language learners can be successful contributors to group activities.

Variations of Cooperative Learning.   Countless books have been written with cooperative learning structures. Among some of the more popular variations are: jigsaw, student teams achievement divisions (STAD), teams-games-tournaments (TGT), think-pair-share, and numbered heads together. Additionally, numerous websites have been dedicated to cooperative learning. Articles and recommended reading–related links can be found at http://www-acad.sheridanc.on.ca/scls/coop/cooplrn.htm and http://www.newhorizons.org/strategies/cooperative/front_cooperative.htm.

Instructional Strategy: Inquiry.   To inquire is to investigate something in an attempt to understand a situation or resolve a problem. The major purpose of inquiry is to teach students how to learn on their own; thus, the process itself often is considered more important than the ends to which it leads. As renowned psychologist Jerome Bruner (1960) said:

> To instruct someone in [a] discipline is not a matter of getting him to commit results to mind. Rather, it is to teach him to participate in the process that makes possible the establishment of knowledge. We teach a subject not to produce little living libraries on the subject, but rather to get a student to think mathematically for himself, to consider matters as an historian does, to take part in the process of knowledge-getting. Knowledge is a process, not a product. (p. 72)

Examples of Inquiry Topics.   Inquiry can be used to explore topics, find information, and reach conclusions. Consider the following examples of topics that could be explored profitably through inquiry:

Primary Grades
- Find out what your grandparents' lives were like when they were six or seven years old.
- Learn about the life of a favorite author, such as Dr. Seuss, Shel Silverstein, or J. K. Rowling.

"IN MY DAY, WE HAD TO WALK THREE MILES UPHILL THROUGH THE SNOW TO THE LIBRARY TO RESEARCH OUR SCHOOL REPORTS."

- Find out how fast snails can move and what they can crawl over.
- List and categorize things that can be recycled.

Intermediate Grades

- Find out how many television commercials are shown during Saturday morning cartoon programs.
- Find out about games that may have been played by children who traveled west by wagon train.
- Investigate what critics say about popular movies suitable for children and then see if students in your school agree with the critics.
- Discover as much about as possible about how computers or digital cameras work.
- Try to learn how the ages of fossils are determined.

Teacher and Student Roles in Inquiry. Students working individually or in groups assume a large responsibility for their learnings during inquiry. Teachers may suggest or present topics, but students decide how they will gather, verify, and interpret information, after which they must demonstrate and explain their conclusions. The teacher may assist in any part of the process. Teachers and students should create the evaluation rubric together.

Strengths of Inquiry.   Inquiry teaches students how to learn on their own without the direct control of the teacher. It teaches them to confront a problem, gather information about it, and compose conclusions. The strategy also encourages critical thinking and open-mindedness because students frequently encounter conflicting information and opinions.

Limitations of Inquiry.   The process is time consuming and requires access to materials and resources. Many teachers would rather devote time to other matters. Students may get stuck or waste time on inconsequential issues.

Usability of Inquiry.   With some modification, inquiry can be used at all grade levels in all subjects, especially science. Primary children and English language learners involved in inquiry require tangible topics and much more teacher guidance than do older students.

Instructional Strategy: Projects.   Projects are activities carried over longer periods of time that usually result in products such as a models, compositions, drawings, or performances. This instructional strategy can bring about intense student involvement, and is especially useful in social studies, science, art, and language.

Examples of Project Topics.   As was the case with inquiry, the variety of suitable topics for projects is virtually limitless. The following are illustrative examples:

Primary Grades

- Make a plan for conserving water in your home.
- List your favorite books. Tell what they are about and why you like them. Make and decorate a title page for your list.
- Make and share a collection of your own drawings, with titles and dates.
- Construct a weather station for your classroom, where temperature, clouds, rain, and snow are recorded and reported daily.
- Plant a class flower or vegetable garden. See what flowers or vegetables you can grow indoors during winter.
- Make a guide of your favorite local restaurants and places of recreation, including what you like to eat or do there.

Intermediate Grades

- Grow vegetables without soil.
- Make a video introduction of your class to send to a pen-pal class in another state or country.
- Produce a class newspaper or literary journal.
- Conduct an oral history investigation of a family member or other adult and learn about an artifact that has particular meaning to that person.
- Maintain cultures of microscopic organisms.
- Plan an imaginary trip to selected places in the world with itineraries, transportation, lodging, meals, places of interest, costs, and so forth.
- Prepare a history of the school, using records, interviews, older photographs, and so forth.
- Write a detailed diary of an imaginary but realistic wagon train trip from St. Louis to San Francisco in 1870.
- Make simulated investments in the stock market. Keep records. Make trades. Follow quotes in the newspaper. See who can make the greatest profit during the semester or year.
- Plan out what you think a good school should be like in twenty years.

Teacher and Student Roles in Projects.   Students do most of the actual work in any project. Though they decide what they want to accomplish, students often require advice from the teacher on how to go about it. The teacher can suggest a number of possible topics, offer suggestions, help students obtain needed materials, set time lines for accomplishment, and arrange for the products to be shown—as advisor, not director. Also, the teacher and students together should create the rubric of expectations for evaluating the project.

"I'll get to the Johnson survey report as soon as I finish my son's homework."

Strengths of Projects.   Gardner says, "Life is a series of projects." Projects classrooms are more student- and thinking-centered. They are more likely to inspire motivation, inquiry, collaboration, reflection, personal accountability, and improved self-concept. Projects enable students to plan on a large scale and carry out plans to fruition.

Most projects help put students in control of their own learning. Though projects are done according to broad guidelines and suggestions from the teacher, students assume the responsibility of planning, organizing, conducting their work individually or in groups, and finalizing the product. Consequently, most in-class activities produce greater student enthusiasm and involvement, in part because they employ a variety of student learning styles and multiple intelligences. Projects that are congruent with curriculum standards and instructional goals and activities lead to better achievement, behavior, and attitude.

Parents and guardians often become involved in their children's projects, too. The resultant products are exciting to students and caregivers alike. Students remember projects as their favorite events in school, and caregivers form high opinions of teachers who use this approach. With the teacher's help, students usually have the opportunity to display their products.

Limitations of Projects.   Projects require a great deal of time. Some teachers question the ultimate value of, say, setting up and maintaining a terrarium, when they consider what could be accomplished if that time were devoted to direct instruction. Caregivers can assume too much of the project work that is done outside the classroom.

Usability of Projects.   Projects can be used to good advantage in all content subjects at all grade levels. Of course, primary children require more direct assistance from the teacher than do older students.

Variations of Projects.   Simkins, Cole, Tavalin, and Means (2002) describe multimedia projects as "project-based multimedia learning . . . in which students acquire new knowledge and skills in the course of designing, planning, and producing a *multimedia product*" (p. 3). In other words, students demonstrate their understandings with technology-based presentations such as computerized slide shows, websites, or video.

Instructional Approach: Technology-Assisted Teaching

The availability of classroom computers and educational software in today's classrooms and homes has produced an upsurge in computerized instruction and distance learning (telecommunications). System, program, and equipment costs have dropped, and the variety and sophistication of educational software have increased. Using television monitors and computers as tools to enhance teacher effectiveness—not replace it—provides new potential for improving schooling and teaching.

Students learning *from* technology differs from students learning *with* technology. Reeves (1998) explains it this way: Students learning *from* media and technology work with instructional television, computer-based instruction, or integrated learning systems. Fundamentally they use computers as tutors to increase their basic skills and knowledge. Students learning *with* technology use technology as a "resource to help them develop higher order thinking, creativity, research skills, and so forth" (p. 2). Technology in this way is a "tool that can be applied to a variety of goals in the learning process, rather than serving simply as an instructional delivery system" (Ringstaff & Kelley, 2002, p. 2).

In recent years word processors have simplified the processes of writing, editing, and revising. Video has expanded the possibilities for visual presentations. The Internet and hypertext links have increased efficiency for accessing and collecting information. Email now allows students to interact and collaborate quickly with persons who are somewhere else. And other tools, including video cameras, digital editing, presentation software, and web-authoring programs are becoming more commonplace.

Now teachers are more easily able to enrich their overall curricula, as well as differentiate their instruction to respond to special needs with more individualized instruction. Programs that provide at least some tutorial assistance are available for students who need extra help or time. Individual students, able to work at their own pace through the plethora of electronic workbooks and tutorials that provide drill and practice, feel more in control of the kind and quality of their work and progress. They also receive more private and timely feedback and interactions regarding their work, which are likely to be less embarrassing than the more traditional methods. Teachers with easy access to several computers are able to instruct small groups at computers simultaneously. Also, television and cable programming made for classrooms now provide additional curriculum opportunities.

Based on research, many believe that technology is most powerful when used as a tool for thinking—problem solving, conceptual development, and critical thinking. This melds with Reeves's thoughts of learning *with* technology, where students work on projects and solve problems by gathering, organizing, and analyzing information.

Learning with technology suggests a shift from student mastery of basic skills to a problem-solving and project-based curriculum. With this goal, teachers and students are in control of the curriculum and instruction, and technology provides assisting tools. "The combination of computation, connectivity, visual and multimedia capacities, miniaturization, and speed has radically changed the potential for technologies in schooling" (Culp, Hawkins, & Honey, 1999, p. 2). Possibilities abound for technology-rich, projects-based classrooms. One example is WebQuest, a model for integrating web use with classroom activities. "WebQuest combines research-supported theories with effective use of the Internet to promote dependable instructional practices" (March, 2003/2004, p. 42). You can find out more about WebQuest at http://webquest.sdsu.edu.

Most students find classroom computers exciting and are intrigued by their color, motion, sound, and interactive capabilities. Jearine Bacon, who teaches upper elementary grades, offers this advice about using computers in the classroom.

Computers are not just for play. One of their main contributions lies in developing logical thinking. Situations can be created for deductive reasoning with the student guiding the lesson and the teacher serving as facilitator.

Sharing ideas and teamwork on the computer can be used for projects and presentations. Multimedia projects involve the use of many different student talents, so the use of cooperative learning benefits the student while it extends the use of technology. Motivating and empowering students to learn are very positive benefits of the computer.

Using the Internet.   Information accessibility via computer is burgeoning. Today most students rely on this medium to investigate, research, document, and communicate their study and projects. Although millions of such resources are readily available, not all are appropriate. It is important that teachers and students be informed consumers and learn to evaluate the information they access. Goldsborough (1997) suggests these five tips for assessing the accuracy and value of information obtained on the Internet.

- Try to find out the credentials and affiliation of the author of the information or creator of the website.
- Try to determine the reason the information is posted. Does the author have a personal agenda?
- Find the creation or modification dates. Usually current information is more reliable and useful than older material, unless, of course, the research is historical.
- Try to confirm the information elsewhere. Reporters are taught to confirm their facts with at least two sources.
- Through personal contacts or review guides, try to learn how others feel about the website.

Strengths of Technology-Assisted Teaching.   Technology- and computer-assisted learning provide several advantages that textbooks cannot. Computers are likely to be more enjoyable because they offer students variety, even novelty, to their studies. They provide easy online accessibility to resources and materials (encyclopedias, journals, newspapers, and so on) and tools such as spreadsheets, word processing, text editing, and desktop publishing. Data and information found by computer is likely to be more up-to-date than textbook resources.

Additionally, many programs now are available that provide for interaction with students. Some programs challenge students to apply complex databases or solve problems through elaborate simulations. These programs pose a problem, give assistance or instruction when students request it, and then provide immediate feedback and consequences to the students' choices. With links to other technologies such as DVDs, CD-ROMs, and hypermedia, computers can surpass conventional print materials with animation, time-lapse photography, and other audiovisual techniques for communicating information and demonstrating processes.

When surveyed, teachers in grades 4–12 who had integrated computerized instruction into their teaching believed that computers had substantially changed their classrooms for the better. As their own experience in using computers evolved, the teachers reported a greater use of word processors (for students creating compositions) and databases (for students doing research) and less use of drill and practice programs. This allowed teachers to expose students to more complex material and provide differentiated and more individualized instruction. This also made classes more student-centered, and allowed teachers to function more as facilitative coaches than dispensers of information (Hadley & Sheingold, 1993).

Limitations of Technology-Assisted Teaching.   Despite its many benefits, technology- and computer-assisted teaching suffer limitations as well. Many teachers are hesitant and ill-informed about proper use of computers, media, and other technology. Many classrooms still do not have enough computers to go around and student access remains limited. Use of the Internet is risky because students can access many sites that are not suitable for them.

Teachers may need to change their beliefs and understandings about teaching and learning and about learning *with* rather than *from* media and technology. Technology needs to be infused into the curriculum and instruction. Technology resources may still be inadequate or inaccessible to teachers or students. And, teachers need adequate training and support to use technology.

Instructional Approach: Differentiated Instruction

Students in today's classrooms bring with them varying languages, cultures, physical considerations, talents, and experiences. In many elementary schools, students work and study in classrooms with other students who are fairly close in age. In other schools students work and study in multi-age classes where they interact with others of broader age ranges and very mixed levels of ability. Whether the class is traditional or multi-age, it is the teacher's responsibility to determine, plan, and begin teaching from where the students are, not from the first page of the curriculum guide. These adaptations are called, collectively, differentiated instruction. For Tomlinson (2000), differentiated instruction is a philosophy—one facet of expert teaching—that rests on a set of beliefs and principles.

- Students who are the same age differ in many ways: their learning styles, academic and reading levels, interests, experiences, and life circumstances.
- These differences have major impact on what students need to learn, including the support they need and the pace at which they need to work.
- The teacher unconditionally accepts all students as they are, attends to their differences, and expects them to become all they can be. The goals for everyone are individual success and maximum growth.
- Assessment is ongoing, responsive to students' needs, and inseparable from instruction. Assessment and instruction are multi-method and multi-source, with student performance determined by individual growth from a starting point.
- The teacher is clear about what is important in subject matter. The teacher adjusts content, instruction, and products based on student readiness, interest, and learning styles. Activities are used that encourage students to use more than one intelligence and encourage teachers to use varied instructional approaches, strategies, resources, and materials.

- All students participate in respectful work and help other students as appropriate. Multiple perspectives are sought and valued.
- The teacher and students collaborate to set both whole-class and individual learning goals, and the teacher equalizes group and individual expectations and standards.
- The teacher and students work together flexibly. Also, time and assessment are flexible and often are linked to students' needs. The teacher guides students toward self-reliance.

Teachers can differentiate instruction in a variety of ways. In primary grades, for example, learning centers and stations allow teachers to set out varied materials and activities and thus differentiate instruction. Learning contracts differentiate instruction for older students. So do tiered activities, in which the teacher keeps the same focus for everyone, but provides opportunities of varying degrees of difficulty.

PLANNING APPROACHES AND STRATEGIES

Bear in mind that all approaches and all strategies require planning by the teacher. You can't rely on any approach to evolve naturally but must envision your expectations and foresee what students are likely to do. Successful instruction evolves from this prior attention.

Long-range plans for the year and for longer units of instruction, discussed in Chapter 2, provide teachers with a map of the year's events, content, and activities. The steps in the backward design process—identify desired results, determine acceptable evidence, and plan learning experiences and instruction—help teachers organize their thinking and plan for the year and longer units.

Good daily lesson plans are needed for day-to-day work and, again, backward design can help. First identify the desired results. Then determine how students will demonstrate these results. As you plan the learning experiences and instruction, consider skills and knowledge the students need to have prior to the lesson. Then think about the beginning (how you will introduce the lesson), the middle (what you and the students will do), and the end (how you will end the lesson, what students will produce, and how you will evaluate and follow up). Here is an outline of considerations for teachers as they make their plans.

Considerations Before the Instruction
- *Facts about the learners:* Who are they? How do they learn? Do they have the knowledge and skills to be successful?
- *Content and context:* Why should my students study this lesson or unit? What is the purpose of this learning? What are the grade level and content area? What content areas can be integrated? Where does the lesson fit into the unit? What are the state and district curriculum standards? What are the learning goals, objectives, and/or essential or guiding questions? How will prior knowledge and skills be assessed before the lesson? What do students need to review?
- *Product and assessments:* How will I be able to tell if students have learned well and enjoyed the work? In what varied authentic ways will students demonstrate accomplishment of the objectives? What criteria will be used to judge students' success?
- *Management and discipline:* What materials and resources are needed? How will technology be used? How will the room be arranged? How much class time is avail-

able? How will students be grouped? How will transitions be managed? How will misbehavior be handled?

Considerations in Opening the Lesson
- How will students be motivated and focused?
- What will make students want to learn this material?

Considerations in Proceeding through the Lesson
- *Teacher input:* How much preparation time is available? How will I describe and model skills? What examples and nonexamples will I provide? How will I teach to the standards and objectives? How will I actively involve all students? What must I modify to make sure all students learn? What teaching skills and strategies will best help my students accomplish the learning? What materials and resources will I need?
- *Guided practice/monitoring progress:* How will students practice alone, with a partner, or in cooperative groups? If students work in cooperative groups, how are the four principles of PIES satisfied? How will I check students' understanding?
- *Independent practice/summative assessment:* How will this occur? What will students do to demonstrate their understanding?
- *Closure:* How will I have students summarize and make meaning of their learning?

Considerations in Following through after the Lesson
- *Transfer:* What opportunities will students have to continue practice and transfer learning? What follow-up activities and homework are appropriate and needed?
- *Reflection:* What went well with the lesson or unit? Was it relevant and worthwhile for the students? What evidence demonstrated this? What teaching skills and strategies worked most effectively? What changes can be made to enhance learning? How will student learning and teacher effectiveness benefit from these changes?

FORMALIZING THE LESSON PLAN

Many experienced teachers plan lessons in their heads and write only fragmented notes in their plan book. Most new teachers need to be more deliberate and are wise to write out detailed plans to ensure coverage and not get lost in the lesson. Such plans can be written in a variety of ways. In fact, some teachers create a master template so they easily can organize and record their planning ideas. Although you will find a format that works well for you, you probably will want to include the following considerations:

- Date
- Standard(s), objective(s), essential or guided question(s), or intended outcomes
- Teacher input and student output
- List of activities or learning experiences, and the time allotted for each
- Modifications for English learners and students with other special needs

- Technology and materials needed for each activity
- Closure
- Follow-up activities
- Evaluation procedures, scoring guides, and criteria
- Management considerations for room set up; material preparation; student groupings; content delivery, procedures, and transitions; and student behavior

Before moving from instructional management to Chapter 7, Managing Students at Work, take time to explore these end-of-chapter activities.

Parting Thought

I talk and talk and talk, and I haven't taught people in fifty years what my father taught by example in one week.

—Mario Cuomo

SUMMARY SELF-CHECK

Check off the following as you either understand or become able to apply them.

❑ Four broad instructional approaches are widely used today in teaching—direct teaching, facilitative teaching, technology-assisted teaching, and differentiated instruction.

❑ In direct teaching, the teacher plans, directs, monitors, and evaluates all aspects of instruction.

❑ In facilitative teaching, the teacher is in charge but allows much more student input, self-guidance, and responsibility.

❑ In technology-assisted teaching, teacher and students assess instruction and resources via computers and the Internet, television, and cable.

❑ In differentiated instruction, the teacher modifies content, instruction and process, and product to best meet the needs and abilities of all students.

❑ Several specific instructional strategies bring about what is intended in learning:
- Among strategies used in direct teaching are direct instruction, concept attainment, and Say, See, Do Teaching.
- Among strategies used in facilitative teaching are cooperative learning, inquiry, and projects.
- Among strategies used in technology-assisted teaching are tutorials, distance learning, and cyberspace connections.

❑ Teaching approach and instructional strategies become translated into daily lesson plans. Experienced teachers often plan lessons in their head, with attention to the following:

- What facts are relevant about the learners? (In particular, consider who they are and their prior knowledge and skills.)
- What should students learn, related to the standards and objectives?
- What activities, materials, and management considerations will serve the students best?
- How much preparation time is available?
- How much class time is available?
- How can students be motivated?
- How should the activities be sequenced?
- How will the lesson be ended?
- What follow-up should there be?
- How will student profitability and enjoyment be assessed?

ACTIVITIES FOR REFLECTION AND DISCUSSION

1. Take a moment to review the statements in the Prediction–Review Guide at the beginning of this chapter. Put a check mark in the Review column next to any statement with which you now agree. How have your thoughts changed since reading this chapter?

2. Interview at least two teachers about how they plan and manage their instruction to satisfy the curriculum standards and the content itself and meet the needs of their students.

3. If you were forced to teach mathematics in either a direct or facilitative approach, which approach would you choose? Explain your reasons, keeping in mind the accuracy, quantity, retention, usefulness, and enjoyment of learning for you and your students. Which approach would you choose for language arts or social studies?

4. In which subjects typically taught in the elementary curriculum do you think you could best use projects? Bearing in mind that projects often are time consuming, how much emphasis would you give to projects (in-class and out-of-class) during the school year?

5. You have just learned that a new species of animal named *zugu* has been discovered in the jungle rivers of Zaire. Devise a lesson plan to teach others verbally (no pictures exist yet) an accurate concept of zugu. Teach your plan to fellow students and check their understanding (and your teaching) by having them draw pictures of zugu.

6. Suppose you decided to teach a haiku lesson by using Say, See, Do Teaching. (A haiku is a poem that is concerned with nature and has three lines of five, seven, and five syllables. The first line often depicts a scene, the second an action within the scene, and the third the aftermath.) Show how you would break the topic into small sequential steps and monitor each student's progress.

7. Describe how you would use technology-assisted teaching in your third-grade science or social studies program.

REFERENCES AND RECOMMENDED READINGS

Armstrong, T. (2000). *Multiple intelligences in the classroom* (2nd ed.). Alexandria, VA: ASCD.
Bruner, J. (1960). *The process of education.* New York: Vintage.

Building classroom relationships [Special issue]. (2003, September). *Educational Leadership, 61*(1). Alexandria, VA: ASCD.

Chamot, A., & O'Malley, J. (1994). *The CALLA handbook: Implementing the Cognitive Academic Language Learning Approach.* New York: Addison-Wesley.

Churma, M. (1999). *A guide to integrating technology standards into the curriculum.* Upper Saddle River, NJ: Merrill.

Cruickshank, D., Jenkins, D., & Metcalf, K. (2006). *The act of teaching* (4th ed.). Boston: McGraw-Hill.

Culp, K., Hawkins, J., & Honey, M. (1999). *Review paper on educational technology research and development.* New York: Education Development Center, Center for Children and Technology.

Goldsborough, R. (1997, August/September). Let the reader beware. *Reading Today, 15*(1), 8.

Hadley, M., & Sheingold, K. (1993, May). Commonalities and distinctive patterns in teachers' integration of computers. *American Journal of Education, 101,* 261–315.

How to differentiate instruction [Special issue]. (2000, September). *Educational Leadership, (58)*1. Alexandria, VA: ASCD.

Hunter, M. (1982). *Mastery learning.* El Segundo, CA: TIP Publications.

Jones, F. (2007). *Tools for teaching: Discipline Instruction Motivation* (2nd ed.). Santa Cruz, CA: Fredric H. Jones and Associates.

Joyce, B., & Weil, M. (with Calhoun, E.). (2003). *Models of teaching* (7th ed.). Boston: Allyn & Bacon.

Kagan, S. (1994). *Cooperative learning.* San Clemente, CA: Kagan Cooperative Learning.

Learning in the digital age [Special issue]. (2005, December/2006, January). *Educational Leadership, 63*(4). Alexandria, VA: ASCD.

March, T. (2003, December/2004, January). The learning power of WebQuests. *Educational Leadership, 61*(4), 42–47. Alexandria, VA: ASCD.

Reeves, T. (1998). *The impact of media and technology in schools: A research report prepared for the Bertelsmann Foundation.* Retrieved August 2003, from www.athensacademy.org/instruct/media_tech/reeves0.html.

Ringstaff, C., & Kelley, L. (2002). *The learning return on our educational technology investment.* San Francisco: WestEd RTEC.

Rogers, C. (1969). *Freedom to learn.* Columbus, OH: Merrill.

The science of learning [Special issue]. (2000, November). *Educational Leadership, 68*(3). Alexandria, VA: ASCD.

Simkins, M., Cole, K., Tavalin, F., & Means, B. (2002). *Increasing student learning through multimedia projects.* Alexandria, VA: ASCD.

Teaching all students [Special issue]. (2001, October). *Educational Leadership, 61*(2). Alexandria, VA: ASCD.

Teaching for meaning [Special issue]. (2004, September). *Educational Leadership, 62*(1). Alexandria, VA: ASCD.

Tomlinson, C. (1999*). The differentiated classroom: Responding to the needs of all learners.* Alexandria, VA: ASCD.

Tomlinson, C. (2000, September). Reconcilable differences: Standards-based teaching and differentiation. *Education Leadership, 58*(1), 6–11.

Tomlinson, C., & McTighe, J. (2006*). Integrating differentiated instruction and understanding by design.* Alexandria, VA: ASCD.

Websites

Cooperative Learning

www.newhorizons.org/strategies/cooperative/front_cooperative.htm

http://www-acad.sheridanc.on.ca/scls/coop/cooplrn.htm

WebQuest

http://webquest.sdsu.edu

CHAPTER 7

Managing Students at Work

A school should not be preparation for life. A school should be life!

—Elbert Hubbard

Prediction–Review Guide

Before you read the chapter, take a minute to put a check mark in the Prediction column next to any statement with which you agree.

	Prediction	Review
1. The problem with routines is that they inhibit individual thinking.	❑	❑
2. In the long run, the best way to begin the day is to allow students to relax and settle in before undertaking the day's arduous work.	❑	❑
3. Authorities agree that if classroom work is worth doing, it is worth being checked carefully by the teacher.	❑	❑
4. The use of classroom monitors is valuable in giving everyone some responsibility for what goes on in the classroom.	❑	❑
5. Usually during independent work it is possible to give students who are stuck all the help they need to resume work in a few seconds time.	❑	❑
6. Signaling devices are preferable to raising hands as a way for students to request the teacher's help.	❑	❑
7. Teachers should not attempt to instruct the class until they have everyone's attention.	❑	❑
8. Modular cluster seating works well for teachers who wish to use cooperative learning.	❑	❑
9. Tattling is a normal part of childhood and therefore should not be a matter of concern for the teacher.	❑	❑
10. Student responsibility is shown adequately when students fulfill duties and obligations promptly, with concern for others.	❑	❑

Support for specific standards found in this chapter:

INTASC Standards

7. Instructional Planning Skills

   The teacher plans instruction based on knowledge of subject matter, students, the community, and curriculum guides.

Danielson's Framework for Teaching

1. Planning and Preparation
   - Demonstrating knowledge of students
   - Selecting instructional goals
   - Demonstrating knowledge of resources
   - Designing coherent instruction

3. Instruction
   - Communicating clearly and accurately
   - Using questioning and discussion techniques
   - Engaging students in learning
   - Providing feedback to students
   - Demonstrating flexibility and responsiveness

NBPTS Standards

2. Teachers know the subjects they teach and how to teach those subjects to students.

NCATE Standards

Apply effective methods of teaching students who are at different developmental stages, have different learning styles, and come from diverse backgrounds.

It might seem that once a teacher has established the physical and psychosocial environments and has taken steps to increase students' desire to learn, students would work diligently with little supervision. Teachers who make that assumption are likely to find that the classroom quickly resembles room 315, described by educational anthropologist Francis Schwartz (1981):

> In room 315 chaos reigns. The room is noisy with the shouting, laughter, and movement of many children. Though most are seated, many are walking or running aimlessly around the classroom. Some stop at others' desks, provoke them briefly, and move on. Several students who are lining up textbooks as "race courses" for toy cars laugh when the teacher demands their attention. As the teacher struggles to ask a question over the noise, few if any students volunteer to answer. When one student does respond correctly, others yell out, "You think you're so smart." (p. 99)

Such classes are familiar to every teacher, and they occur despite good classroom environment and eager students. Missing in room 315 are management procedures that get students to engage in assigned work and stick with it. This chapter addresses management of students at work, giving attention to the following:

1. *Work routines* that involve opening activities, signals for attention, instructions, movement in the room, materials, completed work, student accountability and criterion of mastery, homework, and closing activities.
2. *Providing assistance* through use of student assistants, giving efficient directions and feedback, and directing students in their requests for help.
3. *Incidentals* such as seating, entering and exiting the room, sharpening pencils, using passes outside the room, controlling noise, and dealing with numerous other concerns, including procrastination, tattling, and bullying.

All of these matters can be handled with routines and procedures that students learn as habits and comply with more or less automatically. Jones (2007) and others agree that students' use of time is a major issue. Routine procedures, far from being restrictive, are very helpful in letting students know what to do, as well as how, when, and where to do it, thus reducing confusion and wasted time.

WORK ROUTINES

Opening Activities

How the teacher and students begin the day sets the tone and often sets the behavior. Teachers who are organized and friendly welcome students and get them started on something immediately. Teachers who are preoccupied or unorganized set up themselves and students for a day that is likely to be only minimally productive.

Teachers of younger children often greet their students on the playground and walk them as a group to the classroom. Either on the playground or at the door, the teachers can greet each student individually, tell everyone a little about the day's activities, and remind them as a group of expected behavior.

Teachers of older students often have the children come into the room, stop talking, and get to work immediately on a silent activity, such as reading library books, writing in journals, or seeing how many math problems they can do correctly in a given period of time. While students work, the teacher quietly checks attendance, often using a seating chart. Some teachers have group monitors or table captains report who is absent from their group. Some post a daily opinion poll or survey and have students move their individual photos to indicate how they vote in response to the question for the day. Unmoved photos belong to absent students. Others use a clothespin system in which arriving students clip clothespins with their names to a group chart. Still others use a system in which students take sharpened pencils from loops attached beneath their photos or shadow profiles. The teacher checks attendance by noting which pencils remain.

Choosing, an opening routine that once was widely popular, still is favored by some primary and intermediate teachers. Choosing allows students to move to areas that contain attractive materials and activities when they enter the room. Some students might choose the art center to work with clay, paint, or weaving; others might choose the reading center to read books, magazines, or newspapers; still others might choose the computer center to engage in math or language activities. Once students have chosen their activities, they must be responsible for their conduct, keeping noise down and taking care of the materials with which they are working. This procedure embraces the idea of multiple intelligences (Gardner, 1991, 1993a, 1993b; Kagan & Kagan, 1998) by helping to provide a closer match between student interests, learning styles, and the classroom activities and thereby improve learning and behavior.

Other opening activities popular with teachers are those that go by names similar to *five-a-days*, such as five math problems on the board to try to solve; five vocabulary words to define, learn to spell, and use; or five cities to locate on a map. These are only a few examples of opening activities that students enjoy and that involve them at once. Teachers can use the five-a-days as teasers for content that will be studied that day.

Some teachers open the day with a quick review of the previous day's work and activities. They use the overhead to show key transparencies from the earlier lessons. Others may review the prior day with a mind map of events on transparencies or chart paper, or preview the new day in a similar way. From time to time, opening activities should be changed to avoid a sense of staleness.

CASE STUDY 7.1

THE IMPORTANCE OF ROUTINE

Focus Question
Liz Davis does not have in place a morning routine that sets the tone for a successful day. What management procedures could Liz install to reduce confusion and the amount of wasted time?

Ms. Davis is a beginning teacher. It is 7:55 in the morning and she is reading the revised agenda for the school day that she just received. There will be a fire drill at 10:15, an assembly for only the best citizens at 10:45, and the nurse will check for lice sometime during the day. As Ms. Davis looks for her attendance sheet, which she had placed somewhere in the middle of her desk amid numerous papers, utensils, and miniature toys, she sees an overdue slip for last week's video or film. Somewhere a bell sounds and suddenly thirty-one bright and shining third graders, complete with loud voices, barge through the door.

"Good morning, teacher!" they cry. "Can I open the windows? "Guy," one moans, "you always get to do that!" "Teacher! Here's my permission slip for our field trip!"

Ms. Davis stands there in a daze as thirty-one pairs of hands try to bless her with book reports, late homework assignments, and wilted flowers they picked from neighbors' yards on the way to school. Her students are well-intentioned; Ms. Davis simply hasn't taught them a better way to begin the school day.

Signals for Attention

You never should try to instruct the class when you do not have everyone's attention. Normally, all you have to do is say something like "No talking; everyone's eyes on me" or "Listen carefully." But when students are busy working, especially in teams or groups with talking allowed, you can wear yourself out trying to shout over them. Instead, select and practice a signal that tells all students they are to stop immediately what they are doing and give you their attention. Primary teachers often use auditory signals. They use a clapping rhythm, sound chords on the piano, ring a wind chime, or turn a rain stick. Some ring a bell or say "Freeze!" Other teachers prefer a visual signal and simply flick the lights. Whatever signal you select, discuss it with your students and practice, practice, practice its use.

Instructions

For assigned work it is very important to inform students precisely what they are to do and when and how they are to do it. Every teacher complains about students saying, "I don't know what to do" within seconds after receiving directions. Either students don't listen or there's too much to remember, but both can be avoided by stating what is to be done while jotting reminder notes on the board. For example:

> Boys and girls, all eyes on me. Everyone. Thank you. Listen very carefully. At your desks I want you to do problems 2, 4, 6, 8, and 10 on page 32 of your workbooks. [Jot "p. 32" and "problem numbers" in the corner of the board.] You may work quietly with your partner. [Jot "quiet" and "partner" on the board.] You have twenty minutes to complete your work. [Jot "20 min." on the board.] When you finish, put your papers in the in-basket. [Jot "in-basket."] Then take out your library books and read until time is up. [Jot "library books." Draw a square around what you have listed on the board and point to the notes.] Page 32, problems 2, 4, 6, 8, and 10. Work quietly with partner. Put finished work in the in-basket, and then read your library book until I call time. I'll circulate to help you if you need me. All right, let's get to work.

This procedure can apply to most assignments: Get all students' attention, tell them exactly what they are to do, and post reminders on the board or a chart. To further support the instruction, Jones (2007) advocates the use of VIPs—visual instructional plans (see Chapter 6). You may wish to prepare reminder VIPs and charts beforehand and display them where everyone can see. This may seem unnecessary, but on many occasions it will save you having to repeat yourself several times. Moreover, VIPs eventually will help students learn to be self-directing and take responsibility for their own learning.

Movement in the Room

Movement is necessary before, during, and after many learning activities. Students must move from group to group, obtain and replace materials, turn in completed work, get drinks or go to the restroom, use the wastebasket, come to your desk, perform their monitor duties, and so forth. Older students may be able to sit still for a while, but young students have to move; their natural behavior does not allow them to sit still and quietly for more than fifteen or twenty minutes at a time. Teachers should alternate quiet, still activities with those that allow talk and movement, albeit restrained.

Movement management requires close attention because, although movement is necessary, it has high potential for creating or adding to discipline problems. Even when no trouble occurs, movement can cause congestion, wasted time, and annoyance. Therefore you must discuss—and practice—movement with your students and establish appropriate guidelines. A basic rule should be that students are to remain seated and working unless otherwise directed. Some teachers like to use a code system that they post in the front of the room to remind students of movement expectations for different activities. For example, a red sign tells students they should sit in their seats and talk only when called on. A yellow sign tells students they should remain in their seats, but they may whisper with their neighbors. This is allowed when partners, teams, or small groups collaborate and cooperate on activities. A green sign means that students may do group or individual project work, with quiet talking and movement allowed as necessary for obtaining materials and references.

Materials

Poor materials management can wreck efficiency, especially when it comes to materials that are used daily—textbooks, workbooks, worksheets, paper, pencils, crayons, scissors, glue, paints, and brushes. The logistics of your materials management must allow materials to be stored out of the way yet remain easily obtained, distributed, and replaced.

Storage and Distribution.   Students with desks can keep many of the small materials there, especially textbooks, workbooks, pencils, crayons, rulers, and paper. Teachers use various techniques to encourage students to keep their desks orderly, ranging from simple inspections to procedures intended to be interesting and motivating. For example, some teachers have a box lid or shallow tub for each student that easily slides in and out of the desk space. These have several advantages: they confine the materials that are in the desk, they allow for easy retrieval, and they discourage students from playing with the desk contents when they should be working or listening. The class may earn time toward a preferred activity when they are able to quickly get out their supplies for the next lesson or activity because their desks are tidy and organized. Or, a "desk elf," an imaginary creature, might check all desks at the end of the day. When the elf finds desks that are especially neat, it leaves a small surprise, such as a sticker or a pencil.

When students sit at tables instead of desks, as is typically the case in primary grades, or when space limitations make it difficult for students to keep materials in their desks, other arrangements must be made for the storage of small materials. Some teachers provide each student with a container such as a basket, dishpan, or tub marked with the student's name and kept on a shelf. At appropriate times students go to their baskets for supplies to use at their tables.

In rooms where student desks or tables are arranged in clusters, some teachers prefer to place a large tub or basket in the center of each cluster. The tub contains materials that are arranged in the order they will be used for the day.

Often materials are distributed by the following procedures: (1) Teacher or aide distributes before school, during recess, or at lunchtime, so materials are available for students when they arrive. (2) Monitors are trained to distribute materials as needed at recess, lunch, or during class activities. (3) Students get the materials as instructed.

VIGNETTE 7.1   Managing Materials and Supplies

Ted Saulino describes how he manages materials in his kindergarten class:

I place a small, inexpensive yet durable plastic basket in the middle of each cluster of tables, full of the supplies that students will need on a given day: pencils, scissors, glue, markers, colored pencils, red correction pens, and rulers. The basket sits on top of a folder of good ruled paper and scratch paper.

To avoid arguments and to distribute power at each station, I name rotating team captains. A wall chart, divided into sections representing the workstations, lists the students' names. The name at the top of the list is the first team captain. Next to the captain's name I clip a small star, which I move down to the next name when the week is over. The child whose name is below the captain's acts as the substitute if the captain is absent.

Captains distribute the supplies and distribute and collect all handouts. If someone is absent at a station, captains start an absent folder for the child's return. At the end of each day, captains assess the team's supplies and replenish paper, sharpen pencils, and make sure the team has a clean station.

Upon Reflection

Ted Saulino describes his management for kindergarten. What changes would make his management procedures work better for intermediate or upper grades or for classrooms with individual desks rather than clusters of tables?

Use and Care.   Use and care of materials present opportunities for students to practice conservation. Students should be instructed that they are to make good use of paper, crayons, and pencils, and are not to waste any materials. Likewise, books, workbooks, charts, and other materials that can be reused should be kept clean, undamaged, and orderly. The inherent value in taking proper care of materials is important in itself, especially in times of fiscal difficulties. When supply budgets dwindle, it becomes a matter of necessity for teachers and students alike to make better use of materials.

Replacement.   In addition to efficient distribution and care of materials, good management calls for attention to how materials are to be replaced after use. Typically smaller materials and student work are handled in one of four ways: (1) students themselves quietly return the materials; (2) monitors collect and replace the materials; (3) students place materials in folders or containers that are collected later and scored by the teacher; or (4) the teacher or aide collects, organizes, and replaces the materials.

Large Materials.   Larger materials that play key roles in instruction also must be managed and used efficiently. These materials include maps and screens; reference books such as dictionaries and encyclopedias; globes, smaller maps, models, and art supplies; other items such as materials for aquariums and terrariums; physical education equipment; and audiovisual equipment. Although a few monitors can handle most management duties associated with large materials, many teachers prefer to involve all students in procedures and responsibilities.

Maps and projection screens should be mounted on the wall or above the board so they can be pulled down and used as needed. Maps and screens on rollers can be used to cover material, such as test items and directions that have been written on the board, or to hide larger instructional props or resources until needed.

Reference books should be kept on shelves at the side of the main seating area, also easily accessible to students. Globes and models should be placed where students can easily see and approach them—on countertops or a special table. Art supplies are best kept near the classroom sink in cupboards with closeable doors, and easels should be folded and stacked nearby. Materials for aquariums and terrariums, such as sand, plants, animal food, rocks, and cleaning equipment, should be kept in cupboards and used only by the teacher and designated monitors.

Physical education materials are best kept in a crate or large plastic trash container near or just outside the door until after school; then they are placed in the corner or a closet in the room.

A wheeled cart makes moving audiovisual materials easy. The top shelf can hold an overhead projector or a television (if one is not mounted on the classroom wall). Equipment such as CDs, DVDs, video and audiotapes, and tape or video recorders can be kept on the bottom shelf. Carts also can hold various other projectors in the classroom—motion picture, filmstrip, or slide. However, much of the media now available for teachers' use to supplement instruction has been converted to video, DVD, or CD and is projected through the television monitor. Consequently, unless these projectors are used often for instruction, they are better stored in a central school equipment storeroom and available as needed for teacher checkout.

Completed Work

One of teachers' most time-consuming tasks is dealing with completed work. Teachers commonly take home stacks of daily papers to be checked, graded, recorded, and returned. The following suggestions are intended to help teachers manage this complex and burdensome task.

Should Teachers Check Everything?   It is not necessary that all student work be checked in detail. Much independent work is for practice only, and necessary feedback should be given immediately as the teacher circulates and monitors student efforts.

Teachers should carefully check course work that requires judgment or very accurate correction. However, there is nothing wrong with allowing students to check their own routine work or exchange papers. In fact, as much work as possible should be corrected by students in class, to relieve the teacher as well as to motivate and instruct. Students lose interest when feedback is delayed, and teacher-corrected work, even when returned the next day, has little instructional value. In-class correcting gives prompt feedback on performance and errors. Aides or parent volunteers can check routine student work, but remember this caution: students have the right to privacy regarding their work and progress.

Organizing Completed Work.   Some teachers use a folder system to keep track of student work. The folders are compartmentalized with labels such as *Unfinished Work, Ready for Checking,* and *Completed and Checked* and kept on students' desks. At the end of each day the teacher reviews items in the *Ready for Checking* compartment and moves them to the *Completed and Checked* compartment.

VIGNETTE 7.2   Checking Student Papers

Ginny Lorenz, who teaches a fourth/fifth multi-age class, manages checking her students' work in this way: I like to read carefully student work, but I am not willing to bury myself with thirty papers at a time. I have my thirty students divided into eight groups. Every two weeks, Mondays through Thursdays, I am able to collect, read, and give constructive individualized guidance and feedback to everyone's written work by closely looking at about four papers a day, and we all are able to enjoy Fridays and weekends.

Upon Reflection
What other methods have you seen teachers use to handle the volume of student papers and work?

In classes where folders are not used, monitors collect completed work, perhaps by tables, teams, or groups, and place it in a receptacle. The teacher or an aide checks the work and returns it the next day.

Acknowledging Good Work.   Student work that has been done well should be acknowledged, usually privately through comments or stickers. Barbara Coloroso suggests that teachers allow students to decide themselves if their work needs a sticker. Occasionally, good work should be posted for all to see. This provides a sense of success and is highly motivating to most students, though not all. Be sure to ask the student for permission beforehand. Additionally, samples of completed work—both inferior and superior—should be kept privately in student folders to show parents and guardians at conferences or open house. These work samples are intended to present a well-rounded and accurate profile of the habits and accomplishments of the student.

Student Accountability and Criterion of Mastery

As teachers review student work, they should consider both quality of work and student accountability: How much work is enough? How many math problems should students complete for homework? How many sentences should they diagram? Teachers should answer these questions in terms of a *criterion of mastery.*

Consider the difference in these two sets of instructions. Some teachers say, "Boys and girls, you are to solve the odd problems on this page. Problems you don't finish before recess will be homework." This statement supports a *criterion of speed.* Students will hurry with their work so they can enjoy recess and have no homework. Nothing the teacher said encourages students to be accurate or to learn the concept.

In contrast, other teachers say, "Boys and girls, you are to solve the odd problems on this page. You may stop when you correctly answer five problems in a row." Now students have a genuine interest in accuracy and perhaps even mastery. If they answer the first four problems correctly and miss the next problem, they must begin counting from number one again for their correct five in a row. With this simple instruction, the teacher has encouraged both mastery and student accountability. With each correct response, students become more invested in solving the next problem correctly.

Homework

Most teachers above early primary grades assign homework. The value of homework lies not so much in learning new material as in (1) practicing and strengthening skills already learned, (2) developing an interest in more pleasurable learning activities, such as reading, and (3) allowing caregivers to show interest and support for their child's education.

"I'M GOING TO OUTSOURCE MY HOMEWORK TONIGHT – MATH TO DAD, ENGLISH TO MOM AND SCIENCE TO MY BIG SISTER."

For the most part, homework should focus on activities such as practicing and applying math skills, reading library books or magazines, reading together with an adult, writing anecdotes and reports, drawing pictures related to school work, or making up work missed because of absence.

Such work might encourage, but should not require, caregiver assistance in providing a workplace and insisting that the work be completed. This is particularly true when the caregivers speak a language other than English in the home. When students are weak in a particular skill, such as spelling, the caregiver can be asked to work with the child, perhaps with remedial drill games. Caregivers want to know about homework and how they can help. They should be told that the best things they can do are

- Provide a quiet place for the child to work.
- See to it (good-naturedly) that the child does homework as scheduled.
- Read to or with the child.
- Play games with the child that encourage spelling, math, and other types of thinking—dominoes, Scrabble, Parcheesi, checkers, and Yahtzee.
- Ask and answer questions about news events and a variety of other topics.

Closing Activities

Teachers who simply wait out the last fifteen minutes of the day miss some rich opportunities for teaching and reflecting. Here are some ideas for ending the day: Spend five minutes taking care of closing assignments, notices, cleaning, and tidying so the last ten minutes can be used for review and reflection. Have students give their views on what occurred during the day—accomplishments, high points, excitements, disappointments, things that went well, and things that could be done better next time. Review the day's events by creating a mind map with the students on overhead transparencies or chart paper. Give students a preview of what the next day will bring. Promise at least one interesting surprise and live up to it, so they will look forward to the next day with anticipation.

PROVIDING ASSISTANCE

Student Assistants

Students can assist with many chores in the classroom. Often called *monitors,* these student assistants can take care of tasks such as watering plants, distributing worksheets, and any other routine chores in the room. Some teachers use "one-minute student managers" to handle the variety of jobs that arise from the particular needs for their class. For example, a kindergarten teacher may take advantage of a skilled youngster to serve as "shoelace monitor." This student helps classmates tie their shoelaces, and in doing so, saves the teacher's time and back. These managerial activities add mutual teaching and learning time to the day and allow students to become real partners in the classroom (Freiberg, 1996).

Monitors can be assigned to most routine duties. For example, Mary Martinez, an experienced fifth-grade teacher, identified sixteen categories of responsibilities, which provide jobs for thirty students:

- Class president—manages class business and classroom meetings as needed.
- Flag monitor—leads the daily flag salute and other lessons and activities that have to do with the flag.
- Lights monitor—sees that the lights are turned on and off.
- Window monitor—sees that windows are opened, closed, and shaded as necessary during the day.
- News, weather, and map monitors (two)—report on two or three news items per day, including weather forecasts for city, state, and nation, and locate on the map where the news and weather events occur.
- Class news reporters (two)—make daily entries into the class log about highlights of the day. Kept as a class record, the log is used as a source for the teacher's monthly newsletter to caregivers. From time to time, the students reread the log to affirm their sense of history, accomplishment, and growth.
- Messenger—delivers messages to the office, library, and other teachers.
- Line monitors (two)—head lines and model good behavior for entering and leaving the room and for movement to other parts of the school.
- Physical education equipment monitors (two)—distribute, collect, store, mark, and take care of equipment used on the playgrounds at recess and lunch.
- Table or group monitors (five to six)—manage tables or identifiable groups of students, with such duties as taking attendance, distributing and collecting materials, seeing that the area is kept clean and orderly, and sometimes reporting as the group spokesperson.

- Plant and pet monitors (two)—water and care for plants; clean and care for aquarium and feed fish; and feed and care for animals in the terrarium.
- Materials monitors (two)—handle, store, distribute, and collect small materials such as workbooks, worksheets, pencils, paper, glue, and scissors.
- Audiovisual monitors (two)—obtain projectors, DVD players, and VCRs; operate and return equipment; and manage films, slides, micro-projectors, and models.
- Librarians (two)—manage the class library and the system used for students to check out books, class videos, and other materials. Library monitors are trained to process checkout cards and to keep track of materials.
- Substitute teacher monitors (two)—assist substitute teachers. The teacher keeps these monitors updated on daily routines, the locations of lesson plans and materials, standards of behavior, and the discipline system used in the class.
- Visitors monitor—greets classroom visitors and offers them seating.

Assignments to tasks are made in different ways. Some teachers arbitrarily assign the duties. Others allow students to choose, in alphabetical order or on a first-come basis. Still others have students make written requests or complete application forms and interview for the duties they wish to monitor. In such cases, selection then can be made by the teacher or by class vote.

Directions and Feedback

As students work individually at assigned activities such as seatwork, they invariably encounter difficulties that require teacher help. Effective management requires that teachers provide this help quickly and efficiently so students can stay on task and complete work on time. Jones (2007) says that the teacher's job is to answer the question "What do I do next?" as efficiently as possible. This is accomplished best when the teacher (1) gives clear, understandable directions, (2) posts and reviews reminders and visual instructional plans, (3) uses signal systems for requesting assistance, (4) moves easily and quickly to students in need of help, and (5) provides assistance quickly and efficiently.

Directions and Reminders. Earlier in this chapter you saw how directions can be given briefly and clearly so students know exactly what they are supposed to do, how much time they have, what to do with completed work, and what to do while waiting for the next activity to begin. In Chapter 6 you saw a VIP for long division. By posting this on a wall, most students can work through their math problems with little additional teacher help. Graphic models can be helpful. They can depict spelling rules, paragraph construction, math algorithms, and steps in conducting experiments. Teachers should have students review the graphic models before requesting further help. Other reminders that are not directly pertinent to a given lesson also may be posted, such as "i before e except after c," "keep your area clean," and "invert and multiply." These posted VIPs, graphic models, reminders, and written directions should answer most of the questions students are likely to ask during independent work.

Teacher Movement. Teacher movement and proximity are key factors in managing assistance. The teacher must be able to reach each student as quickly as possible to minimize wasted time and forestall misbehavior. If the desks are arranged with an interior walking loop, or in modular clusters or shallow semicircles, the teacher will be fairly close to all students. Some teachers prefer to move in a predetermined pattern among the desks to be near students, comment on their work, and give help in regular rotation. Others prefer to observe from a central location and move quickly toward any student who show signs of difficulty.

Efficient Help.   Assistance should be given very quickly—in no more than a few seconds time. Jones's research (2007) shows that teachers spend an average of about four minutes per student when giving individual help. In these mini-tutorials, teachers question the student and then wait for a reply, which may be erroneous, fumbling, or nonforthcoming. Jones claims that effective help can be given in twenty seconds or less, as follows: (1) At first contact, quickly find anything the student has done correctly and mention it favorably, such as "Good job up to here." (2) Give a straightforward prompt that gets the student working again, such as "Watch the decimal," "Borrow here," "Look at step three on the chart," or "That word means. . . ." (3) Leave immediately, being sure to pay brief attention to the work of nearby students who have not requested help. Although this third step might appear inconsiderate of the feelings of students needing help, Jones maintains that it has two positive effects: (1) rapid movement gives attention to a greater number of students during work time, and (2) it begins to break down the dependency syndrome and helpless handraising in which students require the teacher's presence before they begin work. As Jones says, "Be positive, be brief, and be gone."

Student Requests for Help

Signals.   We all remember scenes of students congregating at the teacher's desk or sitting dispiritedly at their desks with arms waving limply, waiting for teacher help. Confusion and arms in the air can be avoided through use of signal systems that advise teachers when students need assistance. Some teachers use folded or colored construction paper that students place on the corner of their desk. A variation of this is for students to prioritize and signal their need for assistance by setting a red, yellow, or green cup on their desks.

VIGNETTE 7.3   When Students Constantly Ask for Help

Devora Garrison, a fifth-grade teacher, found this strategy to work with one of her students:
I have one of those students this year who constantly is standing in front of me with a question. She never raises her hand, but feels the need to be under my feet the moment I give an instruction. I discussed ways she could get answers rather than relying on me to do her thinking for her. Finally, to get her to think, I gave her three sticks each day with "Garrison/Anderson" written on them. When she comes up to Mrs. Anderson, my student teacher, or me, she has to give us a stick. When the sticks are gone, she's out of opportunities for the day. There has been an immediate drop in her leaving her seat.

Upon Reflection
What else might Devora Garrison do to help this student and others who frequently request teacher's help?

"I WAS JUST TUGGING ON MRS. STORLIE'S SKIRT TO GET HER ATTENTION. I DIDN'T MEAN TO PULL IT OFF."

Partner Helpers.   A hallmark in differentiated classrooms is that all students participate in respectful work and when they can, they help each other. In classrooms that utilize cooperative learning teams, the strategy of team questions also works well—"Ask three, then me." Both these strategies, in particular, support student autonomy, prompt help from team members, and allow the teacher to circulate and monitor student work without feeling bogged down by "helpless handraisers" and overly dependent students.

Continue Working.   While waiting for the teacher to arrive, students needing help should know they are to move ahead to the next problem or exercise. If this is not possible, they should take out a book and read silently until the teacher arrives to help.

INCIDENTALS

Seating

As mentioned in Chapter 3, various seating arrangements have served teachers well—rows, U-shapes, circles, semicircles, and clusters of various kinds. Most elementary teachers today want space flexibility for different kinds of activities. They also use a good deal of cooperative team and group work and want to be able to circulate easily among students. Modular cluster seating, with four to six students per cluster, usually serves these needs well.

It is best to begin the year with the teacher assigning students to seats and making tagboard name tags for each student. Students should not be allowed to select their own seats until they show that they are capable of self-control.

Entering and Exiting the Room

Most teachers still favor lines for entering and exiting the room, and use various procedures to form them. Once the most common procedure was to have boys and girls in separate lines, but now boys and girls line up together in one or two lines. Let your students know how you want them to form lines and give them ample practice in doing so.

Usually lines for entering the room are formed on a first-come basis. For exiting the room, teachers often excuse students according to (1) where the students sit, (2) alphabetical order by first or last name, (3) arbitrarily by work groups, or (4) as a reward for students or teams who have behaved or worked well. For occasional variety, teachers may have students move according to prompts: "Line up if you are wearing something I can see that is red," "if your birthday is in a month that begins with J," and so on.

Pencil Sharpening

Pencil sharpening can be very disruptive to class instruction. Some teachers keep a large container of pencils sharpened by a monitor before the day begins. If lead breaks or wears down, the student simply exchanges the pencil. Thus the pencil sharpener is not used during the day, and no time is lost because of noise, wandering, or waiting.

Other teachers feel that this system does not encourage self-responsibility. They allow students to keep two pencils in their desks and be responsible for sharpening them at appropriate times, such as before school. Whatever procedure you prefer, it is important to teach the routine to the students and then adhere to it.

Out-of-Room Passes

Passes are used when students must leave the room to go to the restroom, an outside drinking fountain, the library, or the office. Teachers should not allow students to leave the room—with or without permission—unless it clearly is necessary, because there always are students who will look for any excuse to leave the room as often as possible.

Some schools provide teachers with laminated passes on which are written the teacher's name and room number. When this is not the case, teachers provide their own. Some teachers simply purchase pre-made passes at a teacher supply store. Others make their own passes from large pieces of wood that students cannot inadvertently misplace. Six passes should be sufficient: one drink pass, one office pass, two library passes, and two for the restroom—one for boys and one for girls. The number of passes should be adjusted according to classroom need, but usually it is not a good idea to allow two or more students to go together to unsupervised areas such as drinking fountains or restrooms. Students in Julia DePew's fourth/fifth multi-age class use passes she created with clip art and then laminated (Figure 7.1). On the first day of school every student in Julia's class receives a laminated pass with his or her name on it. Students are reminded at that time to use the bathroom before school, at recess, and at lunch. Every morning one student distributes the passes to the others. If students need to leave the room, they return their pass to a small basket near the door. However, if they need to leave more than once, they must sign in for a consequence. Students say, "We like that we can leave once a day if we need to." They also say, "We don't like to sign in, so this lets us be responsible."

Noise Control

Some teachers tolerate noise well; others don't. Regardless of teacher tolerance, every class occasionally (sometimes daily) gets noisy to a degree that greatly interferes with teaching and learning. If this happens in your room, you almost certainly will hear complaints from neighboring teachers.

To keep noise within acceptable limits, discuss with your students the negative effects that loud noise has on learning and teaching. Explain that different levels of noise

FIGURE 7.1   An Example of a Pass for the Bathroom or Drinking Fountain

Source: Julia DePew. Reprinted by permission.

are appropriate and allowable for different activities. For example, there should be no talking during silent reading. During discussions, one person at a time can talk in a normal voice. During cooperative work, quiet talking is allowed as needed. For other activities such as drama and singing, more noise is allowable.

You also should use a clear signal for indicating when the noise level is too high. Consider using a color signal system (visual) or a sound such as a bell or wind chime (auditory) whenever the noise level goes above acceptable limits. Another alternative is to play background music. When you can no longer hear the music, the noise level is too high.

OTHER ANNOYANCES

Several other annoyances drive teachers crazy: procrastination, tattling, messiness, tardiness, and irresponsibility. Teachers also find themselves dealing with some behaviors that are more serious: cheating, lying or stealing, language (swearing), temper tantrums, and bullying. Teachers should model the appropriate behaviors continually and should quickly redirect students when signs of these behaviors occur. The following suggestions help bring these problem areas into manageable proportions.

VIGNETTE 7.4 Silent Signals

Kathryn Krainock teaches second grade in an open classroom. Because there are no doors between classes, she developed silent waves, silent claps, and silent cheers so her students don't distract others. Students give silent waves (index finger gently waving) to a parent or administrator who comes into the classroom. They give silent claps (two fingers quietly clapping) and silent cheers (arms quietly moving up and down as though cheering) for fellow students when they give a speech or do other fantastic feats. Kathryn feels these methods would work successfully in any classroom because they take minimal time and don't distract others.

Upon Reflection

Kathryn Krainock describes silent claps, cheers, and waves in her second grade open classroom. How are students likely to respond to these in intermediate or upper grades or in self-contained classrooms?

Procrastination, Tattling, Messiness, Tardiness, and Irresponsibility

Procrastination. Procrastination, the exasperating habit of putting things off until the last minute, afflicts many students. Everyone has difficulty working at unexciting tasks, and most of us cannot maintain enthusiasm when tasks are overly long or complicated. But when students regularly fail to begin work promptly and fool around instead of working, consider remedies such as the following:

- Keep instructional tasks as interesting and as short as possible while covering what is intended.
- Break long tasks into a series of shorter steps, and place a deadline on the completion of each step. Say, See, Do Teaching, for example, involves students quickly and guides them actively through the learning one step at a time.
- Insert timely brain breaks and energizers into your lesson. For example, have students stand and dance in their teams to music. "The Freeze" is a movement energizer that can be done to music by Greg & Steve on their *We All Live Together* CD (1978), or to other songs the children enjoy.
- Emphasize a time limit and remind students as it passes. One idea is to call out the time occasionally. For example, the teacher might say, "Ten minutes. You should be about half finished." A second idea is to use a Teach Timer, a management tool that displays time (either counting up or down) on the overhead projector. Older students can monitor their progress and the time themselves because they can see the time from anywhere in the classroom. Another idea is to use appropriate background music the children are familiar with and have them self-gauge their progress according to the music—"When this music ends, you should be about half finished." (Take a minute to review the discussion in Chapter 3 about using music to enhance the ambience in the classroom.)

- Use incentives. "As soon as you finish your work (keeping in mind the criterion of mastery discussed earlier), you may . . ." (some quiet preferred activity, such as free reading).
- If other remedies do not work, take the student aside and say, "You just are not getting your work done. I know you can do it. I wonder what we can work out so you will complete your assignments."

Tattling.   Tattling can become a virulent disease that affects almost everyone in the class. It is habit forming and causes students to focus on the negative, lose respect for each other, and forever look to an authority to adjudicate minor problems the students should settle or ignore. For teachers, tattling can become a major irritation. Fortunately, tattling can be controlled rather easily.

Barbara Coloroso (2002) stresses the importance of teaching children to think for themselves and to believe that no problem is so great it cannot be solved. To help students develop decision-making skills she continually encourages them by saying "You have a problem; you can solve it. What's your plan?" Of course the children's age and maturity affect how they handle this conversation. When tattling occurs anyway, and if the matter is insignificant, as most are, proceed to the following steps.

- To help children discern the difference between *tattling* and *telling,* teach them this formula from Coloroso (2002): "If it will only get another child in trouble, don't tell me—that's tattling. If it will get you or another child out of trouble, tell me. If it is both, I need to know" (p. 135).
- For older children, have the tattler write out the complaint, together with a constructive suggestion for resolving the problem.
- Ask the tattler to wait until lunch or after school to make the complaint, assuring the student that you will consider it carefully at that time.
- Have the disputants meet together to discuss the matter and come up with an acceptable solution with which they both can agree.
- Have class discussions or class meetings regarding the nature of tattling, its negative effects on cooperation and good feelings, and the desirability of solving one's own minor differences. Indicate that it is all right to inform the teacher when another student seriously violates one's rights by stealing, bullying, or inflicting physical harm. Role-play tattling behaviors and proper alternatives.

Nelsen, Lott, and Glenn (2000) suggest using classroom meetings as opportunities to practice effective problem-solving skills. After discussion and role-play, students are taught to brainstorm ideas for logical consequences and nonpunitive solutions. Then they vote and act on a suggestion they think will be most helpful. After a reasonable trial period, students reevaluate their solution and make any adjustment that might be necessary.

Messiness.   Messiness is a chronic problem for some students and is evidenced in the work students do and the care they give school materials. Messiness annoys teachers and reinforces unattractive habits in students. To deal with messiness, consider the following suggestions:

- Model neatness. Keep your own work area in order and tidy.
- Have class meetings or discussions about pride in oneself, schoolwork, and the classroom. Talk about how pride often relates to neatness.
- Let students know you are keeping their neatest papers to show parents and guardians.
- Establish an incentive system in which a series of neat papers earns a reward such as a certificate, sticker, or preferred activity.
- Encourage students to exchange ideas about organizing their desks for maximum neatness and efficiency.

Tardiness. Tardiness often occurs for legitimate reasons. However, when it is habitual, tardiness can be annoying and disconcerting, causing the student to miss out on important instruction and instilling a general lack of responsibility. When left unchecked the habit often becomes worse. Chronically-late students may blame the caregiver or an unending series of catastrophes, or they may have fallen into the tardiness habit because it is their nature to procrastinate, they have not yet accepted responsibility for their own educational process, or they are finding something very interesting to do on the way to school.

Although one or two students will arrive late every day, the incidence of tardiness, especially for the chronically late, can be reduced through the following measures:

- Have class meetings or discussions about student responsibilities in supporting and participating in the school program. Make sure students understand the need to arrive a few minutes before school begins.
- Make the opening activities attractive, enjoyable, and important so students will want to participate and will feel left out when they do not. Coloroso (1994) believes in sharing information that is "a little nice to know" first thing in the morning. For example, tell students who are present to answer only the even problems on the day's math quiz.
- Show you mean business by establishing consequences for tardiness and by giving rewards for continued punctuality. Let students help decide the consequences and rewards.
- If other measures do not correct the problem, call the parents or guardians and ask for their input and help.

Irresponsibility. Irresponsibility refers to student disinclination to work up to capacity; mistreatment of materials, equipment, and facilities; and failure to live up to ordinary obligations. An important goal of education is to build within each student a sense of responsibility for one's own acts and for the common good. Responsibility is shown when obligations are fulfilled promptly and correctly with concern for others. To help instill this sense in students who are not otherwise inclined, consider the following:

- Periodically discuss with students what responsibility means and how it contributes to the good of everyone. Also discuss what students should do in the classroom to show they are being responsible.
- Assign specific responsibilities to all class members for helping manage the classroom, as with monitors.

- Assign specific responsibilities to students when they work in cooperative teams. For example, as a team member a student might act as leader, encourager, questioner, researcher, reporter, artist, summarizer, materials collector, or time manager.
- Have students evaluate their own behavior on several points, such as being punctual, completing work, doing their best, taking care of assigned duties, and helping others when necessary. Have them fill out contracts for future improvement, and reward them appropriately when they live up to their promises.

Cheating, Lying or Stealing, Swearing, Temper Tantrums, and Bullying

Sometimes students cheat, lie or steal, swear, or have temper tantrums. Even in the best-run classrooms teachers may not be able to prevent these events. However, some general practices are appropriate:

- Continually model and give opportunities for students to practice honesty, appropriate language, and anger management.
- Have class meetings or discussions about student responsibilities in modeling and supporting appropriate behaviors. Have students role-play behaviors and responses to these situations.
- To the extent possible, plan ahead to prevent the problems.
- Focus on solutions rather than punishment, blame, or shame.
- As you handle the situation, do all you can to keep everyone's dignity intact.

Cheating.   Students cheat on tests for a variety of reasons. Some want to do well and get good grades. Some are afraid of punishment. Some don't want to disappoint their caregivers or their teacher, or they fear they won't have personal value if they don't do well. Others are motivated by rewards. To help students avoid the temptation to cheat:

- Give open-book rather than tests that require memorization of facts, although you can have students quiz each other when they are ready on subjects that require memorization, such as the multiplication tables.
- Distribute test questions in advance so students know what to study.
- Have students brainstorm on ways to solve cheating problems.
- Rather than trying to trick a confession, speak directly to any student involved in cheating by naming the observed behavior ("I noticed you cheated on the math test this morning."). Then invite the student to work with you on a solution so he or she can succeed without cheating.

Lying or Stealing.   Young children may lie or steal because this is part of their normal development. They are learning the difference between what is real and unreal, right and wrong, and they are moving from an egocentric perspective to a broader view of the world. Some have not developed the interest or skills that would prevent them from lying or stealing. Sometimes children lie or steal because they feel hurt—they don't feel they get enough attention and want something from you or others; they don't have friends and try to fill the void by lying or stealing things; or they may feel materially or financially deprived. Some lie or steal because these are actions they observe in adults. Teachers can help students in several ways:

- Model honesty and share openly with the class how it makes you feel when someone lies to you or steals something from you.
- Give the student a chance to correct the untruth or return what was stolen by saying, "We aren't interested in blame or punishment; we just want the truth, or the item returned. We trust this will be done before school ends today."
- Ask what and how questions ("What happened?" "How do you feel about it?" "What did you learn from this?" "How can you use what you learned in the future?" or "What can you do to avoid the problem in the future?") rather than set up questions ("Are you lying to me?" or "Did you steal this?")
- Have the student who told the lie or stole something figure out a way to make restitution that is respectful to everyone. Younger children may need more help: "Would you like to put this where it belongs, or would you like me to?"

"We weren't cheating. I'm Bob's fact checker."

Language—Swearing.   Actually, it is typical that four- and five-year-olds use this type of language when they are discovering and practicing a new-found skill, their ability to startle the adults around them. When adults deal with inappropriate language matter-of-factly and respond calmly, the language tends to disappear in a short time. Older students may continue to use inappropriate language because they still continue to feel rewarded by attention from startled adults, they want to gain status among their peers, or they hear the language elsewhere and really do not know appropriate alternatives. Consider these suggestions:

- Avoid expressing anger or dismay. Rather, simply state that such language is inappropriate, and let students know how this makes you feel: "I feel uncomfortable when you swear, and I would appreciate it if you would choose another word to say what you mean."
- Ask questions to help students discern inappropriate language and consequences: "How does your grandmother feel about swearing?" "What do referees and umpires do when people swear?"
- Young children need guidelines for their behavior. Be firm but kind: "We do not use those words at school." Then walk the child away from the group, but invite him or her to return when he or she will use acceptable words.
- Have children brainstorm acceptable alternatives to swear words.

Temper Tantrums.   Tantrums may have a purpose. A child may want the teacher's attention or the opposite, to get the teacher to leave him or her alone. The child may want to hurt somebody or simply may want to have his or her own way. In some instances the child may not know appropriate ways to communicate his or her needs. Sometimes tantrums are triggered when a child is on cognitive or emotional overload. Read about neurological based behavior and some appropriate management strategies and responses in Chapter 8. Briefly, to help avoid tantrums and soothe students:

- Be there, offer quiet comfort, and speak reassuring words: "It's OK to be upset. It happens to everyone."
- Help the child identify ways to recognize the signs and find alternative ways to communicate: "We need to find a way for you to let me know how you are feeling without hurting yourself or others."
- Always pay attention to the safety of the child and others in the room, including yourself.

Bullying.   Sadly, bullying is a regular occurrence at school, as we discussed in Chapter 4. Bullies are individuals who instill fear in others through physical, verbal, emotional, or sexual bullying, who intend to hurt, and who enjoy it. Elementary-aged bullies may use verbal or physical bullying, or they may ignore or exclude their victims with relational bullying. Bystanders and peers of victims often suffer effects from bullying, along with the victim. Bystanders may appear to follow or support bullies, or do nothing to stop the action, for several reasons: They may feel guilty or helpless because they didn't stand up to the bully. They fear associating with the victim because they are afraid of retribution from the bully. They may not report incidents for fear of being seen as an "informer" or "snitch." Or, they may feel unsafe, with loss of control and inability to take action. Teachers should approach bullying by doing the following.

"I FINALLY TOOK CARE OF THE SCHOOL BULLY. I ASKED HER TO GO STEADY."

- Continually infuse expectations for good character into the way you teach, and model and provide practice for appropriate behavior and acceptance.
- Hold class meetings or discussions, and conduct role-plays and other activities to reduce bullying. For example, create, teach, and practice an action plan to ensure that students know what to do when they observe a bully/victim episode.

- When bullying occurs, gather information directly from students. Do this anonymously and with sensitivity to the students' safety and needs. Follow or establish procedures to investigate reports of bullying, and keep careful documentation. Additionally, listen to family members who report bullying.
- Ask the children what they need from adults to feel safe. Show genuine support and concern for students, and establish "friendship groups."
- Establish, publicize, and follow clear school and classroom rules and consequences for bullying.
- Provide adequate supervision, particularly in common areas such as the playground and lunchroom.
- Inform parents or guardians and try to involve them in solutions of the problem.

This concludes our consideration of the management of students at work and directs us to an examination of how to manage the special needs of students in today's classrooms, the topic of Chapter 8. Before moving ahead, take time to explore these end-of-chapter activities.

Parting Thought

Never, never, never, never give up.

—Winston Churchill

SUMMARY SELF-CHECK

Check off the following as you either understand or become able to apply them.

❏ Good management of students at work contributes greatly to time availability, class control, rapid learning, sense of responsibility, and sense of security.

❏ Routine management calls for attention to
- Work routines
- Opening activities: attendance; sharing; silent reading; journal writing; choosing; five-a-days; clear, succinct instructions for doing work
- Signals for attention
- Movement in the room (traffic patterns, permission)
- Materials: storage and distribution, use and care, replacement, small and large materials
- Completed work: what to do with students' completed assignments
- Student accountability and criterion of mastery
- Homework: its value and purpose
- End-of-day closing: a rich instruction time

❏ Providing assistance
- Monitors: responsibility for everyone
- Helpful directions and feedback: clear directions; visual instructional plans and posted reminders; rapid, effective assistance
- Partner and team help

❑ Incidentals: seating (matched to program); entering and exiting the room; pencil sharpening; out-of-room passes; attention signals; noise control

❑ Other annoyances: procrastination; tattling, messiness, tardiness, irresponsibility; cheating, lying or stealing, language (swearing), temper tantrums; and bullying

ACTIVITIES FOR REFLECTION AND DISCUSSION

1. Take a moment to review the statements in the Prediction–Review Guide at the beginning of this chapter. Put a check mark in the Review column next to any statement with which you now agree. How have your thoughts changed since reading this chapter?

2. Interview at least two teachers about what they do to plan and manage their students at work. Ask them to describe what they do specifically to handle entering and exiting the room and passes, noise levels for various activities, and bullying, as well as some of the other annoyances that occur in their classes.

3. Individually or in teams, describe what you would do to control at least two of the following: tattling, procrastination, messiness, irresponsibility, cheating, lying or stealing, swearing, temper tantrums, or bullying.

4. Think about the schedule of a normal school day. (Refer back to Chapter 2 if necessary.) Decide on the level of noise that you would consider acceptable for the various activities. How would you discuss the topic of noise with the students? What kinds of signaling devices, if any, would you use as reminders? How would you handle this if your students were in another grade (primary, intermediate, upper)?

5. For a grade level you select, decide what classroom monitor duties you want students to fill. How would you make the assignments? How would you instruct monitors concerning their duties and responsibilities? What would you do if a monitor proved to be irresponsible? Likewise, how would you handle monitors if your students were in another grade (primary, intermediate, upper)?

6. Make a list of the various work products that students regularly complete—tests, practice papers, compositions, artwork, and so on. What would you want your students to do with their completed work? Describe how you will communicate and carry out this process.

7. Custom design a ten- to fifteen-minute closing routine (not clean up) that you consider most beneficial to your students and program. What variations might you make during the week? (Some districts provide one shorter day, or *minimum* day, each week to give teachers planning time without students. How would that routine vary from the regular days? Between Monday's routine and Friday's?) What variations might you make from month to month? Also, what variations would you make if your students were at another grade level (primary, intermediate, upper)?

REFERENCES AND RECOMMENDED READINGS

Charles, C. (2008). *Building classroom discipline* (9th ed.). Boston: Allyn & Bacon.

Coloroso, B. (1994). *Kids are worth it! Giving your child the gift of inner discipline.* New York: Avon Books.

Coloroso, B. (2002). *The bully, the bullied, and the bystander.* Toronto, Ontario, Canada: HarperCollins.

Freiberg, H. (1996, September). From tourists to citizens in the classroom. *Education Leadership, 54*(1), 32–36.

Gardner, H. (1991). *The unschooled mind: How children think and how schools should teach.* New York: Basic Books.

Gardner, H. (1993a). *Frames of mind* (10th ed.). New York: Basic Books.

Gardner, H. (1993b). *Multiple intelligences: The theory in practice.* New York: Basic Books.

Jones, F. (2007). *Tools for teaching: Discipline Instruction Motivation* (2nd ed.). Santa Cruz, CA: Fredric H. Jones.

Kagan, S., & Kagan, M. (1998). *Multiple intelligences: The complete MI book.* San Clemente, CA: Kagan Cooperative Learning.

Nelsen, J., Lott, L., & Glenn, H. (2000). *Positive discipline in the classroom.* Rocklin, CA: Prima Publishing.

Olweus, D. (1999). *Core program against bullying and antisocial behavior: A teacher handbook.* Bergen, Norway: Research Center for Health Promotion, University of Bergen.

Schwartz, F. (1981). Supporting or subverting learning: Peer group patterns in four tracked schools. *Anthropology and Education Quarterly, 12*(2), 99–120.

Compact Disk

Scelsa, G., & Millang, S. (1978). *We all live together* (Vol. 2). [CD] Los Angeles: Little House Music.

Managing Special Groups

There is only one child in the world and that child's name is ALL children.

—Carl Sandburg

Prediction–Review Guide

Before you read the chapter, take a minute to put a check mark in the Prediction column next to any statement with which you agree.

	Prediction	Review
1. Fully inclusive education is a fairly new concept, with little history or legal support.	❑	❑
2. Assistive technology refers to tools that enhance the functioning of people with special disabilities.	❑	❑
3. Exceptionality is the term used to identify children who are especially bright, gifted, or talented.	❑	❑
4. Attention deficit disorder (ADD) and attention deficit hyperactivity disorder (ADHD) are best treated with medication because the child is likely to outgrow the order.	❑	❑
5. The term neurological based behavior (NBB) refers to behavior that is outside the student's control and related to the way the brain works.	❑	❑
6. Children who are emotionally disturbed understand the signs and triggers for their outbursts and can learn to control them.	❑	❑
7. Language diversity describes the presence of more than one language in a student's home and has little to do with ethnicity and race.	❑	❑
8. Children of separated or divorced parents are likely to take sides with one parent rather than grieve their loss.	❑	❑
9. Children without permanent housing are more likely to attend school in order to receive the adjunct services such as the free lunch program.	❑	❑
10. Differentiated instruction contributes little toward managing diversity among students.	❑	❑

Support for specific standards found in this chapter:

INTASC Standards

1. Knowledge of Subject Matter

   The teacher understands the central concepts, tools of inquiry, and structures of the subject being taught and can create learning experiences that make these aspects of subject matter meaningful for students.

2. Knowledge of Human Development and Learning

   The teacher understands how children learn and develop and can provide learning opportunities that support their intellectual, social, and personal development.

3. Adapting Instruction for Individual Needs

   The teacher understands how students differ in their approaches to learning and creates instructional opportunities that are adapted to diverse learners.

4. Multiple Instructional Strategies

   The teacher uses various instructional strategies to encourage students' development of critical thinking, problem solving, and performance skills.

Danielson's Framework for Teaching

3. Instruction

   - Communicating clearly and accurately
   - Using questioning and discussion techniques
   - Engaging students in learning
   - Providing feedback to students
   - Demonstrating flexibility and responsiveness

NBPTS Standards

1. Teachers are committed to students and their learning.
3. Teachers are responsible for managing and monitoring student learning.

NCATE Standards

Help all pre-kindergarten through twelfth grade (P–12) students learn.

Apply effective methods of teaching students who are at different developmental stages, have different learning styles, and come from diverse backgrounds.

Children come to school in the United States from diverse cultures and family structures, some speaking languages other than English, some with physical challenges or other special needs, and some with behavior disorders. This is the reality of today's schools. The charge of educators is to provide the best education possible while meeting the needs of *all* children.

As you continue reading, it is important to remember that the students we describe are real persons who have real challenges in life. Consequently, all references are made using person-first language, such as, "students with visual impairments" rather than "blind students."

THE LEGISLATION OF INCLUSION

The United States has long held that all children have the right to a free public education. However, the debate continues as to the best educational approach to meet the diverse needs of all students.

Following the 1954 Supreme Court ruling in *Brown v. Board of Education* and numerous related court cases, schools were opened equally to students of all races and ethnic groups. Subsequently, other federal laws were passed regarding the schooling of non-English speaking children. Included among these are the Supreme Court ruling in *Lau v. Nichols* (1974), Title VI of the Civil Rights Act of 1964, and the Bilingual Education Act of 1974, amended in 1988. As a result of these laws, students with varied languages, skin colors, facial features, heritages, values, and ceremonies now are able to come together for their formal education.

In 1975 Congress passed the Education for All Handicapped Children Act, PL 94-142. The law provided for inclusion of all students in "the least restrictive environment," "to the maximum extent appropriate," and "with the use of supplementary aids and services." One amendment to the law was the Education of All Handicapped Children Act Amendments of 1986 (PL 99-457). Known as "The Preschool Law," this amendment expanded the services to infants and young children who have disabilities or who are at risk in their families. The original law and its amendments merged into the Individuals with Disabilities Education Act (IDEA) in 1990 and the Reauthorization of IDEA of 1997.

The No Child Left Behind Act of 2001 was not written specifically for students with disabilities, but it has several important implications for students and special education. The law requires state testing in grades 3 through 8 in reading and math. It requires accountability for all students' learning, with adequate yearly incremental progress (AYP) toward the goal of 100 percent proficiency in reading, math, and science for all students within twelve years. States and schools that fail to meet the AYP could face corrective measures, including staff replacements, implementation of different curricula, conversion to a charter school, or a state takeover by a hired private management contractor. States and schools that fail to meet the required participation rate in the testing could be considered out of compliance and subject to sanctions. And finally, all teachers must hold full state certification or licensure by 2005, a challenge considering the current teacher shortages in special education.

In recent years, children with special needs have been recognized, supported, and included in regular classrooms (to the extent their abilities allow) for a maximum portion of their day. Thus, children with special physical and intellectual needs are able to join a teaching and learning community where everyone's individual needs are met.

Disabilities that Qualify Children and Youth for Special Education Services

As defined by IDEA, children are considered to have disabilities if they have any or a combination of the following thirteen conditions:

1. Autism, affecting verbal and nonverbal communication and social interaction
2. Deafness

3. Deafness-blindness
4. Emotional disturbance (SED), including schizophrenia
5. Hearing impairment (DHH)
6. Mental retardation (MR), significantly below-average general intellectual functioning, together with inadequate adaptive behavior
7. Multiple disabilities, simultaneous impairments such as mental retardation and blindness
8. Orthopedic impairment (OI)
9. Other health impairment (OHI), chronic or acute health problems, such as a heart condition, asthma, or diabetes, that limit strength, vitality, or alertness
10. Specific learning disability (SLD), visual and auditory processing difficulties including dyslexia and Central Auditory Processing Disorder (CAPD)

MANAGING THE CHALLENGES OF DIVERSITY

CASE STUDY 8.1

Focus Questions

Where does the teacher begin? How can this teacher learn more about her students and their special needs? What support services are available for her and her students, and what is the process to access them?

Mrs. Sanderson was hired to teach a multi-age fourth and fifth grade class. She was one of five teachers in this team. She began her year with twenty-two students in her class but soon added three more. She quickly found that her students had a wide range of ethnic, cultural, and language backgrounds, as well as differing academic and skill abilities.

In addition to Caucasian, ethnic and cultural diversity included students (or their families) from Germany, Japan, Korea, Mexico, Puerto Rico, and South Africa. The six students who were identified as English learners possessed a range of language ability: two had minimal (Pre-production) English-language ability; two were identified as having Early production proficiency; and two were fairly fluent, with Intermediate Fluency. Three of these students lived in homes where family members predominantly spoke a language other than English.

The children ranged in age from a young ten-year-old to a thirteen-year-old boy who had been retained in first grade. Four students were identified as gifted and talented (GATE). Most of the students read at grade level, although four read below and two read at the tenth-grade level.

Several students had identified disabilities. One of the girls was deaf. She had a service dog with her every day, and although she signed and could read lips, a paraprofessional was with her in the mornings. One boy was autistic and worked with the resource specialist three mornings a week. A third child was diabetic, and a fourth had severe asthma. Finally, two children were on behavior contracts.

Eight students lived in divorced or blended families, and another lived with her grandmother. The family of one student was homeless and had been staying in a nearby shelter for the past month.

11. Speech or language impairment (SLI)
12. Traumatic brain injury (TBI), caused by external physical force rather than congenital or degenerative injuries
13. Visual impairment (VI), including blindness

An "established medical disability" also can be a qualifier for special education services. This is defined as a disabling medical condition or congenital syndrome that the individual education program (IEP) team determines has a high predictability of requiring special education and services (California Education Code Section 46441.11(d)).

You can visit the following websites for additional information about IDEA and the qualifying conditions: www.pai-ca.org/pubs/505101.htm, www.cec.sped.org, and www.ed.gov/offices/OSERS/IDEA.

THE CONCEPT OF INCLUSION

Inclusion refers to involving all students in the educational setting that best meets their needs, regardless of background, creed, or level of ability. The intended educational setting is the public school classroom. But inclusion has a broader meaning as well. It refers to a way of life, an attitude, a value, a belief system that holds that all children are entitled to the best education we can provide, *and* that an association of diverse students provides benefits for all. Schools and teachers who embrace the attitude of inclusion show it by their words, decisions, and actions. They strive to make all children feel welcomed and secure. They support the unique gifts and the needs of every child in their school and classroom communities. Their sincere goal is for every child to become successful.

EXCEPTIONALITY

Among the students who present some of the special challenges for teachers are (1) students whose work is academically below or above grade level, (2) students with communication, sensory, physical, behavioral, or emotional challenges, (3) students with limited English proficiency, and (4) students whose family and life experiences lend themselves to potential problems. Ysseldyke & Algozzine (1995) identified twenty-seven different categories relating to exceptional students, those formerly labeled as learning-disabled. Kirk, Gallagher, Anastasiow, and Coleman (2006) consolidated the range of exceptional students that may be in a classroom into six broad groupings:

1. *Intellectual differences* include students who have superior intelligence (such as giftedness) and students who are slow to learn (such as mental retardation).
2. *Communicative differences* include students with communication, speech, or language disorders.
3. *Sensory differences* include students with auditory or visual limitations.
4. *Behavioral differences* include students who are emotionally disturbed or socially maladjusted.

5. *Physical differences* include students with orthopedic or mobility disabilities.
6. *Multiple and severe handicapping conditions* include children who have a combination of conditions (such as cerebral palsy and blindness).

The U.S. Department of Education National Center for Education Statistics (2006b) reported a gradual increase of about 14 percent in 2003–2004 in the number of children being served in programs for the disabled. This increase probably resulted in part from the Education for All Handicapped Children Act Amendments of 1986 that mandated public school special education services for all handicapped children aged three to five. Other reasons for the rise in use of services might be the increased number of children identified as having speech, language, or other impairments and the increased enrollment of children with autism and traumatic brain injuries.

Students of Lower Ability

Some children have achievement rates in certain academic areas that are lower than their general ability levels would indicate. They are apt to be disorganized, forgetful, and frustrated, and they tend toward anger, hopelessness, or low self-concept. To support these students, teachers should do the following:

- Differentiate content, process, or product to best meet student need and ability
- Follow predictable routines and structures
- Model acceptable and appropriate actions
- Signal important information and assistance clues
- Provide ample practice for smaller portions of information
- Have students repeat directions aloud
- Limit confusing trial-and-error activities
- Emphasize students' achievements rather than their mistakes
- Have students keep records of their own work and behavior

Several assistive tools are available for teachers of children with lower abilities. Teachers may use audio books, talking computers, captioned films and videos, and semantic mapping software to help students with their reading. Teachers may have students use word-processing programs with spelling and grammar checks to help them with their writing. Manipulatives and calculators can help students with math and problem solving. Personal organizers, electronic calendars, and a variety of organizing software programs are available to help students with their organization. Finally, the Internet and computer-based instructional programs can help students with their studying and learning.

Students of Higher Ability

Students of higher ability, sometimes referred to as gifted and talented (GATE), are those who significantly surpass the identified norms in achievement. The Gifted and Talented Students Act of 1978 defines gifted and talented students as ". . . possessing demonstrated or potential abilities that give evidence of high performance capability in areas such as intellectual, creative, specific academics, or leadership abilities, or in the performing and visual arts, and who by reason thereof require services or activities not ordinarily provided by the school" (p. 8). The act further distinguishes *gifted* as referring to above-average intellectual ability, and *talented* as referring to excellence in drama, art, music, athletics, or leadership and states that students can have these abilities separately or in combination.

These children require differentiated educational programs and services beyond those normally provided by the regular school. They can be high achievers who are self-starting, persistent, able to work independently, and resourceful. They have direction in their personal learning goals and need minimal guidance to proceed. For these students, management relates to strong articulation of personal goals, of plans to accomplish them, and of tools to assess their progress.

Other students with higher ability, however, may appear more difficult to manage. They are likely to be divergent thinkers who approach situations and problems with perspectives different from those of other students. Teachers often view divergent thinkers either as very creative individuals or as noncompliant students with behavior problems.

Students with higher abilities, both the self-starters and the creative, divergent thinkers, benefit most from open-ended activities. Such assignments allow students to adapt an assignment, a situation, or a problem to match their own uniqueness, ability, and interest. This can be highly motivating for both quality work and behavior. Guided conversations and jointly designed scoring rubrics that clearly set expectations and standards help teachers and students manage a nontraditional approach to curriculum and demonstrations of understanding.

Though these students have the potential to contribute to everyone's learning, they should not be made team teachers for lessons or be kept occupied with busy work. In other words, students who are high achievers should be given *other*, not *more*, and it is especially important that students with higher ability feel valued and appreciated. Additional ideas for students who are higher achievers might include bonus activities, questions, and projects that are motivational, challenging, and meaningful. A helpful resource is www.nagc.org.

Students with Communication, Speech, or Language Disorders

"A person has a communication problem when that person's speech differs from the speech of others to the extent that it calls attention to itself, interferes with the intended message, or causes the speaker or listener to be distressed" (Van Ripper, 1978). Speech impairment is defined under PL 94-142 as "a communication disorder, such as stuttering, impaired articulation, a language impairment, or a voice impairment, which adversely affects a child's educational performance" (*Federal Register,* 1977, p. 42479).

Cartwright, Cartwright, and Ward (1984) distinguish speech (expressive) from language (receptive) disorders: "Speech problems are those associated with the production of the oral symbols of language, whereas language problems are difficulties with the linguistic code or rules and conventions for linking the symbols and symbol sequences" (p. 115).

Many children with speech (expressive) and language (receptive) disorders receive individual help outside the classroom. Sometime during the day, or several times during the week, a speech therapist provides additional assistance to individuals or small groups of students with the same speech or language disorder.

Within the classroom, potential negative consequences of speech and language disorders may affect the child's self-concept and interpersonal relations with peers. To prevent these negative consequences from occurring, teachers should do the following:

- Model acceptance for all children
- Model appropriate language (words, expressions, sounds) at all times
- Encourage all children to talk about activities they participate in outside of school
- Have a secret signal so the student knows you will call on him or her to respond next
- Give children many opportunities to speak without interruption or pressure
- Ask open-ended questions and wait for responses
- Listen attentively to what children have to say
- Plan and deliver instruction so students can rejoin the class easily when they return from their time with the resource teacher

Assistive technology provides a variety of alternative and augmentative communication (AAC) devices for students with communication disorders. AAC devices can be made for individual students and are intended to supplement oral and written language production. They can be electronic or nonelectronic, simple or complex. Communication boards are fairly low tech. High-tech equipment such as speech synthesizers and speech talkers allow individuals with communication disorders to "talk." Machines that create speech and language use icon systems that are accessed by touch or switches. Now with technological advances, AAC devices are smaller (some can be worn on the wrist), more capable, and more affordable.

Students with Hearing Impairments

Hearing impairments fall into two categories—being deaf or having partial hearing (or being hard of hearing). Mild hearing loss may go unnoticed. However, once it is detected, children with hearing impairments usually function well in the classroom, provided certain accommodations are made. For example, some may require a paraprofessional to assist them during the day. Arrangements must be made to accommodate the paraprofessional. Others may use a hearing ear dog as helper. It is crucial that the other children understand the dog is there to work, not to play. It may help to have the owner introduce the dog to the class and share about how they work together. To best help students with hearing impairment, the teacher should

- Ask the student or caregiver what can be done to help him or her. Teachers should not assume that their ideas of help are what the student needs or wants.
- Use adaptive devices such as microphones and receivers, as available.
- Seat the student near the front and center of the room and close to the primary instructional area.

- Always face the student when speaking, particularly when giving important information or instruction, so the student can see your face and read your lips.
- If possible, meet and plan with the paraprofessional, or provide written instructions for his or her reference.
- Use the overhead projector rather than the white- or chalkboard so you face forward as you talk, and provide the student and service provider with a copy of the transparency text.
- Learn and use basic sign language during instruction.
- Consider the lighting in the room and the location of windows and doorways in relation to you as you talk.
- Encourage all students to ask questions.
- Repeat and rephrase instructions, information, questions, and discussion comments made by other students.
- To the extent possible, minimize noise—particularly auditory and visual distracters—both in and outside the classroom.
- Partner the student with someone who will take good, legible notes to share.
- Partner the student with someone who will provide cues about instruction and when to watch the teacher, and who will help in emergency situations.
- Use vigilance in watching and listening to children for signs of behavior, appearance, and complaints that might signal possible hearing impairment.

Assistive technologies for students who are deaf or hard of hearing allow them to experience instruction with amplification or through their other senses. Assistive learning devices (ALDs) include hearing aids, cochlear implants, and a variety of FM (frequency-modulated) transmission devices. With FM technology, the speaker uses a microphone that transmits directly to the student's receiver. This helps overcome the distance and noise problems of classrooms, including background noise that can interfere with appropriate hearing and the hearing of subtle language sounds. Speech-to-print systems, including the teletypewriter-printer device (TTY or TT), telecommunication devices (TDD), and captioning on broadcast and media presentations are other available tools.

Students with Visual Impairments

Students with visual impairments usually function quite well with the use of supplementary aids and services. For example, they may use a cane or a guide dog, use a braille machine, or have a paraprofessional who works with them throughout the day. As with the hearing ear dog, the other children must understand that the guide dog is there to work, not play. If a braille machine is used, arrangements will need to be made in the classroom so it can be placed where it is accessible to the child and not distracting to classmates. IntelliKeys is a newer alternative that enables children with visual (or physical or cognitive) disabilities to access curriculum. The system has a programmable alternative keyboard, a touch pad, braille overlay, and a variety of software applications so children can type, enter numbers, navigate on-screen displays, and execute menu commands with ease. Again, the other children must understand the purpose of the machine. Likewise, arrangements must be made to accommodate the paraprofessional who accompanies the child to class. To best help students with visual impairment, the teacher should

- Ask the student or caregiver what can be done to help him or her. Teachers should not assume that their ideas are what the student needs or wants.
- Seat the student as close to the main instructional area as possible.
- Provide the student with clear oral instructions. If possible, meet and plan with the paraprofessional or provide written instructions for his or her reference.
- Modify lessons to include numerous auditory and tactile experiences.
- Partner the student with others who are able to verbalize or model expectations and procedures, and who will help in emergency situations.
- Use vigilance in watching and listening to children for signs of behavior, appearance, and complaints that might signal possible visual impairment.

Assistive technologies for students who are blind or visually impaired allow them to experience instruction by means of enlarged print or through other senses. Closed-circuit television (CCTV) displays enlarged print on a television monitor. The Magni-Cam, a camera embedded in a mouse-like tool that can be rolled over printed pages, also enlarges print. When it is connected to a computer, the computer screen displays the magnified image. Computer word-processing features allow changes to print style and fonts, and copy machines allow for adjustments to printing size. Some braille machines are more compact, portable, and convenient than before. The Kurzweil 3000, the newest available model, is a personal computer and desktop reading software that turns print into speech. Audio books may be available on request. Finally, bar magnifiers and writing guide sets are relatively inexpensive visual aid tools.

Students with Behavior Disorders

Behavior disorder is a general category in special education for students who exhibit serious and persistent inappropriate behaviors that result in social conflict and personal unhappiness and affect school performance. The term implies that the child is causing trouble for someone else. Sometimes behaviors are described as excesses and deficits. *Excess behaviors* are the more blatant behaviors, such as tantrums and frequent fighting that quickly attract teachers' attention. However, students with *deficit behaviors* (shy or withdrawn students who have few friends or who seldom participate in class) also need attention.

Current research into the brain and how it relates to learning has recognized students who behave as they do because of the way their brains function. Their overall behavior, which is outside the control of the individual, is referred to as *neurological based behavior* (NBB). It appears that NBB results from chemical imbalances, congenital brain differences, brain injuries, or brain diseases that in turn impair normal brain functioning. Two major characteristics of NBB are inconsistency and unpredictability (Kranowitz, 1998). Some students have difficulties in processing information, and their resultant behavior is inappropriate. Students who are diagnosed with NBB or other "mental health issues" usually show high degrees of inattention, hyperactivity, impulsivity, excess emotionality, anxiety, inconsistent emotional responses, unpredictable intense mood swings, withdrawal, and episodes of rage (Kranowitz, 1998; Greene, 2001; Papolos and Papolos, 2002; Hall and Hall, 2003; Cook, 2004a).

It's important to realize that numerous books and journal articles have been written about NBB and mental health disorders. For the purpose of elementary classroom management, fairly succinct discussions follow here and continue in Chapter 9.

Students Who Have Attention Deficit Disorder and Hyperactivity Disorder.   Volumes have been written about attention deficit disorder and attention deficit hyperactivity disorder (ADD and ADHD)—what they are, how to recognize the conditions, and how to treat the problems—and it almost seems that the more we learn about the disorders, the more remains to be learned. Caregivers and teachers say they readily can spot the symptoms. In primary grades, children with ADD have short attention spans or are easily distracted. In the intermediate grades, the children daydream or have difficulty staying focused on work.

Students with attention deficit hyperactivity disorder generally have difficulties with attention, hyperactivity, impulse control, emotional stability, or some combination of these. Children who are hyperactive show excessive, almost constant movement. They jiggle and wiggle and squirm and fuss, blurt out comments and answers, and generally bother the teacher and other students with their noises and movements. Based on their criteria for classification of ADHD, in 2002 the American Psychiatric Association (APA) published statistics showing that approximately 3 to 7 percent of all school-age children may have attention deficit hyperactivity disorder (ADHD) (Root & Resnick, 2003). Figure 8.1 lists criteria identified by the *Diagnostic and Statistical Manual of Mental Disorders (DSM-IV)* for ADHD.

Although attentional distractibility and behavioral hyperactivity often go together, their exact relationship fluctuates. During the 1970s, evidence emerged to suggest that distractibility was the key to the hyperactivity syndrome. However, more recent research suggests that this view overemphasizes the role of attention deficits in leading to hyperactivity problems and that hyperactivity is linked more closely to oppositional and aggressive conduct disorders (Good & Brophy, 2002). Here are three important things to remember: (1) ADD can be diagnosed without hyperactivity but one does not have hyperactivity without ADD, and (2) for the most part these behaviors are not deliberate, and (3) it takes a long time for these children to learn ways to compensate for or control them.

The following are some things you can do to help children who have ADD or ADHD or who show some of the symptoms:

- Differentiate content, process, or product to best meet student needs and ability.
- Be sure you have everyone's attention when giving oral instructions. Make instructions brief and clear and when possible, teach them one step at a time (Say, See, Do Teaching).
- When preparing for a transition, use clear directions and cues (such as a five-minute warning before a transition).
- Have students repeat instructions back to make sure they understand.
- Use visuals in conjunction with oral instructions.
- Carefully monitor work, especially as students begin a new activity or step.
- Adjust work time to match attention spans and provide breaks.
- Insert timely energizers and brain breaks into longer lessons and activities.

Inattention

a. Often fails to pay attention to details or makes careless mistakes in schoolwork, work, or other activities
b. Often has difficulty sustaining attention in tasks or play activities
c. Often does not seem to listen when spoken to directly
d. Often does not follow through on instructions and fails to finish schoolwork, chores, or duties in the workplace (not due to oppositional behavior)
e. Often has difficulty organizing tasks and activities
f. Often avoids, dislikes, or is reluctant to engage in tasks that require sustained mental effort
g. Often loses things necessary for tasks and activities
h. Is often easily distracted by extraneous stimuli
i. Is often forgetful in daily activities

Hyperactivity

a. Often fidgets with hands or feet or squirms in seat
b. Often leaves seat in classroom or in other situations in which remaining seated is expected
c. Often runs about or climbs excessively in situations in which it is inappropriate
d. Often has difficulty playing or engaging in leisure activities quietly
e. Often on the go or acts as if driven by a motor
f. Often talks excessively

Impulsivity

a. Often blurts out answers before questions have been completed
b. Often has difficulty waiting turn
c. Often interrupts or intrudes on others

FIGURE 8.1 *DSM-IV* **Diagnostic Criteria for ADHD**

Source: Reprinted with permission from the *Diagnostic and Statistical Manual of Mental Disorders*, Fourth Edition, TR. American Psychiatric Association.

- Establish and use a secret signal to remind the student when he or she is off task.
- Remind students that accuracy, not speed, is important by encouraging a criterion of mastery (refer back to the previous chapter).
- When students work with printed materials, let them use cards with a cut-out area to frame their attention and cover irrelevant information.
- Allow students to use their fingers as pointers to avoid skipping words or lines.
- Plan for students to move around every few minutes.

- Have a study carrel or area in the room that is free from distractions, and give students the option to go there when they need to.
- Teach relaxation techniques for longer work periods or tests. These might include deep breathing and muscle stretches while sitting.
- If medication is prescribed, monitor and cue students' trips to the nurse as needed.

Students Who Are Emotionally Disturbed

Generally speaking, children who are emotionally disturbed differ from others in the degree of emotionality they exhibit. To better inform yourself about these students, you should read their school histories, if available, and consult with the school psychologist, administrators, and other teachers who are involved with the student, taking note of any recommendations. Children who are emotionally disturbed are easily frustrated and are prone to outbursts of temper. They need your patience and help learning to manage their self-control. Here are some suggestions:

- Differentiate content, process, or product to best meet student needs and ability.
- Learn to recognize clues in behavior that may signal outbursts in order to anticipate a student's loss of control.
- Overlook minor inappropriate behavior, reinforce acceptable behavior, and reduce stressors. (This even means temporarily adjusting expectations if the student is having a bad day.)
- Provide a supportive, predictable, and safe environment.
- Provide a safe and supervised area for the student to cool down.
- Ensure the safety of others, and support their understanding of the occurrence.
- Give the student structured choices whenever it is possible to do so. ("Are you able to concentrate on this work at your desk right now, or would you rather move to the study carrel?")
- Develop an action plan with the principal, counselor, and others for when the student has a tantrum or outburst.
- Avoid dwelling on past outbursts and incidents. Often the student does not understand an outburst and is unable to have meaningful conversations about it. Rather, try to help the student learn from the current incident to prevent future outbursts.

Computers have been found to be especially helpful assistive tools for children with emotional or behavioral disorders. Computers are emotionally neutral systems with which children can interact and engage actively in learning, have fun, and achieve success. Answers in computer-assisted instruction are simply right or wrong. In other words, computers provide safe environments in which children are not judged or criticized.

Students with Physical and Health Impairments

Orthopedic impairments are skeletal and muscle problems that adversely affect a child's educational performance. These impairments might be congenital (such as a clubfoot or absence of a limb); caused by disease (such as tuberculosis); or the result of physical trauma such as cerebral palsy, amputations, fractures, or burns (*Federal Register,* 1977).

Health impairments involve limited strength, vitality, or alertness due to chronic or acute health problems (such as a cerebral palsy, diabetes, epilepsy, heart condition, leukemia, tuberculosis, and others) that adversely affect a child's educational performance (*Federal Register,* 1977).

Many students with physical or health disorders remain in regular classrooms. Because some of these students may need medication or they may miss school for long periods of time, teachers must consider carefully both the academic as well as the social experience of the child. Supportive actions include

- Consulting with the school nurse or occupational or physical therapist, previous teachers, or other resources to understand the condition.
- Asking the student or caregiver what can be done to help with him or her. Teachers should not assume that their ideas of help are what the student needs or wants.
- Spending time helping the class understand the condition and develop realistic attitudes and ways of interacting with the child.
- Differentiating and adjusting assignments and time considerations to allow students to participate and complete work.
- To the extent possible, continuing to support the child who is hospitalized during the school year.
- Allowing sufficient time for catching up and making up work when welcoming a child back to school from an illness.

Students from Diverse Language Groups

Language diversity obviously includes the presence of a language other than English. In addition, however, it includes issues of slang, pronunciation, and usage within a single language, such as African American or Hispanic American English. One in six children of school age in the United States speak a language other than English at home (U.S. Census Bureau, 2003). Their profiles are varied; the children may speak only their native language, be bilingual in both English and their native language, or may speak primarily English. They may have been born in the United States, immigrated, or come as refugees. In 2002, the National Clearinghouse for English Language Acquisition (NCELA) reported that about 4.4 million students have limited English proficiency. The NCELA also reports that between the 1991–1992 and 2001–2002 school years, the number of school-aged language learners increased by 95 percent compared to the total U.S. school enrollment increase of 12 percent.

The report *Language Use and English-Speaking Ability: 2000* found that in addition to English and Spanish, other languages spoken in U.S. homes included Chinese, French, German, Italian, Russian, and other Asian and Pacific Island languages. The report also said, "55 percent of the people who spoke a language other than English at home also reported they spoke English 'very well'" (U.S. Census Bureau Public Information Office, 2003, p. 1). These numbers have great significance for teachers because they will likely have English learners in their classes. To be more specific, in the school year 2002–2003, 3.8 million students (11 percent of all students) received ELL services (National Center for Education Statistics, 2006b). Based on prior history, this number is likely to increase.

Cary (1997) pointed out that in past years language learners were given a variety of negative-sounding labels such as limited-English speaking/non-English speaking (LES/NES) or limited-English proficient/non-English proficient (LEP/NEP). His preference is to emphasize the student's growing resource advantage—having two languages instead of one—by simply referring to them as English learners. Since the 1974 ruling of *Lau v. Nichols,* a variety of philosophies and programs have been put forth for instructing English language learners. Examples include:

- Separate ESL curriculum—grammar, heavy skill and drill, and worksheets (1970s)
- Natural approach—developmental and low stress, with practice of real language meaning and communication (Krashen & Terrell, 1996)
- Submersion—"sink or swim" for language learners who are placed in all-English classrooms with instruction designed for native English-speaking students
- Dual immersion—a 50/50 split of instruction in English and the other language
- Sheltered instruction—another meaning- and communication-based approach to acquiring language. Also known as bridging or Specially Designed Academic Instruction in English (SDAIE), this approach helps language learners acquire core curriculum and expand their English skills by making language understandable through context.

Teachers who follow today's research of language acquisition understand language development differently than their predecessors. They understand that second language learners need many opportunities to practice both their basic interpersonal communication skills (BICS) and cognitive academic language proficiency (CALP), and the practice must be meaningful and with low stress. Teachers also believe that listening, speaking, reading, and writing skills should be linked and developed at the same time. Second language programs that are most common and successful today utilize English Language Development (ELD), Specially Designed Academic Instruction in English (SDAIE), and long-term primary language support and development (Cary, 1997). Instructional strategies and classroom environment can include the following:

- Differentiating and adjusting assignments and time considerations to allow students to participate and complete work
- Providing a concrete, context-rich environment that builds connections of context to objects, manipulatives, models, and multimedia
- Showing rather than telling directions and instructions
- Repeating, summarizing, and paraphrasing
- Using a preview–review format
- Having frequent and varied understanding checks, such as thumbs up, partner sharing, and journal writing
- Providing opportunities for partner and group work
- Offering nontraditional assessment options, such as role-play, media, and art
- Modifying speech so it is slower, with fewer complex sentences, free of idioms and fused words ("okayeveryonedoyahaveanyquestions?"), and using specific naming words

- Having more wait time and think time
- Integrating students' interests, backgrounds, and personal experiences from their home country into the lessons and activities
- Holding high but reasonable expectations, in keeping with the language level of each student

Students from Unstable Family Structures

The areas of diversity that we have just described are well recognized and documented. However, another area of diversity is on the rise, and its very nature also affects the classroom and instruction. Sadly, under a broad category of family and life come hard realities of family structure, involving separation, divorce, blended families, latchkey children, and children who are homeless. Students who come from these situations sometimes (but not always) bring with them other challenges.

Children of Separated or Divorced Parents, Blended Families, and Foster Care. "Half of all children will witness the breakup of a parent's marriage. Of these, close to half will also see the breakup of a parent's second marriage" (www.divorcereform.org). As of 1997, one million children in the United States are involved in a new divorce every year (www.divorcereform.org). Between 1970 and 1996, the number of children under the age of eighteen living with one parent increased from 12 to 28 percent (Teachman, 2004). For some children this means two homes. They spend time with each parent, sometimes split by school year and vacations and summer, but other times split during the school year itself. Another consequence of divorce has been an increase in cohabitation, and now one in three children is born to unmarried parents (www.divorcereform.org). In this situation, or when a parent remarries, children may find themselves members of blended families, with new

---

VIGNETTE 8.1   Working with English Language Learners

Rebecca Cummins works with students with language difficulties in English when she teaches her third graders. For students who cannot speak English, she provides notebooks and encourages them to draw a picture or write in their native language during writing time. The story can be told or read to a buddy who speaks the same language, then told aloud to Rebecca by the buddy. If no one speaks the children's native language, Rebecca shows them that she wants a picture. When the student finishes, Rebecca admires the picture, points out two or three main parts, says the names of those parts, and labels them on the picture. As the children begin learning English, Rebecca has them label parts of their drawings themselves and write summary sentences in English.

Upon Reflection

Rebecca Cummins describes how she works with English language learners. What else might a teacher do if the child is in a primary grade? In an intermediate or upper grade?

"I THOUGHT DRAWINGS OF THEIR FAMILY MEMBERS WOULD MAKE THEM FEEL COMFORTABLE, BUT THEY'VE JUST MADE ME FEEL FAT."

brothers and sisters in addition to a new parent.

Some common responses to divorce have been identified that relate to the development level of the child. Primary-aged children (between five and eight years old) frequently cry and worry about rejection. Boys in particular miss their fathers and often are angry with their mothers for making them leave. Children between nine and twelve are apt to be particularly angry with the parent they believe caused the divorce. They are inclined to side with one parent, often with the mother against the father. They grieve for their loss and are anxious and lonely. Additionally, some children have academic problems and their school performance declines.

Children may be placed in foster care for a number of reasons, including serious abuse or neglect. "About 30% . . . have severe emotional, behavioral, or developmental problems . . . and physical health problems also are common" (AACAP, 2002). Many also have issues of blame or guilt, insecurity, feelings of helplessness or not being wanted, and mixed emotions about attachments.

Teachers with children of separated or divorced parents or from foster care homes should be prepared for the probability of adjustment and custody concerns. Both concerns can affect a child's behavior and academic achievement. As a constant adult for the child, teachers should do the following:

- Recognize and accept emotions.
- Listen and talk to the child, encouraging healthy expression of these emotions.
- Be sensitive in activities and class discussions to a variety of personal and family situations.
- Make information about divorce available to children and their parents or guardians.
- To the extent possible, maintain communication with both parents.
- When possible, consider mentors (such as male teachers who can support children without fathers).

Latchkey Children. For a multitude of reasons, large numbers of children spend time outside school without adult supervision. A report by the National Crime Prevention Council in Washington, DC, published an estimate of from five to twelve million children between ages five to thirteen years are at home and unsupervised before or after school. Current statistics indicate that approximately one of every ten elementary school children spends four and one-half hours a week unsupervised by adults (although younger children may be supervised by an older sibling). These children are referred to as latchkey because they are responsible for letting themselves in and out of the residence. This condition translates into serious realities. When compared to children who are supervised, latchkey children are more likely to experience stress, are more afraid to be alone, are angrier, have more academic and social problems, skip school more frequently, and are more likely to commit antisocial acts founded in peer pressure (Long & Long, 1989; Dwyer, Richardson, Danley, Hansen, Sussman, Brannon, et al., 1990).

Teachers, as well as some communities and business organizations, are working with caregivers and children to reduce unsupervised time for children. Structured before- and after-school activities, Boys and Girls Clubs, homework clubs, and mentors are in place for this purpose.

Children Who Are Homeless.   Fact Sheets published by the National Coalition for the Homeless (NCH) (#2, #10, and #12, 2006) provide statistics regarding children as a fast-growing segment of the homeless population. According to surveys by the U.S. Conference of Mayors (2004) of twenty-seven major U.S. cities, families with children accounted for 40 percent of the homeless population, and homelessness among families continues to increase. "In the United States today, an estimated 1.35 million children [two percent of all children and ten percent of all poor children] are likely to experience homelessness over the course of a year (The Institute for Children and Poverty, 2004)" (National Coalition for the Homeless, 2006b). This is significantly higher than the poverty rate for any other age group. Approximately 25 percent lived with parents who did not have full-time, year-round employment (Annie E. Casey Foundation, 2002).

Approximately 60 percent of homeless women and 41 percent of homeless men had minor children (U.S. Department of Health and Human Services, 2002). In addition to the ravages caused by Hurricanes Katrina and Rita, the increasing poverty and subsequent homelessness among families have resulted from several causes: changes in welfare programs, unstable employment, low wages, loss of benefits, diminishing supply of affordable housing, and the rise in domestic violence.

It's important to remember that these numbers are approximations. A group referred to as the "unsheltered" or "hidden" homeless also exists. These persons are experiencing homelessness but are living with family or friends, or in motels, automobiles, campgrounds, or other places that cannot be counted by researchers and surveys.

Children who are homeless are challenged to enroll in school. The U.S. Department of Education (2004) reports that "residency requirements, guardianship requirements, delays in transfer of school records, lack of transportation, and lack of immunization records often prevent homeless children from enrolling in school." Those who are able to enroll are challenged with regular attendance: ". . . while 87 percent of children and youth are enrolled in school, only 77 percent attend school regularly" (National Coalition for the Homeless, 2006b).

The consequences to children from being homeless can be substantial. Children without permanent housing may suffer physically, emotionally, and educationally. Children who live in cars, shelters, and other such places are more likely than other children who are poor to miss school because of higher mortality rates, more severe health problems, and fewer immunization opportunities.

Communities and programs have come together to support students who are home-less. For example, a magnet school and adult volunteers and mentors in Phoenix provide stability, support, and opportunity for students who are homeless throughout the Phoenix area. The McKinney-Vento Homeless Assistance Act (formerly known as the Stewart B. McKinney Homeless Assistance Act of 1987, amended 1990 and 1994), a federal response to homelessness, protects the educational needs of homeless children. In addition to track-ing attendance and addresses of students who are homeless, The Home, Education, Readi-ness, and Opportunity (HERO) program, developed in 1993 in Nashville, provides parent training, after-school tutoring in shelters, school supplies and clothing, and community locations where children can play with friends. The After-School Corporation (TASC), established in 1998, grants money raised from contributions and foundations to commu-nity-based organizations to run after-school programs in schools. TASC's ultimate goal is to make quality after-school programs available to every child in the United States by 2010. Federal and local programs such as these are working to curtail this cycle, but homelessness is a reality, nonetheless, and teachers are faced with the challenges of students who appear at school one day and then miss the next because they do not have a permanent residence.

Ruby Payne writes and presents extensively about issues of poverty. In her work she gives insight into the hidden rules that govern behavior and decision making of children and adults in poverty, and she describes how schools and educators can understand better the unique needs of children in poverty. You can read more about her work and workshop opportunities at www.ahaprocess.com or www.csba.org/qa/payne.htm.

Teachers can be powerful forces in the lives of children who are homeless, helping them both emotionally and academically. On an emotional level, teachers can

- Recognize and accept emotions.
- Listen and talk to the child, encouraging healthy expression of emotions.
- Be sensitive in activities and discussions to a variety of personal situations.
- To the extent possible, maintain communication with caregivers and provide infor-mation regarding appropriate and available support services.

On an academic level, teachers can

- Partner students with classmates who can help show them the ropes around the school and in the classroom.
- Find volunteers or mentors who can tutor and support the child at the shelter.
- Improvise a portable desk (such as a clipboard or notebook) so the student can do homework at the shelter.
- Offer nontraditional options for students to display their understandings for teachers to assess (such as role-play, media, and art).
- Find appropriate services and donations of clothing and school supplies from local business and civic organizations.
- Be informed of appropriate services from the school, such as the free lunch program.
- Arrange to meet with parents at the shelter rather than at school.
- Minimize enrollment delays.
- Provide shelter staff with copies of homework assignments, newsletters, and calendars.

This has been a discussion of a few of the many special challenges teachers face every day with their students. The list of potential special needs is far from exhausted. The important thing for teachers to remember is that all children are entitled to life, liberty, and the pursuit of happiness. Our job as teachers is to support these rights. We can begin by making all children feel welcome, wanted, secure, and successful.

INSTRUCTIONAL STRATEGIES FOR INDIVIDUAL DIFFERENCES

We now consider some of the broader approaches to managing today's diversity, some of which were mentioned in the previous chapter on managing students at work. However, remember this: Before you do anything with your students, you must get to know them. It is essential that you observe and evaluate your students so you know their special gifts and needs. Then remember to reevaluate frequently the effort and progress of each of your students.

Assistive Technology

Assistive technology—tools and devices that enhance the functioning of individuals with special disabilities—gives students with special needs access to instruction. The Assistive Technology Act of 2004 supports the use of state-of-the-art technology, particularly targeting assistance for children with speech and motor challenges. With this assistance, regular education teachers are better able to include all students in instruction and learning. Some of the available assistive technology was discussed earlier in relation to specific challenges.

Differentiated Instruction

Teachers who differentiate instruction use alternative ways to deliver content instruction. They also vary the process by which students can make sense of the content or they provide various ways for students to demonstrate the understanding and learning they take away from the content.

Multi-Age Classes

When students of varying ages and abilities come together as a community, they are able to contribute to the learning environment. Successful multi-age classes practice differentiated instruction.

Looped Classes

Keeping teachers and students together for two or more years results in increased familiarity and understanding for the teacher, the students, and the caregivers. It increases the teacher's understanding of the students' needs and provides a better-matched academic program for them. It also increases student and caregiver confidence in the teacher.

Team Teaching

Teachers at the same grade level can agree to team teach. They share students, but because they teach specific subjects or ability levels, they may see different students at different times. Team teaching maximizes the teachers' instructional time and energies, but requires cooperation, planning, coordination, and flexibility.

Student Study Teams (SSTs)

The regular education teacher generally initiates these team meetings of interested adults. In addition to the teacher and the parents or guardians, the team may include former teachers, an administrator, and a counselor or other service provider. The primary goal of the participants is to review the student's apparent needs and develop a plan of action to further investigate and then best meet those needs. SSTs, or similar meetings, occur prior to IEP meetings that, by law, require more formal documentation and action.

Individualized Education Programs (IEPs)

PL 94-142 describes the conditions of IEPs. Regular and special education teachers, parents or guardians, and other involved parties come together to develop educational plans for individual students. IEPs must be referenced to the core curriculum. Also, they must include statements of the student's current performance, long- and short-range goals for the student, details of the nature and duration of instructional services for meeting the goals, as well as an overview of the intended evaluation methods.

Supplementary Pullout Instruction

Sometimes students are taught best when they leave their classroom for special instruction. Although this sounds contrary to the essence of inclusion, it is not. For some students, pullout instruction is used to reinforce skills being taught in the classroom. For students with higher abilities, pullout instruction can be another way to enrich their educational program.

Probably the biggest challenge related to pullout programs is organizing the schedule. Schedules must be planned carefully so students do not miss or interrupt important instruction. Teachers must coordinate times with other teachers, service providers, and resource specialists and stay on schedule in their own classrooms.

Transitions also require finessing so they are not disruptive. Teachers must think about students as they leave and return to the class. Because students need to be brought into the current instruction or activity quickly, teachers should do the following:

- Establish and practice routines for transitions: leaving and entering the classroom, locating appropriate materials, and the like.
- Establish and practice clear behavior expectations.
- Post organizers and visual instructional plans for activities and assignments for students to refer to as they begin to work.
- Arrange for partners or buddies to help returning or new students settle into the activity or assignment.

■ Have shorter activities available for the rest of the class to work on while the teacher helps the returning or new students.

Contracts

Contracts provide individualized agreements for student's work, effort, and/or behavior. They include the specific goals or objectives, relevant materials, assessment expectations, and incentives. Furthermore, contracts are agreed to by the teacher and the student. Because contracts are individualized, they give the teacher and student the opportunity to modify the activity or assignment in ways that are best for the student. Contracts also may be extended to involve parents or guardians and align with home behavior and work expectations.

Learning Groups and Partner Learning

Partners or groups of up to six students often provide learning benefits. Spencer Kagan (1994) describes four principles that are essential for true cooperative groups: positive interdependence, individual accountability, equal participation, and simultaneous interaction (PIES). Additionally, teachers should remember two other facts about groups: (1) Groups don't simply happen; group structure must be taught and rehearsed. To be successful, students must learn and practice the skills of cooperation such as listening, sharing, and being responsible. (2) Groups seem to work best when every student in the group has a specific job with specific responsibility to contribute to the group effort and is accountable for that responsibility. For example, literacy circles in groups of five might have a discussion director, a character captain, a summarizer, an illustrator, and a materials manager. (You may wish to revisit the discussion of cooperative learning in Chapter 6.)

"WHAT A DAY! I HAD TO DEAL WITH 23 STUDENTS AND 13 IMAGINARY FRIENDS."

Peer and Cross-Age Tutors and Cross-Grade Partnerships

Most of us learn better when we have to teach someone else. Cross-age tutors and cross-grade partners provide another opportunity for individualized assistance and attention. The experience gives older students the opportunity to be a mentor and a role model to someone younger. The younger children enjoy individual attention from someone who is closer to their age and experience.

Special Programs

Special programs involving community, businesses, and foundation partnerships exist around the country. Several of these were mentioned earlier in the chapter. These programs support academic achievement and social growth and offer enrichment activities for all children.

This brings to an end our consideration of the management of special groups of students. In our next chapter we look deeper into how to manage overall student behavior. Before moving ahead, please take time to explore these end-of-chapter activities.

Parting Thought

Knowledge is of two kinds:
We know a subject ourselves or
We know where we can find information upon it.

—Samuel Johnson

SUMMARY SELF-CHECK

Check off the following as you either understand or become able to apply them.

❑ Inclusion is a way of life, an attitude that values all children.

❑ Exceptionality includes a wide range of students, including
- Students with lower abilities
- Students with higher abilities
- Students with communicative, speech, or language disorders
- Students with sensory challenges such as hearing or visual impairment
- Students with behavioral concerns, including neurological based behavior
- Students with physical and health disorders

❑ Students with attention deficit disorder and attention deficit hyperactivity disorder have difficulties with attention, hyperactivity, impulse control, emotional stability, or some combination of these.

❑ Language diversity is independent of ethnicity and race.
- *English learner* is a more positive label that celebrates the student's resource advantage of having two languages instead of one.
- English learners need many opportunities to practice basic interpersonal communication skills (BICS), cognitive academic language proficiency (CALP), and listening, speaking, reading, and writing.

❑ Family diversity is a broad category of family and life situations that includes challenges related to separation, divorce, and blended families; latchkey children; and homelessness.

❑ Strategies for managing individual differences include differentiated instruction, multi-age classes, looped classes, team teaching, Student Study Teams (SSTs), Individualized Education Programs (IEPs), supplementary pullout programs, contracts, learning groups, peer and cross-age tutors, and cross-grade partnerships.

ACTIVITIES FOR REFLECTION AND DISCUSSION

1. Take a moment to review the statements in the Prediction–Review Guide at the beginning of this chapter. Put a check mark in the Review column next to any statement with which you now agree. How have your thoughts changed since reading this chapter?

2. Interview at least two teachers about their experiences with students with special needs and the support they received from others (administrators, caregivers, support providers, doctors, and professional organizations) when the students were in their class.

3. In your opinion, which of the diversity issues discussed in this chapter pose the greater challenges to the teacher? To the students who are in those groups? To other students in the class? Describe how you will include these students (and their caregivers) in your class community.

4. Anticipate that you have a new fifth grader who is an English learner. How will you instruct that student in language arts and reading? Math? Social studies or science? How will your instruction be different if the student is a primary student (K–2) rather than an intermediate or upper-grade student (3–6)?

5. How will you adapt your classroom, instruction, and activities to include a student who is in a wheelchair?

6. Describe how you will use peer and cross-age tutors and a buddy class for your first-graders. What kinds of activities might you have the two classes work on together?

7. Write a sample contract to use with a student with higher ability who is interested in studying about immigration during the fifth-grade unit on the topic. Write a sample contract to use with a student with lower ability for the same unit.

REFERENCES AND RECOMMENDED READINGS

Annie E. Casey Foundation. (2002). *Kids count data book, 2002.* Baltimore: Author.
Cartwright, G., Cartwright, C., & Ward, M. (1984). *Educating special learners* (2nd ed.). Belmont, CA: Wadsworth.
Cary, S. (1997). *Second language learners.* Los Angeles: Galef Institute.
Children's Defense Fund. (1994). *Child poverty data from the 1990 census.* Washington, DC: Author.
Choate, J. (Ed.). (2004). *Successful inclusive teaching* (4th ed.). Boston: Pearson Education.
City of Mesa. (2006, March). Latchkey children: Young children at home. Retrieved April 2006, from www.cityofmesa.org/police/literature/latchkey.asp (last updated 3/23/06).

Cook, P. (2004a). *Behaviour, learning, and teaching.* Applied studies in FAS/FAE (Distance Education Curricula). Red River College, Winnipeg, Manitoba, Canada.

Cook, P. (2004b). *Sensory Integration Dysfunction. A layperson's guide.* Booklet available from Paula Cook. Internet contact: pcook59@shaw.ca.

Cook, P. (2005). *Rage: A layperson's guide to what to do when someone begins to rage.* Booklet available from Paula Cook. Internet contact: pcook59@shaw.ca.

Delsio, E. (2004, October). Wire Side Chat: How understanding poverty can help low-income children. Retrieved April 2006, from www.education-world.com/a_issues/chat/chat119.shtml.

Dwyer, K., Richardson, J., Danley, K., Hansen, W., Sussman, S., Brannon, B., et al. (1990, September). Characteristics of eighth grade students who initiate self-care in elementary and junior high school. *Pediatrics, 86*(3), 448–454.

Educating language learners [Special issue]. (2004, December/2005, January). *Educational Leadership, 62*(4). Alexandria, VA: ASCD.

Good, T., & Brophy, J. (2002). *Looking into classrooms* (9th ed.). Boston: Allyn & Bacon.

Greene, R. (2001). *The explosive child.* New York: HarperCollins.

Hall, P., & Hall, N. (2003). *Educating oppositional and defiant children.* Alexandria, VA: ASCD.

Hartman, C. (2006, February). Students on the move. *Educational Leadership, 63*(5), 20–24.

Holloway, J. (2002, December/2003, January). Addressing the needs of homeless students. *Educational Leadership, 60*(4), 89–90.

Kagan, S. (1994). *Cooperative learning.* San Clemente, CA: Kagan Cooperative Learning.

Kirk, S., Gallagher, J., Anastasiow, N., & Coleman, M. (2006). *Educating exceptional children* (11th ed.). Boston: Houghton Mifflin.

Kranowitz, C. (1998). *The out-of-sync child.* New York: Skylight Press.

Krashen, S., & Terrell, T. (1996). *The natural approach: Language acquisition in the classroom.* Oxford: Pergamon.

Long, L., & Long, T. (1989). Latchkey adolescents: How administrators can respond to their needs. *NASSP Bulletin, 73*, 102–108.

Papolos, D., & Papolos, J. (2002). *The bipolar child.* New York: Broadway Books.

Payne, R. (2001). *A framework for understanding poverty.* Highlands, TX: aha! Process, Inc.

Rief, S., & Heimburge, J. (1996). *How to reach and teach all students in the inclusive classroom.* West Nyack, NY: Center for Applied Research in Education.

Rubinstein-Avila, E. (2006, February). Connecting with Latino learners. *Educational Leadership, 63*(5), 20–24.

Ryan, K., & Cooper, J. (2007). *Those who can, teach* (11th ed.). Boston: Houghton Mifflin.

The science of learning [Special issue]. (2000, November). *Educational Leadership, 68*(3). Alexandria, VA: ASCD.

Smith, D. (2004). *Introduction to special education: Teaching in an age of opportunity* (5th ed.). Boston: Allyn & Bacon.

Teaching all students [Special issue]. (2001, October). *Educational Leadership, 61*(2). Alexandria, VA: ASCD.

Teachman, J. D. (2004, January). The childhood living arrangements of children and characteristics of their marriages. *Journal of Family Issues, 25,* 86–111.

Van Ripper, C. (1978). *Speech correction: Principles and methods* (6th ed.). Englewood Cliffs, NJ: Prentice-Hall.

Villa, R., & Thousand, J. (Eds.). (1995). *Creating an inclusive school.* Alexandria, VA: ASCD.

Villa, R., & Thousand, J. (Eds.). (2005). *Creating an inclusive school* (2nd ed.). Alexandria, VA: ASCD.

Ysseldyke, J., & Algozzine, B. (1995). *Special education: A practical approach for teachers* (3rd ed.). Boston: Houghton Mifflin.

Legal Actions

Gifted and Talented Students Act of 1978, PL 95-561. (1978).

Individuals with Disabilities Act (IDEA) of 1990, PL 101-476. (1990).

McKinney-Vento Homeless Assistance Act. (Formerly known as the Stewart B. McKinney Homeless Assistance Act of 1987, amended 1990 and 1994.)

Reauthorization of IDEA of 1997. (1997).

Reports and Conferences

American Academy of Child and Adolescent Psychiatry. (2002). *Factsheet 64*. www.aacap.org/publications/ factsfam/64.htm.

Center for the Study of Social Policy. (1992). *What the 1990 census tells us about children*. Washington, DC: Author.

Divorce Rates in Families with Children. (n.d.). Retrieved April 2006, from www.divorcereform.org/ stats.htm.

Federal Register. (1977, August 23). Washington, DC: U.S. Government Printing Office.

National Center for Education Statistics. (2006a). *Digest of Education Statistics, 2005* (NCES 2006-030). Washington, DC: U.S. Department of Education.

National Center for Education Statistics. (2006b). *Public Elementary and Secondary Students, Staff, Schools, and School Districts: School Year 2003–04*. Retrieved October 2006, from http:// nces.ed.gov/fastfacts/display.asp?ID=96.

National Clearinghouse for English Language Acquisition. (2002). *Survey of the states' limited English proficient students and available educational programs and services*. Washington, DC: George Washington University, National Clearinghouse for English Language Acquisition.

National Coalition for the Homeless. (2006a, June). *How many people experience homelessness?* (NCH Fact Sheet #2). Retrieved October 2006, from www.nationalhomeless.org.

National Coalition for the Homeless. (2006b, June). *Education of homeless children and youth* (NCH Fact Sheet #10). Retrieved October 2006, from www.nationalhomeless.org.

National Coalition for the Homeless. (2006c, June). *Homeless families with children* (NCH Fact Sheet #12). Retrieved October 2006, from www.nationalhomeless.org.

Root, R., & Resnick, R. (2003). An update on the diagnosis and treatment of Attention-Deficit/Hyper-activity Disorder in children. *Professional Psychology: Research and Practice*, 34(1), 34–41. www.apa.org/journals/releases/pro34134.pdf.

U.S. Census Bureau. (2003). *Language use and English-speaking ability: 2000*. Retrieved December 18, 2003, from www.census.gov/prod/2003pubs/c2kbr-29.pdf.

U.S. Census Bureau Public Information Office. (2003, October 8). News release. Retrieved December 18, 2003, from www.census.gov/Press-Release/www/releases/archives/census_2000/001406.html.

U.S. Conference of Mayors. (2004). *Status report on hunger and homelessness in America's cities: 2004*. Washington, DC: Author.

U.S. Department of Education. (2004). Education for Homeless Children and Youth Program, 2004. Available at www.ed.gov.

U.S. Department of Education. (2006). Fast Facts: Students with Disabilities. www.nces.ed.gov/fastfacts/ display/asp?ID=64.

U.S. Department of Health and Human Services. (2002). *HHS programs and initiatives to combat homelessness*. Retrieved December 18, 2003, from www.hhs.gov/news/press/2002pres/ homeless.html.

Websites

Assistive Tools

www.intellitools.com

Exceptionality (GATE and Special Education)

www.nagc.org
www.pai-ca.org/pubs/505101.htm
www.cec.sped.org
www.ed.gov/offices/OSERS/IDEA

Families

www.divorcereform.org/all.html

Miscellaneous Facts

www.census.gov/prod/2005pubs/p60-229.pdf
www.tascorp.org/publications/catalog/indrep_a/five_year_report.pdf
www.childstats.gov/americaschildren/pop6.asp
www.childrensdefense.org/data/keyfacts.aspx
www.urban.org/children/index.cfm
www.ncpc.org

Partnerships (schools and families)

www.bridges4kids.org

Poverty and Homelessness

www.ahaprocess.com
www.education-world.com/a_issues/chat/chat119.shtml
www.csba.org/qa/payne.htm
www.ncpc.org
www.nationalhomeless.org/publications/facts/How_Many.pdf
www.nationalhomeless.org/publications/facts/education.pdf
www.nationalhomeless.org/publications/facts/families.pdf
www.usmayors.org/uscm/hungersurvey/2005/HH2005FINAL.pdf

CHAPTER 9

Managing Student Behavior

Everyone stood in awe of the lion tamer in the cage, with half a dozen lions all under the control of his "consequences." Everyone, that is, except the teacher . . .

—June Dostal

Prediction–Review Guide

Before you read the chapter, take a minute to put a check mark in the Prediction column next to any statement with which you agree.

	Prediction	Review
1. Discipline usually heads the list of teacher and public concerns about education.	❏	❏
2. Kounin says successful behavior management relates to withitness and lesson management.	❏	❏
3. Dreikurs and Albert believe that behavior comes from a need to belong, and individuals may choose mistaken goals in order to satisfy this need.	❏	❏
4. The Canters insist that nothing should be allowed to interfere with teachers' rights to teach and students' rights to learn.	❏	❏
5. Glasser contends that cooperative learning teams help meet students' need for belonging.	❏	❏
6. After studying teachers who seem naturally adept at discipline, Jones made his greatest contribution by identifying and focusing on several clusters of teacher skills.	❏	❏
7. Kagan, Kyle, and Scott explain that student positions—the conditions for disruptive behavior—tell teachers *why* students do what they do.	❏	❏
8. Coloroso responds to student mistakes, mischief, and mayhem by applying the three Rs (restitution, resolution, and reconciliation).	❏	❏
9. Marshall says that looking at situations in light of a hierarchy of social behavior removes the action from the person.	❏	❏
10. A good discipline plan meets students' needs; teacher needs are basically irrelevant to its success.	❏	❏

Support for specific standards found in this chapter:

INTASC Standards

2. Knowledge of Human Development and Learning

   The teacher understands how children learn and develop and can provide learning opportunities that support their intellectual, social, and personal development.

5. Classroom Motivation and Management

   The teacher uses an understanding of individual and group motivation and behavior to create a learning environment that encourages positive social interaction, active engagement in learning, and self-motivation.

Danielson's Framework for Teaching

2. The Classroom Environment

   - Creating an environment of respect and rapport
   - Establishing a culture for learning
   - Managing classroom procedures
   - Managing student behavior
   - Organizing physical space

NBPTS Standards

3. Teachers are responsible for managing and monitoring student learning.

NCATE Standards

Help all pre-kindergarten through twelfth grade (P–12) students learn.

Apply effective methods of teaching students who are at different developmental stages, have different learning styles, and come from diverse backgrounds.

Gallup Polls are published annually by Phi Delta Kappa, a professional organization for educators. According to the polls of teacher and public attitudes toward education, for more than three decades discipline (misbehavior in the classroom) has been listed among their top three concerns in public education. (See Gallup polls concerning attitude toward education, published annually since 1969 in *Phi Delta Kappan*.)

Formal attention to classroom discipline began in the early 1950s, and pioneer work at that time laid the foundation for much of today's classroom discipline. Today a number of discipline programs are being used by educators to manage student behavior. In the past, the approach to discipline was fairly strict and teacher-controlled. Teachers could demand, scold, speak sternly, threaten, and keep students in after school—all to force students to conduct themselves appropriately. Teachers also had the backing of administrators, caregivers, and the community. Over time, programs evolved to be more student-centered. In

A TYPICAL DAY FOR SOME

Focus Questions
What are the reasons that students are acting the way they are? What steps should Miss Wilson take to install a discipline plan that will work for her and her students?

Miss Wilson is a beginning fourth-grade teacher. She has twenty-eight students in her class. It's November, and every day seems to be a little worse than the previous day.

Her students are well-intentioned, but most of the children have high energy, and most mornings they yell and push as they enter the room. This morning Zack and Ty are fighting as they enter.

Many of the students dawdle by the cubbies as they remove coats and put away their backpacks. Once they finally sit down at their desks, they conjure reasons to get up and move about the room: "My pencil is broken." "I have to go to the bathroom." "I need a drink of water." "I left my homework in my backpack." "Can I feed the gerbil?"

Often Miss Wilson teaches lessons that are scripted in the teacher's edition of the textbooks. Her routine is to present the new information and give students seatwork to practice the material.

On average it takes about ten minutes for students to line up for recess or lunch. Rather than cut lunch short, Miss Wilson tells students to walk together in straight, quiet lines to the cafeteria.

Maddie often argues when Miss Wilson assigns work or a task. Tim often says, "You can't make me do this." Sasha asks countless questions about every task. Becca pretends to work by doodling on her worksheet.

Finally a bell rings and another day ends.

fact, some would say that today's popular programs have gone to extremes in allowing students rather than teachers to make choices concerning students and school.

HOW SERIOUS IS DISRUPTIVE BEHAVIOR?

Discipline is a serious and ever-growing problem. Many see undesirable trends and conditions in society as contributing factors. Some blame excessive attention to students' civil rights and due process over teachers' rights to teach in a productive and safe environment. Some, including education critic Alfie Kohn, criticize teaching and discipline that do things *to* students rather than *involve* students as partners in the process. Still others, including Canadian consultant Ronald Morrish, even blame current discipline programs, saying that they stress *management* and making the environment functional rather than *discipline* and teaching students to behave properly.

Disruptive behavior in the classroom is any behavior that interferes with productive teaching and learning. Charles (2000) pinpoints disruptive behavior as any behavior that, through intent or thoughtlessness, (1) interferes with teaching or learning, (2) threatens or intimidates others, or (3) oversteps society's standards of moral, ethical, or legal behavior. Fred Jones (2007) notes that teachers in a typical classroom lose about half their teaching time because of students' disruptive behavior. Such behavior is not always bad behavior. In fact, it usually is nothing more than talking, goofing off, or moving about the room without permission. However, disruptions, even those considered benign, lower achievement and often damage class morale. Consider the following:

- Regarding teachers' rights to teach: Disruptive behavior interferes with the teacher's basic right to teach, which also affects student learning and produces much teacher frustration.
- Regarding students' rights to learn: Students who make irresponsible choices disrupt learning for themselves and others, which in turn leads to lowered academic achievement.
- Regarding wasted time: Teachers dealing with classroom disruptions lose enormous amounts of time that would and should be devoted to instruction—50 percent according to Jones's observations.
- Regarding stress, motivation, and energy: Disruptive behavior increases stress and weakens motivation and energy by wearing on teachers and students and perpetuating a poor attitude toward learning.
- Regarding classroom climate: Disruptive behavior can at times produce a climate of fearfulness and stress for students and teachers alike.
- Regarding teacher–student relationships: Disruptive behavior dissolves trust so cooperative relationships never develop adequately.

Many beginning teachers have naïve expectations of students—remember Janna Smart in Chapter 1? They believe that if the teacher is caring, students will make responsible choices and will behave appropriately—they will be orderly, courteous, respectful, honest, considerate of property and others, willing to work, and relatively quiet. But what teachers often encounter are minor but ongoing misbehaviors and even unruliness that in some cases escalate to open hostility, defiance, and physical aggression. As Jones (2007) observed, although 95 percent of disruptive behavior involves little more than talking, moving around the room without permission, and simply wasting time, almost all teachers report that disruptive behavior interferes with their teaching, sometimes greatly.

The disquieting fact is that student behavior, reflective of society in general, continues to worsen. Curwin and Mendler (1997) have observed these trends:

- More students now are behaviorally and academically at risk of failing in schools.
- More students now are disruptive than in the past, and the rate is increasing.
- Children are becoming more disruptive at younger ages.
- Children are more violent.

- Many children lack any feeling of caring or remorse.
- Teachers describe students as more aggressive and hostile.

It is no wonder that teachers and the public have concerns.

IS THE DISCIPLINE SITUATION HOPELESS?

The best elementary teachers have long practiced the Golden Rule to teach their students. They treat children as they want to be treated themselves. They are humane. They care and try. They love their students, or try to, and want to be respected in return.

"It may look ominous, but ever since having it installed, classroom productivity has been up 100%!"

Sadly, that condition is changing. Many children today are self-absorbed, overly indulged, and not held accountable for their behavior. Many children are not taught responsibility or how to behave appropriately. Students have lost their respect for teachers and principals. They can — and do — swear at and argue with the teacher with impunity. Caregivers are likely to side with their child in disputes with the teacher. Principals fear, with good reason, that a disgruntled caregiver will protest before the school board or even file a lawsuit against the teacher, the principal, or the school. The old coercive tactics for enforcing behavior are no longer viable, and teachers who still rely on them, for the most part, are doomed to ineffectiveness and depression.

THE MOVEMENT TOWARD NEW DISCIPLINE

Thousand, Villa, and Nevin (2002) depict effective discipline as a pyramid (see Figure 9.1). Prevention is the base and strength of the pyramid. Prevention is accomplished by establishing a classroom of caring and interdependence, with effective routines and procedures. The next level in the pyramid consists of quick, nonintrusive responses to stop distractions and disruptions the moment they occur. When a disruption cannot be resolved in the classroom, children go somewhere else. In a place away from others, students can calm down, think, and problem solve under adult guidance in order to return to the classroom quickly.

FIGURE 9.1   A Conceptualization for Effective Disciplinary Systems

Source: Villa, R. A., Udis, J., & Thousand, J. S. (2002). Supporting students with troubling behavior. In J. S. Thousand, R. A. Villa, & A. I. Nevin (Eds.), *Creativity and collaborative learning: The practical guide to empowering students, teachers, and families* (p. 143). Baltimore: Paul H. Brookes Publishing Co. Reprinted by permission.

The apex of the pyramid consists of caring individuals who collaborate to establish plans to bring about long-term change in student behavior.

WHAT MAJOR AUTHORITIES SAY ABOUT DISCIPLINE

A number of authorities, past and present, have made suggestions and devised techniques that greatly help teachers minimize disruptive behavior in the classroom. Here we will briefly review selected contributions.

Groundbreaking Authorities

Beginning in the 1950s, several authorities made notable contributions in the area of classroom discipline. Among these groundbreaking authorities were Fritz Redl and William Wattenberg, B. F. Skinner, Haim Ginott, Jacob Kounin, Rudolf Dreikurs, Lee and Marlene Canter, and William Glasser.

Redl and Wattenberg (1951) studied and wrote about how group dynamics influenced behavior and were the first to formalize study when they offered a systematic approach to

"IF YOUR CELL PHONE HAS FIVE HUNDRED
MINUTES, AND YOU USE ONE OF THEM
DURING THIS CLASS, HOW LONG WILL
YOU BE IN DETENTION?"

classroom discipline based on human psychology and humane tactics. Skinner, a behavioral psychologist, investigated how people's behavior and actions were influenced by what happened immediately after they performed an act. Skinner never concerned himself directly with classroom discipline. However, in the early 1960s Skinner's followers created and popularized a program known as behavior modification that was widely used in teaching, child rearing, and human relations. In 1971, Ginott published *Teacher and Child*, where he examined the role of communication—how teachers talk to and with their students—in discipline. Many still regard Ginott's book as one with great influence in the area of classroom discipline.

Jacob Kounin.   Jacob Kounin (1970) was the first to present a detailed analysis of the effects of classroom and lesson management on student behavior. His work was never considered a well-rounded approach to discipline because he did not study techniques used by good disciplinarians to correct disruptive behavior. However, his suggestions on lesson management are incorporated into most of the discipline systems used today.

Kounin explored differences between teachers good at classroom control and those poor at it and found that good managers (1) project an image of being in charge in the classroom and (2) efficiently manage lessons and transitions between lessons.

With regard to being in charge, Kounin isolated two significant skills, which he called withitness and overlapping. *Withitness* is knowing what is going on in every part of the classroom at every moment, in a way that is evident to students. *Overlapping* refers to the ability to deal with at least two issues simultaneously. For example, if the teacher is working with a small reading group and disruptive behavior occurs elsewhere in the room, the teacher overlaps by correcting the disruptive behavior without leaving the reading group or interrupting its activity.

With regard to lesson management, Kounin identified several important skills, among them focus, attention, accountability, pacing, momentum, and efficient transitions between activities. Each skill, if not accomplished well, allows for inattentive dead time that encourages disruptive behavior. *Focus* is obtained by making sure students know what they are supposed to do and why. *Attention* is obtained through motivation and specific directions. *Accountability* (student responsibility) is obtained by calling on students to respond, interpret, comment, discuss, and demonstrate. *Pacing* depends on timing that ensures efficient coverage of activities and ending at the appropriate time. *Momentum* is evident in steady progression through the lesson, without slowdown or frantic rush. *Transitions* from one activity to another depend on established routines that ensure rapid changeover.

Rudolf Dreikurs.   Psychiatrist Rudolf Dreikurs was a contemporary of Ginott and Kounin. His work has been widely acknowledged as beneficial in developing student self-control and responsible behavior. Dreikurs considered discipline to be an ongoing process in which students learn to impose limits on themselves; he was interested in identifying and dealing with the underlying causes of misbehavior. He suggested that teachers and students should collaborate on procedures that offer order, limits, firmness, kindness, freedom to explore, teacher leadership, and frequent opportunities for students to choose their own acceptable behavior.

Dreikurs maintained that all students are motivated by a predominant goal: to feel that they belong—to the group, to the classroom, to the school. Furthermore, they behave acceptably if they attain that goal of belonging. Otherwise, they turn progressively to mistaken goals—attention getting, power, revenge, and withdrawal. For Dreikurs, the essence of classroom discipline involved teachers helping students to gain a sense of belonging and to choose acceptable behavior. Dreikurs made four suggestions for dealing with student misbehavior.

Dreikurs suggested that teachers first establish democratic classrooms that allow students to gain their primary goal of belonging. This will cause most, though not all, discipline problems to disappear. Second, when disruptive behavior does occur, teachers should identify the student's mistaken goal and confront the student with it: "You would like me to pay attention to you, wouldn't you?" or "Could it be that you want to show that I can't make you do this work?" Third, teachers must make sure that disruptive behavior is always followed by reasonable consequences. Consequences, never hurtful acts, are activities students dislike, such as staying after school or completing an assignment at home that should have been done in class. Fourth, teachers must always remain helpful and encourage students to improve.

Linda Albert.   Linda Albert (2003) has built on Dreikurs's work by providing a process that teachers, students, administrators, and caregivers can easily implement. Her approach, called *Cooperative Discipline,* holds that behavior is based on choice, and the choices students make are based on the basic need to belong. To this end, students must feel capable, connected, and able to contribute to the group. Students unable to feel a sense of belonging misbehave in ways that correspond to the mistaken goals Dreikurs described. Albert's program of helping strategies for students also includes a classroom code of conduct, cooperative conflict resolution, school and home action plans, and student and caregiver involvement as partners in the discipline process. For more information about her program, you can visit Albert's website, www.cooperativediscipline.com.

The Canters.   Lee and Marlene Canter are authors of *Assertive Discipline,* a widely used approach to classroom discipline. Their approach, originally published in 1976, was an instant success. Overall, assertive discipline allowed teachers to apply positive support and corrective actions calmly and fairly. The approach provided techniques for teaching students how to behave properly, for gaining student trust and cooperation, and for dealing with students whose behavior is difficult to manage. Canter & Associates merged with Sylvan Learning Systems in 1998. In 2003, the company changed its name to Laureate Education, Incorporated, and focus shifted exclusively to postsecondary education. The Canters no longer produce materials or provide workshops on assertive discipline.

The Canters insisted on teachers' rights to teach and students' rights to learn and said that nothing, especially student misbehavior, should be allowed to interfere with either. They went on to say that teachers have the right to a calm, quiet classroom if that's what they need in order to teach well. Teachers have the right to expect students to behave in ways that do not defeat their best interests. Teachers have the right to expect backing from their administrators and support from parents or guardians. And they have the right to a classroom in which quality teaching and learning can occur.

Teachers appreciated this approach because no one ever so strongly championed their cause before. According to the Canters, the logic of assertive discipline holds that

- Teachers have the right to teach in a professional manner, without disruption.
- Students have the right to learn in a safe, calm environment, with full support of professional educators and others.
- These rights are best met by in-charge teachers who do not violate students' best interests.
- Trust, respect, and perseverance enable teachers to earn student cooperation.

The Canters maintained that these goals can be met by

- Maintaining a calm, productive classroom environment.
- Meeting students' needs for learning and ensuring that their rights are attended to.
- Helping the teacher remain calmly and nonstressfully in charge of the classroom.

William Glasser.   Since 1965, William Glasser, psychiatrist and educational consultant, has developed, popularized, and continually refined an approach to teaching that provides motivation and helps students make good behavioral choices while taking responsibility for their actions. His work continues to the present day. Glasser presents his ideas about "choice theory" (which he originally called "control theory") and quality schools and teachers in several highly acclaimed books: *Choice Theory in the Classroom* (1998), *The Quality School: Managing Students Without Coercion* (1998), *The Quality School Teacher* (1998), and *Every Student Can Succeed* (2001). According to Glasser, choice theory helps everyone become more realistic about human behavior. He describes how choice theory can be used to establish learning environments that lead to success and quality. Glasser believes that quality teaching and learning require depth of understanding and regular and accurate personal assessment. The following are some of the main tenets of his theories:

- All behavior is our best atempt to control ourselves to meet five basic needs: survival, belonging, power, fun, and freedom.
- We can control no one's behavior except our own.
- We cannot successfully make a person do anything. All we can do is open possibilities and provide information.
- All behavior is understood best as *total behavior,* composed of four components: acting, thinking, feeling, and physiology (how we function).
- All total behavior is chosen, but we only have direct control over the acting and thinking components. In other words, we can choose how to act and how to think. Feeling and physiology are controlled indirectly through how we choose to act and think.
- What we do is not determined automatically by external causes. External control does not motivate students to act responsibly or learn. Primarily our actions are determined by what goes on inside us.
- Present-day curriculum and schooling ignore the basic needs and emphasize memorization of isolated facts that are irrelevant to students' lives. Furthermore, quality is judged by how many fragments of information students can retain long enough to be measured on tests.
- Cooperative learning groups help meet students' need for belonging.
- One way to improve behavior and learning is through clarifying what a quality existence would be like and planning the choices that would help that existence. In the classroom, this process occurs best when teachers establish warm, trusting relationships with students.

Applications of choice theory to the classroom are seen in the work of consultants and trainers Kathy Curtiss and Steven English (2003), who have been providing services to schools across the country for many years. Curtiss and English advocate using classroom meetings, integrating character development into curriculum content, and developing instructional strategies that lead to student ownership of learning. They also work on strengthening student reflection and self-evaluation, with the aim of increasing students' responsibility for making the most of their educational opportunity. They recommend the use of portfolios and assessment rubrics (procedures) based on standards, as well as developing stronger partnerships between teachers and students. They point out that these provisions accomplish little unless the classroom is imbued with trust and respect, and students learn to resolve their problems without hurting each other. Instructional strategies that make this possible include cooperative learning, conflict resolution, classroom meetings, and character education. Additional information about their work and Glasser's choice theory can be found at these websites: www.choicetheory.org/directory.html and www.choicetheory.com/links.htm.

Contemporary Authorities

The Wongs.   For years Harry and Rosemary Wong have written about the first days and weeks of school. Their very practical approach, published in *The First Days of School,* is a compilation of valuable ideas from many sources. The Wongs place major emphasis on classroom management, especially the structure and procedures that enable students to work diligently, behave responsibly, and reach high levels of achievement. Here are some of their ideas regarding teaching, learning, and the first days and weeks of school:

- The main problem in teaching is poor classroom management, not poor discipline.
- The most important element for student learning is how a teacher manages the classroom.
- The three most important things a teacher must teach the first days and weeks of school are discipline, procedures, and routines.
- Discipline plans should begin the first day of school. They should be written, posted, reviewed, and practiced with the students, and state the kind of behavior the teacher expects from students.
- Schools should be challenging, exciting, engrossing, and thought-provoking. Schools also must have structure to ensure success. Well-managed schools and classrooms are task-oriented and predictable.
- Effective teachers spend the first two weeks of school teaching students to follow classroom procedures. First they decide what routines will be necessary for the intended activities. Then they list the procedural steps students must follow in order to participate in and benefit from the activities. Finally they teach the procedures by explaining, rehearsing, and reinforcing.

The Wongs believe that an action plan for the first day of school considers and plans for several things. Classroom teacher Sarah Jondahl applies the Wongs's ideas as she anticipates each school year. She prepares the classroom before students arrive. She thinks about academic expectations, class schedules and time frames, and lesson plans and activities for the first days of school. She also considers procedures and evidence to document and evaluate student practice and understanding. She plans steps for maintaining a good learning environment. She also plans ways to establish working relations with students and caregivers.

In addition to their book, the Wongs offer a video series called *The Effective Teacher,* and publish a column on www.teachers.net. Their website is www.effectiveteaching.com.

Fred Jones.   Fred Jones (2007), formerly a clinical psychologist, developed and now directs popular training programs in procedures for managing classrooms and discipline. Jones stresses that the goal of discipline is for students to assume responsibility for their actions. Unlike Kounin and Dreikurs, whose suggestions were valuable but not capable of achieving quick results, Jones intends his program to be effective, easy to implement, and able to produce results quickly.

Jones's research found that although most teachers fear crisis events such as fighting and blatant defiance to authority, these rarely occur, even in hard-to-manage classes. The reality is that about 80 percent of all disruptive behavior is little more than talking without permission and another 15 percent is almost entirely students moving about the room when they should be in their seats or generally goofing off by daydreaming, making inappropriate noises, and the like.

Jones also found that most teachers can regain teaching time that otherwise is lost. They arrange the room to allow them to work the crowd as they move among students during seatwork. They set clear limits through class agreements and effective body language. And they use several clusters of skills—Say, See, Do Teaching; providing incentive systems; and giving efficient help.

Efficient *classroom arrangement* improves the likelihood of successful teaching, learning, and behavior. *Limit setting* involves clarifying the boundaries of acceptable behavior and then formulating *class agreements* of rules and incentives accordingly. For Jones, rules describe procedures—how students are to do their work, what they should do if materials are needed, what to do when unable to proceed on their own, and what to do when finished with an assignment. *Backup systems,* including the school discipline code, will be used when students misbehave seriously and refuse to comply with rules or the teacher's requests.

Body language receives considerable emphasis in this system because, according to Jones, it is the teacher's most effective tool in enforcing boundaries on acceptable behavior. Effective body language projects the message that the teacher means business. Jones claims that teachers can prevent 90 percent of normal discipline problems with nonverbal communication: calm breathing, physical proximity to students, body position, facial expression, tone of voice, and eye contact. Here are two examples:

> An Li stops following the math lesson and is thinking about the new puppies at home. She hears Ms. Eckert pause. She looks at Ms. Eckert and finds her looking at her (eye contact). An Li straightens herself and waits attentively.

> Shawn stops working and talks to Jerry. Suddenly he sees Ms. Eckert's shadow (physical proximity). Immediately he gets back to work, without anything said.

Say, See, Do Teaching keeps students actively involved during instruction by asking them to respond frequently to teacher input. *Incentive systems* work like carrots before the horse's nose. Jones suggests using preferred activity time (PAT) because it offers something students want, and students know they will get it only if they work and behave as they should. Ms. Eckert tells her class that all who correctly finish their homework assignments every day for a week (reinforcing the criterion of mastery mentioned in Chapter 7) can participate in a game of Jeopardy at the end of Friday. Questions used for the game will reinforce what the students study during the week.

Providing *efficient help* is one of Jones's most useful suggestions. Suppose that Ms. Eckert demonstrated a long-division algorithm and students practiced under her guidance before she assigned them problems to complete at their seats. Soon eight students raised their hands. Describing situations such as this one, Jones asked teachers how much time they thought they spent helping individual students during seatwork. Teachers thought one or two minutes, but Jones observed that the actual average was four minutes per student. This is a long time for other students to sit doing nothing—until they misbehave.

To keep students working instead of misbehaving, Jones offers two suggestions. First, teachers should use visual instructional plans and graphic reminders to which students can refer instead of calling for the teacher. Second, teachers should give students enough help in twenty seconds or less to get them back on track. Teachers give this help in three steps: (1) comment on what the student has done correctly (an optional step after the first interaction), (2) give a direct suggestion or clue to get the student back on track, such as "The next thing to do is . . ." and (3) leave immediately. This rapid procedure enables teachers to provide help to all who need it while deterring helpless handraising and the dependency syndrome in which students rely on the teacher's presence before doing their work.

Jones offers a video course of study and a free online study guide entitled *The Video Toolbox* (2005), as well as a companion parenting program. The materials and updated workshop information are available through their website, www.fredjones.com. The website also maintains an active bulletin board of ideas for PAT.

Spencer Kagan, Patricia Kyle, and Sally Scott.   Spencer Kagan and Patricia Kyle have researched and written independently about classroom discipline for nearly twenty years. Together with Sally Scott, they have collaborated to describe an approach they call *Win-Win Discipline* (2004). Kagan, Kyle, and Scott say that the ultimate goal of discipline is for students to be able to manage themselves autonomously and meet their needs through responsible choices. They believe that responsible behavior links closely to curriculum, instruction, and the teacher, and that discipline is something acquired by students, not something done to students. Any behavior that interrupts the learning process reflects a lack of acquired discipline and is a good opportunity for teaching and learning skills of self-discipline and life skills.

Accordingly, win-win discipline emphasizes a "we" approach to working with students to produce long-term learned responsibility. This approach involves three fundamental principles that Kagan, Kyle, and Scott call "the Three Pillars".

- Same Side: teacher understands where the student is coming from and teams up with the student to find discipline solutions
- Collaborative Solutions: teacher and student share responsibility for co-creating discipline solutions
- Learned Responsibility: student acquires long-term responsible behavior that is nondisruptive

Kagan, Kyle, and Scott show teachers how to identify the type of misbehavior as well as the condition that is prompting students to misbehave at any given time. Nearly all disruptions can be categorized into four types of behavior: aggression, breaking rules, confrontation, and disengagement (ABCD disruptive behaviors). They tell teachers *what* students do. What Kagan, Kyle, and Scott refer to as *positions*—the conditions for the disruptive behavior—tell teachers *why* students do what they do. In other words, positions reflect a person's needs at the time he or she acts out. The seven positions are

- Attention-seeking—seeking to be recognized; to receive caring, concern, love
- Avoiding failure—seeking to avoid looking foolish or unsuccessful in front of others
- Angry—seeking to express one's anger
- Control-seeking—seeking to establish the sense of being in charge and able to make one's own choices
- Bored—seeking stimulation
- Energetic—seeking to release excessive energy
- Uninformed—not knowing which behavior is appropriate for the situation.

"YOUR TEACHER DOESN'T MIND A
LITTLE CLOWNING AROUND IN CLASS,
BUT SHE THINKS YOU OVERDO IT."

Positions are neither right nor wrong; they simply are part of the human condition. We all regularly find ourselves in these positions. Identifying and understanding a student's position does not mean that the teacher allows or affirms the disruption. Nor does it mean that the teacher tries to change the position. The teacher deals with the disruption by validating the position and maintaining the student's dignity. The teacher's goal is to help the student toward responsible, nondisruptive ways of behaving when in these positions.

Kagan, Kyle, and Scott give teachers hundreds of concrete structures—step-by-step sequences of interactions—to use for the moment of disruption, follow-up, and long-term solutions. They emphasize preventive strategies aligned with each of the positions. They also place heavy emphasis on the importance of integrating life skill instruction as part of the discipline program. They advocate that teachers and students create jointly written class agreements of rules and responsible alternatives and that teachers develop parent and community alliances to make win-win solutions work for everyone. Additional information on win-win discipline, Kagan structures, and current workshops can be found at this website: www.kaganonline.com.

Barbara Coloroso.   Barbara Coloroso, who writes and consults widely on discipline, believes that all students are worth the effort teachers can expend on them—not just when they are bright, good looking, or well behaved, but always. She asserts that in order for teachers to have good discipline, they must do three things. Teachers must treat students with respect and dignity. They must give students a sense of positive power over their own lives. Finally, teachers must give students opportunities to make decisions, take responsibility for their actions, and learn from their successes and mistakes.

Proper discipline, according to Coloroso, does four things punishment cannot do. First, it shows students what they have done wrong, in contrast with punishment that merely tells. Second, it gives students ownership of the problems. An important goal is for children to develop an inner discipline by learning how to think, not just what to think. To this end, teachers must give students responsibility and ownership by allowing them to make mistakes and by guiding them to accept the natural or reasonable consequences of their actions. The certainty, not the severity, of consequences will have effect for students. Third, proper discipline provides students with ways to solve subsequent problems they may encounter. And fourth, proper discipline leaves students' dignity intact.

VIGNETTE 9.1   Class Agreements

Ginny Lorenz believes that the best statement for allowing students a hand in the writing of classroom rules comes directly from the students. Every year Ginny asks her class to write a letter to the incoming fourth graders. Alex wrote this about class rules: "I will always remember fourth grade because I finally felt good about me. When I came to fourth grade everybody didn't like me because I always got in trouble. Nobody would let me play at their house because they had heard about me at school. This year we talked about rules and picked the ones we wanted. I found out I could be good. I found out I could even be a good student." Alex was correct; he found out that when he controlled his own behavior he could be a good student. Ginny did not control Alex's behavior. He and the other students took care of their own behavior because they felt that they had a say in what was important and they felt that they truly belonged.

Upon Reflection
What might Ginny say when she first meets her new class of fourth graders to involve them in creating a jointly written class agreement of rules and responsible alternatives?

Coloroso explains her ideas on discipline in her books and video series, *Kids Are Worth It! Giving Your Child the Gift of Inner Discipline* (1994) and *Parenting with Wit and Wisdom in Times of Chaos and Loss* (1999). She describes three categories of misbehavior and suggests what teachers can do to help students. The categories are called mistakes, mischief, and mayhem.

Mistakes are simple errors that provide opportunities for learning better choices. When an excited Brent accidentally scribbles on the table rather than his paper, he can help scrub the table clean and the teacher can cover the table with paper to avoid future mishaps.

Mischief, while not necessarily serious, is intentional misbehavior. It provides an opportunity to help students find ways to fix what was done wrong and to avoid doing it again, while retaining their dignity. When Beth tears apart a book because she likes the pictures and wants to keep them in her desk, she should work out a payment plan with the teacher and her parents to replace the damaged book.

Mayhem is willfully serious misbehavior and calls for application of the three Rs for guidance in helping students take responsibility and accept consequences. *Restitution* has the student repair or compensate for the damage. *Resolution* allows the student to identify and correct whatever caused the misbehavior so it won't happen again. *Reconciliation* helps students complete the process of healing the relationships with people who were hurt by the misbehavior. Consider fifth-grader Marcy. When she was not selected for the soccer team, Marcy broke the team captain's arm by willfully pushing her against the wall. With the help of an insightful and supportive coach, Marcy offered to take notes for Amy, the captain, so Amy could keep up in class. In addition to apologizing to Amy and her parents, the coach, and the other team members, Marcy participated in an anger management program sponsored by the neighborhood youth club. There she was able to clarify what she did, why she did it, and what she learned from the experience. She also was able to develop alternative anger management strategies so she could make better choices in the future.

In her book, *The Bully, the Bullied, and the Bystander* (2002), Coloroso examines all the participants in the cycle of violence, a reality in today's schools. Bullies instill fear in others; they intend to hurt, and they enjoy it. Bullies in elementary grades may use verbal or physical bullying, or they may ignore or exclude their targets with relational bullying. Bullying hurts bystanders in addition to the victim. Bystanders or peers of victims may appear to follow or support bullies, or do nothing to stop the action. Teachers must be willing to confront the problem and work with students for awareness, a safe environment, and solutions.

For further discussion on bullying and Coloroso's work, you may want to review the section on bullying in Chapter 7. You also can visit Coloroso's website, www.kidsare worthit.com.

Marvin Marshall.   Marvin Marshall believes that almost all students are inclined to behave responsibly, although they may need help to do so. He insists students cannot be forced to learn or behave responsibly, but they can be influenced to do so through a noncoercive approach. His plan to raise individual responsibility so students choose to do what is right and proper teaches students the four levels of social development. Level A *Anarchy* and Level B *Bothering/Bossing/Bullying* are unacceptable levels of behavior. Level C *Cooperating/Conforming* is acceptable in the classroom, although generally students are relying on external motivation such as peer pressure to guide their actions and behavior. Level D *Democracy and taking the initiative to do the right thing* is the most desirable level and leads to self-discipline. Through the activities Marshall suggests, students learn to make decisions based on internal motivation and take the initiative to do what is right and proper. By focusing on the hierarchy rather than naming misbehaviors, teachers separate actions from students' character. This helps students understand choices and consequences while directing them toward better self-control and self-management.

Marshall's free monthly electronic newsletter, "Promoting Responsibility & Learning," is available via email at www.MarvinMarshall.com. His other websites are www.AboutDiscipline.com and www.DisciplineWithoutStress.com.

Other contemporary authorities offer suggestions and programs to help teachers work with extremely difficult students.

Richard Curwin and Allen Mendler.   Richard Curwin and Allen Mendler, whose primary focus and program reflect Discipline with Dignity, write and consult widely on matters related to discipline and working with challenging youth. Although they seem to be describing older students, sadly, their ideas can be applied to some elementary children. They say that most students who chronically misbehave see themselves as losers, with no hope that education will serve them, and these beliefs put students in serious danger of failing in school. Curwin and Mendler stress that helping students learn to behave acceptably in school is fundamental to teaching, and they ask teachers to do everything possible to instill hope and success in all students, including those who are behaviorally or academically at risk, in a way that preserves everyone's dignity. Teachers must explore ways to ensure success, motivate students, and make learning attractive, interesting, and worthwhile. To this end, Curwin and Mendler describe a systematic approach and concrete suggestions for dealing with challenging students and violence in the classroom. You can find more about their program and suggestions at their website, www.disciplineassociates.com.

Ronald Morrish.   Ronald Morrish was mentioned earlier in the chapter. Morrish feels that teachers today are misguided in their approach to discipline. He believes they focus on behavior management—making the environment functional—rather than on *real discipline*—teaching students to act appropriately, with respect, responsibility, and cooperation. He says that students do not know right from wrong; they do whatever works for them at the time without considering rights or needs of others, and they do not consider consequences.

Morrish believes that teachers must reestablish their authority in the classroom, and that students must be trained to accept and comply automatically with rules, limits, and this authority. He believes that this is accomplished through direct instruction, insistence, do-overs, and practice until the behaviors become habit. *Insistence* is teachers' persistence until students do what they are told to do. *Do-overs* have students repeat the acceptable behavior. In addition to teaching students skills required for school and life success, the ultimate goal of real discipline is for students to be self-disciplined and able to conduct themselves properly even when the teacher is not present. Morrish's discipline tips can be found in his book *FlipTips* (2003) and on his website, www.realdiscipline.com.

BUILDING A SYSTEM OF PARTICIPATIVE DISCIPLINE

You have seen ideas from a number of different approaches to discipline. You can use those ideas to build a system that works for you and your students. In most cases, a participative approach will serve you best. Participative discipline is a system in which teachers and students cooperate in making decisions about expectations, behavior, and consequences for violations of class rules or agreements. To develop a participative discipline plan, you should compile discipline techniques, outline the plan using those techniques, and then fine-tune the plan with your students.

Compiling Techniques

Compile a list of discipline ideas and techniques that suit the needs of your students and that match your philosophy of working with students. For example, you might (or might not) include such ideas as basic rights to teach and learn, rules, withitness, student needs and positions, good lesson management and transitions, efficient help, incentive systems, shared responsibility, the three Rs for guidance, and joint teacher–student ownership of the discipline plan.

Outlining a Plan

Outline a basic plan. From the outset, think of your discipline system as requiring the following seven elements:

- Understanding between you and students
- Balance between your needs and theirs
- Formal agreements between you and them
- Practicality of implementation

- Vitality in ongoing use
- Decorum in application
- Flexibility and renewability

Summarize your ideas clearly, but discuss them with your students before you finalize them. Together, agree on a plan of action.

Launching Your Plan

Implement the class agreement or discipline plan by discussing your ideas with students and asking them for their reactions and suggestions. Some considerations for each of the seven elements follow. The first three points are presented as a sample dialogue to have with students as you launch your plan with the class. The other four are general considerations before you finalize the plan.

Understanding

1. This is our class, and if we work together, we will create a place where each of us feels comfortable and where we all can enjoy the teaching and learning. I have a responsibility to create an environment where this can happen, but I need your help to really make it work. Each of you must know that you are an important member of this class with important responsibilities, and you can help make this a pleasant place to be. One of your important responsibilities is to help us create a positive learning atmosphere, one where everybody's needs are met. To accomplish this, we all must work together. I suggest we begin by creating a class agreement.
2. We all have very important jobs in this class. Your job is to learn as much as you can. That means that you must try your hardest, do your best work, and help everyone in the class do better. My job is to teach you as best I can, to help you, and to make learning as much fun as possible.
3. We all have very important rights in this class, and we must not let anyone interfere with them. You have the right to learn without anyone bothering you. I have the right to teach without anyone bothering me. We must not allow any kind of irresponsible behavior take away your right to learn or my right to teach.
4. Throughout the year, we all must try to do the best we can do—the best teaching from me, the best learning from you, and the best work from all of us, so we can be proud and your caregivers can be proud of you. We can have a good time doing this, working together and getting along and doing excellent work. This is how we make the best of ourselves.

Balance

1. There are many things you need to have in this room in order to do your best. You need good teaching from me, good things to learn, and pleasure in what we do together.
2. There are many things I need in order to teach you best—a calm, quiet atmosphere, good manners from you, and cooperation and helpfulness toward each other.
3. What I need must be balanced with what you need. We can't have a good class if we do everything only to suit me or only to suit you. We have to balance things so that all

of us can have what we need to make this class exceptionally good. That means that all of us must be kind, considerate, and helpful to each other.

Formal Agreement

1. Suppose you were trying your best to learn something in this class. How would you want the other students to act while you were trying to learn? Let's name some behaviors we could choose that would make us happy to be in this class and able to get our work done. (Record student responses, guiding the process so the behaviors are stated positively and apply to everyone.) What are some examples of what these behaviors look like, sound like, and feel like?

2. Do you think we need rules to help us remember how we should behave when I am trying to teach and you are trying to learn? (Discussion.) Let's see if we can think of a rule about how each of us will try to do our work and a rule about how each of us will behave toward others. (Discussion.) These are fine rules. I'll write them here on the board.

3. Let's think about what they mean, about what they tell us to do and not do. How do you feel about this list? (Discussion.) You seem to like these rules, and I do, too. I believe they will help us. Are you willing to adopt them as our class agreement?

4. Now suppose that most of us follow these rules, but one or two students don't. Suppose they talk loudly or run around the room. What should we do if that happens? (Discussion. Record student suggestions, guiding the process so they are stated positively, apply to everyone, and offer solutions, not punishments.) I think your suggestions will be good for our class.

5. You and I need to be on the same side and work together to create a classroom where we all want to be and all can learn. You will be able to have your say and help make decisions about the class. We will learn and practice skills that are important for being citizens in a democratic society. Choosing responsible behavior will be one of the most important things we will learn. Tomorrow I'll have the class agreement, with the rules as well as what happens if they are broken, written on paper. We will sign our names on that paper to show that we agree with the rules and agree to follow them. Then I will make copies for you to take home for your caregivers to see.

Practicality.   Before finalizing the rules and consequences and considering the remainder of your discipline plan, keep this point foremost in your mind: You have to live with the plan. It is supposed to serve your class; your class is not supposed to serve it. It must not be so complicated, difficult, or time-consuming that it enslaves you. Make sure the plan is easy to implement, serves its purpose, requires little extra time from you, and produces minimal irritation, resentment, and lost time.

Vitality.   Ideally, your discipline plan is not something apart from instruction but rather something that is incorporated into instruction, as essential as directions and feedback. Assuming that students see your plan as fair (and that's why you spend so much time discussing it and making sure students buy into it), it will serve wonderfully as you inject interest, novelty, fun, and importance into learning activities. It will earn continued support if you can stop disruptive behavior at once, invoke consequences, and follow through calmly and helpfully, showing the personal support students prize. Also, for your students, it should not be the severity but the certainty of receiving the consequence that has impact. Further, caregivers and administrators will back the plan if it is humane, obviously serves students, and is communicated well.

Decorum. Despite the workload, frustration, and stress with which you always must contend, remember that it is your responsibility to ensure that the classroom is a place of decorum and gentility, where students speak and act courteously, where no one's character is attacked, and where you, especially, serve as the finest model. If you and your students are to prosper, you must make and keep your classroom a good place in which to live and work. This requires ongoing modeling of the qualities of good character and behavior, as well as opportunities for students to practice them.

Flexibility and Renewability. You should begin with what you believe to be best for your students and yourself; then stick by your resolve so long as there is reason to do so. But at the same time, you must remain eminently flexible. If something is not working, try to change it so that it will. Discuss the problem with your students and together come up with an alternative that promises better results. It is good to discuss the class and discipline in regularly held classroom meetings. Some teachers take time at the end of every day for a short discussion of what went well and what did not, and when problems surface they arrange times for longer discussions. They want to know students' views of how things are going and what needs to be done differently. They willingly make new beginnings when warranted, knowing that sometimes a simple change for change's sake is valuable.

This concludes our consideration of discipline—how to manage student behavior so good teaching and learning can occur within an atmosphere of gentility and helpfulness. Before we turn to the topic of how to manage the assessment of student progress, along with record keeping and reporting to caregivers and administrators, take time to explore these end-of-chapter activities.

Parting Thought

Simplicity is an acquired taste. Mankind, left free, instinctively complicates life.
—Katharine Fullerton Gerould

SUMMARY SELF-CHECK

Check off the following as you either understand or become able to apply them.

❑ Disruptive student behavior causes more wasted time, more teacher stress, and more teacher burnout than all other factors combined.

❑ Student behavior is growing worse, as evidenced by apathy, failure to work, disrespect, and open aggression.

❏ The older disciplinary technique of authoritative teacher demands no longer works.

❏ Many valuable ideas in discipline have appeared in the past four decades:
   ■ Pioneering research and work by Fritz Redl and William Wattenberg, B. F. Skinner, Haim Ginott, Jacob Kounin, Rudolf Dreikurs, Lee and Marlene Canter, and William Glasser
   ■ Harry Wong: the first days and weeks of school, procedures and routines
   ■ Fred Jones: setting limits and body language; back up systems; Say, See, Do Teaching; incentive systems; efficient help
   ■ Spencer Kagan, Patricia Kyle, and Sally Scott: Same Side, Collaborative Solutions, Learned Responsibility; ABCD disruptive behaviors; student positions; life skills
   ■ Barbara Coloroso: three categories of misbehavior (mistake, mischief, mayhem); three Rs of guidance (restitution, resolution, reconciliation); the bully, the bullied, the bystander
   ■ Marvin Marshall: external and internal motivation; levels of social behavior (Level A Anarchy, Level B Bothering/Bossing/Bullying, Level C Cooperating/Conforming, and Level D Democracy and taking the initiative to do the right thing); helping students to behave more responsibly
   ■ Richard Curwin and Allen Mendler: behaviorally and academically at risk, rediscovering hope, dignity
   ■ Ronald Morrish: real discipline, teacher's authority, student compliance, do-overs

❏ Teachers typically construct their own systems of discipline, consistent with their personality, philosophy, and needs, and the traits and needs of the students they teach.

❏ Steps in formulating a good personal system of discipline:
   ■ Compile preferred techniques.
   ■ Outline a plan that includes understanding, balance, formal agreement, practicality, vitality, gentility, flexibility, and renewability.
   ■ Fine-tune and publish the plan after discussion with students.

ACTIVITIES FOR REFLECTION AND DISCUSSION

1. Take a moment to review the statements in the Prediction–Review Guide at the beginning of this chapter. Put a check mark in the Review column next to any statement with which you now agree. How have your thoughts changed since reading this chapter?

2. Interview at least two teachers about their discipline plans. To what extent did the teachers and their students work together to create the class rules and consequences? What are their class rules? Consequences? Rewards?

3. Brainstorm a list of disruptive behaviors you might find in an elementary classroom. Categorize these behaviors according to ABCD.

4. Compile a list of specific discipline techniques that you feel best match your personality, philosophy, and needs.

5. Virtually all elementary students will agree that they would like to learn. Why then do they so often misbehave and make no effort to do what teachers provide for them?

6. When you were an elementary student, under which of the various systems of discipline described in this chapter would you have preferred to work? Explain.

7. Review the seven student positions that Kagan, Kyle, and Scott identify. Create kinesthetic signs (and add sounds) to convey their meanings.

REFERENCES AND RECOMMENDED READINGS

Albert, L. (2003). *Cooperative discipline.* Circle Pines, MN: American Guidance Service.

Canter, L., & Canter, M. (2001). *Assertive discipline: Positive behavior management for today's classroom* (3rd ed.). Los Angeles: Canter & Associates.

Charles, C. (2000). *The synergetic classroom: Joyful teaching and gentle discipline.* New York: Addison Wesley Longman.

Charles, C. (2008). *Building classroom discipline* (9th ed.). Boston: Allyn & Bacon.

Coloroso, B. (1994). *Kids are worth it! Giving your child the gift of inner discipline.* New York: Avon Books.

Coloroso, B. (2002). *The bully, the bullied, and the bystander.* Toronto, Ontario, Canada: HarperCollins.

Curtiss, K., & English, S. (2003). Choice theory certification. Retrieved August 2003, from www.kathycurtissco.com/what_we_do.htm.

Curwin, R., & Mendler, A. (1997). *As tough as necessary: Countering violence, aggression, and hostility in our schools.* Alexandria, VA: ASCD.

Dreikurs, R., & Cassel, P. (1972). *Discipline without tears.* New York: Hawthorn.

Dreikurs, R., Grunwald, B., & Pepper, F. (1982). *Maintaining sanity in the classroom.* New York: Harper & Row.

Glasser, W. (1998a). *Choice theory in the classroom* (rev. ed.). New York: HarperCollins.

Glasser, W. (1998b). *The quality school teacher* (rev. ed.). New York: HarperCollins.

Jones, F. (2007). *Tools for teaching: Discipline Instruction Motivation* (2nd ed.). Santa Cruz, CA: Fredric H. Jones.

Kagan, S., Kyle, P., & Scott, S. (2004). *Win-win discipline.* San Clemente, CA: Kagan Cooperative Learning.

Kounin, J. (1970). *Discipline and group management in classrooms.* New York: Holt, Rinehart & Winston.

Marshall, M. (2002). *Discipline without stress, punishments, or rewards: How teachers and parents promote responsibility and learning.* Los Alamitos, CA: Piper Press.

Marshall, M., & Weisner, K. (2004, March). Using a discipline system to promote learning. *Phi Delta Kappan 85*(7), 498–507. Bloomington, IN: Phi Delta Kappa International.

Nelsen, J., Lott, L., & Glenn, H. (2000). *Positive discipline in the classroom.* Rocklin, CA: Prima Publishing.

Olweus, D. (1999). *Core program against bullying and antisocial behavior: A teacher handbook.* Norway: Research Center for Health Promotion, University of Bergen.

Redl, F., and Wattenberg, W. (1951). *Mental hygiene in teaching.* New York: Harcourt, Brace & World. Revised and reissued in 1959.

Rose, L., & Gallup, A. (2005). The 37th annual Phi Delta Kappan/Gallup poll. *Phi Delta Kappan, 87*(1), 41–57.

Thousand, J., Villa, R., & Nevin, A. (2002). *Creativity and collaborative learning: The practical guide to empowering students, teachers, and families* (2nd ed.). Baltimore: Paul H. Brookes.

Websites

Linda Albert
www.cooperativediscipline.com

Barbara Coloroso
www.kidsareworthit.com

Richard Curwin and Allen Mendler
www.disciplineassociates.com

William Glasser
www.choicetheory.org/directory.html
www.choicetheory.com/links.htm

Fred Jones
www.fredjones.com

Spencer Kagan
www.kaganonline.com

Marvin Marshall
www.MarvinMarshall.com
www.AboutDiscipline.com
www.DisciplineWithoutStress.com

Ronald Morrish
www.realdiscipline.com

Harry Wong
www.Teachers.net
www.EffectiveTeaching.com

Managing Assessment, Record Keeping, and Reporting

What we want to see is the child in pursuit of knowledge, not knowledge in pursuit of the child.

—George Bernard Shaw

Prediction–Review Guide

Before you read the chapter, take a minute to put a check mark in the Prediction column next to any statement with which you agree.

	Prediction	Review
1. Authentic assessment places less reliance on testing than traditionally has been the case.	❏	❏
2. Portfolios are synonymous with student work folders.	❏	❏
3. Assessment should be part of the instruction process and should help students learn.	❏	❏
4. Among assessments that guide improvements in student learning are those that teachers administer regularly in their classrooms.	❏	❏
5. Overall, test scores are the most useful records for teachers to keep, since those are what most caregivers understand.	❏	❏
6. Corrective instruction is the same as remedial work.	❏	❏
7. Lists of standards and objectives, as well as continuums, can be found in curriculum guides and in teachers' editions of newer textbooks.	❏	❏
8. Teachers should display comparison records of work and progress as a means of motivating students toward higher achievement.	❏	❏
9. Generally, parents and guardians resent being asked to help with their child's schoolwork at home.	❏	❏
10. Performance should be observed during class time, but records entries should be made in the privacy of the teacher's home.	❏	❏

Support for specific standards found in this chapter:

INTASC Standards

8. Assessment of Student Learning

   The teacher understands and uses formal and informal assessment strategies to evaluate and ensure the continuous intellectual, social, and physical development of the learner.

Danielson's Framework for Teaching

3. Instruction
   - Communicating clearly and accurately
   - Using questioning and discussion techniques
   - Engaging students in learning
   - Providing feedback to students
   - Demonstrating flexibility and responsiveness
4. Professional Responsibilities
   - Reflecting on teaching
   - Maintaining accurate records
   - Communicating with families
   - Contributing to the school and district
   - Growing and developing professionally

NBPTS Standards

3. Teachers are responsible for managing and monitoring student learning.
4. Teachers think systematically about their practice and learn from experience.

NCATE Standards

Reflect on practice, act on feedback, and integrate technology into instruction effectively.

Assessment, record keeping, and reporting are necessary requirements of teaching, but few teachers enjoy dealing with them. Traditionally, these tasks have been seen as unpleasant burdens to be endured while experiencing the pleasures of teaching children. In recent years, legislation and the nationwide push for performance accountability and higher learning outcomes have added to the pressures teachers feel about assessment. But while all this is true, new practices in both teaching and assessment have helped to make these tasks more manageable and achievable to everyone concerned.

This chapter explores assessment methods that are under teacher control, and then discusses effective means of keeping records and reporting to parents and guardians. The following overview summarizes details relevant to the processes of assessment, recording, and reporting.

THE PUSH FOR BETTER ASSESSMENT AND REPORTING

A nationwide movement is underway to ensure positive learning outcomes for our nation's students. In particular, the Goals 2000: Educate America Act (1994) and the No Child Left Behind Act of 2001 have set the tone for curriculum standards and provided an impetus for their development. (Note here that Appendix B lists content-specific professional organizations and their Internet sites where you can find national standards for each specific curriculum area.) This national attention has led to the creation or revision of state learning goals, along with standards for each grade level. These standards relate to the broad areas of content, performance, and opportunities-to-learn. *Content standards* focus on what should be learned in various subject areas, as well as critical thinking and problem-solving skills. *Performance standards* attempt to answer the question "How good is good enough?" They specify the level of satisfactory performance when students apply and demonstrate what they know, often in authentic or real-life situations. *Opportunity-to-learn standards,* controversial because of the potential for more federal involvement, have to do with the condition and resources necessary to give students an equal chance to meet the performance standards (Morrison, 2002).

THE NATURE OF ASSESSMENT

In education, *assessment* refers to the process of finding out, as objectively as possible, how well students are progressing. Because it should be ongoing, assessment often drives instruction as teachers use this information to plan their next steps in instruction. Thorough assessment involves multi-trait, multi-method, and multi-source estimations of student status or progress. In contrast, *measurement* tends to be one-dimensional, often reduced to scores made on short-answer tests. *Grades* are the numbers or letters assigned at the end of a piece of work or a set period of time as a summary judgment statement of the level of student understanding or performance.

Different forms of assessments serve different purposes. *Diagnostic* or *placement assessment* considers "Where are the students now, and where do I begin with my instruction?" This form of assessment, including pretests, helps teachers determine what knowledge and skills the students already have.

Other assessments are fundamental for helping students learn. *Formative assessments* are part of the instruction process. They help teachers determine if students are making satisfactory progress and whether the instruction needs to be modified. They relate directly to instructional goals and should align to state and district standards. Because teachers are testing what they teach, these assessments provide immediate results about both student and instruction success. Types of formative assessment include discussions and questioning, quizzes and tests, writing assignments, and other in-class work that teachers administer regularly.

Summative assessment, occurring at the end of the unit or lesson sequence, helps teachers to determine whether students met the objectives or mastered the content. Summative assessments probe learning—the intended outcomes of instruction. They ask students to produce products and demonstrate skills and understandings in realistic situations and in a variety of ways—through discussion, role-playing, or performance; through conducting investigations or demonstrations; by completing projects or producing tangible products; and by analyzing ideas and procedures. Usually summative assessment is the basis for assigning grades.

In the past, test scores were entered and averaged in the teacher's grade book as evidence to support final grades. But in the movement toward accountability and more satisfactory means of assessment, evidence has been expanded to include the quality of student productivity, often in class or cooperative team assignments. Attempts are made to help students demonstrate nuances of understanding over time, indicate how they think and process information, and show their ability to apply learned skills realistically. Generally this type of assessment is considered to be more genuine, less contrived, and less test-like than former attempts at measurement.

Currently there is considerable controversy concerning the use of standardized testing. The movement emphasizes norm-based measurement (showing how students compare to each other) to establish national standards of performance. For more than thirty years, the United States has used National Assessment of Educational Progress (NAEP) assessments as a national "report card" for educational achievement. Periodic tests, administered to representative samples of students, report achievement in several fields, including reading, writing, mathematics, science, history, and geography. Additionally, states now use other programs and tests such as the Standardized Testing and Reporting program (STAR), the Stanford Achievement Test (SAT 9), and the Indiana Statewide Testing for Educational Progress (ISTEP), intended to measure student achievement of grade-level content standards. Many educators dislike standardized tests because too often they measure only recall and knowledge and provide sparse insight into learning outcomes such as critical thinking and creativity. Furthermore, the tests usually are inadequately aligned with district and state curricula. They believe that as states continue to develop their own assessment tests, reliance on national standardized tests may decrease.

AUTHENTIC ASSESSMENT

Authentic assessment has been gaining favor rapidly among educators. It is explained as that which "involves students in challenges that approximate or at least better represent the 'tests' likely to face them as professionals, citizens, or consumers" (Wiggins, 1994). With feedback from their teachers and others, students analyze, refine, and improve their work over time. In this approach, a student essay might be written and rewritten until polished to high quality. You can see the contrast between this approach and what used to occur—the student wrote an essay, turned it in, received it back with red marks and a grade on it, and threw it away. Authentic assessment encourages students to investigate possibilities, make judgments, rethink efforts, and even redo work until the student considers it a quality product—remember Glasser's thoughts about quality in Chapter 5 and Jones's thoughts about a criterion of mastery in Chapter 7? It is the student, not the teacher, who decides when the work is good enough. The resultant improvement can be as objective an indicator of quality as are grades on tests.

Unlike testing, authentic assessment is at the center of the teaching–learning process. Students are judged by what they do and produce during and after instruction. They do not have to try to translate what they learn into test responses. That fact makes authentic assessment appealing to teachers and students. Taking improvement into account makes the process even more appealing.

Student Portfolios in Authentic Assessment

Students use portfolios to show their work, efforts, and talents, just as models, artists, architects, and others use portfolios to showcase their work. Portfolios play a central role in authentic assessment. Although the name can suggest a large and unwieldy container, a portfolio may simply be a file folder or a three-ring binder that contains work samples as well as written tests from most areas of the curriculum. The important thing is not how they look, but how they are created and used.

A true portfolio requires *collection, selection,* and *reflection.* From a collection of all their work products, students select for inclusion in their portfolios pieces of work—not necessarily their *A* work—that they consider particularly noteworthy. Then they reflect and articulate orally or in writing why they selected each sample—why it is special and what they learned by completing it.

This process has significant benefits for students and teachers. Portfolios make students active participants in the assessment process. They show individual students' ranges of interests, abilities, and achievements over time. This provides teachers, students, and caregivers much to discuss about student learning at school. The process of selection, articulation, and improvement over time provides a broad window into students' experiences and learning and can provide tangible profiles of their growth.

Portfolios also provide concrete examples for parent conferencing. The teacher can say, "Here's what we'd like to accomplish. Here's where your child is. Here are some examples."

Portfolios in Different Subject Areas.   Student portfolios are suitable for use in all subject areas. Examples for the traditional areas of reading, writing, and arithmetic at the sixth-grade level might include

For Reading
- Written responses to reading, such as character or problem analyses
- Book reports
- Literature-based projects or photographs with supporting details of projects
- Audio- or videotapes of dramatic readings

For Writing
- Examples of free or creative writing
- Writing targeted for different audiences
- Writing for different purposes, such as persuasion, information, or entertainment
- Work in a variety of forms, such as poetry, journals, letters, and scripts

For Mathematics

- Math journals
- Projects and investigations
- Diagrams, graphs, charts

Grading of Portfolios.   Portfolios are whole efforts, not exhibits of individual items. The following general criteria are used for grading portfolios (based on Paulson, Paulson, & Meyer, 1991, p. 60):

> *Depth:* Evidence of personal growth through reflection, critical thinking, and insights
>
> *Breadth:* Evidence of personal growth through multiple and varied experiences
>
> *Emphasis:* All entries and reflections contribute to the theme of personal growth
>
> *Unity:* Clear evidence of the process of collection, selection, and reflection
>
> *Mechanics:* Correct sentencing, spelling, capitalization, and punctuation

From the basis of these expectations the teacher is able to make evaluations that ultimately may be converted to grades for records and report cards, described in the broadest of terms as follows:

> *Exceptional achievement,* earned by a portfolio that is particularly well-presented, well-organized, insightful, and technically correct
>
> *Commendable achievement,* earned by an impressive and interesting portfolio that is more loosely organized, less insightful, and not as informative as the exceptional portfolio
>
> *Adequate achievement,* earned by a portfolio that, although acceptable, does not show good organization or display much critical thinking, insight, involvement, or growth
>
> *Minimal evidence of achievement,* earned by a portfolio that lacks depth and is weak in content, thought, and presentation
>
> *No evidence of achievement,* earned by a portfolio that is completely off-track, reveals no insights or other redeeming qualities, or is not the original work of the student

It is important to remember that portfolios are to be viewed as whole products. Although they are made up of individual samples of student work already reviewed and graded by the teacher, it is for the student to determine the items that are noteworthy and that provide evidence of progress and achievement.

The Matter of Grades.   As teaching and assessment practices change, a rethinking of grading also is occurring across the country. Marzano (2000) believes the primary purpose of grading is to provide timely corrective feedback that is as accurate and precise as possible so students can improve their work. Kohn (1999) and others argue that letter grades usually fall short of that goal. Letter grades are symbols, but generally they are not aligned to any common standard and they are essentially arbitrary in levels (A versus B versus C and so on). Further, letter grades do not carry much, if any, information about students'

PORTFOLIOS IN FIRST GRADE

Focus Question

Nancy Rutherford describes how she uses portfolios with first graders. Brainstorm specific ways to use portfolios for assessment in intermediate and upper grades. What suggestions for evidence might students consider to include?

Mrs. Rutherford now uses portfolios with her first-grade students, but when she first heard about portfolios, she thought they were too advanced a concept to be used in first grade. She was put off by the logistics of storing the many oversized projects that were part of her curriculum. She also envisioned the portfolio as purely an assessment tool, so all-in-all the use of portfolios didn't appeal to her.

She since has changed her mind 180 degrees. Mrs. Rutherford finds portfolios to be a great asset in monitoring work in progress. Her students realize that writing is not a one-time try. They learn to look at their work reflectively in terms of predetermined criteria, to assess strengths and weaknesses, and to rewrite accordingly. Her favorite use of portfolios is to show individual progress. Her students review their own work over time and generally are astonished at the differences they find. Even those who had top papers see how much they have improved.

strengths and areas for growth or give any insight into how to help students improve. Consequently, often it is unclear what letter grades represent.

In some districts and schools, teachers are being asked to maintain ongoing records in Internet portals so parents and guardians can use their home computers to check on their child's homework, attendance, and scores, and track their child's progress daily. These programs are intended to strengthen the alliance between teacher and caregivers. To accomplish this, some publishers are providing districts and teachers the needed software with adoption of their materials. In some schools, quarterly paper report cards will continue in addition to this program (Alphonso, 2003).

Educators are seeking better ways to report student accomplishments and areas of growth. Some current recommendations even go so far as to advocate the elimination of letter grades, particularly during the primary years. Teachers are encouraged to monitor student growth in terms of performance, work samples, and long-term projects that show students' capabilities in light of

"I tell my Dad our report cards are now being issued online and he won't admit he can't access them."

predetermined standards and intended learning goals. They then can report this with holistic narratives or continuum checklists of competencies. In the mid 1990s, Vermont was the first state to use portfolios in a statewide assessment program when it required all students in fourth and eighth grade to keep portfolios for writing and mathematics. Fourth and eighth graders took a *uniform test* (timed writing samples and a series of mathematics problems) and presented their portfolios to demonstrate their progress and understandings over time. Well-crafted statewide curriculum standards were developed for judging the portfolios. Although portfolios no longer are collected for statewide data, Vermont continues to support the use of writing and math portfolios for local assessment at several grade levels. To this end, the state promotes writing rubrics and benchmarks based on state standards, statewide professional development meetings, yearly online calibration, and web-based tools to compile the data.

RUBRICS AND THEIR USE

A *rubric* is a scoring guide or assessment scale that is devised to match the standards, objectives, and learning goals of a specific assignment. Because rubrics reflect both broad evaluation standards and specific evaluation criteria, they provide clear descriptions of what students are expected to achieve.

Rubrics can be written for any subject and adapted to any grade level. They require teachers to think more clearly about intended goals and quality work. Well-written rubrics help teachers to score students' work more accurately and fairly. Rubrics match student work to predetermined scoring standards rather than to other students' work (unlike standardized tests) or to expectations held for each individual student. Teachers should share rubrics with students. Students profit from clear knowledge of expectations, and that knowledge then guides their work. It can be very beneficial for teacher and students to discuss learning goals and from those discussions develop the rubrics together.

There are, however, things teachers don't like about rubrics. For one, rubrics don't match other systems, such as letter grades. For another, it takes time to develop successful rubrics, especially those that describe multiple aspects of performance, each with its own criteria and attainment levels. In addition, rubrics can be difficult to explain to caregivers.

The right language is critical when developing rubrics because they must articulate clearly the qualities of student performance that distinguish the levels of work and effort. Over a period of time, teachers may write and refine a project rubric several times in order to make it resemble closely what they actually expect to see in the student work. To ensure the quality of rubric criteria, Wiggins (1994) states this guiding thought: "If a student can achieve a high score on all the criteria and still not perform well at the task, you have the wrong criteria." Depending on grade level, a variety of descriptors can be used:

- Exemplary, proficient, progressing, or not meeting the standard
- Level four, level three, level two, or level one
- Exemplary achievement, commendable achievement, adequate achievement, limited or minimal achievement, or no response
- Star, smiley face, or straight face

▉ RECORDS AND RECORD KEEPING

Ongoing assessment and good records of student progress must be kept to promote effective teaching, good learning, and efficient reporting to caregivers and administrators. Other reasons for keeping accurate records are to furnish data to other schools, to keep attendance (on which financial aid is based), to show student achievement, and to evaluate and modify the district and school curriculum periodically. Additionally, the No Child Left Behind Act requires that records be used in evaluating schools and districts.

What Teachers Want Records to Show

From the teacher's perspective, good records can indicate quickly, at any time during the year, where individual students stand academically and socially. Teachers need this information for teaching, evaluating students, planning for the future, and conferring with and reporting to caregivers and other interested individuals. Records should show the following for individual students: instructional level; progress; unreached standards, goals, and objectives; strengths and weaknesses; and social adjustment.

Instructional Level.   A student's instructional level in any part of the curriculum is the level at which new learning is challenging yet possible. These levels are especially important in classrooms where differentiated instruction occurs. Instructional level is determined through observation, ongoing monitoring of student performance, and occasionally, formal testing. The scores, work samples, and anecdotal comments that serve as indicators are recorded in formats that will be illustrated later.

Progress.   Teachers, students, and caregivers appreciate evidence that the student is making genuine progress. But lack of progress must be noted as well, for this is where replanning, corrective instruction, and second chances begin. Second chances help determine whether the corrective instruction was effective, and they give students another opportunity to be successful in their learning. Progress can be shown in several ways. One of the most common ways is to compare pre- and posttest scores, useful in spelling and math. Another way is to compare samples of work, as in writing and art, done a few weeks apart. Yet another way is to show increased performance through standards and objectives that have been reached and through books that have been read.

Many students enjoy seeing graphic depictions of their improvements. Older students like making the graphs themselves to show increases in scores, quickness, accuracy, and quantity. Because graphs seem to motivate students toward higher performance and are appealing to parents and guardians as well, they are valuable inclusions in individual records folders. These graphs should be individual and private to avoid showing a student in a bad light when compared to others.

Unreached Standards, Goals, and Objectives.   Parents and guardians are interested in their child's progress, as well as in what remains to be accomplished. Well-managed records provide this information, either in a list of standards or objectives that can be checked off when attained or in notations of material to be covered in textbooks.

"SO I MAKE BAD GRADES. IS IT NECESSARY FOR THE SCHOOL SYSTEM TO ISSUE A WRITTEN STATEMENT?"

Strengths and Weaknesses. Student strengths and weaknesses become apparent by examining test scores, other records, and the contents of portfolios or work folders. Teachers note error patterns as they analyze student work, develop ideas for appropriate corrective instruction, and provide opportunities for students to have a second chance to be successful in their learning. Occasionally specialists may be asked to administer diagnostic tests to individual students. Such tests reveal specific weaknesses and error patterns as well as general overall scores.

Social Adjustment. The abilities to relate acceptably and work cooperatively and productively with others are among the most important outcomes of schooling. Evidence of social adjustment is obtained on an informal basis by the teacher, who observes and notes how a student gets along with classmates, shows manners and courtesy, cooperates, takes turns, accepts responsibility, and abides by class rules. Teachers compile this evidence by entering brief comments on progress forms for each student. This information is of special interest to caregivers, most of whom want their child to behave, cooperate, and learn as much as possible.

As older students work more and more in cooperative learning groups and teams, they should be taught to judge the quality of their own work and the efforts of their group. The teacher can help by providing a review sheet such as that shown in Figure 10.1. Note that the contributions of every group member are recorded as positive comments. If a member makes no contribution, the space is left blank.

FIGURE 10.1   Contributions Review

Project Activity _____   Date _____

Leader _____   Contributions _____

Recorder _____   Contributions _____

Member _____   Contributions _____

Member _____   Contributions _____

Member _____   Contributions _____

Member _____   Contributions _____

Problems: Describe any problems the group had and tell what you did to help correct the

problem. _____

Future Instructional Plans.   In every parent–teacher conference, attention should be given to future instructional plans for the student. For the most part these plans will be carried out at school, but sometimes they require assistance at home from the parents or guardians. Student records substantiate the need for assistance, indicate the areas in which it should be provided, and describe how caregivers can help provide assistance.

Forms and Formats for Good Record Keeping

Forms and formats for keeping records include (1) master continuums of standards, objectives, benchmarks, or learning goals; (2) individual student folders; (3) progress forms; (4) graphs; and (5) work samples. It is crucial for teachers to know the state standards, the district expectations and benchmarks, and what is expected on the district report cards.

Standards and Continuums.   Standards or benchmarks may be written statements or checklists. They are listed in newer curriculum guides and teachers' editions of newer textbooks. Objectives are written statements that precisely describe the intended outcomes of instruction—what students will know or be able to do because of the instruction and supporting experiences. When organized into a particular order or sequence, standards or objectives form what is called a *continuum.* Continuums are helpful to teachers in keeping track of student progress. Normally, they are simply checked off when attained.

   Figure 10.2 shows an excerpt from Marilyn's math skills continuum. Codes are frequently used for marking the continuum form. One of the simplest is to enter a slash (/) to indicate that the concept or skill has been introduced. When the student masters the concept or skill, the slash is crossed to make an X. Other systems indicate the date on which the standard or objective was reached, the number of attempts before mastery, and the degree to which the standard or objective was attained—for example, mastery (M), satisfactory (S), and improvement needed (I).

VIGNETTE 10.1   Using Continuums to Document Skill Development

Kindergarten teacher Marilyn Kimbell uses a skills continuum, which she prepares before the school year begins. She lists skills across the top of a grid and the names of her students down the side. Examples of skills are writing name; writing numerals; writing letters; circling objects that are above, below, larger, smaller, and so forth. Children are assessed on these skills by Marilyn, her aide, and trained parent volunteers. Marilyn's aide records the results and Marilyn studies them. She does further assessment if there seems to be a need. Usually the results merely document what Marilyn already has discovered in working with the children. Teachers on her team and her school have tried to correlate the skills continuums with the school report cards. For easy reference, Marilyn makes copies for herself, the parents, and the office.

Upon Reflection
Continuums work for documenting development and learning of skills. Identify other grade-appropriate content and skills that could be documented on a continuum.

FIGURE 10.2   **A Portion of a Kindergarten Math Skills Continuum**

Student Names	Identify and complete pattern	Match set members	Identify set with most	Match set of 6 to numeral	Identify set 1 less than 5	Identify set 1 more than 2	Identify greatest numeral	Identify least numeral	Identify counting order (1–4)	Identify counting order (11–13)

Individual Records Folders.   A personal records folder should be made for each student but kept separate from portfolios that include work samples chosen by students. Records folders contain all essential information about students and are indispensable when conferencing with caregivers and administrators, as well as students themselves. The following suggestions help make folders attractive and useful:

- *Folders.* Use legal-size manila folders. The extra length accommodates most oversized materials.
- *Front cover.* Teacher affixes student name, room number, teacher's name, and grade level. Students decorate the front cover with their own design or artwork. (Have them practice first.)
- *Inside front.* Teacher attaches progress form sheet, such as Figure 10.3.
- *Inside back.* Teacher affixes graph forms (such as Figure 10.4) to indicate individual progress in math, spelling, and other areas.
- *Loose inside.* This area holds samples of student work in penmanship, composition, and art. Special vocabulary and spelling lists plus individual reading lists also can be included. Before and after samples can be stapled together. Work samples should be updated periodically.
- *Student responsibility.* From third grade upward, consider giving students responsibility for recording, graphing, and updating their own folders.
- *Location.* Keep folders in a secure location where they will remain neat and clean and out of the way when not in use.

Records for Various Curriculum Areas

Assessment scores can indicate instructional level, progress made, and particular areas of strength and weakness. Because different areas of the curriculum involve different content

FIGURE 10.3   Student Progress Sheet

Name _____

| | *Pretest* | *Midtest* | *Posttest* |

Reading
   San Diego Quick—level
   Oral Reading Test—level
   Silent Reading Test—level
   Word attack needs _____

Mathematics
   Math grade-level test—
   Basic facts (see graphs)
   Word problem application _____

Language
   Spelling placement
   Word lists and scores (see graphs and samples)
   Capitalization, punctuation, grammar _____
   _____

Composition and Penmanship (see samples) _____
   _____

Social Studies _____
   _____

Science & Health _____
   _____

Art (see samples) _____
   _____

Music _____
   _____

Physical Education (see graphs) _____
   _____

Other _____
Social Behavior _____
   _____
   _____

standards, benchmarks, and goals, they call for different types of records. Those differences are discussed in this section, along with desirable types of records.

Mathematics.   The most useful records for mathematics include a continuum of the standards, benchmarks, or objectives; work samples; and progress graphs. The continuum provides an overview of the mathematics program, together with indications of student progress as student skills and progress are checked off. Student competencies and errors on different types of math problems can be tracked on a record sheet. Graphs such as Figure 10.4 should be kept for certain parts of the math curriculum to show dramatic progress in increments. Graphs are best for recording timed exercises in addition, subtraction, multiplication, and division, as well as word problems.

Reading.   The most valuable records in reading show assessment scores in comprehension and fluency levels, standards or objectives continuums, and lists of books and other materials read by the student. A progress form such as that shown in Figure 10.3 shows areas in which measures are often sought. A reading standards or objectives continuum, illustrated in Figure 10.5, can be used to document specific standards, benchmarks, or objectives reached and not reached by the student. Many students find it motivating to add segments to a bookworm of books read, instead of simply listing titles and dates to correlate the skills continuums with the school report cards. Others like to add leaves or ornaments to a picture of a tree, where each addition shows the title of a book read.

Teachers keep running records of students' reading to assess their reading fluency. After the teacher or trained volunteer records individual students reading aloud, the teacher calculates the percentage of words the student read correctly to determine how well the text matches the student's level at this time. The teacher also analyzes miscues or errors for possible patterns in order to plan mini-lessons, tutorials, and other word study activities. Running records, such as Figure 10.6, are made easier when the teacher makes notations directly on a duplicate copy of the text as the student reads.

Spelling.   Spelling can be treated almost like math facts insofar as records are concerned, as was shown in Figure 10.4. Records for each student should include the scores

FIGURE 10.4   Sample Graph Forms

No.	Week 1	2	4	5	6	7	8	9	10	11	12

Math: Additional facts, number correct out of 50 in five minutes' time.

45–
40–
35–
30–
25–
20–
15–
10–

Spelling: Scores on midweek tests, number correct out of 20.

20–
19–
18–
17–
16–
15–
14–

FIGURE 10.5   Portion of a Reading Objectives Continnuum

Student Names	Consonant sounds	Short vowel sounds	Blends/digraphs	Long vowels, final	Long vowels, double	Vowels modified by letters "r" & "q"	Variant and irregular vowels	Affixes	Main idea	Facts	Cause–effect	Sequence	Prediction	Inference and conclusion	Bases, prefixes, suffixes	Antonyms, synonyms	Contractions	Compound words
	Word attack								Comprehension						Vocabulary			

on weekly spelling tests, showing continuity of achievement and effort. Student work on special word lists or bonus words should be indicated. Teachers also need to assess spelling in written work—are words mastered on the spelling test carrying over to a student's written work?

Grammar and Vocabulary.   For this part of the language arts curriculum, records management changes from recording scores to entering notational appraisals and comments. *Grammar* refers to general language usage, both oral and written, including sentence structure, subject–verb agreement, correct verb tenses, and so forth. The teacher notes errors that seem to recur and makes comments, if needed, on the student's progress sheet (Figure 10.3). The same procedure is followed for vocabulary unless the teacher includes a vocabulary development segment in the language arts program. In that case, students can keep a list of words whose meanings they have mastered, as they do for special spelling words. In some cases, the lists of special spelling words and the new vocabulary are the same.

Writing.   Comments about penmanship and composition are entered here. Composition is further divided into expository and creative writing. Expository writing emphasizes the clear and sequential expression of ideas and involves skills in organization, paragraph construction, the use of topic and subordinate sentences, and so forth. Creative writing stresses the artistic side of writing—expression, novelty of presentation, and varied forms

FIGURE 10.6   Running Record Form

Student _____ Grade _____ Teacher/Rm _____

Date _____ Recorder _____ Comments _____

Competencies (circle predominant behaviors)
1-to-1 matching   Directionality   Fluent Reading

At an unknown word			
Makes no attempt	Seeks help	Reruns	Reads on
Attempt using . . .	Visual	Meaning	Structure

After an error			
Ignores	Seeks help	Reruns	Attempts S/C
Self-corrects using . . .	Visual	Meaning	Structure

Calculations

Error Rate $\dfrac{RW}{E} = 1$

Accuracy % 91%

S/C Rate $\dfrac{E + SC}{SC} = 1$

Level: Easy   Instr   Hard

	Level: 4 **RW:** 53		**Totals:**				
Page	**Cues Used** Title: Where Is My Hat?	**Words:**	**E**	**SC**	**Cues Used** **E**	**SC**
2	"Where is my hat?" said Ben.					
3	Ben looked under his bed. "It is not here," he said.					
4	Mom looked in the closet. "It is not here," she said.					
5	Ben looked in his toybox. "It is not here," he said.					
	He looked and looked.					
6	Mom looked behind the chair.					
7	"Here it is!" she said.					

of prose and verse. In both cases, the records folder should contain samples of the student's efforts, including penmanship. Before and after samples show student progress, though it should be recognized that the contrast (or lack thereof) may be influenced by variations in penmanship that occur normally from day to day.

Social Studies.   The social studies program follows varied paths according to grade level. Numerous topics are covered in a given year, usually including current events plus the history, geography, economics, customs, and so forth of particular communities, states, nations, and continents. Usually, skills with maps, globes, charts, and graphs, plus innumerable construction activities are involved in the social studies program. With emphasis on multicultural and global education, various styles of art, music, clothing, and other cultural items of particular places and times are also highlighted.

Samples of project work done in social studies often reflect team or group efforts and are too cumbersome to be kept as records unless they are photographed or videotaped. Team or group murals or construction projects can be displayed in the classroom for others to see, at which time individual student's contributions can be pointed out. A compilation video or CD of all the students as they work on various projects throughout the year makes a nice addition to the class library and an enjoyable feature at the spring open house.

Science and Health.   Class work in science and health is similar to that in social studies. Large units of study characterize the curriculum and often group projects are undertaken. Some teachers like to have students complete one or more individual science projects, which are displayed for others to see. Notational appraisals entered on forms (Figure 10.3) indicate the type of work done, the student's level of involvement, quality of participation, and any extra efforts that might have been undertaken. Science projects can also be included in a compilation video or CD for the class library or open house.

Art.   Usually the art program consists of two aspects, appreciation and production. Art appreciation is difficult to measure, and records are difficult to keep except for notation of experiences in which the student participated (Figure 10.3). Production art, on the other hand, provides excellent samples, at least two of which should be included in the folder. Before and after samples show artistic growth, and attention can be drawn to the inclusion of various elements such as line, form, texture, composition, balance, and other specific art techniques.

Music.   Meaningful records also are difficult to keep in the area of music. Neither music appreciation nor music production yields scores or products that show relative standing, growth, or attainment of objectives. Notational appraisals can be entered on the progress form (Figure 10.3) to indicate experiences in which the student participated, special talents, and contributions.

Physical Education.   In elementary schools, physical education rarely is presented through formal instruction. Students are taught to play various games and more or less fend for themselves while an adult supervises their play. Some teachers and schools offer programs in running, cardiovascular fitness, and individual sports that promote coordination and muscle tone. For these programs, times, distances, numbers of repetitions, and so forth can be recorded and graphed.

Work Samples.   As noted, work samples are very useful in judging and documenting student performance, but some subject areas do not yield useful work samples. Always try, however, to include something in math, language, social studies, and art, as appropriate for the grade level. At fourth grade, for example, the following should be included:

1. A math worksheet that reflects different skills emphasized at that grade level (such as regrouping, subtracting, adding, and maintaining correct alignment), that reveals certain types of errors that may occur, and that requires knowledge of basic number combinations.
2. A composition that includes many recently taught spelling words and that reveals organization, sentence structure, spelling, and penmanship. Before and after samples of compositions show writing development.
3. Artwork, such as a drawing, that incorporates techniques of line, form, color, contrast, and overall composition—elements that can be analyzed both in isolation and as a total composition.
4. Personal reading lists.

Simplifying Records Management

Good, complete records can be kept rather easily. Record keeping need not be a distasteful and overwhelming burden. Consider the following suggestions:

1. Relate all records directly to the standards, benchmarks, or objectives used in the district, curriculum guides, and/or teachers' editions of textbooks.
2. Use record-keeping forms that require a minimum of marking. Combine and summarize so one form contains the records for many activities. (Many districts now allow the teachers to create and revise forms to better match their needs.)
3. Supplement the forms with samples of student work that show progress toward standards, benchmarks, and objectives.
4. Do most of the record keeping during school time, not at home in the evening or over the weekend. Have aides or volunteers help, and to the extent possible, involve students, as such participation motivates, shares responsibility, and conveys ownership to students of their own education. It also makes for more timely feedback. Remember, however, that students have the right to privacy regarding their work and progress, and because records are legal documents, you alone are legally responsible for their management, recording, and accuracy.
5. Make the individual records folders and portfolios sources of pride for students. They show student accomplishments, capabilities, and progress. Help students see them as extensions of themselves.
6. Save time and work by using computers and software programs to assess and record. They can help organize and manage grades, log standards and objectives that are attained, and print record forms and progress notes for parents and guardians. Learning to make use of the enormous capabilities of the computer can be an exciting adventure for teacher and students alike. Attitude is the key.

Records Needed for Conferencing

Most teachers personally conference with parents or guardians at least once a year. Some conference more frequently, and there are times as well when student study teams and

---

VIGNETTE 10.2   Record Keeping with Technology

Jearine Bacon, who teaches upper elementary grades, uses a computer to manage many aspects of her program. She finds that the computer offers organization and efficiency and can be used to extend and reinforce the lessons. She is able to create forms and templates for use in all aspects of her teaching day. The computer provides statistics in seconds and displays student data in multiple formats. She also finds that she can make parent communications look professional, and they are documented in minutes. Additionally, when she needs to, Jearine is able to update and print substitute teacher plans at a moment's notice.

Upon Reflection
Technology can benefit or hinder a teacher's ability to assess, record, and track student work and progress. In what ways can technology be helpful? In what ways can it hinder?

conferences about particular students must be held with administrators and specialists. The quality of input that regular education teachers bring to these conferences is sharply increased by good records. Suggestions for the conferences themselves are presented in Chapter 4 and Chapter 11. The following materials will help you feel well prepared for any conference.

The Individual Student Folder.   The individual student work folder provides your most useful set of materials for conferencing with or about a student. As suggested earlier, the progress form inside the front cover describes the curriculum in a nutshell, with scores and comments about how the student is doing in each area. Inside the back cover are the graphs that show evidence of progress. Work samples and lists that provide concrete evidence of student effort, accomplishments, and progress are inside.

Notes about Future Plans.   Student strengths and weaknesses, revealed in the records folder, may suggest future instructional plans for the student. Take a moment before the conference to make notes concerning such plans to discuss with the caregiver or administrator.

Notes about Suggestions for Help at Home.   Caregivers should be informed if necessary about how they can help at home with future plans. Their assistance might consist of setting definite uninterrupted study times, working for short periods of time with drill or spelling, listening to their child read aloud, or discussing with the child the plot of a story or book that is being read. Remind caregivers that their involvement normally serves to increase their child's achievement. This information should be made available to parents and guardians in their primary language.

Student-Involved Conferencing.   Some teachers have found student-involved conferences to be very valuable and powerful. These may be goal-setting conferences in the early fall or progress and sharing conferences later in the year. Both teacher and student participate in sharing information with the caregivers, although the teacher's role and degree of participation vary with the purpose of the conference.

For fall goal-setting conferences, students begin a fifteen-minute conference time by sharing their personal goals, describing their learnings, and presenting some of their work. Student, teacher, and caregivers recognize strengths demonstrated by the student's work, and then each identifies an area or two that the student needs to work on. The student states one or two goals for future work, and the teacher and caregivers promise specific help toward meeting the goals. The teacher then answers questions, summarizes, and concludes the conference.

Conferences that occur later in the school year usually serve a much different purpose. Students use their own portfolio with preselected work samples and artifacts to share accomplishments and progress at this time. In preparing for this type of conference, students who self-assess are able to provide remarkable insights into the quality of their work and what they need to do to improve it.

Teachers must prepare students carefully before they schedule student-led conferences. These conferences are most successful when students have actual rehearsal opportunities.

For older students, peers, parent volunteers, and the teacher can listen to the rehearsal. Cross-age tutors and cross-grade partners can be taught to provide helpful feedback to younger students.

It is essential that students and caregivers understand both the learning goals and their roles for either type of conference. Furthermore, they all must be willing to give thought to the student's strengths and areas for growth and how they can participate toward improvement. In any event, student-led conferences bring the focus back to the children.

Ancillary Materials.   The records folder and notes usually are sufficient. However, during the conference, you should have standards, benchmarks, and objectives continuums; a curriculum guide and textbooks; and workbooks and sample worksheets nearby. These materials should not be referred to unless there are questions about standards, benchmarks, objectives, materials, or activities.

This concludes the review of assessment considerations that fall to the teacher's control—authentic assessment, management of high-quality records, and preparation for reporting to parents and guardians. Before moving ahead to Chapter 11, which deals with managing communication with students, caregivers, and others, take time to review these end-of-chapter activities.

Parting Thought

I have learned that success is to be measured not so much by the position that one has reached in life as by the obstacles he has overcome while trying to succeed.

—Booker T. Washington

SUMMARY SELF-CHECK

Check off the following as you either understand or become able to apply them.

❑ Assessment, record keeping, and reporting are requirements of teaching that few teachers enjoy, although with new authentic assessments and technology tools, the tasks are becoming less burdensome and, for some teachers, even enjoyable.

❑ Assessments that relate directly to what teachers cover in class help teachers test more accurately what they teach.

❑ Types of assessment: standardized and normed testing, teacher-created, diagnostic or placement, formative, summative, authentic.

❑ Corrective instruction is part of the instructional process and helps students learn.

❑ Standardized tests are an effort to respond to public concern regarding accountability but may alter curriculum by making teachers teach to the test.

❑ Authentic assessment minimizes the use of tests while emphasizing products that result from student work. Those products provide greater insight into student abilities and accomplishments than do tests, and they can be judged with equal objectivity with the use of carefully designed rubrics.

❑ Records of student performance should reflect the following for any student at any time: academic instructional levels, specific strengths and weaknesses, progress that has occurred, social behavior, future instructional plans.

❑ Formats for keeping good records: continuums of standards, benchmarks, and objectives (simply checked off); progress forms; graphs showing progress, work samples (few in number and specially selected); individual student forms; incentive records; anecdotal narratives.

❑ Record management simplified: Relate records to specific standards and objectives in the curriculum guide and textbooks; use record forms that require a minimum of marking; make most entries during school time; make the individual records folder a source of pride for students; use technology and software programs.

❑ Records are legal documents, and you alone are legally responsible for their management, recording, and accuracy.

❑ Records during conferencing: Use the individual student folder to describe strengths, needs, and progress; make notes about future plans for the student; make notes about how caregivers can help at home. Student-led conferences for personal goal-setting (early in the year) and accomplishments (later in the year) reveal much about student progress and learning.

ACTIVITIES FOR REFLECTION AND DISCUSSION

1. Take a moment to review the statements in the Prediction–Review Guide at the beginning of this chapter. Put a check mark in the Review column next to any statement with which you now agree. How have your thoughts changed since reading this chapter?

2. Interview at least two teachers about their assessment and record-keeping practices. In what ways do they involve students in assessment? What information and records do they find necessary and helpful to keep? How do they use technology tools to help with their record keeping?

3. Describe how you will balance standardized testing and authentic assessment alternatives in a grade of your choosing.

4. Organize a record-keeping system for a grade of your choice. Try to set it up so almost all of the required work can be done at school.

5. Explain how you would use a student records folder to describe to a caregiver in ten minutes or less a child's achievement and needs in your class.

6. You are to conference with parents who have a history of criticizing and berating teachers for unfairly assigning grades to their child. What have you included in the child's folder to counter or forestall the expected criticisms? Explain.

7. Briefly describe a social studies project for a grade of your choice. Create a rubric to score the project objectively.

REFERENCES AND RECOMMENDED READINGS

Alphonso, C. (2003). *The Globe and Mail.* A poor student's worst nightmare. Retrieved August 8, 2003, from www.globetechnology.com/servlet/ArticleNews/TPStory/LAC/20030808/USTUDNO.

Assessment to promote learning [Special issue]. (2005, November). *Educational Leadership, 63*(3). Alexandria, VA: ASCD.

Associated Press. (2003). State gives 'F' to current report cards. Online edition of the *Indianapolis Star.* Retrieved July 28, 2003, from www.indystar.com/print/articles/2/061331-1142-093.html.

Brimijoin, K., Marquissee, E., & Tomlinson, C. (2003, February). Using data to differentiate instruction. *Educational Leadership, 60,* 70–73.

Carr, J., & Harris, D. (2001). *Succeeding with standards: Linking curriculum, assessment, and action planning.* Alexandria, VA: ASCD.

The challenges of accountability [Special issue]. (2003, November). *Educational Leadership, 61*(3). Alexandria, VA: ASCD.

Dunn, L. (2001, July). Online report cards draw high marks. Wired parents can easily peek at kids' grades, when schools supply Web-based reports. *Medill News Service.* Retrieved March 2006, from www.pcworld.com/news/article/ 0,aid,54864,00.asp.

Elmore, R. (2002, October/September). Forum Testing Trap. www.harvardmagazine.com/online/0921.40 .hmtl.

Glasser, W. (1998). *The quality school teacher* (rev. ed.). New York: HarperCollins.

Gusky, T. (2003, February). How classroom assessments improve learning. *Educational Leadership, 60,* 6–11.

Hui, K. (2003, January). Wake expands grading system pilot program. *Newsobserver.com.* Retrieved January 2003, from http://newsobserver.com/news/triangle/story/2072754p-1988740c.htm.

Kohn, A. (1999). *Punished by rewards.* Houghton Mifflin.

Marzano, R. (1998, December). Advances in grading. *Education Update, 40*(8), 4.

Marzano, R. (2000). *Transforming classroom grading.* Alexandria, VA: ASCD.

Marzano, R., Pickering, D., & Pollock, J. (2001). *Classroom instruction that works: Research-based strategies for increasing student achievement.* Alexandria, VA: ASCD.

McTighe, J., & Thomas, R. (2003, February). Toward better report cards. *Educational Leadership, 60,* 52–55.

Moon, T., Callahan, C., & Tomlinson, C. (2003). Effects of state testing programs on elementary schools with high concentrations of student poverty—good news or bad news? *Current Issues in Education, 6*(8). http://cie.ed.asu.edu/volume6/number8.

Morrison, G. (2002). *Teaching in America* (3rd ed.). Boston: Allyn & Bacon.

Narang, S. (n.d.). Standardized tests: What you should know before your child sharpens his #2 pencil. Retrieved March, 2006, from www.scholastic.com/familymatters/parguides/standardizedtest.htm.

Paulson, F., Paulson, P., & Meyer, C. (1991). What makes a portfolio a portfolio? *Educational Leadership, 48*(5), 60–63.

Picciotto, L. (1999, August). Let your students take the lead. *Scholastic Instructor, 109*(1), 33–35.

Ryan, K., & Cooper, J. (2007). *Those who can, teach* (11th ed.). Boston: Houghton Mifflin.

Smithers, R. (2004, April). Pack away those pens, the age of online exams is at hand. *The Guardian Review.* Retrieved April 22, 2004, from http://education.guardian.co.uk.print/0,3858,4906458-108699,00 .html.

Using standards and assessment [Special issue]. (1999, March). *Educational Leadership.* Alexandria, VA: ASCD.

What do we mean by results? [Special issue]. (2000, February). *Educational Leadership.* Alexandria, VA: ASCD.

Wiggins, G. (1994, November). Toward better report cards. *Educational Leadership, 52,* 28–37.

Wilcox, J. (2006, February). Less teaching, more assessing. *Education Update, 48*(2).

Websites

National Center for Education Statistics
www.nces.ed.gov

Rubrics
http://edweb.sdsu.edu/webquest/rubrics/weblessons.htm
www.ncsu.edu/midlink/ho.html
www.rubrics.com

Managing Communication with Students, Caregivers, and Others

The most important thing in communication is to hear what isn't being said.

—Peter F. Drucker

Prediction–Review Guide

Before you read the chapter, take a minute to put a check mark in the Prediction column next to any statement with which you agree.

		Prediction	Review
1.	It is the student's responsibility to communicate with the teacher when concerned about something in the classroom.	❏	❏
2.	The main purpose of the four-way test is to ensure that what you are saying is factual.	❏	❏
3.	Parallel communication in elementary classrooms means that both teacher and student use the "adult" style, as described by Berne.	❏	❏
4.	Supportive feedback and encouragement, as well as appropriate corrective feedback, are valuable to others.	❏	❏
5.	Teachers tend to give less attention to students who behave properly and do their work consistently.	❏	❏
6.	The main purposes of parent–teacher conferences are to become acquainted and to give caregivers the opportunity to talk.	❏	❏
7.	The purpose of win–win conflict resolution is to find a good solution without either disputant feeling put down.	❏	❏
8.	Glasser and Nelsen suggest that class meetings be scheduled whenever the teacher senses a problem that involves the class.	❏	❏
9.	Many disruptive behaviors can be prevented with good communication.	❏	❏
10.	When telephoning caregivers, teachers should try to draw out their feelings, even though the process might take some time.	❏	❏

Support for specific standards found in this chapter:

INTASC Standards

6. Communication Skills

   The teacher uses knowledge of effective verbal, nonverbal, and media communication techniques to foster active inquiry, collaboration, and supportive interaction in the classroom.

9. Professional Commitment

   The teacher is a reflective practitioner who continually evaluates the effects of his or her choices and actions on others (students, parents, and other professionals in the learning community) and who actively seeks out opportunities to grow professionally.

10. Partnerships

   The teacher fosters relationships with school colleagues, parents, and agencies in the larger community to support students' learning and well-being.

Danielson's Framework for Teaching

4. Professional Responsibilities
   - Reflecting on teaching
   - Maintaining accurate records
   - Communicating with families
   - Contributing to the school and district
   - Growing and developing professionally

NBPTS Standards

5. Teachers are members of learning communities.

NCATE Standards

Reflect on practice, act on feedback, and integrate technology into instruction effectively.

What are your memories when you think back to your best school experiences, to those classes or rooms where you learned most and found yourself most engaged in education? Chances are you recall teachers and others who were there, more than what you actually were taught. That's because so much of school learning occurs from exchanges with others. This phenomenon, also present in work and leisure, helps us understand that interaction with others is what makes life most rewarding and memorable.

■ THE VALUE OF COMMUNICATION

When it comes to teaching, communication—the interchange of information, thoughts, and feelings—is the vehicle that moves education forward. It is the means by which teachers motivate, inform, guide, encourage, meet needs, build relationships, and otherwise stir the educational pot. Although we think of communication as verbal, much of it is nonverbal, conveying powerful messages through proximity and facial and body cues (Jones, 2007).

Teachers must communicate routinely with students, caregivers, colleagues, support providers, and administrators. Those who do it well earn cooperation, respect, and even esteem. It is not far-fetched to say that communication contributes more to the quality of teaching than does any other skill. It is no accident that teachers who enjoy the greatest success in teaching also happen to be good managers of communication.

Despite its obvious importance, communication rarely is emphasized in teacher education. Most teachers have to learn how to manage it while on the job. This chapter is intended to help by offering an overview of communication requirements and suggestions for their successful accomplishment.

USES OF COMMUNICATION

Throughout the school day, good communication is repeatedly necessary. Consider the following:

- Giving directions—making them brief and clear
- Conducting instruction—teaching clearly, gently, and patiently
- Holding class discussions and meetings—being receptive, nonthreatening, positive, and helpful
- Meeting with student support providers—being open and collaborative
- Meeting with staff, administrators, beginning teacher support providers, and other teachers—shedding all defensiveness and applying the four-way test, which follows
- Meeting individually with administrators and colleagues—being pleasant, helpful, and supportive
- Conferencing with parents and guardians—treating them as equals who prize their child above all else

The Four-Way Test

The four-way test asks four direct questions that everyone should consider silently as they work on their communication skills. Teachers should keep these questions in mind when they speak with students, caregivers, and others.

1. Is what I am saying true?
2. Is it helpful?
3. Would my silence hurt?
4. Will my saying this build good relationships?

To better understand the magnitude of communication that occurs within the domain of school—the what, how, and to whom school communication applies—review the grid shown in Figure 11.1. Notice the groups of persons—students, caregivers, colleagues, and

FIGURE 11.1 A Classroom Communication Grid

	Persons			
Purposes	**Students**	**Caregivers**	**Colleagues**	**Administrators**
1. Inform	X	X	X	X
2. Instruct	X			
3. Relate	X	X	X	X
4. Control	X			
5. Spirit	X	X		

administrators—with whom teachers regularly communicate and the five primary purposes served by communication—to inform, instruct, build relationships, maintain class control, and build esprit de corps. These points will be explained in the sections that follow.

Although communication is a dynamic two-way engagement, understand that teachers must guide the process. The remainder of this chapter is divided into three parts representing the three groups to whom teacher communication is aimed: (1) students, (2) caregivers, and (3) colleagues and administrators.

COMMUNICATING WITH STUDENTS

In 1964, Eric Berne identified three "states" individuals exhibit when talking with others: the child state, the parent state, and the adult state. The *child state* is shown when we talk with someone to whom we feel inferior. We defer to authority and perhaps behave emotionally. The *parent state* is exhibited when we talk with someone to whom we feel superior. We tend to act as our parents probably did to us—we lecture, correct, admonish, and moralize. In the *adult state,* used when talking with others on a basis of equality, we express our thoughts logically and firmly, without hostility. We should always try to use the adult state of parallel communication when we talk with anyone. The examples of exchanges between teacher and students presented in this chapter reflect adult–adult parallel communication.

Informing Students and Conducting Instruction

Informing. Informing students is mentioned here because teachers do this regularly. All it means is giving routine information orally, then checking that students understand.

Conducting Instruction. When they instruct, teachers use communication to gain student attention, provide motivation, give directions, explain concepts and procedures, pose questions, provide feedback, reteach by providing corrective instruction and second chances, and redirect inappropriate behavior.

THREE STATES OF TALKING

CASE STUDY 11.1

Focus Questions

According to Berne, which adult is using the child state when talking to Luke? The parent state? The adult state? How could the two adults change their comments so they talk to Luke in the adult state?

Luke is having a frustrating day. It seems that everyone is talking to him in a different way.

On the way to school, Daniel the bus driver wanted Luke to sit down and stay seated: "Luke, I'm tired of telling you every single day to sit down. Don't you ever listen to anyone? Sit down. Now."

Then he had a scene with Ms. Janice on the playground before school even began: "Luke, if you don't listen to me this minute, I will not let you play with your friends at recess for the rest of the week. You will have to sit by yourself by the wall."

He liked his teacher, Miss Hummel, though. She always talked to him in a grown-up way, even when he did something wrong. Today when they went to the library for new books, he told her that he left his library book at home. Students cannot check out books until they return the ones they have. Miss Hummel simply said, "Luke, it sounds like you have a little problem. What do you think you can you do to solve it?" Then she listened as Luke made some suggestions.

Gaining Attention.   Frequently attention is gained by making statements such as

- "All eyes on me."
- "Everyone, fold your hands and look at me."
- "Freeze!" (to gain attention of a boisterous class)

Often nonverbal signals such as these are used:

- Bell tone, rain stick, wind chime, or chord on piano
- Flick of lights
- Rhythmic hand clapping

Students should be taught to respond immediately to these words or signals, and no new task or lesson should be started without the attention of every student.

Providing Motivation.   Under ideal circumstances, motivation is inherent in most well-structured lessons. Teachers provide motivation with statements such as

- "Boys and girls, have you ever imagined what it would be like to . . . ?"
- "This is a contest lesson to see if you can set a new record for yourself or for the class."
- "Friends, there is a surprise hidden somewhere in this lesson. Watch and listen for it."

Giving Directions.   Good directions prevent a multitude of problems. Therefore

- Make directions very clear.
- Keep them short.
- Model what you mean and, if appropriate and available, show examples.
- Check to make sure students understand by asking them to repeat back to you.
- If more than two steps are involved, consider writing reminders on the board, using visual instructional plans, or using Say, See, Do Teaching, all described in Chapter 6.

Here are two examples of directions:

- "When I say 'begin,' open your workbooks to page 23 [write page number on the board]. On scratch paper do problems 2, 4, and 6 [write problem numbers on the board]. This is for practice only. I'll come around to see how you are doing. All right, let's get to work."
- "Study your map with your team. You may discuss, but use soft voices only [write "soft voice" or place marker on the soft voice icon]. Using the map, find the answers to the five questions I have given you. When you finish, you may read your library book."

Explaining Concepts and Procedures.   Like giving directions, explaining ensures student understanding; therefore, clarity is essential. For concrete concepts and procedures, common in elementary education, it is best to demonstrate the procedure as you explain it orally. For example:

- "We will cut out our rabbits by starting here at the tail and cutting up and around [demonstrate]. Cut along the line, like this. Jorge, please show us where to begin cutting. Amelia, where do we try to cut? Now let's all do that."
- "When we multiply two negative numbers, the product is a positive number. Watch what I do [demonstrate on board or overhead $-2 \times -2 = +4$]. Minus times minus equals plus. Kwan, try this one: minus 4 times minus 2. What did you get? Why? Remember class, minus times minus equals plus."

Posing Questions.   Questions keep students focused and active. For example, the teacher might ask a question such as the following to encourage student participation: "Who can tell me what *e pluribus unum* means? Thumbs up if you know." (Wait and look around before calling on anyone.)

Questions can force students to use different levels of thought. Benjamin Bloom (1956) listed six levels in a hierarchy of thinking: knowledge, comprehension, application, analysis, synthesis, and evaluation. As you instruct your students, consider posing questions at multiple levels of the hierarchy:

- For recall of information ask factual and literal questions: "In what year did the Spaniards finally drive the Moors from Spain? What else of importance to us happened that year?"
- To show comprehension: "Suppose you have the colors red, yellow, and blue, but you need some green. How could you make green from the colors you have?"

- To show ability to apply learnings: "Let's say you have just written a story. How could you make certain you spelled all your words correctly?"
- To show ability to analyze learnings: "What do you think the colonists were trying to accomplish when they dumped tea into the harbor?"
- To show ability to synthesize from learnings: "How would you go about constructing a map of an imaginary island so we could locate it and identify its various features?"
- To show ability to evaluate: "Do you think Peter Rabbit was doing a good thing when he got into Mr. McGregor's cabbage patch? Why did he do that?"

Some teachers prefer to sort their questions into three categories: literal (find the answer); thinking or reasoning (figure it out); and evaluating, reacting, or feeling (give your opinion). They then teach their students a simple formula to help them understand the types of responses they are expected to make to questions they are asked: "Read the lines," "read between the lines," and "read beyond the lines."

Providing Supportive and Corrective Feedback.   Making helpful comments, sometimes publicly and sometimes privately, while directing a lesson or circulating during student work can provide both supportive and corrective feedback. Comments may focus on errors and corrections, observations, or encouragement. In general, comments should be private if they single out a student and public if they give reminders of procedure or are appropriate to the entire class. Here are a few examples:

Private (Individual Focus)
- "This is some of the best work I've seen you do."
- "You've made a mistake here. How can you correct it?"
- "No, look here: A plus times a minus gives a minus."
- "I don't feel as though you are trying today. I wonder if something else is on your mind. How can I help?

Public (Group Focus)
- "This is some of the best work we've done."
- "It seems that many of you are making the same mistake. Look up here. Let me go through this again before we continue."
- "The secret to doing this correctly lies in looking at the time the driver uses. Think of the problem from that angle."
- "I see improvement today. I see good improvement. We are getting there."

Remember that with very few exceptions, feedback should be positive and helpful rather than faultfinding. When you must reteach, also remember that corrective instruction and second chances support students' success in their learning.

Redirecting Inappropriate Behavior.   Usually when students become inattentive, noisy, disgruntled, or reluctant, or when they dawdle, daydream, and play with objects instead of working, they need only gentle reminders. Negative consequences need not be invoked unless the behavior becomes flagrant or is continually repeated. Normally students can be put back on course through redirection such as the following:

- "Justin." (Just say the student's name quietly.)
- "You need to be finished in five minutes."
- "I know you're tired, but let's see if we can finish this. I'll help you."
- "Please remember our rule about working."

Building Positive Relationships

Another important role of communication is that of building positive relationships. Previous chapters, especially Chapter 4, have explained that students have a primary need to belong, and they should be reassured that they have place, purpose, and acceptance in the class. Students also have a need to be noticed and acknowledged. The quality of their behavior and work merits comment, always with courtesy and consideration.

Emphasizing Belonging and Importance.   What most of us want, really, is to feel appreciated. As a practicing rule, you should make comments that show you value the presence of every student. (Even if you don't, be a convincing actor for the student's sake and yours.) You may even find that such expressions help troublesome students become less troublesome. Be very free with comments such as

- "We are very glad you are in this class, Michael."
- "I like your drawing, Trish. May I put it on the display board?"
- "Class, I just want to tell you how pleased I am with our agreement to make everyone in this room feel comfortable and important."
- "We can't do our best work in these groups unless everyone contributes. We need that from everybody."

Speaking Personally with Each Student.   Teachers good in communication try to speak personally to each student at least once a day. You might feel this personal contact occurs naturally, without conscious effort on your part, but in practice teachers tend to give most of their attention to the few brightest students in their class and to those who disrupt or fail to work. In doing so they overlook other students—usually the majority—who follow directions, complete their work, behave themselves, and show no particular flashes of brilliance.

What do teachers say in these personal communications? They ask questions and make observations, as appropriate. They need not take long, really only a few seconds, and they can be accomplished without using instructional time. Here are some examples:

- "I heard you have new puppies at your home, Teisha. What kind are they?"
- "Today is a hot day, isn't it, Manny? Were you too hot on the playground?"
- "Class, Jimmy has a new baby brother. What's his name, Jimmy? What's it like to be a big brother?"
- "I really appreciate how nicely you worked today, Caitlin. Thank you."

PHONE CALLS THE NIGHT BEFORE SCHOOL

Focus Question

Often children are anxious before the start of the new school year. They worry about many things: Will my teacher be nice? Will I know anyone in my class? Is fourth grade going to be really hard? Karen O'Conner chooses to call all of her students the night before school begins. Write a short script of what she might say to each of them. How do other teachers make students feel welcome?

Mrs. O'Conner is a fourth-grade teacher who takes time to introduce herself and makes each student feel welcome before she meets her class for the first time. She knows that she can't alleviate all of their concerns, but she believes she is able to relax them considerably on the eve of the new school year by calling all her students and personally welcoming each of them to fourth grade and to her class. Each call takes about four minutes. Mrs. O'Conner tells them how much she is looking forward to meeting them and she highlights a few of the major activities and areas of study. She ends the phone call by allowing the children to ask questions and by suggesting that they have a good night's sleep so that they can be ready for a terrific year.

Although phone calls to thirty or more students takes the better part of the evening, Mrs. O'Conner believes the rewards are great. In fact, parents thank her throughout the year for that call and tell her how excited their child was to receive a phone call from the new teacher. On the first day of class the children are less anxious because they have already "met" Mrs. O'Conner. For her, these phone calls are a great way to set the tone for the year.

Commenting on Quality of Behavior and Work. Almost all students like to receive positive comments about their good behavior and work. Younger students like those comments made publicly; older students may prefer that they be made privately so others won't tease them about being teacher's pet or worse. Conversely, no student likes to receive negative comments, especially in front of the class.

It is important that students know when their efforts are appreciated, as well as when they are not. Except for routine comments or sticky notes on their desks that tell the student "good," "fine," "thank you," "right," "you're on target," and so on, personal appraisals should be kept between teacher, individual student, and the student's parents or guardians. If a student does well, find a quiet moment and say

- "You really helped our class today with your comments, Pedro. Thank you for that."
- "Sarah, your paragraph showed that you have learned a great deal in the past week. Keep up the good work."

If the student does poorly, feedback should be honest, even if sugarcoated:

- "I don't think you did your best today, Anna. Is there a problem I can help you with?"
- "I was really bothered by your behavior in class today, Cassie. I wasn't able to teach well because of it. I think we should come up with a plan so we won't have that problem again."

■ "Kevin, you missed eleven spelling words. I'd like to ask your mother to help you at home. I've written a note for her that lists these words and asks if she will work with you tonight."

Sometimes the teacher may choose to write a private note for the student to take home and share. It's important to do this for successes, too. Too often caregivers hear only what their child did wrong. So students won't feel uneasy about notes to their parents or guardians and so the notes actually reach home, it is a good idea to tell them about the content of the note or let them read it.

Stressing Courtesy and Consideration.   Classes tend to reflect the personality of their teacher. Good character among students is more likely when it is infused into the way teachers teach. For example, classes behave much more humanely when courtesy and dignity are emphasized as prime goals, incorporated into class rules, and intentionally taught and modeled.

Younger students readily accept instruction in good manners, meeting people, speaking courteously, saying please and thank you, and offering help. Older students may snicker and groan, but privately they like learning and practicing these things, too. Class meetings and situational role-plays offer opportunities for guided practice.

■ "Don, would you please help Mary? Thank you."
■ "Boys and girls, I'd like to introduce Mrs. Sands, Claire's mother. Welcome to our room, Mrs. Sands."
■ (After instruction on how to introduce people) "Craig, please introduce our guest."
■ "Class, what should you say when someone helps us or does something nice for us? That's right, thank you. Today I will listen hard to hear if any of you say thank you to another student. You listen, too. At the end of the day, we'll discuss what we heard."
■ "Room 12, I believe we have been acting very discourteously during our kickball games. I think this goes for winners and losers alike. No one likes to lose, but usually somebody does. How should we act at such times? How should winners act? Let's practice your suggestions before we go outside today to play."

Maintaining a Sense of Community

Sense of community is emphasized as a means of encouraging students to take initiative, show responsibility, and provide support for each other and the teacher. Class meetings help provide a sense of community in the class.

Class Meetings.   William Glasser (1969) feels that most major problems teachers and students face in the classroom can be resolved with class meetings. Many other authorities in classroom management now place heavy emphasis on classroom meetings. These whole-class meetings are conducted with students and teacher seated in a tight circle so they can see and talk easily with each other. The teacher participates with students but does not criticize or try to direct.

A common purpose of class meetings is to find constructive solutions to problems identified by students—too much noise during work time, assignments too difficult or no fun, students picking on each other, not enough time to complete work, or too much homework.

Three rules are required for meetings to function as intended. First, only positive and constructive solutions can be considered—no complaining, faultfinding, or backbiting is allowed. (This is the only place where the teacher steps in strongly.) Second, every person has the right to express an opinion without being slighted or put down by others. Third, the teacher plays a subdued role, participating to clarify and encourage but not to dominate, lead, or criticize.

Jane Nelsen, Lynn Lott, and H. Stephen Glenn (2000) describe eight building blocks that lead to effective class meetings. Each building block targets a specific skill: forming a circle, practicing compliments and appreciations, creating an agenda, developing communication skills, learning about separate realities, solving problems through role playing and brainstorming, recognizing the four reasons people do what they do, and applying logical consequences and other nonpunitive solutions.

Win–Win Conflict Resolution. Even in the best-managed classes, conflict occurs between students and between the teacher and students. Often in resolution of those conflicts, one person emerges as winner with an urge to gloat and the other as loser with a penchant to pout and hold hard feelings. To improve that situation, Spencer Kagan, Patricia Kyle, and Sally Scott (2004) developed a win–win approach, where all involved get at least part of what they want. For win–win resolutions to occur, teacher and student need to be on the same side, working together toward the same end, and sharing responsibility in the learning process.

COMMUNICATING WITH CAREGIVERS

Caregivers are parents, guardians, or any others who are in charge of children at home. Elementary teachers who are most successful—and who enjoy the highest reputations within the community—are those who communicate well with caregivers. For most caregivers, their child is their most precious possession, their best reflection of themselves, and their best extension into the future. Although appearances nowadays sometimes seem to the contrary, most caregivers expect teachers to hold little Johnny or Jennifer central in their thoughts, and it's no matter that there may be nineteen to thirty-five other children in the class whose caregivers expect the same. The wise teacher keeps this reality in mind.

What Caregivers Expect from Teachers

Caregivers don't expect you to turn their child into an Albert Einstein, a Langston Hughes, or an Amy Tan. But they rightfully expect you to

1. *Care* about their child and give attention to him or her as a person, which you show through acknowledgment of the child's interests, joys, fears, capabilities, and special needs.
2. *Excite* their child about learning.
3. *Teach* their child the basics—literacy and life skills; something of the human condition; correct ways of behaving; and the good, right, and beautiful.

4. *Encourage and support* their child's efforts by nurturing, prodding, and encouraging.
5. *Control* their child to prevent self-defeating behavior, and especially to prevent mistreatment by others.
6. *Inform* them about their child's educational program and progress.
7. *Be dedicated* to doing the best you can for their child.

What Caregivers Need to Know, Will Ask, and Will Say

Caregivers need to know a number of things about their child in school but often never ask about what they really need to know. They tend to shy away from school after their child completes kindergarten and first grade. Many feel they shouldn't meddle. Many feel insecure about approaching the teacher. They don't want to feel embarrassed, or their culture doesn't support such an action. Many would like to help but don't know how. Because English is not their first language, some do not feel able to help. If you take time to inform parents and guardians about what they need to know, you will earn their esteem and support.

Anticipate the questions caregivers are likely to ask, and be prepared to answer them as though their particular child were always in the center of your thoughts.

- "How's my child doing in school?"
- "What is a typical day like?"
- "Is my child progressing as well as expected?"
- "Does my child seem happy?"
- "How does my child get along with others?"
- "How does my child react to trying new things? To making mistakes?"
- "What is my child best at? What is my child weakest in?"
- "Does my child cause problems?"
- "What after-school programs and opportunities are there for my child?"
- "Is there anything I can do to help?"

Most caregivers listen to the teacher's answers but then may respond with additional comments. Teachers who communicate most successfully with caregivers make comments such as the following to the replies caregivers are likely to make.

- "He was never that way before." (Even though he was, your reply should be, "I hope I can count on your help, because I know you don't want him behaving this way.")
- "She was well liked in her other school." (This may or may not be true, but your reply should be, "She will be well liked here, too, if together we encourage her to be more friendly to others. I'm sure with your help we can.")
- "He is just like his father, who has never learned to pick up after himself." (Your reply should be, "Let's see if we can work on this. How can you help?")
- "Her mother is the same way, just loves to talk." (Your reply should be, "I really like her. It's just that her talking sometimes disturbs the class and keeps her from getting her work done. I'm sure you want her learn, just as I do.")

"IT'S A NOTE FROM BILLY'S TEACHER. HE GOT QUITE A WRITE UP."

A Note on Communicating with Caregivers. Most caregivers see teachers as professional, knowledgeable, and communicative. They don't want to think of teachers as wishy-washy, silly, or disorganized, nor do they want to see them behave as long-lost best pals. Of course, they don't want teachers to be gruff and intimidating either.

Focus on how you communicate with caregivers. You want to be approachable and nice, but brief, plain, and businesslike. Be considerate, remain approachable, and show caregivers that you value their collaboration. This is no time to show off your impressive vocabulary or your command of complex sentence structure. Nor is it a time to impress caregivers with the number of acronyms you know (GATE, ELP, IEP, SDAIE, ADHD, and so on ad infinitum). Don't be wordy. Use short, direct sentences with words everyone understands.

Means and Opportunities for Communicating with Caregivers

You never know when a parent may appear at your classroom door and want to talk. When that happens, be sure the unexpected visit does not interrupt your instruction time, and then mostly listen. But for occasions you set and for which you have time to prepare, consider the following opportunities for communicating well with parents and guardians.

Back-to-School Night.   As mentioned in Chapter 2, your school will invite caregivers to visit, and you will be expected to talk about the following:

1. The educational program you plan to provide in your class—a summary of your curriculum, the subject area standards, and special activities. (This doesn't mean that your entire program is to be communicated all at once. You can continue to describe your program through the year using newsletters, websites and home pages, and other means that we describe here.)
2. The expectations you hold for the children, including class work, behavior, homework, attendance and tardiness, makeup work, and so forth.
3. How you intend to enforce your expectations—your discipline system.
4. What caregivers can do to help further the program of their child.
5. Information about special activities and events.

After your presentation, parents or guardians may wish to ask questions and speak with you individually about their child (refer back to questions caregivers ask). It's good practice to schedule this meeting at another mutually convenient time.

Questionnaire.   Some teachers send a questionnaire (written in English and translated into the primary languages used in the homes of their students) in order to receive specific information from caregivers regarding their child and family. Questions might include: Does your child use the same last name as you? What do I need to know to best work with your family? (Are parents separated or divorced? Are there stepparents? Is this a blended family? Are separated parents able to meet together, or is it best to have individual communications?) What special needs does your child have (health, allergies, medications)? How will you be able to participate in the classroom (time, sharing a special interest, helping with field trips or special activities, donating wish list items)? Asking caregivers to describe their child to you can be particularly insightful.

Videotapes and CDs.   Some teachers find opportunities to videotape students as they work on projects and activities in class and then make the videos available in the class library for children to check out and share at home. For these teachers, videotapes or CDs provide a nice alternative option for communicating with caregivers. Many caring adults work outside the home and can no longer volunteer in classrooms during the day. However, they still have the desire to know what their child is doing in school. Videotapes or CDs of the class and activities give parents and grandparents the gifts of time and presence.

Newsletters.   Many teachers send home newsletters every month—or more frequently if possible. Older students can assist with the production of the newsletter within the language arts and computer programs. Results come in the form of parent interest, involvement, and support—well worth the effort.

It is better if newsletters are short and to the point, and caregivers can anticipate them on the same day or week of the month. They should include items such as calendar dates of field trips and other special activities and class accomplishments. Newsletters also may include a question, learning activity, or website of the week. They never should disintegrate into breezy notes that single out a few students.

Notes.   Personal notes are helpful for sending brief messages to parents and guardians, reminders about snacks and money, and for calling attention to responsible student behavior and accomplishments. As we said earlier, students should be allowed to read these notes, or you should read the notes to them; otherwise, if students are uneasy about them, the notes may never reach home. Of course, if appropriate, these notes should be translated into the primary language of the caregivers.

Websites and Home Pages.   More and more schools, teachers, and caregivers are taking advantage of computer technology. Many teachers create web pages for their class and are thereby able to stay in contact with caregivers who have computer and Internet access. Web pages do not have to be fancy or elaborate, but there are several helpful items to include for parents: announcements, homework assignments, and other news and information that may be of interest.

VIGNETTE 11.1   Class Videos

Kindergarten teacher Linda Monedero uses videotapes to communicate with parents and guardians. To prepare parents for this communication, she first sends a letter home to each family listing the purposes of the videotape program and encouraging their participation (which is not mandatory). They are told that the completed videos are usually less than fifteen minutes long; this allows families to view tapes when they come home in spite of busy schedules. Each family is encouraged to keep videos for one or two evenings and return them to school as soon as possible so that other families can view them. The rotation for each video varies because children put their names on slips of paper and the helper of the day draws the name of the student. Video checkout cards or lists are kept in a special location as a record of who has which videotape.

Linda believes three basic rules are necessary to make a video program successful. First, the person filming the video is reminded that the tape will go home with each child; therefore, each child should be taped about the same amount of time. Second, children are told that only acceptable student behavior will be taped. This fosters positive behaviors without having to emphasize the negative, which leads to better overall behavior. Third, a short list of desired activities to be recorded is given to filming volunteers so that the tapes always show children actively involved in learning.

Upon Reflection

Describe how you might use videos or CDs in order to communicate with parents. What would you want to have taped? Who would do the actual taping? How, then, would the tapes be made available to others?

Setting up a web page is not as difficult as it sounds. First you need someone to host the page. Free space is available on the Internet if the school district doesn't have its own server and site dedicated for this purpose. Geocities is an example of a free host. Many service providers now include a free website in their service package. You should be able to find several from which to choose by searching the keywords *free space* or *free web hosting*.

Although the size of the site may be limited, there generally is plenty of room to have several pages of your own. You also will need a way to edit your page. Where your site is housed will determine this; free sites often include the necessary software and instructions online, or you can use a website-editing package such as Microsoft FrontPage. To include student work and photos you will need access to a scanner or digital camera.

Most districts will have a form for parental permissions, but if they don't you can make your own. It's helpful to get separate permissions giving parents and students several options: to include work with first name identification only, to include photo with no name identification, or to include photo and name identification.

Telephone Calls.   Sadly, many caregivers only receive phone calls from teachers when their child is in trouble. It is good to surprise them occasionally with brief, friendly messages. When you finish, you simply say good-bye and hang up, thereby avoiding a lengthy chat from what certainly will be an appreciative caregiver.

VIGNETTE 11.2 Class Web Page and Newsletter

Lynne Harvey finds that her web page and monthly newsletters are effective ways to establish and maintain ongoing, interactive communication between her third grade and home. The number one requested item by parents is a homework page—this simple posting can be done daily or at the beginning of each week, with updates and changes as needed. For Lynne, posting homework on her web page and sending home a monthly newsletter help keep parents informed and provide an opportunity for them to support student efforts.

Lynne always includes a section dedicated to showcasing student work, photos from class, and field trip photos. This gives parents a taste of what goes on from day to day and allows them the opportunity to participate in special events without actually being there. However, before she includes a child's picture and/or name on her website, she makes sure that she has a signed permission form from parents.

Upon Reflection

How do teachers go about setting up a web page in your local school district or school? What permission forms are available and/or required by the school or district? If there are no forms, design something you would use. What would you include on your web page and newsletter to caregivers?

"Mrs. Appleton, this is Miss Cabrera, Leo's teacher. I just wanted you to know that Leo did excellent work in math this week. We all can be very proud of him. Please tell Leo I said so. Thank you for your support, and I'll call you again before long."

On the other hand, messages about concerns should be delivered in a way that requests help:

"Mrs. Engles, this is Mr. James, Rob's teacher. I am calling to let you know there's a problem at school that I need your help with. Rob has received four playground citations in the past two weeks and I am concerned about him. I know you don't want him misbehaving on the playground and endangering himself and others. I am talking with him about following school rules and I'd like to ask you to do the same at home. We don't want to punish Rob. All we want is for him to follow the rules, for his safety and benefit as well as for others. May I count on your support in helping Rob?"

Performances and Displays. Like many teachers, you may wish to put on student performances and displays of student work to be attended by caregivers, relatives, and friends. These events include musical productions, plays, choral readings, readers' theatre, science fairs, art exhibits, and athletic events. Especially for the younger children, caregivers turn out in numbers for these occasions. These events allow teachers to explain further the special activities that contribute to the children's well-rounded education, and lets them to show off what they and the students have done. They also contribute strongly to teachers' good reputations.

Newer schools may have the technology capability to broadcast events over the Internet with video streaming. Video streaming via the Internet requires a media program such as RealPlayer, a free downloadable program that includes a video-streaming tool. Family and friends anywhere are able to view the production online through the school website.

Parent–Teacher Conferences.   As mentioned earlier, most schools regularly schedule conferences that bring the teacher and caregivers together to confer about each child's progress. In Chapter 10 we looked at two types of student-involved conferences. If properly organized, conferences, both teacher- and student-led, can be very productive. In traditional parent–teacher conferences, that duty falls to the teacher, who must set caregivers at ease, communicate without causing affront, draw out the caregivers' ideas, and when necessary, suggest a plan for improving the progress of the child. The following suggestions help make conferences agreeable and useful.

Before the Conference
1. Prepare a folder for each child, with the child's name attractively written on it.
2. In the folder include a summary of work covered to date; a profile of the child's performance in that work; samples, good and bad, of the child's work; and tests and other products that back up your evaluation.
3. Make notes to yourself about anecdotes that provide insight into the child's behavior and progress.

When Caregivers Arrive
4. Greet them in a friendly and relaxed manner.
5. Sit side by side with the caregivers at a table rather than behind a desk. This conveys a message of cooperation.

During the Conference
6. Begin by chatting about the child as a worthwhile person. Mention good traits. This reassures the caregivers.
7. Guide them through the student's folder, commenting on the work samples it contains.
8. Encourage them to talk. Listen carefully. Be accepting. Do not argue or criticize. Caregivers cannot be objective about their own child, and you do not want to cause resentment.
9. Keep in mind that caregivers can be your strongest allies. Let them know you believe this. Show that you, like the caregivers, want the best possible for the child.
10. If appropriate, work together to create a home action plan for them and their child.

FIGURE 11.2   Date and Type of Communication

Surname	Date	Ns	T	Nt	C	U	UCA
_____	____	_____	_____	_____	_____	____	____
_____	____	_____	_____	_____	_____	____	____
_____	____	_____	_____	_____	_____	____	____

Ns = newsletter; T = telephone; Nt = note; C = conference; U = unscheduled talk;
UCA = unsuccessful contact attempt

Ending the Conference

11. End the conference by summarizing what you all accomplished in this meeting, and describing your plans for the student's future progress. Earnestly request their help in supporting your efforts. Thank them for talking with you about the child.

Forming Home Alliances and Home Action Plans

Teachers may find it helpful to involve the parents or guardians as partners to work with the student's progress and behavior. Certainly caregivers can reinforce what teachers do in the classroom. In fact, many current discipline practitioners and authorities stress the importance of home alliances and partnerships and build home communication and cooperation into their programs for managing student behavior. To win parental cooperation, it's important to talk about behavior in clear, objective, nonjudgmental terms; to ask for what is possible to do; and to anticipate success.

Keeping Track of Communication with Caregivers

On index cards or individual sheets of paper, maintain a chart, such as the one in Figure 11.2, for keeping track of contacts with caregivers and to serve as a reminder for contacting them.

A simple variation of the communication log would be to use a telephone message book such as those found in office supply stores. Every entry is duplicated automatically on carbonless paper. The duplicate record remains in the message book as a running chronology of contacts; the original copy is placed in individual student files.

■ COMMUNICATING WITH COLLEAGUES AND ADMINISTRATORS

Much was said in Chapter 4 about how you ought to speak with and conduct yourself around colleagues and administrators so as to ensure support and good working relationships. If you remain concerned about this topic, you might wish to refer back to that chapter. Otherwise, we will bring this chapter to a close with the following brief reminders.

Administrators should be kept informed about programs and problems in your classroom. You may communicate this information orally or via email unless otherwise directed. They may or may not be able to offer help, but in any case, administrators like to know

CASE STUDY 11.3

GRADE-LEVEL TEAM MEETINGS

Focus Question

Grade-level teams can disagree on many things: how something is taught, which supplemental materials are most beneficial to the unit, evidence for assessment, and behavior systems. Identify one area of potential disagreement and describe what teachers can say to negotiate a solution so everyone feels they win.

Ginny Lorenz is a member of a fourth-grade team of teachers. Before the year began at a new school, a meeting with all the team members was set up to discuss grade-level expectations, grading system, school and classroom rules, and other such matters. The discussion was going well until they began to identify the classroom behavior system and classroom rules. Mrs. Lorenz feels strongly that students need to be involved in making the class rules if they are to "buy in." One of her colleagues, however, felt just as strongly that the teacher must be the rule maker. Mrs. Lorenz was afraid they had come to an impasse, but she managed to convince one of her other team members to try her way of writing rules and consequences. While the other person still insisted she had to write the rules, she did agree to identical consequences. This was not a perfect solution, but at least there was some consistency.

At the end of the year the team reflected on their successes, their challenges, and their solutions. Everyone agreed that the compromise regarding the behavior system and rules worked quite well. Substitutes had told team members that it was very easy to substitute in any of their classes because of the grade-level behavior system. Both students and parents seemed to feel that there was a genuine concern for the needs of all students. And in hindsight, the teachers had felt far less frustrated about the need to constantly correct negative behaviors.

what's going on in the school. They detest being caught off guard by calls from upset parents or guardians and not knowing what the caregiver is talking about.

Administrators want to know about your discipline plan, and you should furnish a written copy. Administrators also want to know in advance about class parties, programs, and field trips, and may want to see copies of your newsletter before it is sent home to caregivers. Occasionally administrators will rule against your discipline system or an event you want to organize. By tactfully asking them to suggest alternatives that would accomplish the purpose you had in mind, administrators will feel obliged to help you.

Colleagues such as fellow teachers, paraprofessionals (including service providers for students with special needs), beginning teacher support providers, student teachers, clerical staff, librarians, nurses, psychologists, custodians, lunchroom and playground staff, and others should also be informed of any activities or needs that might impose on them. They do not appreciate your taking their professional duties for granted, especially when they must change plans for your benefit. On the other hand, when you take pains to communicate such matters fully and they are able to help you, most will do so willingly, and your efforts in communicating will have paid off in friendliness, helpfulness, and mutual respect.

This ends our consideration of the effective management of communication. Before moving ahead to Chapter 12, which deals with how to manage the work of other adults—paraprofessionals, substitute teachers, and student teachers—take a moment to explore these end-of-chapter activities.

Parting Thought

What most of us want, really, is simply to feel appreciated.

—Anonymous

SUMMARY SELF-CHECK

Check off the following as you either understand or become able to apply them.

☐ Good communication is what makes good education possible.

☐ Good communication is especially needed in giving directions, conducting instruction, holding class discussions, holding individual conferences with students, conferencing with parents and guardians, and having staff meetings and individual conferences with administrators and colleagues.

☐ When communicating, remember the four-way test:
- Is this true?
- Is this helpful?
- Will my silence hurt?
- Will this build good relationships?

☐ Always use parallel (adult–adult) communication with students and everyone else.

☐ Communication considerations when conducting instruction: gaining attention, providing motivation, giving directions, explaining concepts and procedures, posing questions, providing supportive and corrective feedback, reteaching using corrective instruction and offering second chances, redirecting inappropriate behavior.

☐ Communication for building positive relationships: emphasize belonging and importance, speak personally with each student, focus on quality of work and behavior, stress courtesy and consideration.

☐ Communication for maintaining good behavior: win–win conflict resolution, class meetings.

☐ Communication with caregivers:
- What caregivers need to know from teachers: the educational program, expectations for students, means of enforcing rules, how their child is doing, how they can help, routine information
- Style of communication with caregiver: friendly but businesslike, clear with no jargon
- Opportunities for communicating with caregivers: back-to-school night (the educational program, expectations, means of enforcing rules, how they can help), newsletters, notes, websites and home pages, telephone calls, performances and displays, parent–teacher conferences
- Communicating with administrators and colleagues: keep everyone informed, never take another's services for granted, beginning teacher support providers

ACTIVITIES FOR REFLECTION AND DISCUSSION

1. Take a moment to review the statements in the Prediction Review Guide at the beginning of this chapter. Put a check mark in the Review column next to any statement with which you now agree. How have your thoughts changed since reading this chapter?

2. Interview at least two teachers about their communication with others. How do they communicate with caregivers? What do they include when they prepare for parent–teacher conferences? What do they include in a newsletter or on a web page?

3. What advantages do you see in applying the four-way test to what you say? What dangers do you see? Illustrate with scenarios that involve talking with caregivers, students, and administrators.

4. For a grade of your choice, identify typical contents of a class newsletter you would want to produce. Outline the format. How would you mention and/or include student work? How would you mention as many student names as possible?

5. Write out the telephone messages you might want to deliver to caregivers concerning (a) Maria, whose work quality has been declining; (b) Linda, who has frequent squabbles with other girls in the class; (c) Marta, who always behaves well and offers to help; and (d) Carla, who seems to try hard but continues to do poorly in spelling.

6. You are due to have a routine evaluation conference with your principal. The principal has observed you only three times, and on two occasions your students were abnormally unruly. You expect to be criticized for poor class control. (a) How will you intend to conduct yourself in the conference? (b) What will you say in response if you are criticized for class control? (c) What, if anything, will you say concerning your feeling that you have not been observed sufficiently? (d) What would you intend to say at the conclusion of the conference?

7. Assuming you are able to create one, describe what you would like to include on a web page. What special considerations and permissions will you obtain in order to proceed with this tool?

REFERENCES AND RECOMMENDED READINGS

Albert, L. (1996). *Cooperative discipline.* Circle Pines, MN: American Guidance Service.

Berne, E. (1964). *Games people play.* New York: Grove Press.

Bloom, B. S. (Ed.). (1956). *Taxonomy of educational objectives: The classification of educational goals: Handbook I, cognitive domain.* New York: Longmans, Green.

Coloroso, B. (1999). *Parenting with wit and wisdom in times of chaos and loss.* Toronto, Ontario, Canada: Viking.

Glasser, W. (1969). *Schools without failure.* New York: Harper & Row.

Glasser, W. (1998a). *The quality school: Managing students without coercion* (rev. ed.). New York: Harper-Collins.

Glasser, W. (1998b). *The quality school teacher* (rev. ed.). New York: HarperCollins.

Gordon, T. (1989). *Discipline that works: Promoting self-discipline in children.* New York: Random House.

Jones, F. (2005). *Tools for teaching: Parent edition.* Santa Cruz, CA: Fredric H. Jones.

Jones, F. (2007). *Tools for teaching: Discipline Instruction Motivation* (2nd ed.). Santa Cruz, CA: Fredric H. Jones.

Kagan, S., Kyle, P., & Scott, S. (2004). *Win-win discipline.* San Clemente, CA: Kagan Cooperative Learning.

Nelsen, J., Lott, L., & Glenn, H. (2000). *Positive discipline in the classroom* (3rd ed.). Rocklin, CA: Prima Publishing.

Websites

Communication with Parents
http://teacher.scholastic.com/professional/parentconf/index.htm

Parent Involvement
www.educationworld.com/a_special/parent_involvement.shtml

Parent–Teacher Conferences
www.nea.org/parents/ptconf.html
www.teachervision.fen.com/parent-teacher-conferences/teaching-methods/3683.html
www.education-world.com/a_curr/strategy/strategy046.shtml
www.atozteacherstuff.com/Tips/Parent_Teacher_Conferences

Managing the Work of Paraprofessionals, Substitute Teachers, and Student Teachers

It's easy to get good players. Getting 'em to play together, that's the hard part.

—Casey Stengel

Prediction–Review Guide

Before you read the chapter, take a minute to put a check mark in the Prediction column next to any statement with which you agree.

	Prediction	Review
1. A classroom paraprofessional is someone who takes the place of the teacher.	❑	❑
2. Substitute teaching is considered one of the most difficult teaching jobs.	❑	❑
3. Teachers are expected to provide detailed lesson plans for their substitute teachers.	❑	❑
4. Legally, paraprofessionals may administer, correct, and record student tests and scores.	❑	❑
5. Substitute teachers should not score or grade papers; that is the responsibility and prerogative of the regular teacher.	❑	❑
6. Substitute teachers should be encouraged to teach some of their own lessons that they particularly like.	❑	❑
7. Student teachers technically are paraprofessionals.	❑	❑
8. Paraprofessionals, substitutes, and student teachers, like contracted teachers, can be dismissed from their jobs for reasons of incompetence.	❑	❑
9. The same standards of professionalism are expected equally of paraprofessionals, substitutes, student teachers, and regular classroom teachers.	❑	❑
10. Paraprofessionals and substitutes are advised to discipline students in the way they deem best, so long as they do not infringe on students' rights.	❑	❑

Support for specific standards found in this chapter:

INTASC Standards

6. Communication Skills

   The teacher uses knowledge of effective verbal, nonverbal, and media communication techniques to foster active inquiry, collaboration, and supportive interaction in the classroom.

9. Professional Commitment

   The teacher is a reflective practitioner who continually evaluates the effects of his or her choices and actions on others (students, parents, and other professionals in the learning community) and who actively seeks out opportunities to grow professionally.

10. Partnerships

    The teacher fosters relationships with school colleagues, parents, and agencies in the larger community to support students' learning and well-being.

Danielson's Framework for Teaching

4. Professional Responsibilities
   - Reflecting on teaching
   - Maintaining accurate records
   - Communicating with families
   - Contributing to the school and district
   - Growing and developing professionally

NBPTS Standards

5. Teachers are members of learning communities.

NCATE Standards

Reflect on practice, act on feedback, and integrate technology into instruction effectively.

Enterprising teachers have always looked for help in operating their classrooms. In the old one-room schools, more advanced students helped the less advanced. In today's classrooms, students help each other in cooperative learning teams, differentiated and multi-age classes, cross-grade partnerships, and cross-age tutoring. Increasingly, other adults have begun to help teachers in running their class program. Now it is rare to find an elementary teacher who does not count on the assistance of another adult in the room, at least occasionally. These helpers range from mothers assisting with a class party to full-time employed aides. On occasion when the regular teacher must be away, substitute teachers are present to teach the class and make the day productive for the students. Student teachers also may work in a classroom as teachers-in-training.

Adult helpers who undertake regular, assigned duties commonly are referred to as *paraprofessionals. Para* means alongside of; *professional* refers to the teacher. Teachers have come to rely on paraprofessionals for a variety of tasks. They do clerical work; tutor students; monitor the work of small groups; and supervise in the library, on the playground, and elsewhere in the school. At times, paraprofessionals also deliver basic instruction under the teacher's supervision. Paraprofessionals fall mostly into the following groups: (1) paid instructional aides, (2) paid support providers for students with special needs, (3) caregiver volunteers, and (4) community resource volunteers (such as business liaison volunteers and senior citizens). Student teachers also provide help in many classrooms, but are not referred to as paraprofessionals. The same is true for substitute teachers, district curriculum and instruction mentors, and adults brought in for special purposes, such as to read to children or supervise them on outings. All these adult helpers work under the direction of, or in conjunction with, the teacher, whose responsibility, then, is to manage schedules, duties, and activities of these helpers.

INSTRUCTIONAL AIDES AND SUPPORT PROVIDERS

Instructional aides and support providers have regular work schedules, are salaried, and are expected to meet the same standards of reliability and professional demeanor as contracted teachers. They are recruited, selected, paid, and sometimes trained by the school district before being assigned to or selected by individual teachers. The supply of paid aides waxes and wanes in accord with economic conditions and special programs and grants. When schools have money, they hire more aides. Mandated programs such as special and bilingual education usually provide money to hire skilled support providers. Because of the individual attention required by young students, paid aides are more common at the primary level than at the intermediate.

VIGNETTE 12.1   One Classroom Paraprofessional

As the interpreting aide for children who are deaf or hearing-impaired, Mary Brewer is one type of paraprofessional with whom teachers may interact. Her role as interpreting aide in the classroom is not to teach, but to act as the voice for the student who is deaf or hearing-impaired and to provide ongoing sign interpretation of all voiced communication to that student. Classroom teachers therefore must learn how to use the interpreter's services effectively. Toward that end, it is important that teacher and aide clearly understand their respective roles in working in the classroom.

Upon Reflection:
What paraprofessionals/student support providers are available in your local school or district? What considerations must the teacher make to support students and best use the adult services?

CAREGIVER AND FAMILY VOLUNTEERS

The prime source of volunteer help is from caregivers and other relatives of students in the class. In fact, some schools now require caregivers to spend time helping in their child's classroom. Grandparents and older adults are especially excellent because they have more available time and usually relate well with the young. This has been the case for the Senior Motivators in Learning and Educational Services (SMILES) program in the Salt Lake City School District. (You can find out more about the SMILES program at their website, www.slc.k12.ut.us/depts/comminv/schoolvols.html). However, relatives tend to be hesitant about volunteering their services, so some gentle recruitment may be needed. This can be accomplished informally through hints and expressions of need and with formal notes sent home with children asking for specific kinds of volunteer help. These gentle requests should specify days and times that help is needed and should include a response form.

Caregiver and family volunteers are an extremely valuable, though sometimes a frustrating, source of classroom help. These volunteers may be highly educated and skilled— or barely literate. They may be conscientious or negligent, reliable or undependable. They genuinely may want to help, or they may have little else to do with their time. They may be good models of language, self-respect, good character, and attitude toward others, or they may fall short in these regards. Not all turn out to be what you might hope, but when you get a good volunteer, it's like finding buried treasure.

CASE STUDY 12.1

CLASSROOM VOLUNTEERS

Focus Questions
How will you locate volunteers for your classroom? What specific tasks might you ask of a volunteer? What if the volunteer is not reliable in attendance or performance—how will you handle this?

Teacher Eileen Andreoli finds parent volunteers invaluable in her classroom, and at the beginning of the year she makes it clear during back-to-school night that she greatly appreciates parents' help and welcomes them to share any gifts or talents they have.

Mrs. Andreoli likes to make parents feel welcome when they go to her classroom to help. On a volunteer table in her classroom, she has the work that needs to be done and a clear description of what she needs. She also has files for regular volunteers with notes about things they can do. Mrs. Andreoli also makes sure there is a basket on the table filled with everything the volunteers may need in their work, such as tape, stapler, scissors, glue, paste, and paper clips. This avoids interruptions while she works with the class or having parents search through her desk. Finally, and most importantly, Mrs. Andreoli leaves letters of thanks and appreciations regularly. She believes a little bit of acknowledgment goes a long way.

COMMUNITY RESOURCE VOLUNTEERS

Community resource volunteers can make marvelous contributions to your program, but rarely can you consistently count on their help. They may be representatives from businesses or agencies. They may be volunteers with a local program, such as the Rolling Readers literacy program. Frequently they are retired persons who held occupations that receive attention in the class. Sometimes they are musicians or artists who like to help with the music and arts programs. These individuals tend to be interesting and good communicators, but because they lead busy lives, you cannot count on them regularly.

WHAT IS EXPECTED OF PARAPROFESSIONALS

A common view persists that paraprofessionals mostly do clerical work and help children with their shoelaces and coats, but the actual range of their contributions is almost as broad as that of the teachers. True, they spend substantial time copying materials, checking papers, and keeping records, but many also perform quasi-instructional duties such as directing instructional games and activity centers, monitoring and assisting individual students during seat work, and working with small groups to provide additional practice in basic skills. They may help teachers prepare instructional materials such as flash cards, art materials, visual aides, and worksheets; organize bulletin boards; and administer tests. Or, they simply may be another caring adult with whom students can relate.

Although the primary intent is to provide services that supplement and assist the teacher's efforts by handling many of the miscellaneous time-consuming tasks, skilled paraprofessionals clearly supervise most—and in some cases all—of the instruction in art, music, and physical education. It is common to see paraprofessionals who, at least in particular segments of the curriculum, are as skilled in instruction as the elementary teacher.

It is true that paraprofessionals add to the complexity of teachers' lives, which prompts questions about whether they are worth the extra time they require. Most teachers say they definitely are worth having because paraprofessionals help make their educational programs fuller, richer, and more student-oriented. Teachers are quick to point out, however, that good planning is necessary if the paraprofessional is to be used to best advantage. Paraprofessionals in elementary classrooms may do such things as

- Duplicate materials
- Prepare games and other instructional materials
- Tutor individual students
- Monitor and assist students during centers (such as reading, math, and art) and seat work
- Distribute and collect materials
- Prepare displays and bulletin boards
- Assist students on projects
- Supervise playground activities
- Read stories
- Help with media equipment
- Perform innumerable other duties assigned by the teacher

How Paraprofessionals Are Obtained

Some teachers are known for their ability to attract and maintain an unending supply of qualified paraprofessionals and volunteers eager to work in their rooms. How do they do this?

Word of Mouth.   Word gets around about teachers who like to work with volunteers and are skilled at doing so. Parents and guardians talk among themselves about teachers and programs. A number of these caregivers, and others to whom they talk, like to work in elementary classrooms. They hear about and gravitate to teachers who treat people kindly and in whose rooms children seem to have fun while learning.

Not all teachers enjoy using paraprofessionals and volunteers. It is perfectly acceptable if you prefer to rely on your own abilities to provide a sound educational program. There is no reason to use an aide unless your program is improved by doing so. Sometimes paraprofessionals and volunteers get in the way of instruction, and many teachers do not like dealing with their assorted trials and troubles.

On the other hand, if you enjoy working with other adults, and particularly if you like to provide activities such as plays, field trips, exhibits, and so forth—activities for which aides are especially useful—let your interests be known. Good aides are available. It is simply a matter of making contact with them.

As mentioned, aides and support providers for students with special needs are the only regular paraprofessionals to receive pay, and they are recruited, selected, and given orientation training by the personnel department of school districts. Other aides—parents and guardians, community resource persons, and student tutors—volunteer their services and receive only the pleasures from their work and contribution. Other arrangements are made for substitutes and student teachers.

Universities and High Schools.   Area universities and high schools have many students willing and eager to help in elementary classrooms. Often these students are seriously considering a career in teaching. For admission to teacher credential programs, university students may be required to provide documentation of experience in elementary classrooms. High school students may be in future teachers clubs that maintain connections with elementary schools. Volunteers obtained through these sources tend to be highly motivated to do well and to learn as much as possible about teaching.

"I KNEW IT. THEY HAVE ALL US SCHOOL VOLUNTEERS ON SPEED DIAL."

PTA and PTO Bureaus.   Schools with active Parent–Teacher Associations (PTAs) and Organizations (PTOs) may have bureaus run by parents that are able to furnish qualified parent volunteers to aid in classrooms. Usually teachers provide some basic training for these parent volunteers.

Community Agencies.   Especially in larger cities, community agencies may provide liaison persons from among their employed personnel who make school and classroom presentations upon request. Zoos, museums, newspapers, hospitals, and fire and police departments often have educational departments that provide this service.

OTHER HELPERS IN THE ROOM

As we noted, many other people who are not considered to be paraprofessionals also provide important help to the teacher. They include cross-age partners, cross-age tutors, and student teachers.

Cross-Grade Partners and Cross-Age Tutors

Older students in the school can offer valuable assistance to teachers of younger grades. Also, a hallmark of differentiated and multi-age classrooms is the belief and practice that students help students. As with using cross-grade partnerships, teachers can differentiate instruction in their classrooms in such a way that classmates help one another.

Advocates believe that the use of cross-grade partners and cross-age tutors results in increased achievement and positive attitudes in both the children who are helping and the children being helped. It can be very motivating to younger children to have older students sit beside them, read to them, play with them, and help them with their work. Many teachers say that cross-grade partners and cross-age tutors are among their most reliable, conscientious, patient, and valued helpers.

Cross-grade partners are students from higher grades who befriend and provide encouragement to students in lower grades. In many schools, teachers organize liaisons between older and younger students. This is done primarily for moral support, assistance, and helping young students feel there are older students in the school who will help and listen to them, not just provide additional instructional help.

Some schools have formally established cross-age tutor programs. Where that is not the case, primary teachers desiring tutors should check first with the principal, then approach teachers of older grades for suggestions. In this way, students best suited for tutoring can be obtained.

Cross-age tutors provide younger students help in learning. By fifth or sixth grade, some students think they might want to become teachers. They enjoy younger children, and the young enjoy them in return. Primary teachers prize such students, who are recognized and selected because of their skill, personality, and reliability. However, some teachers are reluctant to make frequent use of these students for fear of causing them to miss out on important parts of the educational program offered by their own teachers. To this end, some primary and upper grade teachers form cross-grade partnerships. As a regular part of their programs, the teachers have both classes come together from time to time to work on projects and share reading and stories.

Substitute Teachers

Substitute teachers fill in when the regular classroom teacher is ill or excused for other duties. Some districts still hire interested persons who have earned, minimally, a bachelor's degree. However, in many districts, qualified substitute teachers must successfully interview in order for their names to appear on an approved master list. Substitutes may also be required to participate in an orientation or training before they can work in the district.

Teachers can request a substitute any time of the day or night. While substitutes may be called directly by a clerk in the district office, many districts now use a twenty-four-hour telephone hotline system. Potential substitutes have the opportunity to check the hotline throughout the day and accept positions at any time. Substitutes may still receive a morning call from this electronic "Subfinder" for last-minute requests.

"THE FOURTH GRADE SUBSTITUTE WON'T BE HERE. SHE CALLED IN CHICKEN."

Substitute teachers have two main obligations—to keep order in the classroom and to further the class's instructional program. The second obligation, which most people consider the more important, cannot occur without the first. Substitutes fulfill these two primary obligations by being prepared, arriving early and obtaining information from the office, and generally making the day productive for the students. Substitutes make the day productive when they take charge in the classroom, clarify expectations about how students are to behave, and emphasize to the students the importance of learning.

Teachers hope that when they must be absent their substitute will control the class and make a normal day's progress in the curriculum. Substitutes hope that they will find a substitute folder with good lesson plans and discipline standards. They also hope they will have the opportunity to use their own special skills—and even teach a favorite lesson or two not in the teacher's plans. An ideal relationship between teacher and substitute incorporates their mutual hopes. The teacher's responsibilities, then, are to

- Plan well.
- Leave an up-to-date substitute folder or easy access to lesson plans and a copy of the discipline plan, current seating chart, and class roster with notations of relevant student information (behavior, students with special needs and any support providers, medication, special schedules and routines, and so on), class schedule and current duty schedule, classroom monitor and volunteer lists, and school map.

■ Teach students how to treat and work with substitutes, and hold students accountable for their behavior.

The substitute teacher's responsibilities are to

■ Follow the teacher's plans carefully unless otherwise allowed.
■ Follow the teacher's system of discipline, or if a plan is not available, quickly establish one before doing further work.
■ Have special lessons ready at all times.
■ Creatively use good time-filler and transition activities.

CASE STUDY 12.2

A TEACHER AND A SUBSTITUTE

Focus Questions

Teachers and substitutes sometimes have different expectations of how the day should go when the teacher is absent. How closely do Janet Beyea's expectations align with Ms. Young's expectations? Will she be able to look back and say that her days in Ms. Young's classroom were productive and successful?

When second-grade teacher Candace Young needs a substitute teacher, she usually wants the substitute to follow her schedule as much as possible. However, Ms. Young recognizes the opportunities substitutes can bring to her class. As often as she can, she makes it clear that variations are not only acceptable but often desirable. Substitute teachers often bring delightful learning activities with them. Some play the guitar and teach new songs; some bring favorite stories; some speak of faraway places; and some teach wonderful games, which the children then teach Ms. Young when she returns. Far more than covering material from point A to point B, Ms. Young expects a substitute teacher in her class to keep students engaged, successful, safe, and she hopes, happy.

As a regular substitute in primary grades, Janet Beyea is used to anticipating a different experience every day she goes to school. She knows first hand that the unexpected is the norm in substituting, and that flexibility and creativity are required.

Substitute teachers always anticipate walking into a classroom and finding no lesson plans. Once Mrs. Beyea showed up to teach music and ended up teaching a sixth-grade class for a week with no lesson plans, no roll book, and no set routines. Because the class had had four teachers in the first six weeks of school, even the students didn't know what they were studying in class.

When she finds no lesson plans, Mrs. Beyea reminds herself that she is not expected to be a miracle worker and turns to several resources. She looks around the classroom and often finds the classroom schedule, the discipline rules, and a job chart posted somewhere. Mrs. Beyea tries to find the teacher's edition of the textbooks because she knows that they will be filled with suggestions. She uses the students and other teachers for guidance. Also, she always has her briefcase where she keeps a book of games and art projects for all grades and some easy-to-use lessons. Mrs. Beyea considers that she was successful if, at the end of the day, the room is tidy, she had no major discipline problems, and the students had some fun.

Student Teachers

Student teachers work with tenured master or cooperating teachers. For many certification programs, student teachers are required to successfully complete field experiences in both primary (K–2) and intermediate or upper (3–6) classroom settings. Because they are training to be elementary teachers, student teachers are present every day and responsible for portions of the educational program as guided by the cooperating classroom teacher and a university supervisor.

Arrangements for student teachers usually are made by the credentialing university or by the district. Occasionally student teachers may request their field placements, although when doing so they must be certain that the experience will fulfill all the state and university requirements for the student teacher to receive a teaching license.

Usually the duties of student teachers are quite clear-cut. While student teachers often carry out some of the same duties as paraprofessionals, there are two main differences: (1) Student teachers are training to be teachers, not teacher helpers, and (2) student teachers, as they progress through their field experiences, usually are assigned fewer clerical and supervisory tasks and ever-increasing amounts of the instructional program. As teacher trainees, they eventually assume all classroom responsibilities from curriculum planning and instruction to management. Under the guidance of the classroom teacher and university supervisor, student teachers typically do the following:

"I'M A VERY GOOD BOY . . . EVEN WHEN WE HAVE A STUDENT TEACHER."

- Plan lessons and units.
- Teach lessons to the whole class and to small groups and individual students.
- Take responsibility for managing student behavior.
- Communicate with caregivers.
- Confer with teachers and university supervisors for suggestions, guidance, and detailed analyses of their efforts and progress.
- Perform on a reduced scale most of the professional activities performed by teachers. These may include extra duties such as lunch or bus supervision.
- Observe and participate for the same hours (contracted hours) as the teachers.

It is important to understand the role the master or cooperating teacher plays in partnership with student teachers. Teachers who are perceived to be highly skilled in instruction and management may at times be asked to have student teachers in their classroom. In this

CASE STUDY 12.3

A MASTER TEACHER AND HER STUDENT TEACHER

Focus Question

Ask several teachers about their student teaching experiences. You just read that cooperating teachers are expected to help with orientation, induction, guidance, cooperation, and reflection. To what extent did the teachers perceive this help during their field experiences?

Ginny Lorenz has taught for more than twenty years and has been a master teacher working with student teachers many times. Although over the years she has seen the education pendulum swing from one side to another and back again, she also has observed that one thing remains constant—the need for a master teacher with whom a student teacher can train and from whom a student teacher can learn.

Mrs. Lorenz sincerely believes that master teachers must be willing to mentor student teachers through all aspects of the educational system. From experience, Mrs. Lorenz knows that this mentoring process takes a great deal of time and effort, and she asks herself whether it is worth all the time and effort. When she is approached to mentor a student teacher, she struggles with a variety of questions and emotions: Do I have enough time to work with a student teacher? Will we (student teacher and I) get along? Will the student teacher have potential? Do I really want to share my students, my class, my time? If the student teacher is not doing well, do I have the expertise to help him or her succeed?

Despite her questions, Mrs. Lorenz ultimately has always agreed to the mentoring process because she feels that if we truly believe in the educational system, we owe it to the new generation of teachers to provide them with a safe place to hone their skills. She believes that veterans—master teachers—must share their love and enthusiasm for teaching and for learning. It is through teaching that we learn. And it is though learning that we continue to grow. Mentoring a student teacher allows veteran teachers to do both.

capacity they may be called master, cooperating, or lead teacher, and as such they mentor, coach, and counsel individuals enrolled in a teacher credential program. The cooperating teacher is perhaps the most important resource for the student teacher during the field experience. The cooperating teacher works closely with the student teacher and university supervisor to provide the best guidance and field learning experience possible. Effective cooperating teachers are expected to do many things. They help student teachers understand the role the classroom plays in their development as professionals and help ease them into the school setting. They help students and caregivers understand the valuable role the student teacher plays in the classroom. Cooperating teachers also help with the following:

- Orientation—helping the student teacher locate key persons; resources; materials; equipment; and district curriculum standards, guidelines, and programs
- Induction—helping the student teacher understand the full-time teaching realities and responsibilities, how children learn, district expectations, and available supports
- Guidance—helping the student teacher with planning, evaluation, lesson delivery, and management; providing demonstration teaching

- Cooperation—through sharing ideas, conferencing and coaching, and accepting and respecting the student teacher both as a learner and a coworker
- Reflection—sharing critical assessments of the student teacher's experience and progress and encouraging the student teacher to use self-reflection productively

REQUIREMENTS FOR PARAPROFESSIONALS AND VOLUNTEERS

The requirements for paraprofessionals and volunteers are not stringent, but all persons under consideration should understand two things from the beginning. First, their services are needed to support the educational program. Their presence at school is not for socializing, drinking coffee in the lounge, or laughing about inappropriate things children sometimes do. This point is tactfully made to prospective helpers, of course. Second, once they are given responsibilities, professional standards apply to them just as to other school personnel. This point also is tactfully made so that no offense is given. (Professionalism is discussed later in this chapter.) With these two understandings in place, teachers look for three additional traits in paraprofessionals and volunteers: (1) a sincere desire to work with students and to help provide a quality educational experience, (2) a personality suited to working with children and other adults in the school, and (3) an assurance of reliability—that the person can and will appear regularly as scheduled.

OPTIMUM NUMBER OF PARAPROFESSIONALS AND VOLUNTEERS

One paraprofessional or volunteer per classroom is desirable; two per room, if they are good, may be better. With more than two, the situation is likely to be counterproductive, cumbersome, and confused. With the exception of support providers for children with special needs, ideally a class profits substantially from the presence of a teacher, one paid paraprofessional present every day, and one caregiver or university student volunteer scheduled as needed. Cross-grade partners and cross-age tutors may be used as needed to work directly with students who require extra help. This amount of assistance permits good instruction and monitoring, individual attention to children, and adequate help so the teacher isn't run ragged.

GROUND RULES FOR PARAPROFESSIONALS AND VOLUNTEERS

There are many expectations of paraprofessionals and volunteers with regards to behavior, authority, and dealing with children. They will not know automatically what is expected of them, especially in professional appearance and demeanor. They will almost certainly know little about legal requirements and danger points. You should be prepared to inform and instruct paraprofessionals and volunteers under your direction, so they are able to function well.

Often expectations of paraprofessionals are stated in handbooks prepared by school districts, and if these are available where you teach, you should see that your adult paraprofessionals receive copies. You should ask that they read the guidelines and discuss the contents with you afterward. If you use parent volunteers, cross-grade partners, or cross-age tutors, take time to explain carefully what you expect. Make sure you discuss with all paraprofessionals and volunteers your expectations concerning authority, reliability, instruction, discipline, communication, professionalism, and legal requirements.

Authority

Adult paraprofessionals and volunteers should be made aware of the lines of authority within the school, which normally flow in the order depicted in Figure 12.1. As the chart illustrates, the principal is in charge of everyone at the school. Below the principal and on an equal level are teachers, librarians, clerical staff, custodians, and district resource personnel such as specialists and psychologists. Classroom paraprofessionals and volunteers are under the authority of the principal and classroom teacher but are directly responsible to the teacher in whose room they work.

The paraprofessional has authority over students only in areas delegated by the teacher. Usually that authority is limited to the classroom and the playground. It should clearly be understood that although the adult may be given considerable latitude, the teacher has final say in all matters related to the class duties of the paraprofessional or volunteer, including instruction, clerical work, the learning environment, and dealings with children and their parents or guardians.

Reliability

Reliability is essential in paraprofessionals and volunteers. Those who are not reliable in attendance or performance of duties are of no value. They need to understand that they must

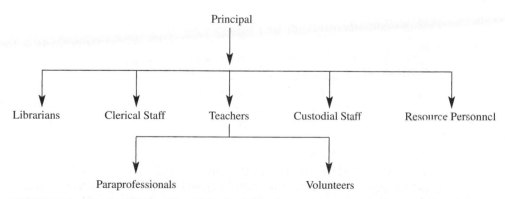

FIGURE 12.1   Lines of Authority within the School

be prepared, that they must function consistently, and that they must let nothing except emergency situations interfere with the performance of their obligations.

Naturally, people become ill and cannot or should not report for work in the classroom, and unexpected emergencies happen to everyone. When these situations occur, paraprofessionals are obliged to inform the teacher as early as possible so the teacher can make other arrangements.

Teachers should not spring surprise duties on paraprofessionals or volunteers that cannot be handled well or gracefully. And they always should anticipate the possibility that the aide may be absent. With a backup plan always in mind, such as change of activity or use of a volunteer, cross-grade partner, or cross-age tutor, the teacher need not panic when an aide will not be present.

Instruction

The instructional program is to be planned and delivered under the direction of the classroom teacher. Many paraprofessionals and volunteers are very good at teaching and do so regularly, but always with the presumption that the teacher has provided suitable guidance. The classroom teacher is not to turn over complete responsibility for significant portions of the instructional program to any paraprofessional or volunteer. The teacher is legally and professionally expected to be in charge of instruction and is responsible for instructional outcome.

Discipline

Technically, paraprofessionals and volunteers are not to discipline students. Discipline is the province of the teacher, principal, and other credentialed persons. In practice, however, teachers cannot expect a paraprofessional or volunteer to work with students but do nothing to manage or help students manage their own behavior. When it is necessary to correct disruptive behavior, the paraprofessional or volunteer should always do so within the parameters of the discipline system in effect in the classroom and with the teacher's permission. By no means should paraprofessionals or volunteers physically punish students, berate them, detain them after school, or force them to do unpleasant tasks as punishment for disruptive behavior. Consequences for disruptive or inappropriate behavior are always for the teacher to provide.

Teachers know that students often consider substitutes fair game. Therefore, they should talk seriously with students about class behavior during the teacher's absence. Teachers should make it clear that the substitute will report on the behavior of the class and individual students. Students should be informed that the substitute may use the teacher's discipline plan or an altogether different one, but that, in either case, students are to behave and be as helpful as possible to the substitute.

Most student teachers arrive at their field placements with ideas about curriculum, instruction, and discipline from their program coursework and textbooks, as well as from their own school experiences. Ideally, the practicum nature of the field experience makes this a time for student teachers to find out what works and doesn't work, with a safety net of sorts provided by the cooperating teacher and university supervisor. Consequently, student teachers might hope to develop and present their own discipline system. This would be done only with the guidance and support of the cooperating teacher.

VIGNETTE 12.2   The Substitute Video

Linda Monedero uses a video activity to prepare her young students and the substitute for a successful day. The videotape created by her students shows the daily schedule and the class rules and is included as part of the materials left for the substitute when the teacher is absent. The substitute and class view this five-minute tape together at the beginning of the school day. Students are accountable because they were involved in making the video and then hear and see it with the substitute.

Students work in cooperative groups to make the short video. Each group draws and labels two signs, one for a subject area (such as "Reading 9:00–10:30") and another for a class rule. The videotape then shows each cooperative group reading its signs. The signs for subject areas are presented in timeline order.

Upon Reflection

Remember substitute Janet Beyea in Case Study 12.2. How likely is it that she would have a productive and successful day with Linda's students?

Communication

Paraprofessionals and volunteers should be taught how to communicate with your students—to speak in a calm, reassuring tone of voice, using words that students understand, and to serve as models of correct grammar and polite language. If your paraprofessional, volunteer, or tutor has a problem in this regard, very tactfully explain that you have a certain way of speaking with children that you would like help with; then demonstrate what you say and how you speak. When you notice improvement, acknowledge the effort with thanks.

Communication between teacher and paraprofessional, volunteer, substitute, or student teacher must be open. This openness permits an easier resolution of problems than when secrecy or hurt is involved, provided neither person is put on the defensive. It is good to remember Berne's three states of communication that were mentioned briefly in the previous chapter—the child state, the parent state, and the adult state. Using adult–adult parallel communication, teachers must take the lead in communicating openly and tactfully, taking as much care as when communicating with students never to disparage or speak brusquely to a paraprofessional, volunteer, or student teacher.

Professionalism

Paraprofessionals and volunteers, certainly those who are paid for their services, should be taught how to behave in a professional manner—that is, with a positive and sincere attitude toward one's status, work, and the children in the class. Professionalism includes dependability and the acceptance of responsibility. In addition, professionalism reflects the styles of dress, speech, and demeanor considered proper for school personnel.

Be sure that you take a moment to discuss with paraprofessionals and volunteers the dangers inherent in gossip. Reportedly over 90 percent of the informal talk that occurs in teachers' lounges is negative in nature. Negative talk that criticizes programs, students, administrators, caregivers, and colleagues may be entertaining, but invariably is counter-productive. It encourages further negativism, diverts energy from productive work, and can lead to personal conflicts. Paraprofessionals and volunteers should be helped to understand clearly that they should either keep quiet or speak positively about children and programs to prevent irreparable damage.

Occasionally frank talk is called for between teacher and paraprofessional, volunteer, or student teacher. Sometimes shortcomings must be discussed, but even then, the teacher must try to point to positive solutions, to better ways of doing things without denigrating the character of others. If you hear paraprofessionals or volunteers at your school speaking derogatorily of school, programs, students, or personnel, take immediate steps to correct the problem. Handle the problem yourself if your own paraprofessional or volunteer is guilty and consider including the university supervisor if your student teacher is guilty. If others are involved, take up the matter with the principal as a school problem. Don't point blame at fellow teachers.

The way one dresses also demonstrates professionalism. Adult paraprofessionals and volunteers, and occasionally, student teachers need to be encouraged to dress neatly, more or less in keeping with how teachers in the school and grade level dress. They will want respect, like everyone else, and they should understand that respect is influenced by appearance. Of course, this consideration applies to a lesser degree for cross-grade partners and cross-age tutors.

Responsibility and dependability have already been mentioned as aspects of professionalism. Responsibility is shown in the assumption of duties and their follow-through without having to be asked. It also is shown through use of common sense, such as paying attention to children when on playground duty. Dependability refers to living up to expectations—doing what one is supposed to do when one is supposed to do it. Of course, it is the teacher's responsibility to clearly inform paraprofessionals, volunteers, and student teachers of expectations, routines, and duties.

Legal Requirements

Paraprofessionals, like teachers, will not be allowed to keep their jobs if they are shown to be incompetent or insubordinate, or to have engaged in criminal or certain immoral activities.

Incompetence refers to an inability or failure to perform satisfactorily those duties normally expected. To be substantiated, this failure must occur repeatedly over a period of time and be documented by the teacher. *Insubordination* means refusal to follow direct, reasonable orders given by a person in authority, or the breaking of a valid school rule in a willful and defiant manner. Generally, *criminal acts* are those activities categorized as felonies under the law—for example, robbery and sale of illegal drugs, but not jaywalking or speeding. *Immoral or otherwise unacceptable acts* come into play only when they directly impact one's job performance or reputation, such as intoxication or drinking while on the job, obscene language at school, and inappropriate sexual activity around the school premises.

Paraprofessionals, like teachers, need to be careful about what they say. While the Supreme Court in 1969 guaranteed teachers and students freedom of expression in the schools, that guarantee does not apply as fully for school personnel as for ordinary citizens. For example, teachers are allowed to speak out on controversial matters, including conditions and policies of the schools. They may not, however, make false or reckless accusations that disrupt the educational process or make abusive and scornful attacks on school officials. Nor are they allowed to use profanity or tell off-color stories within students' range of hearing. It also is forbidden to use the classroom as a forum for expressing personal convictions in sensitive matters such as religion, politics, abortion, or sex education.

Liability for student injury or loss is another legal matter of which paraprofessionals and volunteers should be aware. School personnel have a legal responsibility to protect students from harm and injury. For example, if a student is hurt on the playground and suit is brought to show that the injury occurred at least partly because of negligence, the court will try to determine three things: (1) who was supervising the student at the time of the injury, (2) whether the supervisor exercised reasonable foresight in anticipating danger to the student, and (3) whether the supervisor acted in a reasonable and prudent manner. Teachers, paraprofessionals, and volunteers will not be found negligent unless it can be shown that they violated the requirements of reasonable foresight (e.g., not allowing students to play where there is broken glass or an excavation) and prudent manner (e.g., keeping watch over the students instead of slipping into the lounge for a cup of coffee).

Paraprofessionals and volunteers working in supervisory capacities therefore must be clearly informed that they must be present and attentive, that they must not allow students out of their line of sight while supervising, and that they must make sure students do not play in unsafe areas or use equipment that is obviously unsafe. Paraprofessionals and volunteers should always be informed of legal danger areas and given suitable instruction on conduct.

WHEN PARAPROFESSIONALS MUST BE ABSENT

Most student teachers genuinely want successful field experiences and see them as rich and practical learning opportunities. Many paraprofessionals and volunteers are completely dependable and miss work only out of dire necessity, and they inform the teacher as soon as possible of their pending absence. However, others take all the paid absences available, plus a few extras. Volunteers tend to be even less reliable. And to the teacher's distress, absences appear to occur at times when the aide seems indispensable, causing the teacher to scramble for alternative plans.

This need not be the case. Since you know that your paraprofessionals, volunteers, or student teacher may, at any time, be unavailable, you need only to arrange for substitute aides or extra cross-grade or cross-age tutors. And when that is not possible, you can have backup instructional plans ready.

TRAINING PARAPROFESSIONALS AND VOLUNTEERS

As mentioned earlier, some school districts provide training for the paid paraprofessionals they employ. Such training typically deals with the foregoing matters. However, most paraprofessionals, and almost all volunteers, cross-grade partners, and cross-age tutors are trained on the job, in the classroom by the teacher. As teachers-in-training, student teachers also receive on-the-job training as the cooperating teacher models, mentors, and coaches the routines, management, and instruction of the classroom.

On-the-job training is acceptable—even preferable in most cases—because duties of paraprofessionals and volunteers vary from classroom to classroom. Usually training done by teachers includes an orientation to the classroom; instruction in specific duties; details of where the volunteer is to be stationed, work, or circulate; and demonstration of how duties are to be performed. Legal, ethical, and professional regulations are spelled out clearly. As the paraprofessional or volunteer works in the manner indicated, the teacher provides necessary feedback, both corrections and appreciations.

Paraprofessionals and aides quickly learn procedures and become able to discharge their duties without direct supervision. Still, it is the teacher's responsibility to plan all work and materials included in the instructional program and to supervise these adults at work. Student teachers also learn procedures and over time become more able to perform with less direct supervision, although it is the responsibility of the cooperating teacher and university supervisor to guide and oversee their progress.

ASSIGNING SPACE AND WORK DUTIES

All regular paraprofessionals, student teachers, and aides, whether paid, volunteer, cross-grade, or cross-age, should have a place in the classroom designated as their own. If one is available, this is a desk or table where the teacher provides their notes, materials, or other items. Adults should not be asked to sit in small chairs at low tables used by young children.

Paid paraprofessionals are assigned to the classroom for a specified number of hours, and volunteer work times are scheduled according to teacher need. Volunteers are scheduled by agreement with the teacher, typically for certain days and times. Volunteers should not be left to simply hang around and observe, not knowing what to do with themselves. If a volunteer offers unexpected help on a particular morning, the teacher should accept the offer if it is convenient, but only when there is something productive for the volunteer to do, such as organizing materials, helping individual children, or sorting and filing papers. Otherwise, the teacher should thank the volunteer, explain that no help is needed at the moment, and ask permission to call for help in the future.

Many teachers write specific work assignments on cards for their paraprofessionals and volunteers. These notations need not be made in detail but should indicate duties, sequence, materials, and time allocations. An assignment card might look something like the one in Figure 12.2

Figure 12.2 is written out as it would appear when beginning to work with your paraprofessional. Later, when duties are understood, brief notes suffice, such as

Reading: Tom to center, read story to you; record errors.

Math: Photocopy tomorrow's papers; score today's and enter.

Spelling: Give practice test.

Language: Help monitor.

Usually oral instructions are sufficient when the duties of the paraprofessional or volunteer are mostly supervisory or clerical. Misunderstandings can be avoided by jotting notes on an assignment card. When the duties involve record keeping, remember these

FIGURE 12.2   **Assignment Card for Paraprofessional**

Name: ——————————————   Date: ——————————————

Reading: Take Tom to center and have him read the story aloud to you; keep a record of the errors he makes.

Math: Duplicate tomorrow's papers. Collect today's papers and score them. Enter scores in record book.

Spelling: Give today's practice test to the class. Collect and mark the papers.

Language: Help me monitor students as they write their stories. Help with spelling or other questions they have.

earlier cautions: Students have the right to privacy regarding their work and progress; records are legal documents; and you, as the contracted teacher, are legally responsible for their management, recording, and accuracy.

MAINTAINING PARAPROFESSIONALS' MORALE

Good morale, easily overlooked, is as necessary to paraprofessionals, volunteers, and student teachers as it is to teachers. It affects the quality of their work and the amount of satisfaction derived from it. To keep the morale level high for paraprofessionals and volunteers, give attention to the following:

1. Acceptance—a sense of belonging to the class and educational program, which grows out of appreciative attention and communication from the teacher, and is furthered by assigning specific tasks and work space
2. Meaningful work and clear directions—the paraprofessional or volunteer should not always do menial or tedious tasks; give sufficient guidance so that the work can be done properly
3. Sense of accomplishment—helps paraprofessionals and volunteers to see that their work has been done well and progress was made
4. Evidence of appreciation—for contributions made to the instructional program; need only be a sincere thank-you, but an occasional card or small gift always is welcomed

Remember that student teachers are learners and need morale boosts, too. It is as important for them to hear about what they are doing well as it is to know what they need to change, correct, or improve. Specific positive feedback can be given during planning or conferences, in an interactive journal, or on short notes to the student teacher.

This concludes our consideration of managing the work of paraprofessionals, volunteers, substitutes, student teachers, and other helpers in the classroom. Before moving ahead to Chapter 13, which deals with how to manage two kinds of stress—the stressful emotions of unexpected events and trauma and job-related stress that so badly afflict teachers—take time to explore these end-of-chapter activities.

Parting Thought

Determine that the thing can and shall be done, and then . . . find the way.

—Abraham Lincoln

SUMMARY SELF-CHECK

Check off the following as you either understand or become able to apply them.

❏ Paraprofessionals and volunteers are people who work in the classroom with the teacher to help provide the educational program. Usually they fall into the categories of paid paraprofessional, caregiver or university student volunteer, cross-grade partner or cross-age tutor, or community resource person. Substitute teachers and student teachers are other adults who might work in a classroom.
  - What paraprofessionals can do: tutor, test, supervise, correct papers, duplicate, record, file, prepare instructional materials, assist as directed by the teacher
  - How paraprofessionals are obtained: recruited by schools or by teachers from parents and guardians of students, friends, and relatives; from high schools and universities; from older elementary and secondary students; from parent–teacher associations; from senior citizens' groups; and from community agencies and companies
  - Other helpers: cross-grade partners, cross-age tutors, substitute teachers, and student teachers

❏ Substitute teachers are hired to teach when contracted teachers must be away from the classroom.
  - Teachers leave an updated substitute folder that contains lesson plans and a copy of the discipline plan, current seating chart and class roster with notations of relevant student information, class schedule and current duty schedule, classroom monitor and volunteer lists, and school map.
  - The teacher's obligations: inform students about teacher absences, substitute teachers, how to work helpfully with substitutes, duties of substitute teacher monitors
  - The substitute teacher's obligations: further the program and make the day productive for the students; maintain discipline
  - Mutuality: the ideal relationship between teacher and substitute

❏ Student teachers, who are not properly called paraprofessionals, often are seen working in classrooms.
  - What student teachers can do: plan and teach lessons; take responsibility for discipline; communicate with parents and guardians; confer with teachers and

university supervisors; observe, participate, and perform most of the teacher's activities; responsibilities usually increase with time and experience

❑ Ground rules for paraprofessionals and volunteers
  ■ Authority belongs to the teacher but can be delegated to the paraprofessional.
  ■ Reliability is an essential trait
  ■ Instruction can be provided by paraprofessionals under the teacher's supervision.
  ■ Discipline is the province of the teacher
  ■ Communication is needed for good relationships
  ■ Professional standards are explained and exemplified by the teacher
  ■ Legal requirements require that attention be given to incompetence, insubordination, criminality, immorality; liability for student injury or loss; freedom of expression and subsequent restrictions
  ■ When paraprofessionals must be absent: utilize substitute, cross-grade partner or cross-age helper, backup plan
  ■ Training paraprofessionals: by schools for paid aides; on-the-job training by teachers
  ■ Work space and assignments: designated personal area; work assignments clearly set forth; record-keeping duties closely checked and verified
  ■ Morale of paraprofessionals and student teachers maintained through acceptance, meaningful work and clear directions, sense of accomplishment, evidence of appreciation

❑ Important cautions when the duties involve record keeping: Students have the right to privacy regarding their work and progress. Records are legal documents and the contracted teacher is legally responsible for their management, recording, and accuracy.

ACTIVITIES FOR REFLECTION AND DISCUSSION

1. Take a moment to review the statements in the Prediction–Review Guide at the beginning of this chapter. Put a check mark in the Review column next to any statement with which you now agree. How have your thoughts changed since reading this chapter?

2. Interview at least two teachers about the use of paraprofessionals and volunteers in their classroom. How do they locate and schedule volunteers? When and how do they "train" volunteers? What tasks and responsibilities do they request? How do they show their appreciation?

3. You are told you can choose a paid paraprofessional or substitute teacher from among three available candidates. List in order the criteria you would use in making your selection. How would you determine the extent to which each candidate meets your criteria?

4. For a grade level of your choice, you are provided a paid paraprofessional for two hours a day. Put in order of importance what you would have your aide do during that limited amount of time. Give your reasons.

5. You are ready to instruct your paraprofessional on the ground rules of discipline and professionalism. What would you say and what training would you give, if any?

6. Compile what you will provide in a substitute folder to ensure that the teacher and students have a productive day.

7. Suppose you teach second grade. Two talented but somewhat troubled sixth-grade boys (they talk back to their teacher and sometimes fight with other boys on the playground) think it would be "cool" to work in your room as cross-grade tutors. Their teacher thinks the experience would be good for them. You hesitantly agree to give them the opportunity. What ground rules would you establish for them? If they proved to be good and worthwhile for your program, how would you let them know that you appreciate their work?

REFERENCES AND RECOMMENDED READINGS

Allen, R. (2002, November). Teachers and paraeducators: Defining roles in an age of accountability. *Education Update, 44*(7). Alexandria, VA: ASCD.

Duebber, D. (2000, May). Substitute teaching: Sink or swim. *Educational Leadership, 57*(8), 73–74.

Engaging parents and the community in schools [Special issue]. (1998, May). *Educational Leadership.* Alexandria, VA: ASCD.

Kagan, L., Kagan, M., & Kagan, S. (1997). *Cooperative learning structures for teambuilding.* San Clemente, CA: Kagan Cooperative Learning.

Kagan, M., Robertson, L., & Kagan, S. (1995). *Cooperative learning structures for classbuilding.* San Clemente, CA: Kagan Cooperative Learning.

Kagan, S. (2000). *Silly sports and goofy games.* San Clemente, CA: Kagan Publishing.

Supporting new teachers [Special issue]. (1999, May). *Educational Leadership.* Alexandria, VA: ASCD.

Tannenbaum, M. (2000, May). No substitute for quality. *Educational Leadership, 57*(8), 70–72.

There's no substitute for a great sub! A collection of creative tips and lifesavers from substitute teachers [Back to school issue]. (1998). *The Mailbox Teacher, 27*(1), 32–35.

Websites

The SMILES Program
www.slc.k12.ut.us/depts/comminv/schoolvols.html

National Substitute Teacher Alliance
http://www.nstasubs.org

Trade Books

Allard, H. (1977). *Miss Nelson is missing!* Boston: Houghton Mifflin.

Thaler, M. (1989). *The teacher from the Black Lagoon.* New York: Scholastic.

Managing Emotional Trauma and Job-Related Stress Productively

There have been no dragons in my life, only small spiders and stepping in gum.
I could have coped with dragons!
—Author Unknown

Prediction–Review Guide

Before you read the chapter, take a minute to put a check mark in the Prediction column next to any statement with which you agree.

	Prediction	Review
1. Current brain research suggests that all three parts of the brain work equally in times of stress.	❏	❏
2. The main purpose for crisis intervention and Critical Incident Stress Management is to handle situations that are beyond the resources of the individual or site.	❏	❏
3. Distress is bad for you; however, eustress is good for you.	❏	❏
4. Teaching is considered to be high on the list of stressful occupations.	❏	❏
5. Discipline problems and lack of time are two of teachers' greatest stressors.	❏	❏
6. When prioritizing, it is advisable to finish the easy tasks first so you can concentrate on the more difficult.	❏	❏
7. Selective avoidance is one way to reduce the stress of teaching.	❏	❏
8. Good cooperation and quality achievement almost certainly render a high level of class synergy.	❏	❏
9. A good place to cut back if your workload is too heavy is on communication with caregivers, provided there are no serious problems with students.	❏	❏
10. If the work you assign students is important enough for them to do, then it is equally important that you correct it carefully.	❏	❏

Support for specific standards found in this chapter:

INTASC Standards

6. Communication Skills

   The teacher uses knowledge of effective verbal, nonverbal, and media communication techniques to foster active inquiry, collaboration, and supportive interaction in the classroom.

9. Professional Commitment

   The teacher is a reflective practitioner who continually evaluates the effects of his or her choices and actions on others (students, parents, and other professionals in the learning community) and who actively seeks out opportunities to grow professionally.

Danielson's Framework for Teaching

2. The Classroom Environment
   - Creating an environment of respect and rapport
   - Establishing a culture for learning
   - Managing classroom procedures
   - Managing student behavior
   - Organizing physical space

3. Instruction
   - Communicating clearly and accurately
   - Using questioning and discussion techniques
   - Engaging students in learning
   - Providing feedback to students
   - Demonstrating flexibility and responsiveness

4. Professional Responsibilities
   - Reflecting on teaching
   - Maintaining accurate records
   - Communicating with families
   - Contributing to the school and district
   - Growing and developing professionally

NBPTS Standards

1. Teachers are committed to students and their learning.

NCATE Standards

Reflect on practice, act on feedback, and integrate the technology into instruction effectively.

In this chapter we explore two aspects of stress. We begin with a topic that relates ever more strongly to our lives today—the effects of emotional stress that result from unexpected events such as tragedy and trauma, with attention to managing that stress. Later we will explore suggestions concerning management of stress that normally accompanies teaching.

MANAGING EMOTIONS OF UNEXPECTED EVENTS AND TRAUMA

"The best laid plans of mice and men . . ." How many times have we planned and prepared and showed up ready to teach, only to find that something or someone has put an enormous obstacle in our path. It may be something as simple as having to change the schedule for the day, despite its effects on your program. Certainly the move of a best friend or the death of a pet can affect a child's attention and interrupt the flow of your plans. But increasingly it seems that obstacles are taking on a more imposing nature: an accident with fatalities involving a school bus and its passengers; the sudden death of a beloved teacher; the kidnapping and death of a local child; the shooting at a local high school; terrorist attacks on New York and Washington, DC; natural devastations such as fires, hurricanes, tornadoes, and floods; and the other disasters that overflow the newspapers. All such events produce strong emotional reactions in our students and us. While we can't change the events, we can manage the associated emotions in a way that allows our students and us to cope with them more easily.

State laws give districts the legal responsibilities for emergency preparedness, school safety, and risk management. Further, the Field Act of 1933 requires that schools are to be available as post-disaster shelters. To this end, districts have plans in place for such major events. Generally, public school employees are sanctioned as disaster service workers, and as such, teachers are responsible for giving care and support to students in a crisis. In other words, teachers may have to deal with the effects of emotional stress.

Important Definitions

In order to understand the nature and results of events that require special care or intervention, we should be familiar with the following terms.

Stress.   *Stress* is anything that causes continuing physical, mental, or emotional strain or tension. In this chapter we will explore how stress can be positive (eustress) or negative (distress). Here we will talk about distress.

Trauma.   *Trauma* is a physical or emotional injury or shock from experiencing a disastrous event outside the range of usual experience. In this chapter we focus on emotional trauma. Anyone can experience high emotions when traumatic events occur. Teachers are faced with two important questions: How can we manage these emotions, especially in our children? And how do we take care of ourselves as well?

Critical Incident and Crisis Intervention.   Childs (2002) defines a critical incident as "any emotionally significant event that overwhelms the coping abilities of exposed individuals or groups" (p. 3). Crisis intervention is the "assistance rendered after a critical incident" (p. 3). As a short-term response to a critical incident, a crisis intervention has several goals:

- Interventions attempt to decrease or relieve adverse reactions of individuals or groups affected by trauma.
- Interventions are intended to impact or address the individual or group's ability to cope and assist in identifying and assessing available support structures.

- They normalize reactions to the event or crisis.
- They assess the individual or group's capabilities and need for further support or referral.

Crisis intervention is not therapy for the individual or group. Teachers do not have the training for that task. Rather, it is to assess and then assist with the immediacy of an event in order to return the individual or group to a normal level of functioning.

Critical Incident Stress Management (CISM).   *Critical Incident Stress Management* is a systematic crisis intervention model that has become a standard of care for traumatized persons. The model and its structure were conceived by Dr. Jeffrey Mitchell, a military doctor who studied emotional trauma of individuals involved in a crisis. For additional information and links to related articles, resources, workshops, and training opportunities regarding CISM, go to www.icisf.org.

Stress and the Triune Brain

Knowledge about human brain physiology helps us understand how to provide crisis intervention. In the 1980s, Paul MacLean, the former director of the Laboratory of the Brain and Behavior at the United States National Institute of Mental Health, introduced the triune brain theory. MacLean describes the human brain as being three brains in one, having evolved in that manner in response to various needs. Although each of the three brains, or layers, specializes in a separate function, all three layers interact.

Simplified, the three areas of the brain work in this way. The primary function of the brain stem and cerebellum, also called the reptilian complex, controls physical survival and body maintenance (digestion, reproduction, circulation, breathing, and movement). The middle brain controls emotion and survival acts, such as eating, drinking, and sleeping. The outer brain (neocortex) is responsible for language, higher-order thinking, and ability to see ahead and plan for the future. The neocortex seeks a balance of emotions (meaning none becomes extremely high), and until this balance exists, the cortex has a reduced capacity to process information and use logical reasoning.

Here is how all this relates to stress. In times of undue stress or threat, the brain tends to bypass reason. Instead of allowing us to assess situations and plan ahead, it hammers us first with a fight, flight, or hide response—we fight back or we try to escape or hide from the situation. In other words, we react first, after which logic, reasoning, and decision making seem to follow. This explains why we may behave the way we do during a critical incident— why we may forget the name of our best friend or feel driven to clean the house and polish the silver.

Signs and Symptoms of Emotional Stress

Fear and anxiety are debilitating emotions for everyone. Human reactions to disaster differ from person to person. In general, under situations of threat or excitement our bodies undergo chemical changes—rapid pulse, increased blood pressure, muscle tension, and

"I'M SO OVERSCHEDULED THE ONLY DOWN TIME I HAVE IS THE TIMEOUT CHAIR."

perspiration. Along with these physical reactions, adults reacting to disastrous events often engage in a natural grieving process that begins with denial, then anger, and finally a degree of resignation. If their distress is great, they may demonstrate symptoms of what now is called post-traumatic stress disorder (PTSD), in which they reexperience the event, either in dreams or in a related context; avoid talking about it; numb their emotions; or assume a high-alert state of being.

Children's reactions to trauma also may be varied. For example, they may detach from the pain of the moment in emotional shock and be seen as having an apparent lack of feelings. They may regress to immature behaviors, needing to be held, rocked, or remain close and clinging to a caregiver or someone important to them. They may act out behaviorally, venting feelings of anger, terror, frustration, or helplessness. They may repeatedly ask questions or require a lot of extra reassurances.

The Nature of Crisis Intervention

Critical incidents generally involve traumatic loss (death, serious injury, hostage situations), social unrest or racial conflicts, and manmade or natural disasters. Critical incidents are judged by the reaction to the incident, not by the magnitude of the event.

Today many districts and schools have teams of district and community members trained to assist in the aftermath of a critical incident. A *Crisis Response Team (CRT)* is called when the event overwhelms the school's ability to handle a situation and operates with consent and concurrence of the site administrator. The CRT command leader meets with administration and keeps them informed as the team carries out the approved plan. Typically the team provides direct crisis intervention services to students in the classrooms, in whole or small-group settings, and to individual students as needed. The team also is prepared to assist teachers and school personnel in handling student reactions and provide personal support to them. Additionally, the CRT can provide consultation services to administration and give information and community resources to parents and guardians.

The CRT responds to what individuals need right in the moment. Their interventions deal with the here and now, are designed to prevent further emotional and behavioral disturbances, and are short-term. Team members are facilitators who use active and direct strategies and responses. CRT members are not counselors, bound to invest in long-term care and treatment. They will make referrals to counselors and other community resources, as needed, so individuals receive the best long-term support.

When Crisis Teams Are Not Available

Crisis Response Teams are not always available when needed. In those cases, it is up to the teachers and school personnel to help others cope. Most school districts provide some advice concerning how personnel are to function at those times, recognizing they do not have adequate training or understanding. Here are some things schools do. When applying any of these tactics, one must keep in mind students' emotional maturity and needs.

Through a question and response guide, Berman, Diener, Dieringer, and Lantieri (2003) coach teachers and caregivers about ways to discuss exceptional events with children. These discussions are varied in accordance with the age and maturity of the children, as well as their personal connection to the event. Most children appreciate talking with adults they trust and see as supportive, caring, and sensitive. Among the guidelines for discussions are the following:

- Ask the children what they already know, what they think they know but are not sure about, and what questions they have. Ask open questions: "What do you know about . . . ?" "What is upsetting you the most?" "Are you saying that . . . ?"
- Listen and respond to their questions and concerns with facts, in simple language, and without extraneous details for which the children may not be ready. Simply and factually correct misinformation. Allow children to respond to each of your comments.
- As you listen to and observe the children, respond to what you hear and see in a supportive and sensitive way. Children are reassured when they know you are listening and you care about them.
- Avoid talking to children about adult concerns that would likely raise new questions and fears, limit their own expressions, or simply be over their heads.
- Use active listening to clarify without judgment, help you understand the children, and help the children sort out their ideas. Because children may be unable to say what they feel or what they say may mean something different to you than they intended, paraphrase what you hear and invite them to elaborate or clarify: "Can you tell me more about that?" or "What do you mean by that?"
- In addition to talk, provide children with opportunities to explore and express themselves through writing, play, drawings, and props such as clay or puppets.
- Look and listen for nonverbal messages such as facial expressions, gestures, posture, and fidgeting; also notice voice rate and tone and watch for significant increases in anxiety, distractibility, despair, or fear.
- Help children explore their feelings. Listen closely for underlying concerns such as personal and family safety.
- Validate that their feelings are OK: "You seem sad when we talk about this. I feel sad too."
- When closure to discussion of feelings is difficult, simply thank the children for sharing and affirm that you care.
- Identify and monitor children with personal connections to the event and inform the counselor.
- Finally, look for and accept support from other adults who can help you (a caregiver, mentor, and others).

RESPONDING TO CRISIS

Focus Question
What action plan does your local school or district have in place to handle serious or crisis events?

Sherry Coburn, a sixth grade teacher, is also the team coordinator who prepares the yearly telephone tree that is used to contact all staff when a serious event warrants their knowledge. She describes crisis response at her school.

Gilmore's Crisis Response Team originally was designed to aid students in crisis—suffering from such losses as a sibling, parent, or relative. As time has gone on, its purpose has increased. We have been called on to service children who had been friends with someone shot and killed by gang involvement and gang retaliation. We once had to deal with many students when a popular student was hit by a train and killed. We also had an incident when a teacher was killed due to domestic violence.

Our crisis team has had to branch out within the past few years to anticipate problems and work out solutions prior to their happening in order to make our school a safe place for both students and staff. We devised and held the first intrusion drill in our state and continue to hold them on a monthly basis. We believe that this drill must be second nature to our students, just as a fire drill is.

Last year when a large hall fight broke out we devised a plan to deal with this new type of incident. We called it a "Code Hall Sweep." When teachers hear this over the PA system, they close their classroom doors and do not allow anyone in. Administrators and hall assistants then can handle the situation by rounding up anyone involved.

Of the numerous strategies that have been proven effective, several are fairly easy to remember and implement by teachers, including the SEA-3 Method and the SAFER Method, described in the following paragraphs. As you read these strategies, keep in mind that they can be applied to anyone in need, adults as well as children. Also remember that as the classroom teacher, you know your students. Because you are familiar with your students' behavior and maturity prior to situations of stress or trauma, you will be able to gauge any of the changes listed in the paragraphs below.

SEA-3 Method

This is a method that considers five areas to assess the functioning of individuals—children or adults—in situations of stress or trauma. SEA-3 stands for speech, emotion, appearance alertness, and activity.

- *Speech.* Listen to the child's speech. To what degree is it slurred or rapid?
- *Emotion.* Evaluate the child's emotion, considering both mood and affect. For example, to what degree is the child depressed or euphoric? Is the child's display of emotions flat or inappropriate? What emotions, if any, are being expressed? Does the

child laugh or make jokes about a sad situation? Does the child show overwhelming emotion, such as excessive crying or hysteria?

- *Appearance.* Consider the child's appearance—neat, disheveled?
- *Alertness.* Pay attention to the child's alertness. Do the child's thoughts seem normal? What is the child's level of abstraction—concrete or conceptual? Is the child hallucinating? How accurate is the child's orientation to time, place, and others? What is the child's judgment and capacity for insight? The teacher can assess the child's alertness and judgment by using nondirective responses to what the child says.
- *Activity.* What is the child's activity—lethargic, hyperactive?

SAFER Method

This is a very useful intervention method, which teachers often use without knowing they do. The SAFER method is designed to stabilize the situation by (1) removing the person in crisis from the source of stress, (2) reinforcing cognitive processing and what is natural in time and place, (3) reinforcing the individual's own coping skills, and (4) referring the person for additional care, if necessary. This process may take only a minute or less to perform. In simplified terms, here is what you do:

1. *Stabilize the situation.* Reduce the situational stressors by removing the child from the situation. Turn the child away from the scene or take him or her into another room.

2. *Acknowledge the crisis.* Ask the child to describe what happened or describe personal reactions. The teacher's role is to assist the child in talking about what happened and putting words to the reactions and emotions. Using active listening, the teacher would ask the child to describe what happened and then retell what he or she heard the child say ("I heard you say . . .").

3. *Facilitate understanding.* Using language appropriate to the developmental and emotional maturity of the child, explain what is going on. This helps the child understand the situation. Validate the child's reactions as being natural, but avoid the word "normal." For example, you might say something like: "That was probably really scary for you to hear the sirens when they came into the parking lot."

4. *Encourage adaptive coping.* While continually assessing the child's ability to function, teach the child reasonable and appropriate basic stress and crisis management strategies. Identify appropriate coping skills ("What do you do when you are scared?"); consider personal, school, family, and community resources ("Is there someone at home now who can come for you?"); and develop a reasonable action plan ("Would you like to put some water on your face or lie down in the nurse's office for a few minutes before you go back to class?" "I know Sarah is your friend. I just talked to Sarah's mother, and after school you can go to their house until your parents arrive home.")

5. *Restore or refer.* Your goal is to help the child return to normal functioning. If you feel your efforts are not producing that result, you should consider referring the child for additional care.

Attention-Refocusing Strategies

Attention-refocusing strategies also assist teachers as they work with children in stressful situations. This can be done by asking questions that require the person in distress to use the five senses or that draw attention to the outdoor natural environment. The teacher or helper may begin this strategy by telling the distressed person, "I'm going to ask some silly questions to help you become less upset." Before returning the child to the class or situation, it's important for the helper to ask, "Do you feel you are ready to go back to class?"

Up Shifting

Up shifting strategies are intended to shift the child from an emotional focus to a cognitive focus. These strategies involve quick actions and sounds, such as having students echo rhythmic clapping led by the teacher, or blend counting with a word. For example, as students count in sequence, they replace every multiple of five with the word *buzz*.

Other Subtle Techniques

Several other subtle techniques can be used to advantage. Examples include:

- Physical contact by gently touching the individual's hands or shoulders
- Physically turning the individual away from the event or distraction
- Speaking in a calm, quiet, unemotional voice
- Prompting deep rhythmic breathing
- Relating only relevant facts, not details
- Paraphrasing the individual's last sentences and using nondirective responses
- Asking specific questions to check what the individual understands and how the individual is doing
- Asking the individual what has helped in past upsetting situations
- Asking the individual what he or she needs to help settle down now
- Reiterating the paradigm: Who was involved? What happened? What comes next?

Throughout the entire contact, the teacher or helper behaves naturally and authentically.

Taking Care of Self

Through all these efforts, it is crucial that teachers and helpers take care of themselves and each other, whether they are individual teachers working with their students or members of a Crisis Response Team. This is necessary because helpers and team members are susceptible to direct or vicarious traumatization when responding to a crisis event and when providing support services for victims.

Self Care.   Make sure that all adult helpers utilize tools to help them manage their own stress more effectively. These tools include proper diet, exercise, and rest; journaling and/or counseling for themselves; reduction of other distractions; and moderation of alcohol and medication.

Debriefing.   Debriefing is a structured process through which adults involved in crisis intervention are helped to process their experience in such a way as to avoid symptoms of PTSD or vicarious traumatization. Debriefings, conducted by trained personnel, are essential for everyone's well-being and should occur regularly.

MANAGING JOB-RELATED STRESS

Now we turn attention to stress normally associated with teaching. Teaching can be a good and rewarding job, one that contributes to individual and collective good and brings participants into contact with many fine people. But it is no secret that teachers' lives are filled with stress. Teaching makes one nervous and tired, and if students do not behave well, teachers are certain to experience headaches, anxiety, apathy, and an occasional desire to escape from it all.

Teaching used to be easier than it is now. As recently as the 1950s, nearly all teachers taught to age sixty-five. Many retired at that time, but others continued on to age seventy and beyond. Teachers can't do that anymore. You rarely see a teacher remain in service until sixty-five; most now accept reduced pensions and retire much earlier, just to escape the pressure. Teachers say the job wears them out, especially now that they no longer can count on the success, respect, and dignity that once came with teaching.

What has caused this unfortunate change? Most teachers say students have become more recalcitrant and increasingly difficult to motivate and manage. Today's students are influenced by countless interests outside of school, often lack a cohesive family structure, are less responsive to adult authority, and are more willing to test limits, which they do with regularity. Increasingly, parents and guardians either seem to do little to support the school program and their child or they are overbearing and demanding in their expectations.

But teachers are not only worn down by unruly students or difficult caregivers. In the 1990s, surveyed teachers considered the school setting and workload pressures more stressful than direct contact with students (Pullis, 1992). Teachers everywhere now complain of too much to do and too little time to do it. They see the curriculum change yearly, for varied reasons—sometimes academic, sometimes political. They constantly are required to retool in order to teach in accord with programs, standards, and tests that come into vogue. The No Child Left Behind Act and national and state tests and standards mentioned in Chapters 2 and 10 all are examples of prevailing political influences. Teachers also are responsible for fulfilling nonteaching duties that were unheard of three decades ago. Add to that shrinking funds for supplies; inclusion into regular classes of students with special needs, including children with physical and emotional challenges, English language learners, and exceptionally difficult-to-handle students; endless in-service workshops; and the increased criticism they endure because of lackluster student achievement, and you can see why teachers feel they are expected to do more and more with less and less, and yet, get less respect for it. Such perceptions, correct or not, bring with them heavy loads of stress.

Stress and Its Effects

We have noted that stress is a state of bodily and mental tension. At times the pressures associated with stress become intense. That is not to say that stress is always bad. Life without any stress at all would be incredibly dull. Stress prepares us for action. As suggested earlier, under situations of threat or excitement, our bodies undergo chemical changes that are manifested in rapid pulse, increased blood pressure, muscle tension, and perspiration. In modest amounts, these changes give us vim and vigor. Stress only becomes harmful when it reaches such proportions that it produces deleterious effects.

Source: Artwork reprinted courtesy of Jody Bergsma Galleries: www.bergsma.com.

Thus, stress is seen as consisting of two parts—distress and eustress. *Distress* is negative. It occurs when one feels unable to cope and produces a number of undesirable side effects. *Eustress,* on the other hand, is positive. It occurs in the presence of interesting, challenging, yet resolvable problems. Eustress energizes, enlivens, and excites. It would be incorrect to put forth the impression that teachers need no stress in their lives. What they need is eustress. Unfortunately, too much of what they get is distress.

What Bothers Teachers Most

Generally speaking, most teachers share common needs and hopes. They need to establish and maintain positive relationships with parents and students. They need for students to behave responsibly and hope they will do so courteously. They need supportive relationships with caregivers. They hope for student success. And they need time to manage and accomplish all the personal and professional tasks that come with the profession. Additionally, most teachers sense a growing amount of pressure or unease when any of these goals is not being reached. The yearly Gallup polls and other studies identify time pressures and management of disruptive children as prime sources of teacher stress. It should be noted that the concerns identified in research produce only modest stress, though the level increases as the problems remain unresolved.

But far worse stress occurs when teachers receive poor teaching evaluations, experience verbal or physical attacks from students or caregivers, endure job transfers, and contend with lawsuits. While most teachers never experience most of these events, they say they frequently feel the threat of them.

What Energizes Teachers

You might think that teachers would be energized by conditions opposite to those that bring stress—that is, they would be very happy if given adequate time, well-behaved students, high student achievement, close affiliation with colleagues, and cooperation from satisfied caregivers. It has been found, however, that while removal of major stressors results in job satisfaction, it does not in itself motivate teachers to invest greater amounts of effort into their work.

Sadly, few schools make significant efforts to provide positive motivation for teachers. Teachers rarely have the opportunity to do work in areas of special personal interest. They have almost no opportunity to advance unless they move out of teaching into administration or counseling. Given those facts, teachers must find job rewards within teaching itself. Teachers sometimes have classes, and frequently several students, who are fun to work with. Occasionally caregivers express gratitude, sometimes students thank their teachers and show appreciation, and once in a while administrators or fellow teachers make favorable comments. Some teachers are recognized as master or lead teachers and asked to work with and mentor student and beginning teachers. But self-satisfaction, in these hectic days of teaching, is too weak to motivate a continual push for excellence in most people. Slowly, most teachers begin to question the value of their efforts, especially as frustration builds.

Stress Management for Teachers

Much can be done to make teachers' professional lives better, despite the increasing number of stressors with which teachers must contend. There remains hope that someday school districts may decide that education proceeds better when teachers are contented and hard working than when they are stressed and struggling for survival. To accomplish a transformation in teachers' lives, schools need only free up time for teachers, require less busy work, trust teachers' judgment concerning how to teach and manage student behavior, support home and community alliances that lighten teachers' burdens, and energize teachers through recognition of effort and success.

But let's be practical. If teachers want to improve their existence, they must take charge of the matter themselves. Among steps they can take to relieve much of their stress are prioritizing, accepting a new perspective regarding perfection, selective avoidance, time management, discipline, communication with caregivers, and maintenance of physical well-being. Discipline and communication, though discussed previously, are mentioned here once more.

Prioritizing. To prioritize is simply to put things in order of importance and then to focus on items that require immediate attention while leaving those of lesser importance until later. It means considering the best use of time at this moment. Most persons operate the other way around—they attend to inconsequential matters first, thinking that when they get them out of the way they can concentrate better on more important matters. Unfortunately, with time restrictions as they are, the important matters never receive the attention they should. Stress comes from not getting to the matters that really need attention, or that others expect one to do expeditiously. It doesn't come from skipping the junk mail.

Accepting Less Than Perfection.   Many teachers want perfection. They want students to be perfect and they want themselves to be perfect. They set high goals and push everyone to reach them. Certainly nothing is wrong with holding high expectations. The stress arises when individuals fall short, and they will, for a variety of reasons. Therefore it is best that we acknowledge that perfection simply isn't possible. Football coach Vince Lombardi summed it up this way: "Practice doesn't make perfect. Only perfect practice makes perfect."

Using Selective Avoidance.   At a conference that dealt with the major problems that teachers have to face, one speaker suggested several ways teachers could deal with stress, the best of which simply is to avoid it. The audience laughed, but the speaker was serious. He explained that teachers can learn to say no as a way to prevent overburdening themselves with an insupportable load of tasks. They can avoid associating with chronic complainers who find fault with everyone and everything and thus adversely affect the attitudes of those around them. They can set aside the trivial matters that consume so much time. They can learn not to take work home with them every night so that once in a while they can enjoy the luxury of thinking and talking about nonschool topics. Finally, they can give students greater responsibility in helping manage the classroom and the instructional program. Here are some suggestions.

Say No.   Most teachers, particularly new teachers, are unwilling to say no to their principal, and most are reluctant to say no to colleagues and caregivers. They want to impress others with their willingness to shoulder the load; they want the principal, caregivers, and colleagues to think and speak highly of them. And often they are afraid that a displeased administrator will give them a bad evaluation or assign them to unpleasant duties. That eventuality is unlikely if the teacher says, "I'd like to help, but my schedule is packed. I'll do it if you can help me get a little more time." (Often, administrators can reduce a teacher's duties to make the time available.) Similarly, teachers often are afraid that caregivers and colleagues will dislike them if they decline personal requests. Again, say, "I'd like to be able to help you, but I'm so pressed for time. Do you have any suggestions?" Sometimes caregivers and colleagues will surprise you with their willingness to relieve you of certain tasks in order to obtain your assistance with their problems.

Remember this—teachers by nature want to be helpful. After all, they have chosen a profession based on helping others. But sometimes one has to say no to balance rewards against ravages of overload. It's also important to remember that there are many tasks that teachers simply must assume. You can't say no to meetings, keeping good records, filing required reports, planning lessons, obtaining necessary materials for teaching, and so forth. But if you list the incredible number of tasks that teachers routinely contend with, you would find that many of them could be left aside without any negative consequences.

Seek Occasional Solitude.   Teachers probably can accomplish far more if they find a space that is quiet and away from the activity of others. The space should be furnished adequately with the materials and supplies they need for the task at hand.

Avoid Time Robbers and Use Time Savers.   Too much to do and not enough time to do it—that is the teacher's chronic complaint. But let us now bring up a matter that teachers

---

CASE STUDY 13.2

TIME ROBBERS

Focus Question
Here Mr. Monroe gives in to several time robbers. List them. How can he better organize his tasks and time to avoid them?

Mr. Monroe, a sixth-grade teacher, works in his room for two hours each day after school. Two hours of concentrated work should be more than enough time to take care of all the matters that significantly impact his program. But Mr. Monroe spends the time reading memos, emails, notices, advertisements, and other pieces of mail received at school. He goes to the faculty lounge for coffee and on the way stops to talk with the custodian about a ball game. In the lounge he finds the principal and they chat, tell jokes, and talk about politics. Then he returns to his room; waters the plants; feeds the rat, hamsters, and rabbits; and cleans their enclosures. He dislikes messiness, so he picks up scraps, arranges books, cleans the sink, and tidies his desk. While looking for reference materials for the next day's lesson on ancient Greece, he comes across interesting material on money, coins, mints, and various monetary systems, which he reads though they have nothing to do with Greece. Before he knows it, five o'clock arrives and only a few of his necessary tasks have been done. He still has papers to grade, so he takes them home.

"JUST TEACHERS' LOUNGE
WILL SUFFICE, ED."

tend to overlook. Most of them could save large amounts of time simply by not wasting time they have available to them.

Time robbers eat up a large portion of teachers' time and give little in return. One such robber is teachers' tendency to deal with matters that could just as well be delegated or even left aside indefinitely. Oftentimes dealing with the trivial, talking instead of working, and working in a disorganized way compound the reality of time robbers.

In contrast to time robbers, time savers are steps and shortcuts that enable teachers to get necessary work done, while leaving some time for personal needs, including quiet relaxation time to socialize with colleagues. The most valuable time savers are working efficiently, delegating work, reducing paper checking, and controlling the number and length of faculty meetings.

Efficiency begins with prioritizing tasks as described earlier, giving attention only to tasks that are absolutely necessary—such as planning, scoring selected papers, preparing instructional materials and activities, keeping adequate records, and preparing for conferences with students and caregivers. Difficult tasks should be completed first and the fun work left for later.

Once you establish priorities, work hard during the time you have set aside. Avoid temptation to chat, gossip, daydream, or gaze out the window. Though these activities are quite restful and valuable, they should come after the work is finished. Review papers and update records quickly and efficiently and then plan for the next day. Normally you can do all this in an hour of concentrated work.

Assign routine tasks such as watering plants, cleaning the room, feeding animals, dusting, straightening, and so forth to students. It's good for them. If students are too young, have aides or volunteers help.

Be Realistic about Paper Checking.   Checking work students turn in consumes monumental amounts of time for most teachers. This task can be greatly reduced with no detriment to students. Most teachers believe that if they assign written work they are honor bound to mark every single paper carefully. But there are strong counterarguments to this view. First, many written tasks are given to students for practice only. By circulating during independent practice time, you can observe students at work and know how they are doing, identify problems they are encountering, and provide the help they need. Two side benefits accrue

VIGNETTE 13.1   Managing Student Work

Ginny Lorenz teaches a 4/5 multi-age class of thirty-two students. During her first year of teaching upper grades, Ginny would read student papers four nights a week.

During her second year of teaching this grade, Ginny did something new. She added a Writer's Workshop where parents and guardians helped with the editing of student work. When students had a piece in final draft form, they put a check next to their name on the board. Once Ginny had eight or ten names with check marks, she took that group home and read for grades. This worked well for both Ginny and her students.

Upon Reflection

Ginny Lorenz described another procedure for managing student work in Chapter 7 (Vignette 7.2). Compare both her methods with what you have experienced or have seen other teachers do.

from circulating around the room. You are close to students and proximity helps maintain discipline. Also, by working the crowd you can provide efficient help (as Fred Jones advocates, in twenty seconds or less). When students have completed their work and you have made notations as necessary on your clipboard, collect the papers and discard them later.

A reality is that students profit little, if any, from the marks you make so conscientiously and meticulously. Even by the next day, students will have lost the context of what they were doing and your marks will mean little to them. Their errors should be corrected as they are being made. Moreover, students do not like to receive marked-up papers. Their first and often final inclination is to crumple it and throw it away, unless of course it has a star or happy face on it. If you insist on going to such lengths in scoring student papers, you need to go back over the papers with students, in detail, when you return them. Students don't like this, but that's the only way you can make them learn much from all your hard work.

This is not to say that you should never carefully correct student papers. Toward the end of units, when students are asked to show what and how much they have learned, you can expect them to do their very best work, which you should then check carefully.

A note of caution, however: If you are going to send corrected papers home with your students, make sure you mark them accurately! Caregivers invariably find the mistakes you make.

Streamline Record Keeping.   As discussed in Chapter 10, tasks related to record keeping can consume great amounts of time. You can reduce this workload by doing four things: (1) keep only those records that truly are necessary; (2) train students to assist in keeping their own records; (3) have an aide or volunteer help with recording and filing, and (4) use available computer technology for records management. Remember these two cautions, however—students have the right to privacy regarding their work and progress, and you are legally responsible for the accuracy of these records.

Take a Proactive Role in Faculty Meetings.   If faculty meetings at your school tend to be too long and tedious, you can take steps to shorten them. You can request agendas for the meetings, and when discussions stray from the agenda, you can suggest that, in the interest of time, the agenda be followed. Faculty members can ask to be excused from the meetings when the topics do not apply to them—for example, there is no need for primary teachers to attend meetings that deal with sixth-grade outdoor camp. Also, teachers can agree as a staff to limit the length of discussions.

Remove the Stress from Teaching.   As explained in Chapter 9, disruptive student behavior not only severely cuts into teachers' time but also is a major source of frustration and stress. You can use a number of different tactics (many described in Chapter 9) to reduce dramatically the stress usually associated with discipline. You and your students will very much appreciate the results.

Streamline Communication with Parents and Others.   In Chapter 11 you were urged to communicate well with caregivers as a means of securing family and home support for your efforts. Although they can be time intensive, avoid the temptation to bypass communications with caregivers as you look for ways to free up some time. Rather, remember that communication with caregivers is worth the effort involved and should be given high priority. You can streamline the communication process by using a class website that describes expectations you hold, your discipline system, how parents can help, and provides updated information regarding class activities and assignments. Add email capability so parents can initiate or exchange communication with you, to which you can respond briefly. If you need to call a parent on the phone, say, with utmost courtesy and respect, something like, "Hello Mrs. Nichols. This is _____, Betsy's teacher. How are you this evening? I'd like to talk with you for a moment about Betsy. I only have five minutes right now. Is this a convenient time for you?" Prior to calling, rehearse what you want to say and anticipate questions and comments from the listener.

Keep Yourself Physically Fit.   Make sure you have adequate rest, good nutrition, some recreation, and some physical exercise, all of which help in combating stress. Your brain needs food (glucose) and oxygen, and exercise and "brain breaks" help with this. Drink plenty of water to keep your brain hydrated. Get enough sleep. Sleep is critical in order for the brain to process, think, and remember. Also, do some isometric exercises and stretches throughout the day. When possible, work in natural light; fluorescent lights may cause eyestrain and anxiety. Additionally, involve students. It will help them, too.

Take Occasional Brain Breaks.   Throughout your daily class routines, take time to nourish your brain (and your students' brains, as well). The human brain is not designed to hold constant focus on something for a lengthy period of time. Brain breaks can involve short periods of rest, listening to calming music, thinking about something entirely different, telling a joke or story, and standing and stretching.

ACTIVITIES THAT PRODUCE POSITIVE STRESS

The first part of this chapter concentrated on the damaging effects of emotional stress caused by unexpected events and trauma. The second part of this chapter dealt with on-the-job stress, and gave you a number of suggestions for removing unwanted stress in your work. We now turn attention to what you can do to increase the positive, useful stress, known as *eustress*.

Moderate amounts of stress energize us, give us a sense of direction, make us pleased with our jobs and ourselves, provide a sense of accomplishment and importance, and in so doing positively affect our morale. The following paragraphs review sources of eustress that teachers find most readily available in teaching—group efforts, student achievement, newsletters and literary journals, public performances and exhibits, shared responsibility, and class synergy.

Group Efforts

Many teachers enjoy working with other teachers. However, unless they belong to a collaborative grade-level team, they seldom have incentive to do so. When they decide to collaborate on a task or activity such as a field day, art exhibit, or simulated archaeological dig, they find excitement and joy, not only for themselves but for students as well. The eustress they experience is inherent in the activity itself, but another good payoff is student involvement and parental appreciation. Remember, teachers can be resources to one another; they simply need to learn to ask and learn to share.

Student Achievement

Achievement is mainly what schooling is all about. Teachers of high achievers usually feel successful, while those of lower achievers feel somewhat defeated. It is important to realize that student achievement actually can be increased through the way recognition is given. For example, when outstanding student work products such as art, compositions, and scale models are put on public display, students become motivated to accomplish work of still higher quality. When students keep personal charts that graphically depict how much they have read or how skilled they have become in math, they strive to reach even greater heights, especially when the results are communicated to caregivers.

To emphasize student achievement, you need to discuss with students what achievement—and quality—mean, show them what makes it possible, illustrate how progress is documented, and explain how results are shown to caregivers and others. Then as students strive to achieve, and later to surpass previous levels of achievement, you will find that everyone's motivation to excel increases.

Newsletters and Literary Journals

Teacher- and student-produced newsletters and web pages, described in Chapter 11 as vehicles for communicating with parents and guardians, also provide marvelous opportunities for enlivening teaching and learning. The same is the case for class literary journals. Intermediate- and upper-grade students can contribute to the writing and production of newsletters and journals, as writers, designers, and artists, with their names listed somewhere in the work. Teachers can assist in primary grades, but from third grade onward students can do most of the work in print, and they are highly motivated to do their best writing, spelling, grammar, and artwork. Caregivers eagerly read such

VIGNETTE 13.2   Class Newsletters

Kindergarten teacher Kay Ballentine creates a short weekly class newsletter titled *Kindergarten Korner.* It tells about activities during the week and upcoming events she wants parents to be aware of. Kay tries to mention as many children by name as possible each week, and she makes sure every child is mentioned frequently. Parents read the newsletter avidly and go out of their way to write or tell her about it. They seem to think it proves that she cares about their child, which of course she does.

Ronda Royal is a third-grade teacher who uses her newsletter to keep everyone informed. She always gives a copy of her newsletter to the principal and to any volunteers who do not have children in her room. Her weekly newsletter is solely her production, although she often includes snippets of student work to show parents what the children are creating in her room. Ronda always writes her news in complete sentences and full paragraphs. Many parents say they appreciate this type of complete communication because it shows that she is putting effort into informing them of events of her room, of ways to assist their child, and of upcoming guests and activities.

Upon Reflection

Both Kay and Ronda use newsletters to communicate with caregivers. Describe how you would use newsletters. What would you include? How would you involve students in their production?

materials, taking pride in their child's work and crediting the teacher for the documented accomplishments.

Public Performances and Exhibits

Most schools encourage teachers and their classes to present performances such as plays, readers' theatre, holiday skits, and musicals, as well as exhibits of art, science projects, and social studies projects. Generally these events produce high levels of excitement and motivation, and students willingly work hard to prepare for them.

Most often performances and exhibits are seen in conjunction with back-to-school and open house nights. But displays of student work for students, teachers, and visitors to see, such as artwork and models, can be posted at any time in various locations in the school. Some performance events may even be broadcast through a local cable station or via the Internet. Some people may think of exhibits and performances as frills outside the core program, but once you see the level of motivation and pride they engender, you will want to make them prime components of your class's educational program.

Sharing Responsibility with Students

From the beginning of the school year, you should impress on your students the roles and responsibilities they are to assume in regard to their own education. Students can be shown how to take an active stance in learning to be participants rather than recipients. As they move into this shared responsibility, a spirit of self-direction and self-responsibility develops that teachers find very satisfying.

Achieving Class Synergy

When you are able to bring about an attitude of shared responsibility and then add to it the desire for significant accomplishment and evidence, that elusive condition of *class synergy* may occur—when members of the class energize each other through cooperative group efforts (Charles, 2000). This effect binds students together, spurs them on, and makes school a time of pleasure and fulfillment. Synergy, or esprit de corps, is one of the best things that can happen in a classroom. Classbuilding and teambuilding activities do much to foster synergy. Class work becomes joyful instead of tedious, and students involve themselves actively rather than comply lethargically. School days end with a satisfied glow instead of wretched fatigue. As students experience synergy, they provide much positive energy to teachers. As a bonus, word quickly gets to caretakers, who react positively to their child's educational program, and become in the process more supportive of the teacher.

Before moving ahead to the Epilogue, take time to explore these end-of-chapter activities.

Parting Thoughts

Yet do I hold that mortal foolish who strives against the stress of necessity.

—Euripides

Rule #1: Don't sweat the small stuff. Rule #2: It's all small stuff.

—Dr. Michael Mantell

SUMMARY SELF-CHECK

Check off the following as you either understand or become able to apply them.

❑ Stress and trauma affect teachers and students.

❑ Critical incident—any emotionally significant event that overwhelms coping abilities.

❑ Crisis intervention—short-term response to a critical incident with the goal of helping.

❑ Crisis intervention is not therapy.

❑ Critical Incident Stress Management (CISM)—a systematic crisis intervention model.

❑ The three areas of the triune brain interact as we react to a critical incident.

❑ Signs and symptoms of emotional stress: children may shut down their feelings, regress to immature behaviors, act out behaviorally, ask questions, require lots of extra reassurances.

❑ What teachers and schools can do:
- SEA-3 Method: speech, emotion, appearance, alertness, activity
- SAFER Method: stabilize the situation, acknowledge crisis, facilitate understanding, encourage adaptive coping, restore or refer
- Attention-refocusing strategies
- Up shifting
- Subtle techniques
- Take care of yourself
- Debriefing

❑ Stress—some is needed, but too much is harmful.
- Distress—inability to cope; overwhelming, hurtful
- Eustress—a challenge; interesting, helpful

❑ What stresses teachers most: disruptive student behavior, lack of time, too much to do, lack of student success, poor relationships with caregivers.

❑ What energizes teachers most: student achievement, recognition, interesting work, possibilities for growth and advancement.

❑ Stress management for teachers: prioritize (take care of important matters first), accept that perfect isn't possible, avoid selectively (learn to say no; learn to hide), manage time efficiently (avoid time robbers), develop a nonconfrontive discipline system, communicate well with caregivers, give close attention to your physical well-being.

❑ Steps toward positive stress: build meaning and spirit; engage in group efforts; work toward student achievement; produce newsletters, web pages, and journals; have your class put on public performances; work for shared responsibility with students; seek class synergy.

ACTIVITIES FOR REFLECTION AND DISCUSSION

1. Take a moment to review the statements in the Prediction–Review Guide at the beginning of this chapter. Put a check mark in the Review column next to any statement with which you now agree. How have your thoughts changed since reading this chapter?

2. Interview at least two teachers about their experiences with stress, both stresses that come from unexpected or traumatic events, as well as on-the-job stresses. Also ask what activities bring them eustress as opposed to distress. How do they deal with the things they find stressful?

3. Investigate the crisis response plan at a local school and share your findings with your class.

4. List six important tasks that call for your attention today. Prioritize those tasks by their importance. List nonessential tasks that try to draw you away from your important tasks. How will you deal with them?

5. Do you know a teacher who appears to have reached burnout? Assess that person as to how he or she looks, talks, relates to students and others, prepares for teaching, maintains discipline, and participates in school activities.

6. The text suggests that your teaching life would be more enjoyable if your class produces newsletters, a web page, and journals, and puts on public performances and displays. Evaluate that contention objectively. To what extent would those suggestions *add* stress rather than reduce it? List and discuss your pros and cons.

7. Suppose you are put in charge of teacher morale and appreciation in your school. Within reason, what would you do and emphasize in order to make teachers' professional lives more joyful and rewarding? Explain your program to the class.

REFERENCES AND RECOMMENDED READINGS

Allen, R. (2005, March). Who cares for the caregivers? Helping administrators and faculty cope with a crisis. *Education Update, 47*(3).

Berman, S., Diener, S., Dieringer, L., & Lantieri, L. (2003). *Talking with children about war and violence in the world.* http://life.familyeducation.com/war.parenting/36559.html.

Charles, C. (2000). *The synergetic classroom: Joyful teaching and gentle discipline.* Boston: Addison Wesley Longman.

Childs, G. (2002). *Workshop and crisis response team guidebook: Critical Incident Stress Management Program.* Poway, CA: Poway Unified School District.

Everly, G., & Mitchell, J. (n.d.). A primer on Critical Incident Stress Management (CISM). www.icisf.org (with links to related articles and resources, and links to training information).

Fuery, C. (2005). The new winning year one: Jump-start student success from day one K–12 (9th ed.). Captiva, FL: Sanibel Sanddollar Publications.

Jensen, R. (1998). *Teaching with the brain in mind.* Alexandria, VA: ASCD.

Johnson, S., & Johnson, C. (1986). *The one minute teacher: How to teach others to teach themselves.* New York: William Morrow.

Kagan, S., & Minor, J. (2002). *Boost achievement through brain-based instruction: Course workbook.* San Clemente, CA: Kagan Publishing.

Levin, D. (2003, April). When the world is a dangerous place. *Educational Leadership, 60,* 72–75.

PBS Parents. (n.d.). *Talking with kids about war and violence: Learn how to answer children's questions by seeing the world through their eyes.* Retrieved December 2003, from www.pbs.org/parents/issues advice/talkingwithkids/war and http://life.familyeducation.com/war.parenting/36559.html.

PTSD: What is Posttraumatic Stress Disorder. National Center for PTSD. http://en.wikipedia.org/wiki/PTSD.

Pullis, M. (1992). An analysis of the occupational stress of teachers of the behaviorally disordered: Sources, effects, and strategies for coping. *Behavioral Disorders, 17*(3), 191–201.

Waddell, D., & Thomas, A. (1998). *Disaster: Helping children cope: A handout for parents.* National Mental Health and Education Center. Retrieved December 2003, and March 2006, from www.naspcenter.org/safe_schools/coping.html.

Wilcox, J. (2005, December). Handling disasters takes a team approach. *Education Update, 47*(12).

Wolfe, P. (2001). *Brain matters: Translating research into classroom practice.* Alexandria, VA: ASCD.

Websites

Teacher Stress

www.nea.org/neatoday/0401/stressed.html?mode=print
www.untrammelled.co.uk/teacherstress
www.channel4.com/health/microsites/0-9/4health/stress/saw_teachers.html

It's Your Turn

The present is the only thing that has no end.

—Erwin Schrodinger

*Every child is an artist. The problem is
how to remain an artist once he grows up.*

—Pablo Picasso

PULLING EVERYTHING TOGETHER

Now it's your turn to pull together everything you have read, observed, discussed, and analyzed. In the preceding chapters you investigated good management skills. It is hoped that the additional information and resources presented in the appendixes that follow will help you step confidently into your first classroom. The cumulative skills development activities below are extensions to the appendixes.

This edition of *Elementary Classroom Management* ends with a Capstone Activity where you can reflect on the nature and operations of your own classroom.

ACTIVITIES FOR REFLECTION AND DISCUSSION

1. Obtain five or six good resource books for teachers. Review and compare contents. Present your reviews for class information and discussion.

2. Visit five or six teacher-related websites. Review and compare contents. Present your reviews for class information and discussion.

3. Obtain copies of five or six widely read professional journals and teacher magazines in education. Review and compare the contents. Present your reviews, along with subscription information, for class information and discussion.

4. Contact various professional organizations and inquire about their mission, cost of membership, and benefits. (Usually this can be done via the Internet or at the local level by contacting organization representatives or members for information.)

5. Obtain a resource that provides information on overseas employment. (Probably your university or college placement office can furnish this information.) Share the information with the class. If possible, speak with a teacher or professor who has taught abroad and obtain his or her impressions of the advantages and disadvantages of the experience.

6. Obtain a reference that outlines teacher certification requirements in various states. Compare the requirements for four or five states and present them to the class.

CAPSTONE ACTIVITY

As a team or individual activity, select a grade level and outline in three or four pages the components of classroom management you would intend to employ in your overall operation of the classroom. Explain briefly how your selections reflect your personality and beliefs about teaching and learning, as well as the needs of students at this grade level.

Parting Thought

When you reach for the stars, you may not quite get one, but you won't come up with a handful of mud either.

—Leo Burnett

The journey of a thousand miles begins with one step.

—Chinese Proverb

Resources for Expanding Horizons and Opportunities

Live a balanced life—learn some and think some and draw and paint and sing and dance and play and work some every day.

—Robert Fulghum

Prediction–Review Guide

Before you investigate the appendixes that follow, take a moment to put a check mark in the Prediction column next to any statement with which you agree.

		Prediction	Review
1.	Education differs from other professions in that it uses jargon that is easily understood outside the profession.	❑	❑
2.	In reality, educators would do better to avoid jargon and use plain English that everyone understands.	❑	❑
3.	Quality teacher resource books and websites of ideas and activities can be found in abundant supply.	❑	❑
4.	Resource books and websites are intended to help supplement existing curricula, not provide a curriculum of their own.	❑	❑
5.	Among the professional journals available, more elementary teachers are likely to be interested in *Instructor* and *The Mailbox* than *Gifted Children Quarterly*.	❑	❑
6.	One of the most widely read journals of general interest to educators is the *Phi Delta Kappan*.	❑	❑
7.	Each state has one head education official whose office normally is located in the state capital.	❑	❑
8.	Department of Defense teaching opportunities exist worldwide.	❑	❑
9.	Teaching positions overseas, in which instruction is given in English, rarely are available to teachers from the United States.	❑	❑
10.	Teacher certification requirements are essentially the same in every state.	❑	❑

In 1988 Robert Fulghum's best seller *All I Really Need to Know I Learned in Kindergarten: Uncommon Thoughts on Common Things* seemed to capture many of life's truths, as exemplified in the epigraph presented above. Fulghum reminds us that by the end of kindergarten he and the rest of us had learned such things as: Play fair. Don't hit people. Put things back where you find them. Clean up your own mess. Don't take things that aren't yours. Say you're sorry when you hurt somebody. Fulghum's book is wonderful and reassuring for teachers to read, as are many of the other resources presented in the following appendixes, but it doesn't include all that teachers need to know about teaching. It does not help novices understand the special language that teachers sometimes speak. It does not identify helpful resources and tools. Nor does it help recently licensed teachers take the next step in their career.

In the appendixes that follow, we move beyond the ordinary parameters of classroom management to information that is of particular value to teachers new to the profession. This section includes:

- Appendix A: brief explanation of frequently heard educational terms
- Appendix B: contact information for professional organizations
- Appendix C: some of the professional journals that teachers have found useful
- Appendix D: selected websites, music, and teacher resource books that contain especially interesting curriculum ideas, activities, and reproducible pages
- Appendix E: contact information for head education offices of each state
- Appendix F: a brief list of contacts for overseas teaching opportunities
- Appendix G: the comprehensive list of references and recommended readings

Education Talk

I was still learning when I taught my last class.
—Claude M. Fuess, Phillips Academy educator

If you are around schools as a teacher, student, paraprofessional, or volunteer, you hear a number of terms and expressions that may not be understood by anyone outside of education. It almost appears that teachers have a language of their own. These special words and labels aren't purposefully used to confuse others, but are conveniently used to refer to all manner of special programs, materials, and procedures that would wear educators to exhaustion if they had to say all the names in full.

All professions use unique jargon, with words, letters, and language patterns understood for the most part only by persons in that profession. For those new to teaching, a brief list of special terms is offered here to ease the rites of passage. This list presents a beginning; it is far from exhaustive. As you hear people use other words and expressions you don't recognize, swallow your pride and ask what they mean.

Term	Meaning
Assistive technology	Devices and tools that assist individuals with disabilities. The Assistive Technology Act of 2004 supports the use of state-of-the-art technology, specifically targeting assistance for children with speech and motor challenges.
Attention deficit disorder (ADD)	A learning disability, characterized by difficulty in concentrating or paying attention for long periods of time, that affects ability to concentrate on learning.
Attention deficit hyperactivity disorder (ADHD)	A learning disability, characterized by hyperactivity, impulsivity, and/or distractibility, that affects ability to concentrate on learning.

Authentic assessment	Assessing students' learning, problem solving, and ability to analyze, apply, synthesize, and evaluate, by having them work on tasks they might experience outside the classroom.
Average daily attendance (ADA)	A record kept for administrative and budgeting purposes.
Back-to-school night	A scheduled event, usually early in the school year, when parents and guardians visit schools to meet the teachers, see the classrooms, discuss programs, and ask questions.
Backward design	Teachers identify desired results and acceptable evidence before planning instruction and learning experiences.
Beginning Teacher Support Program (BTSA)	One name for a district-sponsored program that matches beginning teachers with veteran teachers for support and guidance.
Bilingual education	Varied approaches to educate students who speak a primary language other than English.
Certified personnel	Teachers, administrators, and sometimes librarians and media specialists whose positions require a credential or license earned through programs of higher education and issued by the state in which they are employed.
Charter schools	Self-governing public schools that operate outside the boundaries of existing district and union structures according to a special contract or charter that often is made by educators in the local community.
Classified personnel	Nonteachers who make up the support staff, including secretaries, custodians, attendance clerks, aides, and other school employees.
Combination class	A class of two grade levels in which a teacher instructs independent grade-level programs; homogeneous, usually fewer discipline problems, and less instruction time for each grade level because of the dual curricula.
Convergent thinking	A type of thinking that focuses on finding a single correct response, answer, or solution; the opposite of divergent thinking.
Cooperative learning	An instructional approach in which students work together in groups to accomplish a common task or learning goal and are accountable for their individual effort and learning.
Criterion-referenced	Test and grading system based on achievement in subject matter; the opposite of norm-referenced; for example, scores and grades (89%; B+) that are made on tests that include only information taught in a given class.
Critical thinking	Thought processes requiring higher levels of thought, such as analysis, synthesis, and evaluation.
Curriculum mapping	A process of identifying redundancies and gaps within a total curriculum program.

Differentiated instruction	Modified content, instructional process, and product designed to accommodate all children.
Distance education	Use of technology to connect students and teachers or speakers who are separated by location.
District office	The head offices of a school district where the top administrators are located.
Divergent thinking	A type of thinking that expands outward in seeking multiple correct responses, answers, or solutions; the opposite of convergent thinking.
EL	English (language) learner.
Engaged learning time	Time during which students are engaged actively in learning, as opposed to involvement in numerous other kinds of activities (or nonactivities) that comprise the school day.
ESL	English as a second language.
ESOL	English for speakers of other languages.
Gifted and talented education (GATE)	Children who show evidence of high achievement or potential in academic, creative, artistic, or leadership areas.
Home schooling	A growing trend (although a longtime practice) of parents educating their children at home for religious or philosophical reasons.
Inclusion	Commitment to educate every child to the maximum extent possible in the regular school and classroom.
Individualized Education Plan (IEP)	Plan approved by parents or guardians that clarifies and organizes the educational program and related services to meet a student's individual needs.
Individuals with Disabilities Education Act of 1990 (IDEA)	Federal legislation requiring that all students with disabilities be accommodated in regular education classrooms to the extent possible.
In-service	A class, workshop, program, or the like provided for professional growth of employed teachers.
Instructional technology	Tools that support and expand the computer's usefulness in appropriately delivering content and instruction to exceptional children.
Interstate New Teacher Assessment and Support Consortium (INTASC)	A consortium that has developed standards and an assessment process for initial teacher certification.
Limited English proficient/non-English proficient (LEP/NEP)	Used for students and/or programs or materials.
Limited English speaking/non-English speaking (LES/NES)	Used for students and/or programs or materials.
Looping	An educational practice in which teacher and students remain together for two or more years.

Magnet school	An alternative school that offers specialized programs in science, performing arts, or other areas, so constituted as to attract students from diverse ethnic and racial groups.
Master teachers	Teachers, perceived to be highly skilled in their instruction and management, who have student teachers in their classroom; may be called master, cooperating, or lead teachers.
Mentor teachers	Teachers designated because of their unusual expertise or involvement in a special project to assist other teachers in developing proficiency (e.g., reading, math, or technology mentor).
Mind map	Any graphic, easy-to-read diagram that combines the information of a word outline with the clarity of a picture to show how to organize an idea, solve a problem, or perform a series of steps.
Minimum day	An instructional day shortened for various reasons, most commonly so teachers can participate in grade-level planning activities and in-services during the afternoon.
Mission statement	A statement that spells out the goals of a school or district, together with the plans for achieving them.
Multi-age classes	Heterogeneous classes with all ability and discipline levels, in which students are grouped and work at levels according to their progress over time and their developmental growth rather than their chronological ages.
Multicultural curriculum	Practice of including and honoring cultural diversity to promote appreciation and understanding of diversity by making differences and similarities, respect, and affirmation explicit parts of the curriculum.
Multiple intelligences	A theory that identifies eight intellectual capacities that people use to approach projects and problems and create products.
National Board for Professional Teaching Standards (NBPTS)	A nonprofit agency that has developed five core propositions regarding what experienced teachers should know and be able to do and that awards professional certificates for this ability.
National Council for Accreditation of Teacher Education (NCATE)	An accrediting agency that has identified six criteria for prospective teacher performance in a context of professional and liberal arts studies.
National Education Goals	U.S. education goals that were intended to be reached by the year 2000; legislated by Congress after they were established by the president and the fifty state governors.

Neurological based behavior (NBB)	Behavior that occurs because of the way the brain functions; it is outside the control of the individual.
No Child Left Behind Act of 2001	President George W. Bush's reauthorization of The Elementary and Secondary Education Act (ESEA of 1965); emphasizes standards and annual testing of all children to document progress toward meeting standards, district report cards of student achievement, and the goals that all schools provide quality and competent education and that newly hired teachers be NCLB certified.
Norm-referenced	Tests and grading systems that compare a student's performance against the performances of many other students; the opposite of criterion-referenced; for example, grading on a curve and reporting achievement test scores in terms of percentiles or grade-level equivalencies.
On-task	An expression used to indicate that students are working at assigned learning activities rather than daydreaming or goofing off.
Open house	A function usually held toward the end of a school year, when parents and other interested persons are invited to visit the school and classrooms.
Opportunity class	Self-contained classroom for students who have shown problems of behavior and/or attendance.
Outcomes-based education (OBE)	Educational plans that focus and organize the school's programs and instructional efforts around very specifically defined learning outcomes that all students are expected to achieve, rather than topics to be covered.
Praxis Series	A series of tests to assess skills and knowledge of beginning teachers, from entry into the profession to actual classroom performance.
Prep period	Time during the school day for teachers to plan lessons, prepare materials, and handle administrative tasks; elementary teachers rarely have prep periods; middle and high school teachers usually do.
Public Law 94-142	Education of All Handicapped Children Act of 1975; intended to ensure that all children receive an appropriate public education in the least restrictive environment (the regular classroom, when and to the extent possible); incorporated into the Individuals with Disabilities Education Act of 1990 (IDEA).
Reflective teaching	Thinking that is focused on a prior act or occurrence to understand better what did and did not occur, and why, and to identify changes that could lead to future improvement.

Resource specialist	A teacher highly qualified in one or more subject areas, such as reading, language, or mathematics, who provides assistance to other teachers or works with students who qualify for extra assistance.
Scope and sequence	Characteristics of the overall school curriculum; scope refers to the subject matter and activities, sequence refers to the order in which topics and activities receive attention.
Service learning	Opportunities for students to learn helping skills and provide service to others.
Sheltered	Students who, because of language limitations or other traits, require specialized instruction (frequently used for students with limited English proficiency); now referred to as SDAIE, Specially Designed Academic Instruction in English.
Special Day Class (SDC)	A class for students who are handicapped and unable to profit from attendance in the regular classroom.
Specially Designed Academic Instruction in English (SDAIE)	Teaching approaches and strategies used to help students with limited English proficiency.
Standards	Generally, what students need to know or be able to do, as related to content, performance, and opportunity-to-learn.
Student Study Team (SST)	A team of interested adults, initiated by the regular education teacher, to review the student's apparent needs and develop a plan of action to further investigate and then best meet the needs.
Team teaching	An arrangement where two teachers collaborate and teach the same students.
Title I	A section of the 1965 Elementary and Secondary Education Act; a federally funded program established to address special learning needs of disadvantaged children by, among other things, providing monies to improve student performance in reading and math.
Title VII	A federally funded program to assist students who have limited English proficiency (LEP).
Vouchers	An educational plan option that gives caregivers a receipt or written statement that they can exchange for the school (public or private) they feel is most desirable for their child.

Professional Organizations

If the only tool you have is a hammer, you tend to see every problem as a nail.

—Abraham Maslow

Teachers have available to them membership in many professional organizations. Organizations such as the National Council for Teachers of English (NCTE) focus on specific content areas. These organizations, especially the larger ones, have national, state, and local chapters. Membership can be of value to teachers for several reasons. Such organizations usually publish journals that investigate current issues and trends and supply information on the latest materials and techniques. They offer members reduced rates for materials available for sale. They inform members of national and area conferences and extend reduced attendance rates. Organizations such as the American Federation of Teachers (AFT) and the National Education Association (NEA) deal with and lobby for education in general. Other organizations such as the Association for Supervision and Curriculum Development (ASCD) and Phi Delta Kappa give broader coverage to curriculum, instruction, technology, assessment, and other topics of interest to educators.

Here are the web home pages for several professional organizations that might be of interest to elementary teachers.

CONTENT-SPECIFIC ORGANIZATIONS

National Art Education Association   www.naea-reston.org
National Council of Teachers of English   www.ncte.org
American Council on Teaching of Foreign Languages   www.actfl.org
American Alliance for Health, Physical Education, Recreation, and Dance   www.aahperd.org
National Council of Teachers of Mathematics   www.nctm.org
National Association for Music Education   www.menc.org
International Reading Association   www.reading.org
National Science Teachers Association   www.nsta.org
National Council for the Social Studies   www.socialstudies.org

OTHER ORGANIZATIONS OF INTEREST

American Federation of Teachers (AFT)   www.aft.org
   AFT was founded in 1916 to "represent the economic, social, and professional interest of classroom teachers. It is an affiliated international union of the AFL-CIO."
National Education Association (NEA)   www.nea.org
   NEA, "the nation's largest professional employee organization, is committed to advancing the cause of public education."

National Parent Teacher Association   www.pta.org

The National PTA "is the largest volunteer child advocacy association in the nation."

National PTO Today, Inc.   www.ptotoday.com

PTO Today was founded in 1999 to provide resources and services to help parent group leaders help their schools. School Family Nights is a unique PTO program.

American Educational Research Association (AERA)   www.aera.net

AERA's mission is "concerned with improving the educational process by encouraging scholarly inquiry related to education and by promoting the dissemination and practical application of research results."

Association for Supervision and Curriculum Development (ASCD)   www.ascd.org

ASCD is an international nonprofit nonpartisan organization of educators that "addresses all aspects of effective teaching and learning—such as professional development, educational leadership, and capacity building."

Phi Delta Kappa International (PDK)   www.pdkintl.org

PDK is an international association of professional educators whose mission is to "promote quality education, in particular publicly supported education, as essential to development and maintenance of a democratic way of life . . . accomplished through research, service, and leadership in education."

National Association for the Education of Young Children   www.naeyc.org

NAEYC is "dedicated to improving the well-being of all young children, with particular focus on the quality of educational and developmental services of all children from birth through 8" . . . and committed to helping teachers in their daily work on behalf of all young children.

National Association for Gifted Children   www.nagc.org

NAGC directs its resources to "training teachers, encouraging parents and educating administrators and policymakers on how to develop and support gifted children and what's at stake if high-potential learners are not challenged and encouraged."

International Society for Technology in Education   www.iste.org

A nonprofit professional organization with worldwide membership, dedicated to providing "leadership and service to improve teaching and learning by advancing the effective use of technology in K–12 education and teacher education."

Professional Journals

Learning is like rowing against the stream; if one does not advance, one falls right back.

—Vietnamese Proverb

Professional journals are intended to keep members of the profession current about new research, discoveries, studies, ideas, materials, and best practices related to their field of practice. Educational journals range from highly theoretical, esoteric research journals to practical resources written for and by classroom teachers. Some educational journals focus on single content areas; some are aimed specifically at elementary, middle, or high school teachers; others publish articles and thematic issues for the broader educational community. The following are some of the most widely read journals and teacher magazines in education. In most cases the websites are to home pages of the publishing organization, where you will find the link to their publications (and in many instances, to other helpful resources and information).

JOURNALS OF GENERAL INTEREST TO ALL EDUCATORS

Educational Leadership, Association for Supervision and Curriculum Development (ASCD)
www.ascd.org
Intended primarily for leaders in elementary, middle, and secondary education, but is also for anyone interested in curriculum instruction, supervision, and leadership in schools. Published monthly September through May, except bimonthly December/January.

Phi Delta Kappan, Phi Delta Kappa   www.pdkintl.org
Articles concerned with educational research, service, and leadership; issues, trends, and policies are emphasized. Published monthly, except July and August.

Edge: The Latest Information for the Education Practitioner, Phi Delta Kappa   www.pdkintl.org
Bimonthly magazine issued five times a year. Each issue features a single article; articles focus on timely educational programs and practices, preferably that apply across grade levels and subjects.

JOURNALS AND MAGAZINES OF GENERAL INTEREST TO ELEMENTARY TEACHERS

Highlights for Children www.highlights.com
Monthly (index issue, December). "Wholesome fun dedicated to helping children grow in basic skills and knowledge, in creativity, in ability to think and reason, in sensitivity to others, in high ideals, and worthwhile ways of living."

Instructor, Scholastic www.scholastic.com/instructor
New ideas and teaching devices for language arts, reading, science, social studies, math, computers, and other subjects, and recent research and innovation related to child development. Eight issues annually.

The Mailbox Teacher www.theeducationcenter.com/cgi-bin/tec/guest.jsp
> Magazine of ideas and activities for kindergarten and elementary teachers. Four issues a year.

National Geographic Kids, National Geographic Society www.nationalgeographic.com
> Published monthly. Combines learning and fun with puzzles, games, and stories about wildlife, adventure, other kids, sports, science, places around the world, and more.

Teaching preK–8, Early Years, Inc., a subsidiary of Highlights for Children, Inc. www.teaching-k-8.com
> Magazine (formerly *Early Years*) published monthly except June, July, August, and December with feature articles, ideas, and reproducibles for teachers of young children.

JOURNALS AND MAGAZINES OF TOPICAL INTEREST TO ELEMENTARY TEACHERS

Arts and Activities Online Publishers' Development Corporation www.artsandactivities.com
> Stimulating material on photography, children's art, and art ideas for teachers who have not had extensive art training.

Gifted Child Quarterly, National Association for Gifted Children (NAGC) www.nagc.org
> Scholarly articles dealing with theory and research related to psychology and the education of children who are gifted.

The Horn Book Magazine, Horn Book www.hbook.com
> "Independent, opinionated, and stylish." Bimonthly reviews of the newest children's literature, articles, editorials, and columns related to aspects of children's books.

Language Arts, National Council of Teachers of English www.ncte.org
> Deals with topics related to teaching of English at the elementary school level. Eight issues per year.

The Reading Teacher, International Reading Association www.reading.org
> Articles dealing with the teaching of reading at the preschool and elementary school levels. Eight issues per year, with an annual index included in the May issue.

Science and Children, National Science Teachers Association www.nsta.org
> Practical emphasis for kindergarten through ninth-grade science teachers; includes projects, experiments, book reviews, and audiovisual and software information. This is a member benefit, not available by subscription.

Social Studies and the Young Learner, National Council of Social Studies www.socialstudies.org
> Articles on teaching social studies in the elementary grades. Published quarterly September through May.

Teaching Children Mathematics (*TCM*), National Council of Teachers of Mathematics www.nctm.org
> Published nine times a year as a resource for elementary school students, teachers, and teacher educators. "The focus . . . is on intuitive, exploratory investigations that use informal reasoning to help students develop a strong conceptual basis that leads to greater mathematical abstraction."

Young Children, National Association for the Education of Young Children www.journal.naeyc.org
> Bimonthly publication "organized around topical clusters that devote special attention to issues in the field of early childhood education."

Zoobooks, Wildlife Education, Ltd. www.zoobooks.com
> Monthly themed issues feature an animal or wildlife family.

Resource Websites, Music, and Books of Interest

Don't be apprehensive if some of your attempts seem risky. This is appropriate, since so much of life involves taking risks—for you as well as the children. That's how we grow.

—Anonymous

Honestly, resources abound. In fact, it is quite easy to get lost in the jungle of potential websites, music, and resource books. It is our intent to offer a few select resources that teachers have found helpful. You will find links to other websites, and if you visit teacher stores and general bookstores, you probably will discover many other wonderful resources. *Best advice:* Be open to possibilities, but remember the realities of time and practicality. In other words, investigate and then carefully select what best suits your needs at the moment, but also what will help with the larger picture of your teaching experience.

WEBSITES OF INTEREST

www.accessexcellence.org/AE/mspot
> A variety of teacher-developed interactive mysteries that can be solved by science (on- and offline activities).

www.bluewebn.com
> Web resources and pages across grades and curricula that you can bookmark and access from anywhere.

www.brainpop.com
> An educational program with content spanning science, math, English, social studies, health, and technology, developed and aligned to national standards (NCTM, NSES, and NCTE). Offers informative animated short movie clips and quizzes across subject areas "that speak to kids in a language and voice that they understand. . . . BrainPOP's topics present students with an engaging, enlightening, and entertaining view of a given subject." BrainPop at school and home, in English and Spanish.

www.cooltext.com
> Free online graphics generator for web pages and other things. Create web banners, fun fonts.

www.discoveryschool.com
> Links to puzzle maker and study starters, lesson plans, teacher tools, curriculum center, homework helpers, and others.

www.education-world.com
> Designed as a resource for educators by educators, with the goal of making it easy for educators to integrate the Internet into the classroom. Includes lesson planning, professional development, technology integration, school issues, and more.

www.eed.state.ak.us/tls/frameworks/mathsci/ms5_2as1.htm

A collection of classroom-based assessment strategies, including interviews, observations, creative performances, and self and peer evaluations. Part of the ongoing documentation of student ability relative to Alaska content standards.

www.funbrain.com

Fun for kids. Teachers can post quizzes for their class.

www.geosense.net

A geography game that students can play with other students around the world, plus links to numerous other related sites.

www.gsn.org

Global SchoolNet is a not-for-profit organization that partners with schools and organizations to "co-develop free or low cost programs to help students become literate and responsible global citizens, and to prepare them for the workforce." *The Global School House*: Online collaborative learning, collaborative projects, communication tools, and professional development.

www.inspiration.com and www.kidspiration.com

Inspiration: Helps learners to organize and rearrange information in varied formats (outline, narrative text, and concept map with pictures or symbols). *Kidspiration*: Helps kindergarten through fifth-grade learners develop strong thinking skills through brainstorming, planning, organizing, and creating.

www.kathimitchell.com/rubric.html

"A bunch of rubrics," including rubrics for math and science.

www.kidlink.org/english/general/intro.html

"Non-commercial, user-owned organization helping children understand themselves, identify and define goals for life, and collaborate with peers around the globe, individually or through school . . . free educational programs are for children and youth in all countries . . . most users are between 10–15 years of age."

www.kn.sbc.com

"The *Knowledge Network Explorer* (KNE) began in 1992 in response to the needs of California teachers, librarians, and students." Links to lessons and webquests and Filmentality, "a fill-in-the-blank tool that guides you through picking a topic, searching the Internet, gathering good Internet links and turning them into online learning activities."

www.nationalgeographic.com/xpeditions

National Geographic Xpeditions: Activities and resources to learn geographic concepts and issues and help integrate U.S. Geography standards into the classroom. Blue-Ribbon Links to other resources for teaching online and learning geography.

http://nie.yumasun.com

Newspapers in Education (NIE) is a worldwide program that promotes the use of newspapers in the classrooms. www.post-newseducation.com links to the Denver Newspaper Agency. Other sites link to other newspapers.

www.scholastic.com

Links to tools and resources, including online activities, lesson plans, and strategies.

www.songsforteaching.com

"A host of educational experts bring you tested ideas for using the magic of music in your lesson plans." Educational songs from popular artists are presented by subject.

www.teachingideas.co.uk

Teaching ideas for primary teachers (of children ages 5–11). Literacy, science, music, history, geography, art, PE, and more.

www.thinkquest.org

> Sponsored by the Oracle Education Foundation, "ThinkQuest is all about students thinking and learning together. Students work [and compete] in teams to create the best educational websites and compete for exciting prizes, including a trip to ThinkQuest Live, an educational extravaganza celebrating their achievements."

www.themoonlitroad.com

> Member of the Storytelling Ring, a group of websites dedicated to the art of storytelling. Ghost stories and folk tales from the American South.

http://tryscience.org

> Virtual field trips (video camera clips and narration) to international science centers and museums.

http://webquest.sdsu.edu

> A resource site for those who use the WebQuest model to teach the Web. "WebQuest is an inquiry-oriented activity in which most or all of the information used by learners is drawn from the Web. WebQuests are designed to use learners' time well, to focus on using information rather than looking for it, and to support learners' thinking at the levels of analysis, synthesis, and evaluation."

■ MUSIC FOR ELEMENTARY CLASSROOMS

Music can set a tempo for transitions, but as we said in an earlier chapter, teachers also can select the right type of music for the desired objective—thinking, productivity, relaxing, learning, de-stressing, concentration, and inspiration. Enjoy!

Don Campbell. *The Mozart Effect: Music for Children* [CD].

> Mozart's music stimulates the intellectual and creative development of students, increasing verbal, emotional, and spatial intelligence along the way. Appropriate for all ages.

J. Feldman. *All Day Long with Dr. Jean* [CD].

> Music and songs to guide children through the numerous activities of the day.

Clint Klose and Larry Wolfe. *Developing Character* [CD and lyrics].

> Positive character traits taught through music. Students sing to learn about citizenship, compassion, cooperation, courage, friendship, honesty, perseverance, pride, respect, and wisdom.

Clint Klose and Larry Wolfe. *Social Studies Lyrical Lessons* [CDs and lyrics and cassettes].

> Curriculum songs integrate music across curriculum. Appropriate for primary grades K–3 and intermediate grades 3–6.

Clint Klose and Larry Wolfe. *Monthly Melodies* [CD and lyrics].

> Fun teachable moments out of calendar events for grades K–3.

Mark Krantz. *Story Songs* [CD].

> Words directly from classic children's stories, including *Where the Wild Things Are, The Polar Express,* and *Goodnight Moon.* Appropriate for early grades.

Gary Lamb. *Music for the Classrooms: Sixty Beats per Minute* [CD]. LifeSounds Music catalogue. www.musicandlearning.com.

> Piano music to increase concentration, productivity, and higher-level thinking for all grades.

Gary Lamb. *Music for the Classrooms* (*Watching the Night Fall, A Walk in the Garden Distant, Fields Language of Love, Love Themes*) [CDs]. LifeSounds Music catalogue. www.musicandlearning.com.

> Piano-based instrumental recordings with original music at sixty beats per minute. Appropriate for all grades.

Putumayo Kids. *World Playground: A musical adventure for kids.* Putumayo World Music. www.putumayo.com/playground.html.
>"Compilation takes children and their families on an inspiring musical and cultural journal around the world."

Raffi. *Rise and Shine. Raffi with Ken Whiteley.* Cambridge, MA: Troubadour Records Ltd.
>Popular songs by Raffi.

Greg Scelsa and Steve Millang. *We all live together* (Vols. 1–4) [CDs].
>Singable lyrics and catchy melodies. For example, Volume 2 teaches children basic concepts and Volume 4 includes songs "It's a Beautiful Day," "Hand Jive," and "The Ugly Duckling."

The Sound Health Series: *Music for Thinking; Productivity; Relax; Learning; De-Stress; Concentration; Inspiration; Motivation* [CDs].
>Music based on clinical research of the effect of music and sound on the human nervous system. Performed by the Arcangelos Chamber Ensemble.

Stewart, G. *Playtime parachute fun for early childhood.* Long Beach, NJ: Kimbo Educational.
>Parachute and imaginary play to develop gross motor skills and spatial awareness. Original music and lyrics. Adaptable for special education.

"You'd never won it if I was easy to teach."

TEACHER RESOURCE BOOKS

An astonishing number and variety of resource books exist that can help teachers strengthen their curriculum and generally make their classrooms more lively and enjoyable for themselves and their students. It is well worth several visits to teacher and general bookstores to see the types and varieties of such materials. The following titles have been selected as a few examples of the many excellent resources available.

Arnold, C., Davis, L., Feist, M., Hansen, A., Kugler, C., Kugler, K., McMahon, M., Rawlins, P., Richards, L., & Swain, L. *The original summer bridge activities* for P–K, K–1, 1–2, 2–3, 3–4, 4–5, 5–6, 6–7, 7–8. (2006). Greensboro, NC: Rainbow Bridge Publishing.
Fun organized educational materials for parents to help children bridge the gap over the summer months. Each book includes activities for reading, writing, math, and language arts skills. "Meets National Standards. Recommended by teachers. Designed by parents."

Bauer, K., & Drew, R. (1992). *Alternatives to worksheets: Motivational reading and writing activities across the curriculum K–4*. Cypress, CA: Creative Teaching Press, Inc.
Reproducible activities, projects, and patterns for K–4.

Cicciarelli, J. (Ed.). (1998). *The giant book of bulletin boards for all reasons and seasons K–3*. Cypress, CA: Creative Teaching Press.
Teacher-tested ideas for creating a learning environment that showcases student accomplishments.

Despard, Y. (2004). *Easy file folder reports*. Monterey, CA: Evan-Moor Corp. www.evan-moor.com.
"Easy successful report writing . . . 27 reports—9 each for social studies, science, holidays, and celebrations." Reproducible report forms and covers.

Evans, J., & Moore, J. (2001). *Bulletin boards every classroom needs. Grades K–6*. Monterey, CA: Evan-Moor Corp. www.evan-moor.com.
Thirty-two bulletin boards ideas (with color patterns and letters) to display student work.

Finch, K. (1992). *File folder games: Reading and math*. Greensboro, NC: Carson-Dellosa Publishing Company, Inc.
Blackline pages that can be copied onto tag board and laminated to make 42 reusable manipulative math and reading games for grades 3 and 4.

Fry, E., & Kress, J. (2006). *The reading teacher's book of lists* (5th ed.). San Francisco: Jossey-Bass.
" . . . places at your fingertips over 190 of the most used and useful lists for developing instructional materials and planning lessons for elementary and secondary students." Organized into sections, including: "Phonics," "Useful Words," "Vocabulary," "Assessment," and "References."

Lang, A. (2004). *Spanish and English comments for report cards and notes home*. Greensboro, NC: Carson-Dellosa Publishing Company, Inc.
Over 350 constructive comments in both English and Spanish for academic progress (language arts, math, science, social studies, art, music, and physical education), "behavior, attendance, work/study habits, peer relations, personal development, and character development."

Pressnall, D., & Malecha, L. (1998). *The big book of music games*. Grand Rapids, MI: McGraw Hill Children's Publishing.
"[A]ctive learning games and reproducible board games . . . that strengthen basic music concepts and reading skills."

Pica, R. (2001). *Wiggle giggle & shake: 200 ways to move and learn*. Beltsville, MD: Gryphon House, Inc.
Thirty-eight classroom themes of "movement-inspiring activities for children 4–8 [that] encourage children to think and solve problems, to recognize and explore their feelings, and to participate physically in their own learning."

Ryall, M. (2003). *Readers' theatre. Grade 6*. Monterey, CA: Evan-Moor Corp. www.evan-moor.com.
Reproducible scripts that are "tied to grade-level curriculum concepts in science, social studies, character education, language arts, and more." Also for grades 1, 2, 3, 4, and 5.

Sevaly, K. [Shelley Price, Ed.] (2003). *September idea book: A creative idea book for the elementary teacher*. Teacher's Friend Publications, a Scholastic Company. www.teachersfriend.com.
One of a series of eleven monthly idea books filled with blacklines/reproducibles for elementary teachers to use throughout the month and year.

Silberg, J. (1995). *500 Five Minute Games.* Beltsville, MD: Gryphon House, Inc.
"Quick and easy activities for 3–6 year olds" that teach essential skills, including counting, guessing, alphabet, and birthday games.

Skrabanek, D. (2003). *Science projects, grades 3–4.* Steck-Vaughn Company. www.svschool supply.com.
More than seventy science projects and ideas for setting up attractive displays for science fairs. Includes projects for life, physical, earth, and space science that align to FOSS standards. Also for grades 1–2 and 5–6.

Wilmes, L., & Wilmes, D. (2000). *Parachute play for indoor/outdoor fun.* Elgin, IL: A Building Blocks Publication.
Revised fifty new games for imaginative play and learning. "Uses cooperative games to build language and listening, fine and gross motor skills, and spatial awareness, along with imaginative play." For ages 3–8. Activities are adaptable for special education.

BLOCK PEOPLE, PUPPETS, GAMES, AND OTHER STUFF

Block play people. Carson, CA: Lakeshore. www.lakeshorelearning.com.
"Experience the diversity of block play!" Each set has six or eight or twelve free-standing figures.
Other Block Play People: Black, Native American, Asian, White, Hispanic families, and block people with differing abilities. Also, community workers and storyteller block people.

Let's talk kids puppets. Carson, CA: Lakeshore. www.lakeshorelearning.com.
Puppets for children, with moveable arms and mouth, machine washable, sewn-on features. White, Hispanic, and black girl and boy.

Learning well inference [a reading comprehension board game]. Baltimore, MD: WORLD*CLASS Learning Materials Inc. www.wclm.com.
Game objective: Be the first player to go from elementary school through college while answering inference questions.
Other board games: Around the World; Getting the Main Idea; Cause & Effect; Context Clues; and Reading for Detail.

Reading rods phonics activity set: Letters and sounds. Learning Resources. www.learning resources.com.
Other Phonics Activity Sets: Sentence Builders; Word Building. Versions in Spanish are available.

Rock 'N Learn, Inc. Conroe, TX. www.rocknlearn.com
CDs, cassettes, and books for children to "enjoy learning to read with a variety of cool songs." Other products are available for early childhood, math, science, social studies, and Spanish and French.

Judy/Instructo. (1999). Grand Rapids, MI: School Specialty Children's Publishing. www.Frank Schaffer.com.
The original Judy clock with synchronized analog and digital displays.
Other products by curriculum areas and class kits are available in stores and through the catalogue.

Carson-Dellosa Publishing. A variety of colorful pocket charts and cards for organizing the classroom. www.carsondellosa.com.
Books, classroom management and decoration materials, and catalogue are available.

Learning Resources. www.learningresources.com.
A variety of color-coded pocket charts and cards for organizing the classroom.
Products, newsletter, and catalogue are available for teachers and parents.

U.S. State and Territory Departments of Education

The journey of a thousand miles begins with one step.

—Chinese Proverb

All states, the District of Columbia, and the territories of American Samoa, Guam, the Northern Mariana Islands, Puerto Rico, and the Virgin Islands maintain their own departments of education. Home pages or licensing websites for most are listed here. While all websites have links to licensing and job opportunities, note that some are designed for easier search and access.

Alabama: www.alsde.edu
Alaska: www.eed.state.ak.us
Arizona: www.ade.state.az.us/certification
Arkansas: www.arkansased.org
California: www.cde.ca.gov
Colorado: www.cde.state.co.us

Connecticut: www.state.ct.us/sde
Delaware: www.doe.k12.de.us
District of Columbia: www.k12.dc.us
Florida: www.fldoe.org
Georgia: www.public.doe.k12.ga.us
Hawaii: http://doe.k12.hi.us

"I'm reporting you to the Department of Education!"

Idaho: www.sde.state.id.us/certification
Illinois: www.isbe.state.il.us
Indiana: www.doe.state.in.us
Iowa: www.state.ia.us/boee
Kansas: www.ksbe.state.ks.us
Kentucky: www.education.ky.gov
Louisiana: www.doe.state.la.us
Maine: www.maine.gov/education
Maryland: www.marylandpublicschools.org/msde
Massachusetts: www.doe.mass.edu
Michigan: www.michigan.gov/mde
Minnesota: www.education.state.mn.us
Mississippi: www.mde.k12.ms.us
Missouri: www.mo.gov
Montana: www.opi.state.mt.us/cert/index.html
Nebraska: www.nde.state.ne.us
Nevada: www.doe.nv.gov
New Hampshire: www.ed.state.nh.us/education
New Jersey: www.state.nj.us/education
New Mexico: www.sde.state.nm.us
New York: www.nysed.gov

North Carolina: www.dpi.state.nc.us
North Dakota: www.dpi.state.nd.us
Ohio: www.ode.state.oh.us
Oklahoma: www.sde.state.ok.us
Oregon: www.ode.state.or.us
Pennsylvania: www.pde.psu.edu
Rhode Island: www.ridoe.net
South Carolina: www.scteachers.org
South Dakota: www.doe.sd.gov
Tennessee: www.state.tn.us/education
Texas: www.tea.state.tx.us
Utah: www.usoe.k12.ut.us/cert
Vermont: education.vermont.gov
Virginia: www.pen.k12.va.us
Washington: www.k12.wa.us
West Virginia: http://wvde.state.wv.us/certification
Wisconsin: www.dpi.state.wi.us
Wyoming: www.k12.wy.us
Guam: www.doe.edu.gu
Puerto Rico: phone 787-754-0060
Virgin Islands: phone 340-774-0100

Overseas Teaching Opportunities

Your imagination is your preview of life's coming attractions.

—Albert Einstein

Overseas teaching positions in English-speaking schools are available in many parts of the world and have considerable appeal for those who would like to live and work in a foreign country. Included among the numerous programs are the following. You can link to program information through the websites below.

European Council of International Schools (ECIS)   www.ecis.org

Fulbright Teacher and Administrator Exchange Program, sponsored by the Bureau of Educational and Cultural Affairs, United States Department of State   www.fulbrightexchanges.org

International Schools Services, annually publishes *The ISS Directory of Overseas Schools* www.iss.edu

Japan Exchange and Teaching Programme (JET)   www.embjapan.org

Search Associates www.search-associates.com

United States Department of Defense Dependent Schools   www.dodea.edu

Parting Thought

The Essence of Teaching

What nobler profession than to teach the next generation—
to see children hold your understanding in their eyes,
your hope in their lives,
your world in their hands.
In their success you find your own
And so to them you give your all.

—Author Unknown

APPENDIX G

Comprehensive List of References and Recommended Readings

A teacher is someone who knows the way, shows the way, and goes the way.
—Unknown

Albert, L. (2003, 1996). *Cooperative discipline.* Circle Pines, MN: American Guidance Service.

Allen, R. (2002, November). Teachers and paraeducators: Defining roles in an age of accountability. *Education Update, 44*(7). Alexandria, VA: ASCD.

Allen, R. (2005, March). Who cares for the caregivers? Helping administrators and faculty cope with a crisis. *Education Update, 47*(3).

Alphonso, C. (2003). *The Globe and Mail.* A poor student's worst nightmare. Retrieved August 8, 2003, from www.globetechnology.com/servlet/ArticleNews/TPStory/LAC/20030808/USTUDNO.

Annie E. Casey Foundation. (2002). *Kids count data book, 2002.* Baltimore: Author.

Armstrong, T. (2000). *Multiple intelligences in the classroom* (2nd ed.). Alexandria, VA: ASCD.

Assessment to promote learning [Special issue]. (2005, November). *Educational Leadership, 63*(3). Alexandria, VA: ASCD.

Associated Press. (2003). State gives 'F' to current report cards. Online edition of the *Indianapolis Star.* Retrieved July 28, 2003, from www.indystar.com/print/articles/2/061331-1142-093.html.

Berne, E. (1964). *Games people play.* New York: Grove Press.

Berry, M., principal investigator. (2002). Healthy school environment and enhanced educational performance, prepared for Carpet and Rug Institute. Report is available at www.jjcommercial.com/ pdf/10-CharlesYoungElementary.pdf.

Bloom, B. S. (Ed.). (1956). *Taxonomy of educational objectives: The classification of educational goals: Handbook I, cognitive domain.* New York: Longmans, Green.

Brimijoin, K., Marquissee, E., & Tomlinson, C. (2003, February). Using data to differentiate instruction. *Educational Leadership, 60,* 70–73.

Brophy, J. (1987). Synthesis on strategies for motivating students to learn. *Educational Leadership, 45,* 40–48.

Brophy, J. (1998). *Motivating students to learn.* Boston: McGraw-Hill.

Bruner, J. (1960). *The process of education.* New York: Vintage.

Building classroom relationships [Special issue]. (2003, September). *Educational Leadership, 61*(1). Alexandria, VA: ASCD.

Bureau of Education. (1918). *Cardinal principles of secondary education* (Bulletin #35). Washington, DC: Department of the Interior, Bureau of Education.

Campbell, D. G. (2000). *The Mozart Effect for children: Awakening your child's mind, health, and creativity with music.* New York: HarperCollins.

Campbell, D. G. (2002). *The Mozart Effect: Tapping the power of music to heal the body, strengthen the mind, and unlock the creative spirit.* New York: HarperCollins.

Canter, L., & Canter, M. (2001). *Assertive discipline: Positive behavior management for today's classroom* (3rd ed.). Los Angeles: Canter & Associates.

Carr, J., & Harris, D. (2001). *Succeeding with standards: Linking curriculum, assessment, and action planning.* Alexandria, VA: ASCD.

Cartwright, G., Cartwright, C., & Ward, M. (1984). *Educating special learners* (2nd ed.). Belmont, CA: Wadsworth.

Cary, S. (1997). *Second language learners.* Los Angeles: Galef Institute.

The challenges of accountability [Special issue]. (2003, November). *Educational Leadership, 61*(3). Alexandria, VA: ASCD.

Chamot, A., & O'Malley, J. (1994). *The CALLA handbook: Implementing the Cognitive Academic Language Learning Approach.* New York: Addison-Wesley.

Chan, T., & Petrie, G. (1998). *The Brain Learns Better in Well-Designed School Environments.* www.nea.org/teacherexperience/braik030312.html.

Charles, C. (2000), *The synergetic classroom: Joyful teaching and gentle discipline.* New York: Addison Wesley Longman.

Charles, C. (2008). *Building classroom discipline* (9th ed.). Boston: Allyn & Bacon.

Children's Defense Fund. (1994). *Child poverty data from the 1990 census.* Washington, DC: Author.

Childs, G. (2002). *Workshop and crisis response team guidebook: Critical Incident Stress Management Program.* Poway, CA: Poway Unified School District.

Choate, J. (Ed.). (2004). *Successful inclusive teaching* (4th ed.). Boston: Pearson Education.

Churma, M. (1999). *A guide to integrating technology standards into the curriculum.* Upper Saddle River, NJ: Merrill.

City of Mesa. (2006, March). Latchkey children: Young children at home. Retrieved April 2006, from www.cityofmesa.org/police/literature/latchkey.asp (last updated 3/23/06).

Coloroso, B. (1994). *Kids are worth it! Giving your child the gift of inner discipline.* New York: Avon Books.

Coloroso, B. (1999). *Parenting with wit and wisdom in times of chaos and loss.* Toronto, Ontario, Canada: Viking.

Coloroso, B. (2002). *The bully, the bullied, and the bystander.* Toronto, Ontario, Canada: HarperCollins

Cook, P. (2004a). *Behaviour, learning, and teaching.* Applied studies in FAS/FAE (Distance Education Curricula), Red River College, Winnipeg, Manitoba, Canada.

Cook, P. (2004b). *Sensory Integration Dysfunction. A layperson's guide.* Booklet available from Paula Cook. Internet contact: pcook59@shaw.ca.

Cook, P. (2005). *Rage: A layperson's guide to what to do when someone begins to rage.* Booklet available from Paula Cook. Internet contact: pcook59@shaw.ca.

Cruickshank, D., Jenkins, D., & Metcalf, K. (2006). *The act of teaching* (4th ed.). Boston: McGraw-Hill.

Culp, K., Hawkins, J., & Honey, M. (1999). *Review paper on educational technology research and development.* New York: Education Development Center, Center for Children and Technology.

Curtiss, K., & English, S. (2003). *Choice theory certification.* Retrieved August 2003, from www.kathy-curtissco.com/what_we_do.htm.

Curwin, R., & Mendler, A. (1997). *As tough as necessary: Countering violence, aggression, and hostility in our schools.* Alexandria, VA: ASCD.

Delsio, E. (2004, October). Wire Side Chat: How understanding poverty can help low-income children. Retrieved April 2006, from www.education-world.com/a_issues/chat/chat119.shtml.

Doll, R. (1995). *Curriculum improvement: Decision making and process* (9th ed.). Boston: Allyn & Bacon.

Dreikurs, R., & Cassel, P. (1972). *Discipline without tears.* New York: Hawthorn.

Dreikurs, R., Grunwald, B., & Pepper, F. (1982). *Maintaining sanity in the classroom.* New York: Harper & Row.

Duebber, D. (2000, May). Substitute teaching: Sink or swim. *Educational Leadership, 57*(8), 73–74.

Dunn, L. (2001, July). Online report cards draw high marks. Wired parents can easily peek at kids' grades, when schools supply Web-based reports. *Medill News Service.* www.pcworld.com/news/article/0,aid,54864,00.asp.

Dwyer, K., Richardson, J., Danley, K., Hansen, W., Sussman, S., Brannon, B., et al. (1990, September). Characteristics of eighth grade students who initiate self-care in elementary and junior high school. *Pediatrics, 86*(3), 448–454.

Educating language learners [Special issue]. (2004, December/2005, January). *Educational Leadership, 62*(4). Alexandria, VA: ASCD.

Eisner, E. (1985). *The educational imagination: On the design and evaluation of school programs* (2nd ed.). New York: Macmillan.

Eisner, E. (2002). *The arts and creation of mind.* New Haven, CT: Yale University Press.

Elmore, R. (2002, September/October). Forum Testing Trap. www.harvardmagazine.com/online/0921.40.hmtl.

Engaging parents and the community in schools [Special issue]. (1998, May). *Educational Leadership.* Alexandria, VA: ASCD.

Everly, G., & Mitchell, J. (n.d.). A primer on Critical Incident Stress Management (CISM). www.icisf.org (with links to related articles and resources and links to training information).

Evertson, C., Emmer, E., Clements, B., Sanford, J., & Worsham, M. (2006). *Classroom management for elementary teachers* (7th ed.). Boston: Allyn & Bacon.

Finn, C. E., Jr., & Ravitch, D. (2004, September 29). *The mad, mad world of textbook adoption.* Washington, DC: Thomas B. Fordham Institute. www.edexcellence.net/institute/publication/ publication.cfm?id=335.

Fraser, B., & O'Brien, P. (1985). Student and teacher perceptions of the environment of elementary school classrooms. *Elementary School Journal, 85*(5), 567–580.

Freiberg, J. (1996, September). From tourists to citizens in the classroom. *Educational Leadership, 54*(1), 32–36.

Freiberg, J. H. (Ed.). (1999). *School climate: Measuring, improving and sustaining healthy learning environments.* New York: RoutledgeFalmer.

Fuery, C. (2005). *The new winning year one: Jump-start student success from day one K–12* (9th ed.). Captiva, FL: Sanibel Sanddollar Publications.

Gardner, H. (1991). *The unschooled mind: How children think and how schools should teach.* New York: Basic Books.

Gardner, H. (1993a). *Frames of mind* (10th ed.). New York: Basic Books.

Gardner, H. (1993b). *Multiple intelligences: The theory in practice.* New York: Basic Books.

Gardner, H. (1997). Reflections on multiple intelligences: Myths and messages. *Phi Delta Kappan, 77*(3), 200–209.

Gilbert, L. (2005, May). What helps beginning teachers? *Educational Leadership, 62*(8), 36–39.

Ginott, H. (1972). *Teacher and child.* New York: Macmillan.

Glasser, W. (1969). *Schools without failure.* New York: Harper & Row.

Glasser, W. (1998a). *Choice theory in the classroom* (rev. ed.). New York: HarperCollins.

Glasser, W. (1998b). *Control theory in the classroom* (rev. ed.). New York: Harper & Row.

Glasser, W. (1998c). *The quality school teacher* (rev. ed.). New York: HarperCollins.

Glasser, W. (1998d). *The quality school: Managing students without coercion* (rev. ed.). New York: HarperCollins.

Glasser, W. (2000). *Every student can succeed.* Chatsworth, CA: Author.

Goldsborough, R. (1997, August/September). Let the reader beware. *Reading Today, 15*(1), 8.

Good, T., & Brophy, J. (2002). *Looking into classrooms* (9th ed.). New York: Allyn & Bacon.

Goodlad, J. (2004, 1984). *A place called school: Prospectives for the future.* New York: McGraw-Hill.

Gordon, T. (1989). *Discipline that works: Promoting self-discipline in children.* New York: Random House.

Greene, R. (2001). *The explosive child.* New York: HarperCollins.

Gusky, T. (2003, February). How classroom assessments improve learning. *Educational Leadership, 60,* 6–11.

Hadley, M., & Sheingold, K. (1993, May). Commonalities and distinctive patterns in teachers' integration of computers. *American Journal of Education, 101,* 261–315.

Hall, P., & Hall, N. (2003). *Educating oppositional and defiant children.* Alexandria, VA: ASCD.

Hartman, C. (2006, February). Students on the move. *Educational Leadership, 63*(5), 20–24.

Harvey, S., & Goudvis, A. (2000). *Strategies that work: Teaching comprehension to enhance understanding.* New York: Stenhouse Publishers.

Hathaway, W., Hargreaves, J., Thompson, G., & Novitsky, D. (1992). *A study into the effects of light on children of elementary school age—A case of light robbery.* Unpublished manuscript, Planning and Information Services, Alberta Department of Education, Edmonton, Alberta, Canada.

Hebert, E. (1998, September). Designing matters: How school environment affects children. *Educational Leadership, 56*(1), 69–70.

Holloway, J. (2002, December/2003, January). Addressing the needs of homeless students. *Educational Leadership, 60*(4), 89–90.

How to differentiate instruction [Special issue]. (2000, September). *Educational Leadership, (58)*1. Alexandria, VA: ASCD.

Hui, K. (2003, January).Wake expands grading system pilot program. *Newsobserver.com.* Retrieved January 2003, from http://newsobserver.com/news/triangle/story/2072754p-1988740c.htm.

Hunter, M. (1982). *Mastery learning.* El Segundo, CA: TIP Publications.

Jacobs, H. (1989). *Interdisciplinary curriculum: Design and implementation.* Alexandria, VA: ASCD.

Jacobs, H. (1997). *Mapping the big picture: Integrating curriculum and assessment K–12.* Alexandria, VA: ASCD.

Jacobs, H. (2004). *Getting results with curriculum mapping.* Alexandria, VA: ASCD.

Jensen, E. (1998). *Teaching with the brain in mind.* Alexandria, VA: ASCD.

Jensen, E. (2000). *Music with the brain in mind.* San Diego: The Brain Store.

Johnson, D., & Johnson, R. (1998). *Learning together and alone* (5th ed.). Boston: Allyn & Bacon.

Johnson, S., & Johnson, C. (1986). *The one minute teacher: How to teach others to teach themselves,* New York: William Morrow.

Jones, F. (2005). *Tools for teaching: Parent edition.* Santa Cruz, CA: Fredric H. Jones.

Jones, F. (2007). *Tools for teaching: Discipline Instruction Motivation* (2nd ed.). Santa Cruz, CA: Fredric H. Jones.

Joyce, B., & Weil, M. (with Calhoun, E.). (2003). *Models of teaching* (7th ed.). Boston: Allyn & Bacon

Kagan, L. (2003). *The successful dynamic trainer: Engaging all learners course workbook.* San Clemente, CA: Kagan Publishing.

Kagan, L., Kagan, M., & Kagan, S. (1997). *Cooperative learning structures for teambuilding.* San Clemente, CA: Kagan Cooperative Learning.

Kagan, M., Robertson, L., & Kagan, S. (1995). *Cooperative learning structures for classbuilding.* San Clemente, CA: Kagan Cooperative Learning.

Kagan, S. (1994). *Cooperative learning.* San Clemente, CA: Kagan Cooperative Learning.

Kagan, S. (2000). *Silly sports and goofy games.* San Clemente, CA: Kagan Publishing.

Kagan, S., & Kagan, M. (1998). *Multiple intelligences: The complete MI book.* San Clemente, CA: Kagan Cooperative Learning.

Kagan, S., Kyle, P., & Scott, S. (2004). *Win-win discipline.* San Clemente, CA: Kagan Cooperative Learning.

Kagan, S., & Minor, J. (2002). *Boost achievement through brain-based instruction: Course workbook.* San Clemente, CA: Kagan Publishing.

Keene, E., & Zimmermann, S. (1997). *Mosaic of thought: Teaching comprehension in a reader's workshop.* Portsmouth, NH: Heinemann.

Kirk, S., Gallagher, J., Anastasiow, N., & Coleman, M. (2006). *Educating exceptional children* (11th ed.). Boston: Houghton Mifflin..

Kohn, A. (1999). *Punished by rewards.* Houghton Mifflin.

Kounin, J. (1970). *Discipline and group management in classrooms.* New York: Holt, Rinehart & Winston.

Kranowitz, C. (1998). *The out-of-sync child.* New York: Skylight Press.

Krashen, S., & Terrell, T. (1996). *The natural approach: Language acquisition in the classroom.* Oxford: Pergamon.

Learning in the digital age [Special issue]. (2005, December/2006, January). *Educational Leadership, 63*(4). Alexandria, VA: ASCD.

Levin, D. (2003, April). When the world is a dangerous place. *Educational Leadership, 60,* 72–75.

Lieberman, A., & Miller, L. (1999). *Teachers—Transforming their world and their work.* New York: Teachers College.

Long, L., & Long, T. (1989). Latchkey adolescents: How administrators can respond to their needs. *NASSP Bulletin, 73,* 102–108.

Mandel, S. (2006, March). What new teachers really need. *Educational Leadership, 63*(6), 66–69.

March, T. (2003, December/2004, January). The learning power of WebQuests. *Educational Leadership, 61*(4), 42–47. Alexandria, VA: ASCD.

Marshall, M. (2002). *Discipline without stress, punishments, or rewards: How teachers and parents promote responsibility and learning.* Los Alamitos, CA: Piper Press.

Marshall, M., & Weisner, K. (2004, March). Using a discipline system to promote learning. *Phi Delta Kappan, 85*(7), 498–507. Bloomington, IN: Phi Delta Kappa International.

Marzano, R. (1998, December). Advances in grading. *Education Update, 40*(8), 4.

Marzano, R. (2000). *Transforming classroom grading.* Alexandria, VA: ASCD.

Marzano, R., Pickering, D., & Pollock, J. (2001). *Classroom instruction that works: Research-based strategies for increasing student achievement.* Alexandria, VA: ASCD.

Maslow, A. (1943). A theory of human motivation. *Psychological Review, 50,* 370–396.

McCann, T., Johannessen, L., & Ricca, B. (2005, May). Responding to new teachers' concerns. *Educational Leadership, 62*(8), 30–34.

McTighe, J., & Thomas, R. (2003, February). Toward better report cards. *Educational Leadership, 60,* 52–55.

McWilliams, P. (1995). *The portable life 101.* Los Angeles: Prelude Press.

Moon, T., Callahan, C., & Tomlinson, C. (2003). Effects of state testing programs on elementary schools with high concentrations of student poverty—good news or bad news? *Current Issues in Education, 6*(8). http://cie.ed.asu.edu/volume6/number8.

Morrison, G. (2002). *Teaching in America* (3rd ed.). Boston: Allyn & Bacon.

Narang, S. (n.d.). Standardized tests: What you should know before your child sharpens his #2 pencil. www.scholastic.com/familymatters/parguides/standardizedtest.htm.

Nelsen, J., Lott, L., & Glenn, H. (2000). *Positive discipline in the classroom.* Rocklin, CA: Prima Publishing.

Newmann, D. (1997). *The compleat teacher's almanack: A daily guide to all 12 months of the year.* New York: Fine Communications.

Olweus, D. (1999). *Core program against bullying and antisocial behavior: A teacher handbook.* Bergen, Norway: Research Center for Health Promotion, University of Bergen.

Papolos, D., & Papolos, J. (2002). *The bipolar child.* New York: Broadway Books.

Paulson, F., Paulson, P., & Meyer, C. (1991). What makes a portfolio a portfolio? *Educational Leadership, 48*(5), 60–63.

Payne, R. (2001). *A framework for understanding poverty.* Highlands, TX: aha! Process, Inc.

PBS Parents. (n.d.). *Talking with kids about war and violence: Learn how to answer children's questions by seeing the world through their eyes.* Retrieved December 2003, from www.pbs.org/parents/issuesadvice/talkingwithkids/war and http://life.familyeducation.com/war.parenting/36559.html.

Pearpoint, J., & Forest, M. (1992). Foreword. In S. Stainback & W. Stainback (Eds.), *Curriculum considerations in inclusive classrooms: Facilitating learning for all students* (pp. xv–xviii). Baltimore: Paul H. Brookes.

Picciotto, L. (1999, August). Let your students take the lead. *Scholastic Instructor, 109*(1), 33–35.

PTSD: What is Posttraumatic Stress Disorder/National Center for PTSD. Retrieved October 5, 2006, from http://en.wikipedia.org/wiki/PTSD.

Pullis, M. (1992). An analysis of the occupational stress of teachers of the behaviorally disordered: Sources, effects, and strategies for coping. *Behavioral Disorders, 17*(3), 191–201.

Rauscher, R., Shaw, G., Levine, L., Ky, K., & Wright, E. (1993). Music and spatial task performance. *Nature, 365,* 611.

Reeves, T. (1998). *The impact of media and technology in schools: A research report prepared for the Bertelsmann Foundation.* Retrieved August 2003, from www.athensacademy.org/instruct/media_tech/reeves0.html.

Rief, S., & Heimburge, J. (1996). *How to reach and teach all students in the inclusive classroom.* West Nyack, NY: Center for Applied Research in Education.

Ringstaff, C., & Kelley, L. (2002). *The learning return on our educational technology investment.* San Francisco: WestEd RTEC.

Rogers, C. (1969). *Freedom to learn.* Columbus, OH: Merrill.

Rosales-Dordelly, C., & Short, E. (1985). *Curriculum professors' specialized knowledge.* Lanham, MD: University Press of America.

Rose, L., & Gallup, A. (2005). The 37th annual Phi Delta Kappan/Gallup poll. *Phi Delta Kappan, 87*(1), 41–57.

Rubinstein-Avila, E. (2006, February). Connecting with Latino learners. *Educational Leadership, 63*(5), 20–24.

Ryan, K., & Cooper, J. (2007). *Those who can, teach* (11th ed.). Boston: Houghton Mifflin.

Schools as safe havens [Special issue]. (1997, October). *Educational Leadership.* Alexandria, VA: ASCD.

Schwartz, F. (1981). Supporting or subverting learning: Peer group patterns in four tracked schools. *Anthropology and Education Quarterly, 12*(2), 99–120.

The science of learning [Special issue]. (2000, November). *Educational Leadership, 68*(3). Alexandria, VA: ASCD.

Silver, H., Strong, R., & Perini, M. (2000). *So each may learn: Integrating learning styles and multiple intelligences.* Alexandria, VA: ASCD.

Simkins, M., Cole, K., Tavalin, F., & Means, B. (2002). *Increasing student learning through multimedia projects.* Alexandria, VA: ASCD.

Siris, K., & Osterman, K. (2004, December). Interrupting the cycle of bullying and victimization in the elementary classroom. *Phi Delta Kappan, 86*(4), 288–291. Bloomington, IN: Phil Delta Kappa International.

Smith, D. (2004). *Introduction to special education: Teaching in an age of opportunity* (5th ed.). Boston: Allyn & Bacon.

Smithers, R. (2004, April). Pack away those pens, the age of online exams is at hand. *The Guardian Review.* Retrieved April 22, 2004, from http://education.guardian.co.uk.print/0,3858,4906458-108699,00.html.

Supporting new teachers [Special issue]. (1999, May). *Educational Leadership.* Alexandria, VA: ASCD.

Tannenbaum, M. (2000, May). No substitute for quality. *Educational Leadership, 57*(8), 70–72.

Teaching all students [Special issue]. (2001, October). *Educational Leadership, 61*(2). Alexandria, VA: ASCD.

Teaching for meaning [Special issue]. (2004, September). *Educational Leadership, 62*(1). Alexandria, VA: ASCD.

There's no substitute for a great sub! A collection of creative tips and lifesavers from substitute teachers [Back to school issue]. (1998). *The Mailbox, 27*(1), 32–35.

Thousand, J., Villa, R., & Nevin, A. (2002). *Creativity and collaborative learning: The practical guide to empowering students, teachers, and families* (2nd ed.). Baltimore: Paul H. Brookes.

Tomlinson, C. (1999). *The differentiated classroom: Responding to the needs of all learners.* Alexandria, VA: ASCD.

Tomlinson, C. (2000, September). Reconcilable differences: Standards-based teaching and differentiation. *Education Leadership, 58*(1), 6–11.

Tomlinson, C. (2002, September). Invitations to learn. *Educational Leadership, 60*(1), 6–10.

Tomlinson, C., & McTighe, J. (2006). *Integrating differentiated instruction and understanding by design: Connecting content and kids.* Alexandria, VA: ASCD.

Traver, R. (1998). What is a good guiding question? *Educational Leadership, 55*(6), 70–73.

Tyler, R. (1949). *Basic principles of curriculum and instruction.* Chicago: University of Chicago Press.

Udavari-Solner, A. (1995). A process for adapting curriculum in inclusive classrooms. In R. Villa & J. Thousand (Eds.), *Creating an inclusive school* (pp. 110–124). Alexandria, VA: ASCD.

Useem, E., & Neild, R. (2005, May). Supporting new teachers in the city. *Educational Leadership, 62*(8), 44–47.

Using standards and assessment [Special issue]. (1999, March). *Educational Leadership.* Alexandria, VA: ASCD.

Van Ripper, C. (1978). *Speech correction: Principles and methods* (6th ed.). Englewood Cliffs, NJ: Prentice-Hall.

Villa, R., & Thousand, J. (Eds.). (1995). *Creating an inclusive school*. Alexandria, VA: ASCD.

Villa, R., & Thousand, J. (2005). *Creating an inclusive school* (2nd ed.). Alexandria, VA: ASCD.

Waddell, D., & Thomas, A. (1998). *Disaster: Helping children cope: A handout for parents.* National Mental Health and Education Center. Retrieved December 2003 and March 2006, from www.nasp-center.org/safe_schools/coping.html.

What do we mean by results? [Special issue]. (2000, February). *Educational Leadership.* Alexandria, VA: ASCD.

Wiggins, G. (1994, November). Toward better report cards. *Educational Leadership, 52,* 28–37.

Wiggins, G., & McTighe, J. (1998). *Understanding by design* (expanded 2nd ed.). Alexandria, VA: ASCD.

Wilcox, J. (2005, December). Handling disasters takes a team approach. *Education Update, 47*(12).

Wilcox, J. (2006, February). Less teaching, more assessing. *Education Update, 48*(2).

Wolfe, P. (2001). *Brain matters: Translating research into classroom practice.* Alexandria, VA: ASCD.

Wong, H., & Wong, R. (2001). *How to be an effective teacher: The first days of school* (17th ed.). Mountain View, CA: Harry K. Wong Publications.

Ysseldyke, J., & Algozzine, B. (1995). *Special education: A practical approach for teachers* (3rd ed.). Boston: Houghton Mifflin.

Series

Hirsch et al: *What your _____ grader needs to know*.

Trade Books

Allard, H. (1977). *Miss Nelson is missing!* Boston: Houghton Mifflin.
Collins, M., & Tamarkin, C. (1990). *Marva Collins' way*. New York: G. P. Putnam's Sons.
Sollman, C., Emmons, B., & Paolini, J. (1994). *Through the cracks*. Worcester, MA: Davis Publications.
Stuart, J. (1949). *The thread that runs so true*. New York: Simon & Schuster.
Thaler, M. (1989). *The teacher from the Black Lagoon*. New York: Scholastic.

Compact Disc

Scelsa, G., & Millang, S. (1978). *We all live together* (Vol. 2) [CD]. Los Angeles: Little House Music.

WEBSITES

Chapter 2

Character Counts!
http://charactercounts.org
Curriculum Designers
www.curriculumdesigners.com

Chapter 4

Discipline
www.positivediscipline.com
Inclusion
www.inclusion.com
www.circleofinclusion.org
Professional Development
www.kaganonline.com

Chapter 5

Fred Jones
www.fredjones.com
Howard Gardner and Project Zero
www.pz.harvard.edu/index.htm
Kathy Curtiss and Choice Theory
www.kathycurtissco.com
Ruby Payne and Students of Poverty
www.educationworld.com/a_issues/chat/cjat119.shtml
www.csba.org/qa/payne.htm
Spencer Kagan
www.kaganonline.com
William Glasser and Choice Theory
www.choicetheory.com/links.htm

Chapter 6

Cooperative Learning
www.newhorizons.org/strategies/
cooperative/front_cooperative.htm
http://www-acad.sheridanc.on.ca/scls/coop/
cooplrn.htm
WebQuest
http://webquest.sdsu.edu

Chapter 8

Assistive Tools
www.intellitools.com
Exceptionality (GATE and Special Education)
www.nagc.org
www.pai-ca.org/pubs/505101.htm
www.cec.sped.org
www.ed.gov/offices/OSERS/IDEA
Families
www.divorcereform.org/all.html
Miscellaneous Facts
www.census.gov/prod/2005pubs/p60-229.pdf
www.tascorp.org/publications/catalog/
indrep_a/five_year_report.pdf
www.childstats.gov/americaschildren/pop6.asp
www.childrensdefense.org/data/keyfacts.aspx
www.urban.org/children/index.cfm
Partnerships (Schools and Families)
www.bridges4kids.org
Poverty and Homelessness
www.ahaprocess.com
www.education-world.com/a_issues/chat/
chat119.shtml
www.csba.org/qa/payne.htm
www.nationalhomeless.org/publications/
facts/How_Many.pdf
www.nationalhomeless.org/publications/
facts/education.pdf
www.nationalhomeless.org/publications/
facts/families.pdf
www.usmayors.org/uscm/hungersurvey/
2005/HH2005FINAL.pdf

Chapter 9

Linda Albert
www.cooperativediscipline.com
Barbara Coloroso
www.kidsareworthit.com
Richard Curwin and Allen Mendler
www.disciplineassociates.com
William Glasser
www.choicetheory.org/directory.html
www.choicetheory.com/links.htm

Fred Jones
www.fredjones.com
Spencer Kagan
www.kaganonline.com
Marvin Marshall
www.marvinmarshall.com
www.aboutdiscipline.com
www.disciplinewithoutstress.com
Ronald Morrish
www.realdiscipline.com
Harry Wong
www.teachers.net
www.effectiveteaching.com

Chapter 10

National Center for Education Statistics
www.nces.ed.gov

Chapter 11

Communication with Parents
http://teacher.scholastic.com/professional/
parentconf/index.htm
Parent Involvement
www.educationworld.com/a_special/
parent_involvement.shtml
Parent–Teacher Conferences
www.nea.org/parents/ptconf.html
www.teachervision.fen.com/
parent-teacher-conferences/
teaching-methods/3683.html
www.education-world.com/a_curr/strategy/
strategy046.shtml
www.atozteacherstuff.com/Tips/
Parent_Teacher_Conferences/

Chapter 12

National Substitute Teacher Alliance
www.nstasubs.org
The SMILES Program
www.slc.k12.ut.us/depts/comminv/
schoolvols.html.

Chapter 13

Teacher Stress
www.nea.org/neatoday/0401/
stressed.html?mode=print
www.untrammelled.co.uk/teacherstress
www.channel4.com/health/microsites/
0-9/4health/stress/saw_teachers.html

▪LEGAL ACTIONS

Gifted and Talented Students Act of 1978, PL 95-561. (1978).

Individual with Disabilities Act (IDEA) of 1990, PL 101-476. (1990).

McKinney-Vento Homeless Assistance Act (formerly known as the Stewart B. McKinney Homeless Assistance Act of 1987, amended 1990 and 1994).

Reauthorization of IDEA of 1997. (1997).

▪REPORTS AND CONFERENCES

American Academy of Child and Adolescent Psychiatry, *Factsheet 64.* www.aacap.org/publications/factsfam/64.htm.

Center for the Study of Social Policy. (1992). *What the 1990 census tells us about children.* Washington, DC: Author.

Divorce Rates in Families with Children. (n.d.). Retrieved April 2006, from www.divorcereform.org/stats.html.

Federal Register. (1977, August 23). Washington, DC: U.S. Government Printing Office.

National Center for Education Statistics. (2003a). *Digest of Education Statistics, 2002* (NCES 2003-060). Washington, DC.

National Center for Education Statistics. (2003b). *Overview of Public Elementary and Secondary Schools and Districts School Year 2001–02.* Retrieved December 18, 2003, from http://nces.ed.gov/pubs2003/overview03/table_10.asp.

National Clearinghouse for English Language Acquisition. (2002). *Survey of the states' limited English proficient students and available educational programs and services.* Washington, DC: George Washington University, National Clearinghouse for English Language Acquisition.

National Coalition for the Homeless. (2005a, June). *How many people experience homelessness?* (NCH Fact Sheet #2). Retrieved April 2006, from www.nationalhomeless.org

National Coalition for the Homeless. (2005b, June). *Education of homeless children and youth* (NCH Fact Sheet #10). Retrieved April 2006, from www.nationalhomeless.org.

National Coalition for the Homeless. (2005c, June). *Homeless families with children* (NCH Fact Sheet #12). Retrieved April 2006, from www.nationalhomeless.org.

U.S. Census Bureau. (2003). *Language use and English-speaking ability: 2000.* Retrieved December 18, 2003, from www.census.gov/prod/2003pubs/c2kbr-29.pdf.

U.S. Census Bureau Public Information Office. (2003, October 8). News release. Retrieved December 18, 2003, from www.census.gov/Press-Release/www/releases/archives/census_2000/001406.html.

U.S. Conference of Mayors. (2004). *Status report on hunger and homelessness in America's cities: 2004.* Washington, DC: Author.

U.S. Department of Education. (2004). Education for Homeless Children and Youth Program, 2004. Available at www.ed.gov.

U.S. Department of Health and Human Services. (2002). *HHS programs and initiatives to combat homelessness.* Retrieved December 18, 2003, from www.hhs.gov/news/press/2002pres/homeless.html.

NAME INDEX

SUBJECT INDEX